An Economic History
of Sweden

This book represents the first recent attempt to provide a comprehensive treatment of Sweden's economic development since the middle of the eighteenth century. It traces the rapid industrialisation, the political currents and the social ambitions, that transformed Sweden from a backward agrarian economy into what is now regarded by many as a model welfare state.

Based upon comprehensive and original research, *An Economic History of Sweden* represents an invaluable resource for both economic historians and students of economic theory. Its central narrative provides a wealth of historical material reaching right up to the modern era, including an analysis of the more troubled recent past of the 'Swedish model'. In addition, the author's discussion of the driving forces of Sweden's industrial development offers an important contribution to recent theoretical debate on the role of institutions for economic development and growth.

Lars Magnusson is Professor of Economic History at Uppsala University, Sweden. He has written extensively on the history of industrialisation and the history of economic ideas. He is the author of *Mercantilism: the Shaping of an Economic Language* (1995)

Routledge explorations in economic history

An Economic History
of Sweden

Lars Magnusson

London and New York

First published 2000
by Routledge
2 Park Square, Milton Park, Abingdon, Oxon, OX14 4RN

Simultaneously published in the USA and Canada
by Routledge
270 Madison Ave, New York NY 10016

Routledge is an imprint of the Taylor & Francis Group

Transferred to Digital Printing 2006

Typeset in Garamond by
Exe Valley Dataset Ltd, Exeter

British Library Cataloguing in Publication Data
A catalogue record for this book is available
from the British Library

Library of Congress Cataloging in Publication Data
Magnusson, Lars, 1952–
    An economic history of Sweden / Lars Magnusson.
        p.   cm. — (Routledge explorations in economic history.   16)
    Includes bibliographical references and index.
    1. Sweden—Economic conditions.   I. Title.   II. Series.
HC375.M25   2000
330.9485—dc21   99–39725
                                                        CIP

ISBN10: 0–415–18167–4 (hbk)
ISBN10: 0–415–40703–6 (pbk)

ISBN13: 978–0–415–18167–9 (hbk)
ISBN13: 978–0–415–40703–8 (pbk)

Contents

Figures and tables

Figures

Tables

Foreword

Fernand Braudel, the French economic historian, coined the term *la longue durée* to express the importance of the long waves of history, the waves that move beneath the surface The history that deals with short-term events, the movements on the surface, he called *l'histoire événementielle*. This book attempts to shed light on the long waves in economic history; the long-term trends whose workings are often hidden, but which have a decisive effect on the way our society evolves. What may appear on the surface to be crucial events that cause drastic changes in our lives may, in fact, have a lesser impact on the way we provide for ourselves and on the structure of our society than the long-term changes, changes that we cannot clearly identify in the bustle of daily life.

This in no way means that history is made up only of long-term trends and structures. All history is also about change, about the way structures are disrupted and transformed. In history, structures always interact with the forces that change them, either swiftly or over a longer time. Innovations and innovators therefore play a very important part in history. Accordingly, this book gives as much attention to innovations and innovators as to the forces that work over long periods of time. To attempt a description of the way changes occur is a task for every historian that is as tempting as it is challenging.

The aim of this book is both modest and ambitious. It is modest in that it cannot hope to give a comprehensive picture of Sweden's economic history. The space available limits me to a presentation of some of the main trends, a general outline. Neither can I attempt, by drawing on recent research, to offer a completely new picture of the economic history of Sweden. Such a work is to be found in Eli Heckscher's monumental *Sweden's Economic History since Gustav Vasa*, (1935–1949). All efforts to improve on this work have failed; it may be that it simply cannot be bettered. On the other hand, this may be an excessively ambitious goal. From its inception, my work has been guided by the thought that it must be possible to capture and highlight the most important trends in the swarm of complex events that make up Sweden's economic history. By the same token, I have taken the liberty of picking and choosing among the vast resources of present-day research in this field. There has been an enormous increase in the volume of research since the days of Eli Heckscher, to both the delight and vexation of anyone attempting to present an overview of the economic history of Sweden. I had no intention of compiling a brief summary of this research. If that had been the case, I fear that instead of writing a book, I would have produced a compendium. The picture of economic history painted here is therefore entirely my own, and no-one can deprive me of either the responsibility for this work or the pleasure it has given me.

This book is an abridged version of the Swedish edition, which also covers the period before 1750. This English edition begins with the agrarian revolution – in many respects the most important prerequisite of the industrial breakthrough that followed in Sweden. Certainly well before that period as well as later, developments in Sweden were propelled to a considerable extent by economic change and transformation elsewhere in the world. As early as the seventeenth century, Sweden was part of the emerging capitalist world economy. When we speak today of 'globalisation', we must not forget that in this sense Sweden has been an open economy for several hundred years. Hence, its development has been shaped by a combination of external and internal processes of development that have made the country what it is today.

A foreword of this kind allows me to express my gratitude to many people. My warm thanks to my teachers, Professor Karl Gustaf Hildebrant and Professor Bo Gustafsson, now my friends and colleagues, who inspired me to become as good an economic historian as they (presumably without success). I also thank all my colleagues and friends at the Institute of Economic History in Uppsala and in other academic circles. I would like to thank Jan Ottosson, who helped me with the tables in this book. Above all, my thanks go to all the students whose lively participation in classes and seminars over the years has taught me most of what I believe I know about Sweden's economic history. My thanks also go to Struan Robertson, who translated the text into English, work which included the introduction of some clarifications and improvements on the original text. Finally, my deepest and most heartfelt thanks to my family, Margaretha, Karl, Erik and Sigrid, who have tolerated my intermittent trips abroad to find the peace to write this book.

Uppsala, January 2000
Lars Magnusson

Introduction

In the summer of 1799 the famous English clergyman and economist Thomas Robert Malthus was one of a group which travelled in Scandinavia to gather material for the second edition of his *Essay on the Principles of Population* . . ., the first edition of which had attracted considerable attention when published the previous year. After visiting Norway the company crossed the border to Sweden. During their travels from Värmland to Stockholm the travellers were struck by the extent of the poverty they saw. On his return to England one of the group, Edward Clarke, described his observations in detail.

> To add to the general wretchedness of the country, a greater dearth had prevailed, during the former winter, than the oldest people ever remembered. . . . The people had saved themselves from starving, by eating the bark bread, and a grass we afterwards found to be sorrel. . . . In everything, the appearance of the people was strangely contrasted with that of the Norwegians. The latter wear red caps. The Swedes, in their broad-brimmed hats, without any buttons upon their black coats, looked like so many Quakers in mourning.[1]

In Malthus's view, the fact that the Norwegians appeared to enjoy better conditions than the Swedes must ultimately be attributable to population pressure. And in Norway this pressure was lighter than in Sweden – mainly because Norwegians usually married rather later than Swedes. Supported by numerous similar observations in other parts of Europe, Malthus felt confident in his conclusion that it was the relationship between the size of the population and the availability of land (and thus food) that was the basis for all human societies up to that time. The balance between these two factors was both delicate and fragile, he said. Everywhere, rapid population growth threatened to outstrip existing land availability. The result was poverty and misery of the kind Malthus and his companions found such plentiful evidence of in 1799. W. H. B. Court, the British economic historian, phrased it clearly: 'Crude physical scarcity therefore plays and has played a great part in economic history.'[2] Hence the daily struggle for survival has been an ever-present feature in the history of mankind. The provision of food, shelter, fuel and clothing have been primary human activities since time immemorial.

And this is, of course, still the case in many countries and regions where mass famine is far from eliminated. For many people in the world outside Europe, the USA and south-east Asia – the third world – the struggle for daily bread is still very much a fact of life. At the same time, the kind of 'mass consumption society' that has emerged in the West in the past century is only a very short interval in the history of mankind. We may think that we have eliminated once and for all, at least in our part of the world, the conditions that produce purely physical poverty. But we cannot be certain about this. Basic changes may occur in our conditions as a result of population migration, environmental and natural disasters or war which may once again create physical want. In this context we should also remember that it is little more than a hundred years since the last great famine hit Sweden – the famine in the province of Norrland in the 1860s. This repeated an historically stereotyped and sombre pattern: people on the move, desperately searching for food, children with distended stomachs, high mortality, particularly among small children, and the scourge of typhus epidemics.

In a 1936 essay, Eli Heckscher, a pioneer in Swedish economic history research, defined the essence of this work. He said that his task was 'to study the way people have provided for themselves through the ages'.[3] Heckscher concentrated on 'material' provision. Provision is of course not limited to food, clothes and shelter. It extends to include the satisfaction of cultural and recreational needs and the need for some work-free time (leisure time). The term 'provision' is related to needs and preferences that change over time.

The science of economic history does not postulate that there should be any particular 'material' or 'economic' reality that may be distinguished from other human activities and be made the subject of separate study. This also means that it is too limiting to say, as does Carlo Cipolla, for example, that economic history is the study of past economic events.[4] For what is an 'economic event'? Can an economic event actually be separated from other historical 'events'? Is it not better to say that economic history research gives a *perspective* to the study of man's social behaviour in the past. Its point of departure is that in providing for themselves, people make economic choices, i.e. they choose from various scarce resources. In an absolute sense, human needs may appear to be unlimited. This is the background to the fact that people in all kinds of societies are compelled to choose, on the basis of their 'preferences', between different types of essentials, cultural or consumer goods, or between work and leisure time. These 'preferences' are largely socially determined, but they also show individual characteristics.[5]

Throughout history people have done their best to meet such needs – whatever they may have been. Man's ability to satisfy his needs has always been related to the resources available to him. These resources are the availability of labour, various natural resources (land, water, precipitation, raw materials, etc.) and some capital stock. Of course it is more poetic to speak of human cultivation and material cultures instead of 'capital stock'. No matter what terms we use, this 'stock' or 'cultivation' is expressed in material or mental artefacts that determine and limit our scope for action: we become 'path-dependent'. Artefacts exist in the form of houses, roads and infrastructure and, more widely, in geography, topography and cultural attitudes. In general it is striking how we humans are influenced by the aggregate historical result of our own cultivation – more than one social thinker has mentioned a 'tyranny of artefacts'.[6] Each new generation inherits these resources from its predecessors. Each generation in its turn ensures that the resources grow – or are dissipated. The choices we make today determine whether the next generation will inherit a greater material 'cultivation' or not.

It is important to realise that economic history studies economic choices in a social and historical context. Ever since the days of David Ricardo economists have referred to 'economic choices' in terms of choices made among limited assets. But at the end of the nineteenth century economics changed to become principally a science of static conditions. Among other things, this means that economists have dealt largely with preferences and needs as given. When the 'economic man' of the economists enters the market he is already equipped with a pre-determined scale of preferences from which he makes his choices. If, instead, we take the view of economic history, we can no longer deal with needs and preferences as given. As history unfolds they change and assume new forms. They are expressed in different ways in different geographic, cultural and social environments. They are shaped by society and culture – but are also dependent on aggregate resources (the 'artefacts') in any particular society. In this sense there is a grain of truth in what Friedrich Engels once said, 'Freedom is realised necessity'. This means that in their wishes and preferences people consider what they perceive as being possible to achieve. Therefore, many economic historians refer to a kind of 'ecological' balance between natural resources and perceived needs, particularly in relation to older types of society. For this reason, we must emphasise the importance of a process of interaction. In economic history our needs are governed by our use of scarce resources, but our scarce resources also govern our needs and preferences. This constant interplay between 'perceived' (!) needs and resources is at the core of economic history. This interplay creates the conditions for change over time in the way people provide for themselves and meet their material and other needs. When people learn to economise and make better use of their scant resources, they increase the production potential of their community. We usually refer to this kind of increase in terms of raised productivity. Higher productivity means we can produce more in a given period of time or with given resources. This then allows a greater division of labour in the community.

Fewer people will need to be employed in the so-called primary sectors (agriculture, animal farming, hunting and fishing) and can instead turn to secondary occupations (handicrafts and manufacturing) or even tertiary activities (services production). This greater division of labour alters people's needs and preferences, which in its turn causes the market to expand and prompts people to both manage their resources better and improve their production capacity.

But people learn more than the best way to manage scarce resources – or to ensure that these resources become less scarce. As Adam Smith, the Scottish philosopher and the father of economics, so often said, man is also a social being. To satisfy one of his most basic social needs – for security and companionship – man creates societies. Man has an inherent *appetitus socialis*, according to Samuel Pufendorf, the seventeenth-century natural law theorist.

A society may be said to consist of a complex set of social institutions. These 'formal institutions' are made up of sets of detailed laws and regulations, but also 'informal institutions', i.e. norms, conventions and unwritten rules.[7] The former are expressed in the laws and regulations which, in the form of legislation to regulate competition or consumption, affect the way we act in the market. The latter are expressed in behaviour patterns, standards and ethical rules which may also be manifested in our behaviour, for example in the market, whether or not we are aware of them. As both John Commons, the American economist, and Karl Polanyi, the Hungarian–British anthropologist, and others have emphasised, the 'market' is in fact a very complex historical 'artefact' whose existence presupposes the emergence of social norms, conventions and behaviour patterns.[8]

This book is an attempt to present a general overview and introduction to Swedish economic history from 1750 to the present day. It includes parts 2 to 4 of the Swedish edition, which also deals with the history of the early Medieval period up to 1750. Certainly, Swedish economic history post-1750 bears traces of this early history. Hence, for example, Sweden, during the Medieval and Early Modern period, was characterised by its lack of feudal political institutions. For most of this period, a free land-owning peasantry dominated the countryside while the nobility – with the exception of the seventeenth century – was quite weak both socially and politically. Instead, the state was much more omnipotent than in most comparable European lands during this period. Moreover, this also meant that – except for a number of territorial changes in its peripheries – Sweden remained a coherent national and administrative structure. Although Sweden became a 'great power' in the seventeenth century – expanding eastwards and south-wards – this did not really change this general picture. In this context the most important territorial changes were the incorporation of former Danish lands (Skåne, Halland, Blekinge, Gotland, Härjedalen, Jämtland) in the middle of the seventeenth century and the subsequent loss of Finland to

Russia in 1809. Thus Sweden was both socially, ethnically and, to a large extent, culturally homogenous. Moreover, towns were small in Sweden and mainly dominated by its agrarian hinterland. This meant that it took a long time for a domestic and independent class of burghers to develop in Sweden. Hence, in general, Sweden was only very slowly and impartially drawn into the emerging capitalist world economy. The main – and for a long time the only – important sector dominated by an international merchant capitalism was the iron mining industry. The activities of such a group of exporting and importing merchants could only be spotted in a small number of cities, mainly Stockholm, but from the seventeenth century also Gothenburg. At least up to the seventeenth century Sweden was characterised by its small, rural economy. However, from then on, forces set in which would fundamentally alter this situation. In the long run, Sweden would become the kind of small but open economy which it is today – but including, however, a number of social and political peculiarities which perhaps can be traced back to its earlier past. It is this line of development we shall attempt to trace here.

1 The agrarian revolution

It would be a mistake to regard the period from the Middle Ages up to the eighteenth century as static. The expansion of Sweden's international trade drew the country into a process of international capitalist growth. The rural peasant communities became part of an expanding export sector and in the cities the country blacksmiths, for example, were forced to place themselves under the supervision of foremen in centralised armament factories. But this capitalism, still in its infancy, lacked the strength to break down the powerful resistance of the household-based market economy with the village community and the peasant household as its foundations. In all important respects, an economy that rested on individual financial management, with some distribution of labour and market contacts, continued to be predominant. Of course, at bottom, this economy had relations with an 'outer' world of politics and the state. In this context it is important to bear in mind the fact that, from a subordinate perspective, the increase in capitalist features appeared to be deliberate interventionism in which the government, not least, played an important part. This view, that capitalism is something imposed by government and other centres of power, is not without foundation. It is a system which often acts as the very antithesis of the simple market economy. In its exchange of surplus products and local specialities, the simple market economy finds its own paths. Capitalism, by contrast, requires regulation, often at the national level, which places constraints on the way the household-based market economy operates; farmers are forced to make charcoal, they are not allowed to forge in their own workshops in the rural areas, they are banned from maritime trade, etc. This process is usually driven by a vigorous government that attempts to gain benefit for itself – but regulation and coercion are as essential to the new capitalist actors as the very air they breathe.

The stability of the long-cycle economy ultimately rests on the low level of per capita agricultural production. Despite some advances in agricultural technology, there were no major breakthroughs from the Middle Ages to the eighteenth century, largely because individual improvements were not followed up in other parts of the agricultural technology system. As a result, productivity measured as crop yield remained low. This in turn left very limited scope for a more sophisticated division of labour. Most of the harvest went to provide for the inhabitants of the village and the small surplus was eaten up by taxes and dues. This pattern was accentuated by a number of social institutions which a later and more unsympathetic generation referred to collectively as 'village community pressure' and which introduced rules that created security and the conditions required for the households' reproductive capacity.

It was the agrarian revolution that finally managed to break up this structural system with its social and institutional 'iron cages' (Max Weber). The term 'agrarian revolution' may be used in various senses. Our point of departure here should, however, be what this revolution really achieved – a growth in agricultural production – rather than the breakthrough of a particular technology. Thus it is feasible to speak of an agrarian revolution which increases per capita food production so much that there is a major rise in production surplus in the agricultural sector over an extended period of time. In other words, what is needed is a growth in agricultural production capable of causing major disruptions in the cycle of crises and the traditional institutional arrangements.

The importance of the institutions may be illustrated here by the theory of the 'peasant economy' formulated in the 1920s by Chayanov, the Russian economist, which draws largely on conditions in Russia. Chayanov emphasised that the peasant economy could easily experience periods of rising per capita growth. But the system of social regulations surrounding this economy ensured that such a rise in growth resulted mainly in a fall in labour supply and/or the dissipation of the profit on festivities and other luxury consumption. By the same token, a fall in yield caused a sharp increase in the villagers' work input. Another variation on this theme is Malthus' theory, which postulated that a rising surplus will result in rapid population growth. Thus in both Chayanov and Malthus we find the basic idea that within the framework of the peasant economy, higher incomes do *not* generate an increase in savings and investments.

Growth can certainly be absorbed, as Chayanov describes, for short periods, particularly if it is regarded as temporary and unstable. We know that actors are reluctant to change their behaviour. But they are sometimes compelled to, at least under certain conditions. In this case it is conceivable that rapid agricultural growth, coupled with the realisation that the gains are not short-term, may have been strong enough motivation to change behaviour in the long term, for example towards using a larger surplus for investments.

Whatever the case may be, it may be said that an agrarian revolution is the ultimate prerequisite for the economic expansion which began in the eighteenth century in Sweden and in the whole of Western Europe. Rising per capita production will in the long term create the conditions for a more extensive division of labour, increased market production and a process of social differentiation in the agricultural sector. This makes a not insubstantial contribution towards laying the foundations for an increase in capital formation as well as for institutional reforms and long-term political processes that, although difficult to measure, are of great importance in the long run.

Agricultural growth, 1720–1870

In the absence of reliable production statistics from earlier than 1860 it is difficult to make an exact estimate of the growth in agricultural production in this period. Most of the figures have been more or less educated guesses. However, it is most likely that only after the 1720s can we trace a *long-term* upward trend. Eli Heckscher assumed that grain production went up by about 75 per cent from 1720 to 1815. Gustaf Utterström also assumed that between 1815 and 1860 'the production of grain and potatoes . . . must have risen by substantially more than 60 per cent, perhaps closer to 100 per cent'.[1] If this is the case, annual growth for the whole of this period may be fixed at 1.0 to 1.2 per cent. Since the average population growth for the same period was 0.6 per cent a year, the increase in production per capita in round figures was 0.4 to 0.6 per cent a year.[2] More recent researchers have presented somewhat different figures, but have, by and large, arrived at the same levels. Lennart Schön, for example, has estimated the annual growth in vegetable production from 1815 to 1850 to be 0.5 per cent a year.[3] Sture Martinius has calculated a slightly higher figure for the years from 1830 to 1860, giving an annual per capita increase of 0.6 to 0.9 per cent. However, Martinius refers here to agricultural work productivity per capita, which means that he subtracts a possible 10 per cent of the population who were directly employed in agriculture during this period.[4] Another way to measure the increase in production is the crop yield figure (the weight of harvest yield against a given amount of seed sown), which rose during this period, although not by much. For the end of the 1860s David Hannerberg calculates a grain figure of 6.9 for autumn wheat, 6.4 for autumn rye, 6.6 for corn and 5.5 for oats. These figures are at least two points higher than those of a hundred years earlier.[5] But that may of course be pure chance. Some crop yield calculations for farms in east central Sweden, for example, show no dramatic changes at all from the mid-eighteenth century until the middle of the following century.[6]

The above deals with the production of cereal (including potatoes). However, potatoes cannot be wholly equated with grain. Since the nutritional content of potatoes is higher than that of grain and will therefore support more people per acre, replacing grain with potato crops will fill more stomachs. And from the early nineteenth century there was a very sharp rise in potato production.[7]

When it comes to animal production, we have even less reliable figures to fall back on. However, there is no indication of a more long-term increase in animal products per capita before the 1850s. Instead, the data available point to a fall in production, particularly in the eighteenth century. A major cause

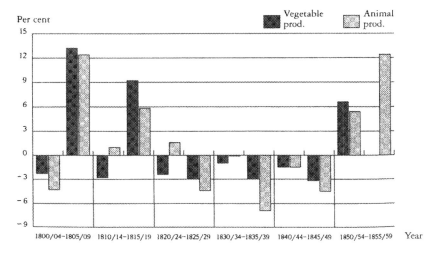

Figure 1.1 Per capita increase in food consumption, 1800–1860. Percentage change in consumption per consumption unit of vegetable and animal produce.

Source: L. Schön, *Agricultural Transformation and Consumption Trends 1800–1870*, Lund 1985, pp. 39, 44.

of this fall was the increase in cereal cultivation and the attendant cultivation of grazing land. Neither, for example, can Lennart Schön find any direct increase in animal production for the first half of the nineteenth century. The change that took place remains largely within the framework of the growth in population.[8] However, some data suggest a moderate relative increase in output. For example, the increase in livestock on Sweden's large estates – particularly in the eastern part of central Sweden – from 1750 to 1850 exceeded population growth.[9] But it may be that conditions on these estates were special and did not conform to the general pattern.

The figures quoted thus far may seem modest if we are talking of an 'agrarian revolution' during this period. But we should bear in mind that these figures represent an average over a very long period. We also know that growth was unevenly spread over this period; for some years no growth at all could be reported. The years from 1770 to 1790 in particular are often referred to as a period of evident decline, as was most of the entire period from 1820 to 1850. On the other hand, 1720 to 1760, 1800 to 1820, and 1850 onwards are classed as periods of growth. There was another decline in the 1860s, clearly expressed at the end of the decade in what has been called Sweden's last period of famine. We must also remember that the rate of growth was different from one region to the next, and the variations could be very large. From 1720 to 1870 growth in what were rather sparsely popul-ated areas was far greater than in the communities on the plains. To give an example, between 1750 and 1850, grain and potato production in the southern Dalarna parish of By increased by probably up to 3 per cent a year.[10] In Krokstad parish in northern Bohuslän, per capita production rose by 1.5 per cent from 1800 to 1835 and then fell to a figure that was 'probably over 1 per cent between 1835 and 1850. It then fell drastically.'[11] Thus the dramatic increase in production was mainly in the communities located in terrain that offered a mix of arable and forest land. Growth also seems to have been higher in west Sweden than in east Sweden, at least if we mean by the latter the provinces bordering Lake Mälaren.

Foreign trade statistics clearly indicate that agricultural production must have grown in the hundred years up to the middle of the nineteenth century. When agricultural expansion started in the eighteenth century, Sweden had a shortage of grain and imported large quantities of cereals, mainly rye, from the other Baltic countries. However, after 1830 the import requirement was replaced by fairly substantial exports. These were made up, however, almost exclusively of the export of oats to Britain from west and south Sweden. Most of this trade went though the ports of Gothenburg and Uddevalla. In the 1880s grain export peaked in relative terms, when it made up about 18 per cent of the total value of the country's exports, second only to wood products. Thus for a brief period, grain exports outstripped iron, for example.[12]

The reasons for the agricultural growth from the mid-eighteenth century have been the subject of much discussion. A purely theoretical explanation

Figure 1.2 Periods of famine still occurred in the mid-nineteenth century. In his 'Illustrations of Current Events, 1849' Fritz von Dardel says: 'He who, suffering from starvation, carries out unlawful actions shall not therefore be liable to punishment.' The writing at the bottom of the illustration says: 'Sorry, but we are starving to death!' 'And we shall too!' KB.

Figure 1.3 Work in the fields. After Petter Strandberg, *The Reason for Agricultural Improvement* (1749). An engraving by J. E. Rehn after a colour drawing in the Bellinga Collection. NMA.

may be the aggregate effects of growth in the production factors of labour, land and capital. If growth is greater than can be wholly explained in this way, it should have occurred as the result of the kind of advances in technology or organisation that increase production. Let us examine each of these production factors in turn.

It is clear that growth in the *labour* factor cannot fully explain the increase in agricultural production. Gustaf Utterström assumed that 83 per cent of population growth from 1820 to 1860 was in the agricultural sector.[13] Assuming that the population doubled in this period, the agricultural workforce grew by perhaps 0.4 per cent a year. If this is the case, about half the increase in production remains unexplained – or, in other words, there was a sharp rise in production per worker in this period.[14]

Clearly, our method of measuring work productivity is very approximate. The number of people 'employed' in agriculture gives us no direct information about their actual work input. First, we do not know what percentage of the potential workforce was actually active in agricultural production. Second, we do not know if employment expressed in hours or days per year rose or fell during this period. For example, organisational and technical innovations in the agricultural sector may have made agricultural work more intensive and less seasonal than before. Third, and last, we have insufficient data about the 'quality' of the labour that was used and what changes, if any, took place here. One might, however, venture to say that the 'quality' improved in pace with advances in literacy and more extensive information exchange regarding agricultural technology.

When it comes to the second question, most people maintain that during this period more intensive use was made of the available workforce. Most technical innovations introduced were, as we shall see, hardly labour-saving; on the contrary, they required a higher work input. New methods of cultivation, including crop rotation and intensified crop sequences, and – perhaps above all – the more intensive cultivation of the soil though the use of the plough, harrow and field roller had the same effect. Furthermore, the higher production of grain and potatoes also required a great deal of land reclamation which, given a technology that produced no labour savings, must have required a higher work input. In light of this, should we assume that the work supply increased by more than the 0.4 per cent a year mentioned above? This is not certain. It depends in its turn on the way the increase in work intensity is related to the amount of underemployment in the agricultural workforce. It is, for example, quite likely that underemployment increased during this period, i.e. a growing percentage of workers were only loosely involved in direct agricultural work and, instead, occupied themselves with woodcrafts and the like. It is difficult to say how these opposing tendencies may be weighed against each other. Yet we may venture the conclusion that although the supply of work increased, it does not fully explain the rise in production.

In some ways, measuring the *land* production factor and the importance of its effect on production growth is even more difficult. This factor is commonly defined as the 'natural' yield from a piece of virgin land. The growth of this factor is thus the result of, for example, an increase in cultivation. But in practice it is almost impossible to identify this 'natural'

Figure 1.4 New land comes under cultivation in Bergslagen in 1809. At the edge of the wood under the hill is the crofter's cottage. Coloured drawing by Gustaf Silverstråhle. NMA.

yield from the yield related to different kinds of investment in the land, i.e. capital. An estimate of the extent of land reclamation operations can give us an idea of the importance of this factor for growth. In the case of Sweden, Hannerberg guesses that the total land area under cultivation rose from 1.5 to 2.6 million hectares from 1800 to 1850 alone. If we err on the side of caution and assume that the rate of land reclamation was less in the eighteenth century, we may hazard a guess that the area of land under cultivation doubled between 1750 and 1850, in which case the increase in arable land would have been 0.7 per cent or 0.2 per capita, if we also assume an annual population growth of approximately 0.4 per cent (geometrical average). In this case the figure gives the contribution of the 'land' factor to production growth, provided the reclaimed land had as high a 'natural' quality as land previously reclaimed, and that it gave the same yield.

This last assumption is, of course, a little doubtful. The theory that the marginal yield of land tends to fall as land reclamation increases is, as we have seen, well founded to say the least. Yet it is not certain that it is generally true. It is claimed in various quarters that the massive land reclamation of the nineteenth century actually brought better land under cultivation. Improved drainage, better implements (ploughs) and stronger draught animals (horses) allowed former wetlands to be farmed. Particularly in the plains communities this meant that agriculture could be extended down to the fertile clay soil areas. This soil has a higher 'natural productivity' than the more mixed moraine areas that had earlier come under cultivation for cereal production, for example. As Gustaf Utterström emphasises: 'As late as around 1800, in many parts of the country it was often not the best but the most easily drained and prepared land on the upper slopes that had been used as arable land.'[15]

Whatever the case may be, land reclamation was indisputably an important factor in the growth in production. We may assume that the first land to be reclaimed was 'moss-covered, infertile natural meadows, former forest land, for example by means of shifting cultivation, rooting-out etc., but only a limited amount of marshland.'[16] According to Carl-Johan Gadd, ploughing up grassland, using up to ten draught animals, was the most common method of land reclamation in the eighteenth century. Other methods, slash-and-burn in particular, became more widespread in the nineteenth century. This was a labour-intensive method in which the grass on the soil surface was broken up with hoes and the turf then burnt and the ash spread. According to contemporary estimates 100 square ells could be hoed in a day. Thus reclaiming an acre of land required 140 man days.[17] The real wetlands could not be reclaimed until well into the nineteenth century. Cultivation of this land required more sophisticated implements, and steam power. Tackling clay soil swampland also required a completely different set of implements than those available up to the mid-nineteenth century. Before then most of the land reclaimed was old meadowland.

Of course, the amount of land reclaimed varied from region to region. Once again, we find the greatest activity in the forest areas or the communities on the wooded uplands. Maths Isacson calculated that in the parish of By in south Dalarna the area of arable land increased more than threefold over a 100-year period from the middle of the eighteenth century.[18] Similarly, Folke Karlsson reports a 70 per cent increase in arable land in western Småland between 1800 and 1850.[19] Urban Herlitz calculates the increase in Krokstad parish in Bohuslän as roughly 150 per cent for the same period.[20] The difference between land reclamation in the plains and forest communities is evident from the above-mentioned Gadd survey: from the 1780s to the 1850s there was an approximately 80 per cent increase in arable land on the western Skaraborg county plains, while the increase in the Sandhem forest parish between 1765 and 1850 was as high as 180 per cent. Other sources give even higher figures. Gunnar Bodvall assesses the increase from 1640 to 1780 in the Ljusdal parish in northern Hälsingland to be fourfold![21] The long period quoted here gives an indication of the risk involved in regarding land reclamation as something that only took place in the eighteenth and nineteenth centuries. In many areas this process went on for a far longer period. Yet it is clear that there was a real breakthrough in land reclamation from the middle of the eighteenth century, and it was particularly intensive in the nineteenth century. As a result, a large part of the available land area came under cultivation. Most of this area was meadowland, but also some of the so-called wasteland (land that had fallen into disuse when the great plague decimated the rural population) was now farmed more intensively.

We call the third production factor *capital*. In concrete terms, it is difficult to separate capital from the land factor because land reclamation often involves various kinds of capital investment to improve on the 'natural' quality of the soil. Thus we count as 'agricultural capital' first and foremost the resources invested in ditching, land consolidation, stone clearance, enclosure, etc., all of which improve the production capacity of the land. Gadd, for example, writes the following about the important work of stone clearance:

> In the forest villages and some plains villages such as Falbygden, the introduction of new implements such as the scythe and the plough required the fields to be cleared of stones, including the mounds of stones from earlier clearance work. One result of this activity was the stone-walled farms that are typical of the woodland and mixed forest/plains villages of present-day southern Sweden, most of which were built in the nineteenth century.[22]

Second, we include under the heading of agricultural capital items such as farm buildings, implements and machinery, livestock holdings and storage.[23] When discussing the contribution of agricultural capital to the increase in cereal and potato yield, it is factors such as the significance of improved

Figure 1.5 A plough with adjustable mouldboard. Introduced in Swedish agriculture in the eighteenth century, it became widely used in the nineteenth century. NMA.

agricultural implements and buildings that we must consider. In older descriptions of the agrarian revolution in England, for example, technical innovations were put squarely in the foreground. Later research has questioned the decisiveness of their role. This does not mean that, taken together, important innovations could not have caused a rise in production.

The technical innovation usually mentioned here is the spread of the use of the iron plough. The simple wooden plough had long been the universal tool of cultivation. But different types of plough became more widely used in the eighteenth century. They were usually of wood but fitted with an iron-tipped ploughshare. The great advantage of this plough was that it could usually cut a deeper furrow than the wooden plough. This in its turn improved the potential yield of the soil and reduced the risks of damage from mild frosts, cloudbursts, etc. The most important innovation in Sweden in the eighteenth century was the plough with a curved mouldboard, probably first used in the Netherlands in the seventeenth century. Before that a straight mouldboard had been used. A curved mouldboard turned the ploughed furrow instead of simply pushing the soil to one side.

The iron plough as such was not a real innovation in the eighteenth century. There is firm evidence that earlier models were in use in Western Europe, and ploughs were also in use in south and west Sweden in the Middle Ages. During the eighteenth century they were hardly used at all in an area made up of the provinces of Uppland, east Södermanland, Östergötland, east Västergötland, Småland, Blekinge and north-east Skåne. It is difficult to find a general explanation for the strength of the resistance of the wooden plough in this area. Reference has sometimes been made to the 'general backwardness' of eastern Sweden compared to the west and south of the country. Another common assumption is that the spread of innovations from Europe was from the south-west of Sweden and northwards through the country. But not even at that time did innovations spread so slowly – at least not if they were considered to be of any use. This hypothesis is also contradicted by the fact that the curved mouldboard plough was in use in Dalarna in the early eighteenth century. At Christopher Polhem's estate in Sjärnsund,

Dalarna, the so-called Sjärnsunds plough, with its curved mouldboard, was manufactured and sold during this period. If we accept the theory of a slow spread of innovations from the south-west upwards, it would have 'jumped' the more central parts of east Sweden. A more likely explanation is that the older ploughs with straight boards were too heavy and could hardly be used on the moraine soil that formed a large part of the arable land in east central Sweden. They were not even particularly easy to use on clay soil. They were still not robust enough to differ in any decisive way from the wooden plough in terms of their function. They quite simply did not bite in to clay soil any better than the wooden plough. Yet they were big and cumbersome and had to be pulled by a large number of draught animals. This is probably why the plough was used mostly on the more easily worked soils of the south Swedish plains. There were also larger communities here, with more hands and many draught animals. The advantage of the plough was probably also greater when it was fitted with the curved mouldboard – and also when it began to be made entirely of iron. As these advantages gradually came to be understood, the use of the iron plough spread, even in east central Sweden.[24] The plough, especially the Dalarna plough, became more prevalent in Norrland and on the island of Gotland, where the wooden plough had previously been entirely dominant.[25] However, the plough with the curved mouldboard was not widely used at first. An expert in this field even said of the eighteenth century that 'generally speaking, roughly the same plough was in use at the end of the century as at its beginning'.[26] It was not until the nineteenth century that this innovation became popular. As already noted, it was not until this time that ploughs became less cumbersome, more reliable and, not least, cheaper. These improvements were, in their turn, closely linked to an upswing in the domestic manufacture of ploughs. A number of estates and farms began to manufacture ploughs in earnest from the early nineteenth century. The first to do so was C. G. Stjernsvärd, who began to manufacture the so-called Scottish plough at Engeltofta in Skåne in 1803. Larger-scale production of similar types of plough began later on the estates (which became Sweden's rural industrial communities or 'bruk') at Uddelholm, Djurholm and Furudal (the 'Furudal plough'), Åkers styckebruk and Brefvens bruk – and Överums bruk, shortly after 1851, when it started production, became Sweden's biggest manufacturer of ploughs.[27]

In addition to the plough, several other implements were introduced, or to be more precise, improved, from the eighteenth century onwards. Already in the eighteenth century, for example, harrows were equipped with iron teeth, which improved their performance. In the early nineteenth century the more large-scale manufacture of harrows also began in the rural estates and workshops, for example at the Degerberga manor estate in Enskede – by the well-known agricultural innovator, Alex Odelberg – and at Överum.[28] The same was true of rollers and clod-crushers, which also began to be more widely used in the nineteenth century. All this equipment led to more intensive cultivation of the soil, which in turn produced better harvests.

Figure 1.6 Överums bruk. Sweden's largest manufacturer of ploughs in the second half of the nineteenth century. From: *Sveriges industriella etablissementer* 1872. KB.

Parallel with more sophisticated soil preparation, other innovations were introduced which had the long-term effect of improving the agricultural sector. The eighteenth century became generally known as a century of vigorous experimentation in agricultural technology. A host of ideas were discussed and tested, and many of them were spread to an interested public through the Royal Academy of Sciences and its numerous publications. Later, a number of county agricultural associations were established which published their own journals, brochures and local magazines.[29] The Patriotic Society, founded in 1767, directed its energies towards modernising agriculture, focusing particularly on the encouragement and distribution of information on inventions in the field of agricultural technology. Publications from societies of this kind contained articles on, for example, a sowing barrow designed by Parson Westbeck (The Royal Swedish Academy of Sciences papers, 1741), a wooden plough with three ploughshares (The Agricultural Journal, 1779), a rotary harrow with iron teeth (The Agricultural Journal, 1776) or C. J. Cronstedt's five-row sowing machine (The Royal Swedish Academy of Sciences papers, 1769). At the same time, the Model Room, which contained collections of agricultural equipment, was set up on the initiative of The Patriotic Society to serve as a source of inspiration for innovators. This was also true of the best-known of the model collections from the eighteenth century, that assembled by Anders Berch, who was the first to take the professorship at Uppsala University in the new subject of economics.

We must avoid exaggerating here the significance of the optimism about technology. The more fanciful ideas, at least, were hardly of any practical use.

One example was the sowing machine which had already appeared in several designs in the eighteenth century, but which was hardly used even in large-scale farming before the 1850s.[30] Up to the middle of the nineteenth century there was only one improvement that was a genuine form of 'mechanisation', i.e. a labour-saving invention. This was the threshing machine which in time came to replace the laborious process of hand-threshing. The first so-called threshing wagons were to be found in Norrland from the mid-eighteenth century, and were attributed to a notable inventor, a university lecturer called Magnus Stridsberg, of Härnösand. The real so-called cylindrical threshers, an invention of the Scotsman Andrew Meikle, came into use in 1788, but they were expensive and therefore usually only installed on the large estates and manor farms. By 1814 Stjernsvärd at Engeltofta in Skåne had manufactured seventeen of these threshers, three of which were in use on his own farm. There were other reports of threshers in use in Småland, Västergötland and on the island of Gotland, but they were still far from common.[31]

Thus there was no real breakthrough in agriculture based on the more advanced use of farming implements and machinery until the second half of the nineteenth century. As we have noted, neither was the technology that came into use during this period genuinely labour-saving. Capital, to the extent that this factor contributed to production growth, largely took the form of investments related to land reclamation, ditching, fencing and so on. We may therefore note that per capita increase in agricultural production from the mid-eighteenth century was partly due to an increase in work input on land reclamation. But whether or not this is the full explanation is open to question.

There is a fourth production factor whose impact is even more difficult to measure. This factor is made up of different technological and organisational *improvements* within the limits of a given set of production factors. We have already discussed the 'quality' of the workforce as a possible improvement of this kind. We have also seen that farming equipment became more sophisticated during this period. There was a great deal of interest in innovations, and it is most likely that the size and quality of the country's stock of farming equipment improved. There were also a number of improvements in agricultural buildings. Several sources show improvements in the design of barns during this period, allowing better animal husbandry and storage. Lastly, there are signs of some improvements in livestock. During this period the livestock became larger and gave more meat, butter, etc. We have already mentioned in this context that in the eighteenth century the horse replaced the ox as the main draught animal in many areas. Although this change was not universal, it could be clearly identified as a long-term trend. Since the horse had more stamina than the ox, this change undoubtedly made a great contribution to an increase in production. Larger areas could now come under cultivation, the land could be cultivated more intensively and (heavier) ploughs could be used more widely.

Figure 1.7 Bondelycka. Oil painting by unknown artist, mid-eighteenth century. NMA.

We must also consider a number of other improvements that may have contributed to growth and progress. During Sweden's Age of Freedom people became more aware that encouraging organisational change and introducing favourable laws and regulations paved the way for improvements in agriculture. Perhaps the most important organisational change in the agricultural sector was the gradual move away from the old tried and tested forms of farming to a system that may be described as *crop rotation*. Although the old system of continuous cropping of two or three cereals was, it is true, still in use until the middle of the nineteenth century,[32] as Utterström and others point out, it had begun to be phased out far earlier, partly because crops like potatoes, turnips and peas were grown more on fallow land and partly because more wasteland was being brought under the plough. Other important new crops were the forage crops and oats, the cultivation of which now rose sharply. Without doubt the change to crop rotation meant that the 'land' factor was used more intensively. The important point was that adding crops to the rotation sequence allowed the fallow periods to be shortened.

Particularly in the older literature, the great land reforms were considered to play a central part in giving agriculture the new vigour it enjoyed from the eighteenth century onwards. The first such reform, the great redistribution of land holdings (the *storskifte*) was introduced as early as 1749. It is usually associated with one of the foremost agricultural reformers of the time, Jacob Faggot, Secretary of the Royal Academy of Sciences and Chief Inspector of the National Land Survey Board. In all likelihood it was Faggot who wrote in *Obstacles and Assistance in Swedish Agriculture* (1746) a critique of the old village system with its open-field farming. Under the Field Consolidation Act that followed, the small narrow strips of farming land were to be consolidated to form larger units. Another basic principle was that the common areas of wasteland were to be dissolved and added to individual tax farms (*skattejord*, farmland owned freehold by the peasant who worked it, who was obliged to pay taxes and charges – often in kind – to the Crown, hence the name tax land/tax farm). Under an Ordinance passed in 1749 the National Land Survey Board was to be called in and the land consolidated when a petition was submitted by all the village landholders. Of course, the voluntary nature of this approach slowed the implementation of this reform. Faggot also wanted a less liberal approach, his view being that land could be redistributed on the petition of a single village landholder. This more radical line was also expressed in the stricter provisions added to the Ordinance in 1757 and contained in the 1783 Land Survey Ordinance. Ordinances were passed in 1749 and 1757 which permitted only one reallocation of land per tax farm. However, this regulation was supplanted by the Ordinance of 1762 which allowed the tax farms' fields and meadows to be consolidated in more than one parcel of land.

The extent to which the *storskifte* land reform was carried through and the effect it had, has been the subject of much debate. Heckscher, for example, tended to regard the *storskifte* as a rearrangement that was initiated 'from above', and which had no real practical significance. Where this reform was carried out, it was, in his view, on the initiative of landowners of a certain standing and under strong protest from the peasantry. He also suggested that the peasantry's resistance was an expression of their general conservatism. However, although it is difficult to establish the impact of the *storskifte* in terms of the overall growth in production, it is clear that these redistributions of land occurred in many places – often, however, in the modified form set out in the Ordinance of 1762, which allowed land to be dispersed in more than one parcel. Neither was the peasantry quite so conservative as Heckscher described. In many cases they acted more as instigators of this process. Birgitta Olai, who studied land reform from 1776 in the parish of Ekebyborna in Östergötland, says, for example, that 'no direct resistance to starting the land redistribution process can be seen among the Ekebyborna peasantry'.[33] Ronny Pettersson came to the same conclusion in his study of the subsequent statutory regulation of land redistribution, the *lagaskifte*, in Halland in the mid-nineteenth century. In his view, the position of the peasantry was usually one of 'positive reactions and a general desire for change'.[34] The first *storskifte* reforms were in the plains villages of Uppland, Östergötland and Skåne, and also in Värmland and Gästrikland. Some time into the nineteenth century a total of two-thirds of all the arable land in the southern and central parts of the country had been consolidated under this great redistribution of landholdings.[35]

The more radical version of the *Storskifte* Ordinance, the *Enskifte*, which could be enacted on the petition of a single village landowner, was, however, more of a decree from above. On 2 February, 1807 the General *Enskifte* Ordinance was issued. It was based largely on local regulations that had been issued earlier in Skåne, in 1803. This Ordinance limited the maximum number of land parcels per farm to three and required the villages to be dissolved. Outside Skåne, this reform was not widely enacted; it was, however, carried out to a limited extent in Skaraborg, on the island of Öland and in Blekinge.[36] Rather inappropriately, this Ordinance is associated with the celebrated Rutger Maclean, master of Svaneholm Castle in Skåne. Maclean was both an ardent advocate of the ideas behind the French Revolution and a tough and practical agricultural reformer. In addition to running his farm estate as a home-farm with the help of peasant labour hired on a daily basis, he owned fifty-one freehold farms in four villages in Skurup. He had the land divided into seventy-three farms of 40 acres each, the land being divided into even squares with the farmhouses in the middle. His aim was to achieve more than simple land consolidation: he intended to found a model community. Although his visions were bolder than those of the average landowner in Skåne, he attracted many followers.

However, the radical transformation caused vociferous protests from the peasantry in the form of the so-called *Frälsebonderörelesen* (a movement of peasants who farmed land held by the nobility and who therefore paid their land taxes to the nobility) mentioned in Skåne in 1810, which had as its

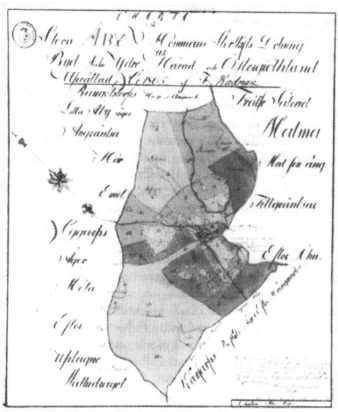

Figure 1.8 A map of the storskifte land redistribution in Stora Åby, Östergötland, drawn up in 1805. The National Land Survey Board.

main target the effects of the *Enskifte* land reform and the wave of rationalisation that spread through the great estates of Sweden's southern counties.[37] Skåne was, in any case, in the vanguard of the process of land reform in Sweden. As early as 1822, half of all the land in Malmöhus county, for example, had been partitioned and consolidated.[38]

In the rest of Sweden, however, it was the 1827 *laga skifte* Ordinance on the legal partitioning of land holdings that triggered a really extensive and radical wave of land reform. Throughout the nineteenth century the great majority of tax farms underwent the process of legalising the redistribution of their land holdings. But there was considerable resistance, particularly in Dalarna, which meant that there was no land redistribution in some of the villages in this area until well into the twentieth century. The *laga skifte* land reform legislation extended and superseded the earlier Ordinances on land redistribution. Under this new legislation, land reform would be carried out

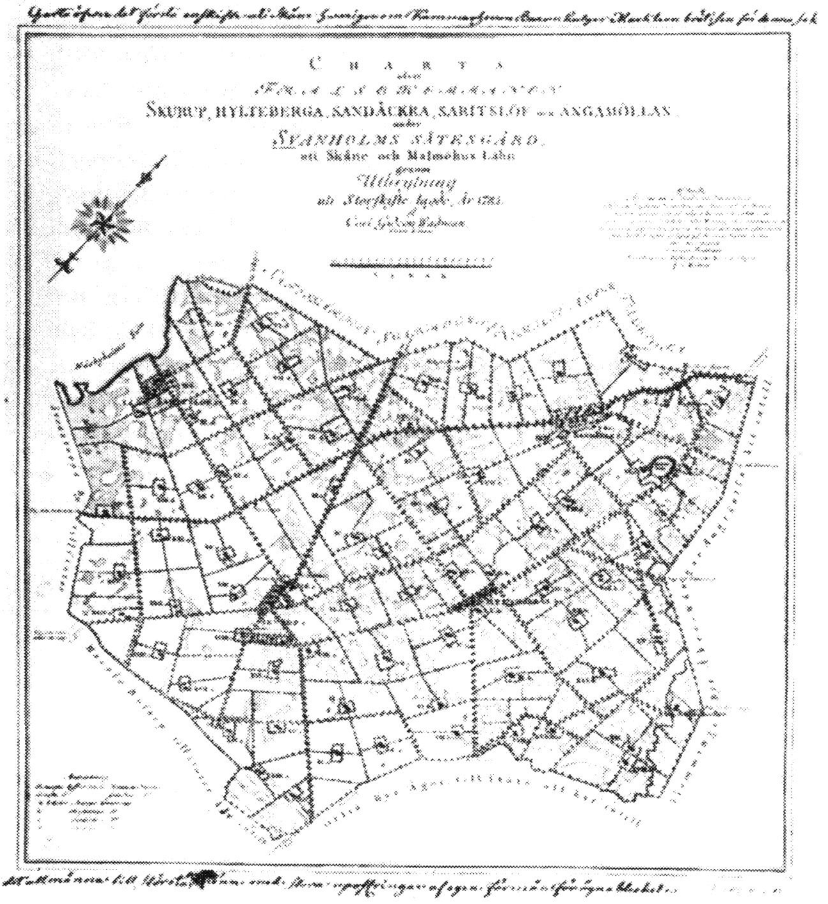

Figure 1.9 The Svaneholm Map. The handwriting round the border says: 'A map of the first Enskifte land redistribution in Skåne, by which means Baron Rutger Maclean broke the ice in this matter to the greater good of the commoners but at great personal sacrifice in the short term.' KB.

in such a way that the tax farms' land was consolidated to form larger units, and the wasteland was parcelled out. The intention was to dissolve the villages. Plots of land and farms were to be close to parcels of the farmland, which usually meant that some villagers had to move out of their villages. The results of this dissolution of the villages varied from case to case. When only one or two farm sites were moved out, many of the villages remained more or less intact. In other cases the effects were more far-reaching. No consistent system of isolated farms developed in the wake of the *laga skifte* legislation – so we must look for other reasons for Swedish solitude!

Taken together, the land redistribution regulations meant that the very foundations of the old village communities were slowly but surely undermined. However, the reason may have been less the dissolution of the villages and more the allocation of wasteland and the cessation of the fallow system. As already noted, the effect of land reform on agricultural growth was the subject of lively debate. Its effects are difficult to measure, yet it is probable that by creating more efficient farming units and strengthening the rights of private land possession, this reform had a positive impact on the process of agricultural growth, the reasons for which we are examining here.

It is important to point out that land redistribution was not the only institutional change that strengthened the right of land tenure. The entire complex of laws had this effect from the eighteenth century onwards, which we shall discuss further in Chapter 3. Of particular importance in this context was the constitutional change of 1789 that paved the way for almost unlimited rights of possession and disposal of tax land. Land possession had formerly been closely linked to the concept of specific social rights. This concept now gradually disappeared, and what we may call a modern form of land title began to take shape. As part of this reform, the abolition of the special rights to tax-exempt land on feudal terms, which had been enjoyed by the nobility, would be given special attention. This exclusive monopoly was withdrawn in 1789. The stronger position of farmers as landowners was perhaps most evident in the wave of tax land purchases that started in the eighteenth century and which subsequently became even more extensive.

In addition, the change in attitude towards land redistribution and croft (*torp*) tenure came to assume considerable significance in the process of agricultural growth, primarily in the lifting of the restrictions that had previously impeded the division of freehold farms. The main purpose of the old restrictive policy had been to ensure that all the farms were occupied. The authorities feared that an extensive division of freehold farms could cause impoverishment and a consequent loss of tax revenue. To give an example, an Ordinance from 1684 with the telling title of 'A Bill on How All Tax Farms are to be Occupied and Worked to Avoid Their Destruction by Dissolving Them into Too Many Small Parts', said that people who owned less than a quarter of a 'mantal' (a unit of land measurement that varied with local usage, based on the capacity of the land to support a family – similar to the English 'hide') were not entitled to farm it. They would be compelled to offer for sale, or 'cede', their land to those who owned more than a quarter of a mantal of land.[39] The legislation governing the creation of crofts was also very restrictive. The 1734 Forestry Ordinance only allowed crofts to be formed on tax land 'as an exception'. Existing crofts were either to be classed as tax land or 'demolished'.[40]

There was, however, a shift in perspective during Sweden's Age of Freedom. Influenced by the economic debate in England and France, attention focused on the relationship between a large population, agricultural growth and military power. It was thought that for this equation to balance, it must be

made easier to divide up the tax farms. Another reason was that the formation of crofts and further division of farms would prevent a sector of the
population from becoming landless – which would otherwise be the consequence of further population growth.[41] This reversal in attitudes towards the
'break-up of the farms' produced the 1747 Ordinance that allowed farmland
leased from the Crown and tax farmland to be divided into parcels of less
than a quarter of a mantal. However, the authorities were still to ensure that
the peasant was a landholder, i.e. that he was still able to support himself,
otherwise there remained the obligation to 'cede' the land as mentioned
above.[42]

A similar change was made for crofts in the Resolution of 1743, which
allowed, for example, more crofts to be formed when new land was reclaimed. An underlying motive here was, of course, the 'promotion of
cultivation'. The threat of demolition or that the Crown would take over the
croft hardly encouraged farmers to set up crofts on their land. Now the
farmer's right of title to the croft was guaranteed. There was, of course, also a
fiscal motive behind this, as Valter Elgeskog points out. The new arrangement allowed the farmland to continue to be taxed, while the Crown could
also count on additional revenue from personal taxes, i.e. imposts that were
not linked to the land, from the crofters. This applied to crofts on meadowland or wasteland which formed part of a parcel of land. The restrictions
remained in force when it came to forming crofts on unredistributed land
and on residual common land. Here, the village landowners had the authority to forbid the creation of crofts. To some extent this issue was resolved
by the continuing process of land redistribution, which eventually turned
most wasteland into private land holdings. The constitutional reform of
1789, which guaranteed the farmer of tax land unrestricted rights of
possession and disposal, allowed the landowner to continue to do as he
wished on the allocation of crofts. Taken together with the removal of the
restrictions on dividing tax farms, this was a strong stimulus for land
reclamation and for an increase in the rural population.

We have discussed the importance of the different production factors in the
very marked increase in agricultural production from the 1720s onwards. No
simple explanation can be found for this upswing. Yet it seems clear that the
rapid rate of growth is *mainly* attributable to an increase in land reclamation.
Land reclamation in its turn required changes in the complex of regulations
of the time, including a relaxing of the restriction on the division of tax
farmland and on the formation of crofts. At first glance the rise in per capita
growth appears to refute the assumption that the work production factor had
some impact. In fact, we may assume a very sharp increase in work input in
this period, for example in land reclamation, but also through the more
intensive farming methods which went hand in hand with changes in the
system of cultivation which improved the efficiency of crop rotation. The
importance of the potato should also be mentioned here. Compared with

cereal crops, potatoes could support the same number of people from a smaller arable area. And as the most important staple food in the population's diet, it was at least partly interchangeable with cereal crops. Finally, there were various improvements in farming equipment, although advances in this area were not as great as has perhaps been supposed.

The roots of agricultural transformation

In light of the above we need to establish the real reason for the vigorous expansion of the peasant economy in the eighteenth century. Why did the peasantry begin to cultivate new land and work as never before? We must look for the answer in the sweeping changes that occurred after 1720. The main feature of the post-1720 period was the improvement in the position of the peasantry in the political, economic and social spheres. This was without doubt both a precondition for and a result of the growth and transformation of agriculture during the period up to the mid-nineteenth century.

The reasons for this new vigour in the agricultural sector should be sought in the political and social changes that followed the introduction of absolute supremacy of the monarch and the end of Sweden's era of 'great power policy'. The system of absolutism had accentuated a development which had, it is true, already begun in the seventeenth century: the transformation of the nobility from an independent estate of the realm to a power that was in the service of the state. The gradual relaxing of the traditional boundaries between the four estates was in fact essential to absolutism. We have already mentioned, for example, that Karl XII's tax reform of 1713 had as its main point of departure the equal treatment of all the estates of the realm.

The decision for the Crown to repossess land that had been held by the nobility, the so-called reduction process, was an important driving force in the introduction of absolutism. This decision also had far-reaching consequences for Sweden's agricultural history, the most immediate being that nobles could no longer apply the strategy they had followed, at least in part, in the seventeenth century, of appropriating tax farmland to form larger estates. A Diet Resolution of 1680 withdrew the right of the nobility to bequeath land, as well as the option to change tax farmland or Crown farms into *frälsejord* (land possessed by the nobility that was exempt from taxes payable to the Crown). Around 1700, about one third of the country's total arable land was in the hands of the nobility. This proportion fell towards the end of the eighteenth century, when the sole right of the nobility to tax-exempt land was withdrawn. Individual nobles or other persons of rank could, it is true, purchase Crown farmland as freehold, and a substantial amount of land changed hands under this system. But in the long term a move towards large estates of the type that emerged in the Baltic countries and Denmark was still blocked. On the other hand, the reduction did not mean that the nobility ceased to be landowners or carry on agriculture. On the contrary, the restrictions of the reduction encouraged a change from the widespread operation of large estates made up of numerous freehold farms to the more intensive working of manor farms. Thus for many nobles the operation of a home-farm with the help of a relatively small number of peasants – who were, in some cases, worked harder – was an alternative to the more grandiose plans that were in place before 1680.[43] The links between the nobility and agriculture were also strengthened by the military allotment system, under which officers were allocated special country properties as their homes and their incomes came from levies on a special group of peasants, the *rusthållarna*, who undertook to fit out a cavalryman, for example, in return for fiscal concessions from the Crown.

Taken together, the factors of absolutism, the reduction and the allotment of soldiers also had other significant effects that directly improved the status of the peasantry as one of the estates of the realm. An important result of the reforms of the 1680s was the change in the tax system and the collection of tax revenues. Under the new system, Crown taxes were directly linked to stated purposes, both civil and military. This applied both to the officers in relation to the *rusthållarna*, and to the infantry who occupied soldiers' tenant holdings and collected revenues directly from the peasants. The individual occupants could not, of course, make arbitrary changes to the tax levy. Any changes in tax could only be made through the political process. Until the abolition of absolutism this power of decision rested with the absolute monarch. In the Age of Freedom, with its ineffectual kings and council, it was the Diet of the Estates (*Ståndsriksdagen*) that had to be consulted. However, a recalcitrant peasant estate, often supported by the clergy and sometimes even by the burghers, made it difficult to enact any increases in taxes. Therefore, as H. L. Rydin wrote, the stability of land imposts was actually 'a corollary of the system of military allotment'.[44]

Initially, the new tax system certainly increased the burden of tax on the individual freehold farmer. The military allotment system described above went hand in hand with a general improvement in the efficiency of tax collection. The tax burden grew even heavier during the Great Nordic War, when it was accompanied by frequent levies for new soldiery.

From the 1720s onwards, the static tax rate had a different effect. We may follow the way the value of the levy on farmers' working tax and Crown land gradually came to be eroded. First, this seems to be related to the inflation that occurred as early as the 1730s, but that rose steeply in the 1750s. Then in the 1760s price increases – here we refer mainly to the price of cereals – were replaced by a downturn in prices. Prices then rose again in the 1770s and in the 1790s in particular.[45] The aggregate effect was an annual average increase in cereal prices of 2 per cent from 1732 to 1775. The greater part of the land register tax and 'mantal' (poll) tax were payments-in-kind and therefore not affected by inflation. A part of the tax was payable in money and the value of this part of the payment was eroded. Lars Herlitz found that in the Skaraborg county in the 1730s, 27 per cent of basic taxes were paid in money. From the 1730s to the 1770s the total tax levy in this area per 'mantal' fell from 19.45 to 17.5 barrels (*tunnor*, 1 tunna=156 litres), i.e. by about 10 per cent.[46] In the same area the price of tax land rose as a result of the fall in taxes. Tax land quite simply became more attractive to own. In the eighteenth century the current value of a mantal of tax land increased eightfold while Crown land increased only threefold. There were no such effects on the price of exempt land. There is no evidence of a lightening of the tax load. This was largely because owners of manor farms were able to change the tax levy to keep pace with inflation.

However, the rising land prices are reason to suspect some other cause other than falling land rents. The long series of good harvests in the 1720s and 1730s and again in the 1770s and 1790s made what were in theory fixed land rents a lighter load to bear. Another factor is that in this century land reclamation increased the actual area contained in a mantal. A large proportion of the tax was still linked to the mantal, and the earlier experiments with income tax in the years of Karl XII's reign had not been continued. In summary, we may therefore note that the real tax burden, at least on tax land, fell. After the Peace of Nystad in 1721 the constant war levies also ceased. Neither was it necessary to continue the frequent votes of supply to finance a war machine that during the 'great power policy' period had always been hungry. The decay of Sweden as a great power and its dreams of empire in the seventeenth century undoubtedly led to a redistribution of income that benefited the peasantry. This was particularly true of the peasants on tax farmland, but presumably also of those farming Crown lands. As we have already said, the trend was less uniform for the noble landowners. However, the trend in the county of Skaraborg indicates that the noble landowners did not benefit in the same way as their peasant counterparts, as may be seen from the more modest increase in the price of exempt land, less land reclamation, the dispersal of tax farms and the formation of crofts.

During the eighteenth century the improved status of the peasantry became noticeable in every way. We have already mentioned the importance of the obligation to 'cede' land for purchase. Heckscher, in particular, considered these purchases to be a general sign of the 'renewed vigour of the peasant class'.[47] Some of the sales of rights to farms on Crown land occurred as early as the seventeenth century. But it was not until the Tax Land Purchase Resolution of 1701 that these land sales became better ordered and more common. The reason was, as usual, fiscal. The initiative appears to have been taken by the Crown Lands Judiciary Board, which complained of a general shortage of funds. Accordingly, Karl XII, in his camp in Lais in Livland, dictated a letter on February 20, 1701 setting out the conditions for the sale of the title to tax land.[48]

These sales were to continue throughout the eighteenth century, with the exception of the period from 1773 to 1789, when such purchases were banned. As a result, some 14,000 mantal went from Crown lands to tax land. Land sales peaked in the twenty years after the Tax Purchase Resolution and again in the 1750s and 1760s, when there was a 'dramatic upswing' in the purchase of 'ceded' tax land.[49] Most of these purchases were, of course, in counties with a high percentage of Crown land. First among these was Östergötland, but these purchases were also common in the counties of Kalmar and Älvsborg.[50]

Most of these acquisitions were made by farmers who were now in a position to extend their land holdings. At least in western Sweden, this wave of 'ceded' land purchases was like an epidemic: when a farmer of Crown lands purchased tax land, his neighbours were tempted to follow suit. But, particularly during the initial period, a fairly substantial proportion of these purchases were made by the nobility. In the western counties most land purchases were not in the outright agricultural communities: they were by people who had already bought 'ceded' land in, for example, the Götaälv area, while the plains of Skaraborg were still hardly affected. The end of the eighteenth century, however, saw a sharp upswing in the percentage of 'ceded' land bought by peasants. This change in the distribution of land holdings between the nobility and peasants must be related to the amount of benefit different groups could be assumed to derive from acquiring land in this way. Until 1789 the main right a peasant had was that he could bequeath and trade the title to his land. But land title was strictly regulated in other respects. As Jörgen Kyle writes, 'The right of disposal of the assets of the freehold (tax) farms were limited in important respects by the rights of the Crown and the tenant holder, the village community and the legislation on inheritance and the right to sell, mortgage, exchange or give away the land.'[51] The legal process which began in the Age of Freedom and began to be widely applied in 1789 strengthened the rights of possession and disposal. At this point the old rules on eviction, which had been a threat to every farmer of tax land whose tax payments were in arrears, were lifted. From 1789 farmers also enjoyed the statutory right to hunt and to fell the forests on their land. As early as 1766 new legislation on fishing had given the holders of land bordering on the sea or lakes better fishing rights. The compulsory assessment of property and the obligation to give the Crown first refusal when selling land was also lifted. The relaxation of controls concerning the formation of crofts has already been discussed. These reforms were followed by a relaxation of the old regulation which put a maximum on the number of the (often unpaid) live-in workers allowed on each farm.[52] These legislative reforms made ownership of a freehold title even more attractive. This also applied to the miners in the mining areas. The old mineworking laws which had, for example, compelled the peasants in a certain district to supply coal as tax and sell coal to the ironworks, were gradually repealed. Undoubtedly this made possession of tax land a definite advantage for the miners as well.

It is, perhaps, not surprising that the percentage of tax land bought by peasants (and miners) increased over time. Furthermore, it is certain that the improvement in the peasantry's financial situation also had a part to play. Good harvests and a lighter tax load allowed them to retain a growing

Figure 1.10 Baron Rutger Maclean, Svaneholm (1742–1816). KB.

surplus which could, for example, be used to purchase 'ceded' freehold land. Despite the restrictions on the right of land possession in the early eighteenth century, an individual farmer could certainly improve his position by changing his farm from Crown land to tax land.

The strong interest of the 'persons of rank' in buying freehold land remains to be explained. In the mining communities the ironworks made active efforts to increase their land and forest holdings. In the county of Örebro, particularly in Linde and Nora, the purchase of tax land therefore became a race between the ironworks and the peasants. Even in western Sweden the ironworks played an important part. Other groups, such as government officials, merchants and so on, were also active in buying tax land. The considerable interest in acquiring tax land around Gothenburg and along the River Göta valley may be seen as an expression of the commercialisation of the entire region that occurred in conjunction with the upswing in trade and timber in the eighteenth century.[53]

The agrarian revolution, commercialisation and social change

The good harvests, the stronger position of the peasantry and the relative fall in tax levels laid the foundations for an increase in the agricultural surplus at people's disposal, a surplus that could be used for investment, land reclamation and a higher work input. That the purely economic gains were accompanied by political and social advances were certainly a decisive factor in the surplus actually being invested in productive activities. Measures including stronger rights of possession and the land redistribution and consolidation process, allowed people to enjoy the fruits of their own labour in a more evident way than before. The optimism on the subject of agriculture that prevailed among the élite of society was also reflected among the peasantry. The better times were not short-lived; they would continue. Neither was there any new outbreak of a great war to spoil the picture. As a result, some of the surplus was invested in future improvements. The picture of a static peasant economy where a short-term surplus was eaten up by luxury consumption and festivities does not agree very well with the actual conditions in Sweden in the eighteenth century and the first half of the nineteenth century.

This increase in surplus had far-reaching and long-term consequences. Investments generated even greater increases in production. We see the 'agrarian revolution' we mentioned earlier. Parallel with this revolution came a commercialisation of the agricultural sector and widespread social change in the rural areas. The peasants had, of course, long been part of a simple market economy in which goods changed owners over relatively long distances. But the increase in the production of cereals and other agricultural products generated higher incomes which, in their turn, stimulated an expansion of the market. One visible result was the export of oats in particular, that began to gain pace a few years into the nineteenth century. But the domestic market expanded as well. From the mid-nineteenth century the five-year accounts kept by the County Governors give a wealth of examples of the way the peasants' growing incomes generated a strong demand for, not least, consumer goods. This was especially true of the economic boom of the 1850s. To give an example, the Kalmar County Governor's five-year accounts for 1851–55 reports the following about forest workers in Kalmar county: 'A few years have been enough to take the forest peasantry from a calm simplicity into the middle of the noisy world of commerce.'[54] The same County Governor's accounts also say that: 'The wealthy peasants spend a great deal on their clothes, their means of transport and the like; they live above their station, often consuming foreign drinks, and have in recent times shown a deplorable appetite for gambling, which they indulge during their visits to Kalmar.'[55]

Although this is surely an exaggerated picture, it is still clear that the peasantry's market relations were intensified in the first half of the nineteenth century. In the rural areas the traditional markets' range of goods increased and in the market squares of towns where the country folk sold their goods, the stalls became steadily more numerous. One manifestation of this was that peasants began to travel more. A diary kept by Johan Fredrik Isakson of Hälla farm in the parish of Folkärna in southern Dalarna allows us to map his travels from market to market. For the seven years the diary covers, 1876–83, he made a total of 296 journeys outside his parish. Most of these journeys were of no great distance; he travelled to By to visit the church and attend an auction, to Avesta to visit the market square, sell coal and go to the bank, and to Norberg to sell hay, potatoes and meat. There were also a number of journeys to markets that were farther afield.[56]

In the areas surrounding the large cities this commercialisation led to specialisation. Particularly from the 1820s, Stockholm, for example, became an important market for milk, meat and other animal products, resulting in more intensive specialisation in domestic livestock in an area within a radius of 30 to 40 kilometers from the city centre, the 'milk miles'.[57] The intensified commercialisation of agriculture was also expressed in a particularly buoyant land market and in the emergence of different credit institutions to supply the agricultural sector with capital, foremost of which were the credit societies formed by the large-scale farmers, which began to make a serious impact in the 1830s, the pioneer being the Skånska Credit Association founded in 1836. A not insignificant proportion of the credit banks' capital came from foreign debenture loans. The real breakthrough for these banks came in the 1840s and 1850s. Individual freehold farmers – initially the most wealthy – could obtain credit for land reclamation etc. by mortgaging their own landholdings.[58] There is no doubt that this more vigorous commerce in the agricultural sector had an important effect on the burgeoning industrialisation of the nineteenth century – which we shall address in the next chapter.

This agrarian expansion, taking place at the same time as commercialism began to flourish, also led to social advances. The other most important driving force was the sharp increase in the population, which can, however, scarcely be understood without the agricultural expansion. The underlying reasons for the rapid rise in Sweden's population figures from 1750 to 1860, from about 1.8 million to 3.5 million, is debatable. There is, for example, no simple link between production growth, on the one hand, and population growth, on the other. Some researchers have chosen to regard the growth in population as a separate force, with a falling mortality rate and a constant nativity level resulting in a larger population. According to this interpretation, it was, not least, the relative infrequency of plague epidemics and wars that produced this positive result. Furthermore, referring to Ester Boserup, the well-known agrarian researcher, it is widely thought that it was the growing population that forced the growth in agricultural production and not vice-versa.[59] The question of whether production or population was the driving force is something of a 'chicken-and-egg' problem. We must be content to note that this is a process in which the two factors reinforce each other: a better economic situation leads to population growth, which in its turn stimulates an increase in production and so on.

We may in any case note that there was a very rapid process of social differentiation. Between 1751 and 1850 the number of peasant households increased by about 10 per cent, while the number of crofters, 'hill-cottage occupiers', live-in workers and other landless people in the rural areas more than quadrupled. A growing percentage of the rural population was partially or wholly without land and thus incapable of supporting themselves by their own farming. A large part of the livelihood of many of these partially or wholly landless people was from paid work for farmers and the large estates. The crofters at least had some patches of arable land and could also keep cows and other livestock. The 'hill cottage occupiers' landholdings were usually far more meagre than those of the crofter. In their case, work, paid either in money or in kind, was even more dominant. The *statare* (farm workers contracted on an annual basis) were another group with no land of their own. These workers were usually employed by the larger manor farms and estates. As a rule they were simple labourers, receiving payment in kind in the form of food, accommodation and fuel.

The background to this process of differentiation is open to a number of interpretations. The emergence of a landless 'proletariat' in the rural areas is often seen as a direct result of the rapid upswing in population figures. With more and more children surviving to adulthood, not everyone can be a peasant or a peasant's wife. Similarly, it has often been assumed that the multitude of country folk without land was the result of the high birth rate in this group. The historical-demographic studies that have been carried out do not, however, allow such a conclusion. On the contrary, available data suggest that the birth rate was in general higher among people with more substantial economic resources, i.e. the landed peasantry. In what is now acknowledged as a classic study of three parishes in Västergötland from 1778 to 1830, Christer Winberg showed that the average marriage age for landless women was 29.3 years old against 27.6 for peasants, while the average for living children born in wedlock in peasant households in one of the parishes – Dala parish – was 4.35 against 3.15 for the landless inhabitants. We may add here that child mortality in this area was higher in peasant households, which supports the theory that the rapid population growth was *not* the result of a tendency for landless people to 'breed like mice in a barn', a prejudiced description by Richard Cantillon, the Irish economist of the eighteenth century.[60] However, this is not to say that at the bottom of the social structure there were not families who lived in the most miserable squalor and with an appallingly high rate of child mortality.[61]

At least in Västergötland it was evident that a significant part of the growing agricultural proletariat were recruited to the farms. By 1850 the heads of half the landless households under the age of 55 were from the peasantry, according to Winberg's study.[62] However, the fall in social mobility during this period was certainly a more general phenomenon. On the other hand, it was obviously a consequence of the rapid growth in population. The most common claim here is that 'proletarianisation' was due to the population growing quicker than the ability to support it, i.e. there was quite simply not enough arable land. As we have seen above, during this period the area of cultivated land grew at a faster rate than the population. There was thus no question of a 'democratic' distribution which would give everyone access to some land. At the same time as the population grows, a process of social differentiation occurs that strengthens the position of the peasants as landowners. Strengthened by better rights of possession, the process of land redistribution and consolidation, etc., a group of peasants emerges who jealously guard their property and do not want to see their land divided up.

Figure 1.11 The Löfsätra Estate in Roslagen, 1760. Ink drawing by Fredrik Felt. The estate belonged to Principal Assistant Secretary Harald Appelbom. KB.

The same differentiation process widened the gap between those with land and those without. Of course, there had long been some differences in the amount of land farmers held and the incomes they had. There is, however, every indication that these differences became more pronounced during this period. The rising surplus and growing commercialism, taken together with the better opportunities for individual disposal of income, is likely to have led to some benefiting more than others. A good labour supply, personal initiative or sheer good fortune may have been decisive factors. In this way, small differences could lead to cumulative long-term changes. In the long run, this kind of differentiation process caused the emergence of a group of relatively well-to-do peasants on the one hand, while some people were reduced to being without land on the other. In some areas land reform will certainly have accentuated this process. But there is nothing to suggest that it was the worst-off peasants, for example, who had to move out of the villages following the *laga skifte* statutory land reform – the reverse was not infrequently the case, as many well-off and enterprising farmers saw the benefit of relocating to gain access to consolidated parcels of more fertile land. Neither does the land redistribution process in itself seem to have led to any extensive marginalisation of the less well-off peasants. In general, the process of social differentiation we are discussing here seems hardly to have led to the widespread emergence of large-scale farming. At least, no large group of farmers emerged with considerable landholdings who made extensive use of paid workers. In the period we are discussing here, social differences were still relatively minor. But they probably grew and were to continue to grow. Neither was there any massive dispersal of small units of land with the aim of combining them with the larger farms. Although this occurred – perhaps more often than we know – people most commonly found themselves without land because there was not enough arable land for all the peasant children. In addition, those without land added to their numbers by forming families and producing children.

The end of the Malthusian cycle

Sweden's rural communities underwent an agrarian revolution from the 1720s onwards. In the cycle of crises that affected the early agrarian society, an upswing in production could be linked to an even faster rise in population, which in time caused an agricultural crisis. But the agrarian revolution appears to confound this cruel logic. From the 1720s, production increased faster than the population. This trend was also accentuated in the first half of the nineteenth century with the dramatic rise in the crop yield figure. The last, more traditional type of famine occurred at the end of the 1860s – but that was a regional phenomenon.

The production downturn of 1760 to 1790 has, it is true, been interpreted as the final expression of the old crisis cycle. After several decades of agricultural expansion, the 1760s saw a return of the typical crisis phenomena of famine, epidemics and an increase in child mortality. Land reclamation during the previous period had, however, been particularly extensive,[63] and this time the greater pressure on land resources only caused a relatively

Figure 1.12 The beginning of the end of an era: the agricultural proletariat have organised and demand the abolition of the regulations governing live-in workers and better pay. The landowners respond by dismissing the farm workers and crofters and evicting them. This illustration is from the eviction of some fifty farm workers at the Trolle-Ljungby entailed estate, Skåne, 1909. KB.

Figure 1.13 The stone-walled farm to the right is typical of the times (detail from Figure 1.3).

short-term crisis. At the end of the eighteenth century agriculture expanded once again. Land reclamation quite simply improved agricultural productivity. The most important long-term effect of this was that the conditions that caused the cycle of agricultural crises ceased to exist.

2 Early industrialisation

The word 'industry' is from the Latin *industria*, which means roughly 'assiduous activity or work'. But it is used in many ways. In its narrowest sense it means factory production. It is sometimes used in a broader sense, to denote manufacture before the emergence of factories. Before the factory system became established, 'industry' signified all non-agrarian production carried on in rural areas, with the exception of the guild-based crafts. Another term for the same thing is 'protoindustry'. This term, however, does not include rural handicrafts, as it refers to products that were marketed outside the village in which they were produced.

Making non-agricultural products such as clothing, household implements and kitchen utensils, simple agricultural equipment and other useful articles was, of course, a well-integrated part of the simple village-based market economy. These activities were adequately covered by the old heading in economics statistics of 'agriculture and associated activities'. The widespread individual management of the household's economy required most of the articles the household needed to be manufactured in the home. There were usually a number of specialists in the villages – the blacksmiths, cobblers and tailors who supplied households with the articles they needed – and there was some specialisation among peasant households; some, for example, were known as particularly skilful carpenters while others might work at digging wells.

In addition to these activities there was an early form of protoindustry which marketed its products outside its own local economy. Our definition of terms is further complicated here by the existence, even before the Middle Ages, of communities in which peasant households concentrated on a particular kind of handicraft production for trade. In some respects, household handicraft production is a better term than protoindustry, because that term may lead people into the false belief that protoindustry was an essential stage in the progression towards 'real' industrialisation in the nineteenth century. However, protoindustry was more that just a step towards a modern industrial society. It was a self-evident part of the older agrarian economy. In regions with special 'natural' conditions such as access to raw materials, crafts had long been practised that supplied customers over fairly large areas.

There is evidence in Sweden of several of these early important proto-industrial areas or districts where the handicrafts of peasant households were produced for trade in distant markets, markets which underwent major expansion in the eighteenth century. The three main districts are the Sjuhäradsbygden in Västergötland, an area covering the north of Skåne and southern Småland, Dalarna and, particularly, the Siljan district. The villages of these regions had highly developed household handicraft production which employed a large proportion of the population.

The Sjuhärads district was an early centre of extensive linen manufacture, but other crafts, particularly wood and metalworking, were also represented. From the 1820s, cotton gradually came to replace linen. People spun and wove everywhere in the rural communities. At its peak in the 1870s as many as 50,000 people are estimated to have been involved in textile crafts. After that time, rural household handicraft production gradually lost ground as it was out-competed by growing factory-based production. Before the nineteenth century, casks, sieves, baskets, barrels, furniture, scythes, wagons, etc., were also produced for sale. As we shall see later, the dominant linen and cotton craft was organised as 'a putting-out system', in which merchants from Borås placed orders with rural producers.

The district on the borders of Småland and Skåne was another important handicraft area, which reached up towards the Sjuhärads district in south-west Västergötland. It was known particularly for its extensive metalworking and woodcrafts, which centred on the parish of Gnosjö. Wire-mill and stretching-hammer works produced semi-finished goods which were finished in peasant homes to produce carding brushes, needles, hooks, etc. There were also bayonet-forgers, coopers, carpenters, clockmakers and the like, in Gnosjö in the nineteenth century. But household handicraft production was well-developed elsewhere as well – the manufacture of weaver's reeds, scythes, tongs, etc., in Markaryd, linen further north in the Sunnebo area and forging (including ploughshare manufacture) and foundry work in Osby in north Skåne and elsewhere. Household handicraft production was also common in the forest villages in the county of Kristianstad. Göinge and Åsbo specialised in various woodcraft products, including casks, furniture, wheels, chests and rakes. Göinge, in particular, had rough forgers and fine metal workers, and copper and bronze castings were made for trading.

Yet it was probably Dalarna, particularly the Siljan district and the area to the north, that was the country's main household handicraft production region before the mid-nineteenth century. The Handicraft Commission's interim report of 1918 looks back with nostalgia at the conditions that obtained before the real breakthrough of factory-based industry:

It is likely that southern Dalarna was characterised very early as the centre for forging by virtue of its iron resources and its widespread mining activities, while south-east Dalarna is known mainly for its painters and wooden vessels, north-east Dalarna for its clocks and other metal crafts centred on Mora, grindstones from Orsa, baskets in Värmhus, casks in Venjan and Älvedalen, and boats in Venjan and Sollerön.[1]

The Siljan district was particularly well known for its vigorous homecraft production, with considerable specialisation in the different villages and parishes. Våmhus was the centre for articles made from animal hair – even beyond Sweden, to Russia, for example. Boats were built on the island of Sollerön, and Hjulbäck in the parish of Leksand was 'a centre for turned goods' such as rolling-pins, spinning-wheels and bowls. But the most diversified handicrafts were to be found in the parish of Mora. Here, too, there was a clear division of labour among the villages. 'Almost every village had specialised in a certain type of manufacture, with divisions almost as strict as those of the guilds', writes Dag Trotzig, for example.[2] Thus, casks were made in Garsås, weaving looms in Noret, basketwork in Bonäs, combs in Selja, casks and weaving reeds in Gopshus and Oxberg, and Östnor specialised in clocks and other metalwork. Östnor was also the home of the popular Mora clock, which was produced by a highly decentralised cottage industry. A number of different specialists, among them smiths, foundrymen, carpenters and clockmakers, were required to make a Mora clock. In the first half of the nineteenth century, close to a thousand Mora clocks were made here without the work being co-ordinated by any putting-out system merchant or manufacturer. From the metalworking crafts of Östnor emerged an extensive factory-based industry which still operates on a large scale today.

In addition to these three main districts, household handicraft production for trade was carried on in many other areas. The well-known linen craft that was common in Hälsingland and Ångermanland, for example, employed thousands of producers in the rural areas at the beginning of the nineteenth century. The same is true of southern Gästrikland where wood and metal craft goods produced for the market were common, such as horseshoes and horseshoe nails from the parishes of Torsäker and Årsunda, or fox traps from Ovansjö. Lerbäck parish in Närke was famous for its forged wheel hubs, Kumla for its cobblers, Våla and Harbo in north-east Västmanland for furniture (chairs), Halland for wool and knitted goods, and Lindome in Halland for traditional furniture.

The organisation of rural handicraft production

This early division of labour thus meant that household handicraft production was deeply rooted in the old agrarian society. As we have suggested above, these handicrafts appear to have emerged mainly in districts whose natural geographic features made it difficult for agriculture to support a large population. The Mora area is an interesting example. There is firm evidence of a relatively dense population in this area already in the Middle Ages – far too dense in relation to the limited possibilities this area offers for farming. This high population density can only be explained by the early concentration of the production of handicraft goods for the market. In the districts around Mora there was plenty of wood as a raw material, and iron could be bought from the mining regions of southern Dalarna or from Gästrikland. This combination allowed people to become highly skilled in the production and further refinement of goods to be sold to households or in markets all over the country.

These industries were notable for the considerable ingenuity used in organising these activities. Articles were either produced as part of the farmer's household activities or by peasants in their own homes. Up to the end of the eighteenth century the former was probably the most common form, while the nineteenth century saw the emergence of separate households that supported themselves by producing craft goods. But there is no clear boundary here. In the nineteenth century it was still common in the linen-producing districts of Hälsingland and Ångermanland for much of the spinning and weaving to be done by housewives, children, maids and farm-hands. However, we may assume that in many areas a significant proportion of the labour force, particularly in the case of textile products, consisted of single women living in their own homes. In the same way, in the eighteenth century it was already common in the Sjuhärads district, for example, for handicraft production to give crofters and even landless peasants a basis on which to form their own households. Christer Ahlberger writes: 'It was typical in this area that a weaver's household also had a little land to farm: the family usually had several sources of income. The men would work as day labourers on the farms and at making craft goods while the women wove.'[3]

As a number of researchers have emphasised, it is difficult to ascertain the extent to which production was organised as part of the farmer's household activities or that of other households. The main reason is that it is not so easy to establish what is meant by the term household. In the pre-industrial agrarian society there were several categories of people such as widows, the sick, the elderly and the 'destitute', all of which were provided for as members of the farmer's household but who in fact lived in their own little cottages. At least in the Delsbo area of Hälsingland, widows and poor women with children formed an important part of the workforce. They spun and even wove at home in their small cottages or at the farmhouse. In the nineteenth century, in the Sjuhärads district, there was also a group of women weavers who were entirely separate from the croft or farm households, the so-called fourth-part weavers, who were clearly in the category of paid workers, their pay being one fourth of the value of the quantity of cloth they wove.[4]

It has been claimed in international research that the emergence of the widespread household production of handicraft goods (protoindustry) led to a sharp growth in regional populations. The opportunity to support oneself from protoindustrial activities paved the way for a change in the demo-graphic pattern. As it was easier to make a living in the protoindustrial regions, people could marry younger and set up their own family homes. And since the number of children born was closely linked to the marriage

age of women, the result was a rapid rise in population, according to Franklin Mendels, the economics historian who studied the early cloth industry in Flanders.[5] But this was, of course, only true where protoindustry caused new households to be formed. In areas where rural handicraft production continued to be organised by, and as a part of, the farmers' households, these demographic effects were by no means self-evident.

In Sweden these protoindustries therefore had no powerful impact on demographic trends until the nineteenth century. A possible exception is, once again, the Sjuhärads district, where crofters and the landless appear to have formed households with handicraft production as an important means of livelihood. Here, too, according to many observers, the population upswing in a number of parishes was already 'noticeably strong' in the early nineteenth century.[6]

There were three main ways of selling handicraft products. The first may be called the *peasant system*, in which the producers themselves – often collectively – marketed their goods. In the Sjuhärads district, goods were sold by peddling on a large scale. Even before the eighteenth century the peddlers of this area, either themselves or through representatives commonly known as 'västgötaknallar', sold their wares all over the country. But their most popular period was in the eighteenth century, particularly at the end of that century. In 1796 alone these peddlers took out over a thousand trading licences and although the number then fell, there were still four hundred itinerant peddlers in the 1840s, travelling far and wide to sell their goods.[7]

The marketing of linen produced by the peasants of Hälsingland and Ångermanland was by a form of peddling known as 'sörköreri'. The peasants

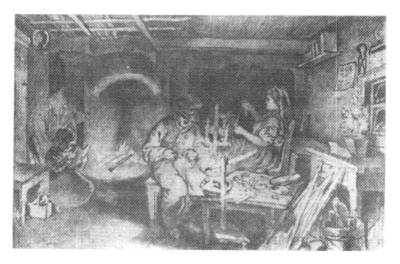

Figure 2.1 The interior of a croft located between Eksjö and Rödjenäs in Småland. Tinted ink drawing by Kilian Zoll in his sketchbook 1845–77. NMA.

of Ångermanland and Hälsingland had long carried on trade direct with Stockholm and other large market towns such as Sala, Västerås, Uppsala and Norrköping. The peasants joined forces and fitted out wagons and sledges with leather goods, hides, butter and game birds and, above all, flax and linen, to 'thereby dispose of their own and the farmer's products', as it was written in a trading licence issued in 1809.[8] Until 1810 this peddling was carefully controlled. Journeying from Nätra, Sidensjö and Själevad (and other places), the people the licences called 'peasants' could only have with them the produce of their own farms according to the rules that governed all forms of 'rural trade'. Around the turn of the century a typical peddler (sörkörare) from Nolaskog carried his own household's products and goods from two or three other households as well.[9] Particularly after the so-called lower excise duty (on domestic trade) was lifted in 1810 it became common for these peddlers to buy goods from other farming households. There then emerged, parallel with the old collective forms of marketing, a special group of 'peasant-merchants' who established regular business contacts in the towns.

A number of these merchants came to specialise in the linen trade, and in the first half of the nineteenth century took over the peddlers' trade in linen. This presumably meant that the farmers' trade in linen cloth expanded even more. Many of the peasant-merchants managed to combine their trading

Table 2.1 Linen purchases in selected years. Quantity, value and average price. Prices in riksdaler, skillings and runstycken

Year	Linen cloth of all qualities		
	Ell	Value in rdr and sk	Average price in rdr, sk and rst
1811	2662	1721:10	31:1/2
1812	3046	3902:37	1:13:6
1813	2484	2439:45	:47:2
1814	3369	3288:47	:40:1 1/2
1817	5422	6192:12	1:6:10
1821	5798	6060:29	1:2:2
1826	5556	5475:29	:47:3 1/2
1841	11518	11294:27	:47:1
1842	9661	9103:12	:45:2 1/2
1864	1485	1450:47	:46:11
1865	2173	2002:15	:44:3
1866	2677	2407:–	:43:2
1867	2102	1485:28	:33:11
1868	1616	1014:33	:30:1: 1/2
1869	1107	827:44	:35:11
1870	1604	1141:17	:34:1 1/2

Source: M. Morells, *Bondeköpman, Sörkörarnas avtagare*, Örnsköldsvik 1982, p.110.

Note: The amounts are rounded up to whole ells, values to riksdaler riksgäld (a slightly lower value riksdaler) and skillings.

with farming. One of the most important peasant-merchants in Ångermanland in the mid-nineteenth century was Eric Norberg from Kornsjö in Nätra. He progressed from trading in linen goods as a secondary interest to devoting most of his time to this trade. Each year he had large consignments of linen shipped to Stockholm, and made frequent visits to oversee the trade. In the capital he bought other goods which he then disposed of in his home district.[10]

The system by which the merchants bought up household handicraft products is usually called the *'kauf' system*, or buying system. We have seen that specialised peasant-merchants played an important part in the sale of linen from Hälsingland and Ångermanland. However, it is likely that most of the linen was sold through a city merchant acting as a middleman. In the Hälsinge parishes, merchants from Söderhamn and Hudiksvall bought up large consignments of linen which they sold on further south. In Hudiksvall, for example, there was the Dahlbom merchant house, which was one of several medium-sized outworker businesses in the city. At the beginning of the nineteenth century this merchant house bought up linen cloth from a number of parishes around the Dellen lakes in Hälsingland, namely Delsbo, Norrbo, Bjuråker and Forssa.[11] Under the same system the merchants of Härnösand bought up a large proportion of the linen cloth produced in Ångermanland.

The kauf system was not a uniform one – there were different kinds of producer–merchant relationships. In Hälsingland and Ångermanland the town merchants bought up large quantities of linen cloth in markets in, for example, Bjuråker, Färila, Järvsö (Hälsingland) and Näske (Ångermanland). In this case it is likely that the linen producers were fairly independent of the individual merchants. Similarly, it was common in many areas for the peasant producers to supply goods themselves to different buyers in the town. But there could also be stronger bonds in the kauf system. Many producers had a one-year contract with a particular merchant. If the producer also found himself in debt to the merchant, the merchant could be quite confident that he had the sole right to that producer's product. These arrangements could also be found in Hälsingland, where the peasants/ producers had a strong hold on linen manufacture. To take an example, the relationships between the linen producers and the Dahlbom trading house in Hudiksvall were clearly very stable. There was a permanent core of suppliers who can hardly have sold any significant amount of linen over and above the quantities they supplied to Dahlboms. But there were also producers who supplied their linen on a less permanent basis.[12] In other areas, fairly close and durable ties between producer and merchant were even more common. This was true not least of the linen industry (and later the cotton industry) in the Sjuhärads district, where as early as the eighteenth century the merchants of Borås had gained a fairly strong hold over the rural producers.

In the Sjuhärads parish, in particular, a third form of production, the *putting-out system*, developed. As with the word 'industry', the term 'putting-out system' (German: *verlagssystem*) has a number of meanings. It is sometimes used to mean simply a relationship between merchant and producer in which the merchant has a very strong position, for example by virtue of the producer's debt to him. But in a kauf system, peasants could also be in debt and thus dependent on their merchants. In the strict sense, in a putting-out system an entrepreneur 'puts-out' raw materials or semi-finished goods to individual producers who process the material and deliver the finished or semi-finished product to the same merchant for sale or further processing. There were, of course, variations on this theme. For example, a producer could be supplied with raw materials by a merchant but purchase other raw materials himself. Sometimes the producer took money instead of raw materials and bought all his raw materials himself. Here, it is almost impossible to draw a clear line between the kauf system and the putting-out system.

In the strictest sense, however, the putting-out system was not widespread in Sweden for a number of reasons. The degree to which the merchants were involved in the sale of household handicraft production reflected the local position of social power that the peasant producers could attain. For example, their position was generally considered to be stronger in Hälsingland and Ångermanland with their relatively unimportant towns than it was in the Sjuhärads district which was close to the more important towns of Borås and Gothenburg. But other factors were also important, in particular the availability of raw materials and/or other input goods. In Hälsingland and Ångermanland most of the flax was grown in fluvial soil which was unsuitable for other cultivation – in other words the linen industry had access to a local raw material. This meant that the merchants did not control the raw material supply. The reverse situation obtained in the Sjuhärads district. A lot of flax was grown, particularly in the Marks area and along the river Viskan, but most of the flax was brought in from outside the district. This was even more true of cotton, the supply of which was almost wholly controlled by the merchants.

Thus the Sjuhärads district saw the early development of a putting-out system which linked rural producers with town merchants. But particularly after 1820, when cotton began to make real advances, the putting-out system expanded rapidly. Paradoxically, this expansion began to undermine the earlier role of the Borås merchants as co-ordinators of the putting-out system. In the eighteenth century it was common for these merchants to supply the raw material direct to the producers, who returned the finished product. After 1820, however, a new middleman, the putting-out farmer, often called the 'joint buyer', appeared, who in practice took over the role of the merchants of Borås. This kind of putting-out system was common along the Häggån valley between Kinna and Fritsla.[13] Special storehouses were built on some of the larger farms in this area from which the weavers collected cotton and returned the finished (cotton) cloth.[14]

Some of the smaller putting-out farmers continued to buy on credit their raw materials from Borås or Gothenburg, which they then put out to the village weavers. The finished product was then sold to the Västgöta peddlers on a twelve-month credit.[15] The larger putting-out farmers also arranged their own imports of cotton from England and organised their own retail trade. In time, some of these independent putting-out farmers invested their capital in factories and machinery and became manufacturers. One such putting-out farmer was the well-known Sven Ericsson, who in 1834 set up the country's first mechanical cotton-mill at Rydboholm outside Borås. Another was the putting-out farmer Johannes Johannesson Mark, who founded the Gamlestaden factories in Gothenburg.[16] Sven Ericsson came from an old family of putting-out farmers from this area. His mother, Kerstin Andersson, known simply as 'Mother Kerstin', owned the Stämmevad putting-out house in Kinna, which became one of the biggest in the Sjuhärads district, with an extensive network of suppliers (weavers). Sven Ericsson founded his own putting-out business at Rättargården in the same parish, with a network of over a thousand home suppliers.[17] In 1851 the prominent putting-out farmers Anders Larsson and Sven Andersson of the parish of Örby collected cloth from 204 weavers. Altogether there were 474 households in the parish that wove for one of the putting-out farmers.[18]

Central government policy

The seventeenth century saw the introduction of a 'town economic' policy, a feature of which was a strict ban on rural trade. Under this policy, the authorities regarded the trade in handicraft goods with suspicion, particularly if carried on by the peasantry. A Royal Resolution of 1734, however, drew a clear line between what was permitted as rural trade and what was forbidden. This resolution said that the peasant was entitled to sell his own products but any buying of farm produce etc. for trade in the country was forbidden. When the general freedoms and rights of the peasantry were improved in 1789, peasants were allowed to add their neighbours' produce to their own. Many observers thought this concession was simply formal recognition of what was already a traditional practice.[19] The abolition of the lower excise duty on domestic trade in 1810 opened up wider opportunities for unrestricted rural trade. Until the final repeal in 1846 of the resolution that outlawed rural trade the peasantry were in theory only entitled to sell their own and their neighbours' produce. Furthermore, up until 1860, peasants had to have a special licence issued by the County Governor in order to travel to market to sell their produce. It is difficult to know what practical effects these restrictions had. Clearly they did not seriously hamper the direct trade from the flax districts of Ångermanland and Hälsingland, nor prevent these peasant peddlers from becoming peasant-merchants.[20]

The main purpose of the statutory ban on rural trade was to draw a clear line between the urban and rural economies. In the eighteenth century there was widespread scepticism about extensive rural household handicraft

Figure 2.2 The cradle of Sweden's textile industry, the cottage industry village of Kinna in the Sjuhärads district before 1880. Photo-engraving. From Mannerfelt, O. and Danielsson, H.; Sven Ericssons and the Rydboholms factory (1924). KB.

Figure 2.3 The Rydboholm factories before the arrival of the railway. From *Sveriges industriella etablissementer* 1870–76. KB.

production and trade. Craft and industrial production were regarded as indisputably urban sources of livelihood. Centralised urban manufacture was therefore preferred. Some, who better recognised the realities of the situation, were prepared to accept peasant handicrafts, but the products were to be bought up by the town merchants to be sold on, i.e. a putting-out system. The ban was not intended solely to favour urban manufacture and commerce: it was widely believed that agriculture would suffer if peasants were permitted to 'dabble' in other occupations.[21] Despite the numerous resolutions restricting rural trade, the infringements were many. It is only against this background that we may understand the torrent of complaints about illegal rural trade lodged in the second half of the eighteenth century in particular. As late as 1810, Carl Nieroth, County Governor of Härnösand, complained about peasants who

> travel about and make clandestine purchases of others' produce from near and far which, in the hands of the peasantry become trade goods; they also secretly acquire all kinds of knick-knacks and groceries that are distributed in equal secrecy in their local districts, this being part of the disorder which, difficult as it is to prevent, is undoubtedly harmful to the cultivation of the land.[22]

The merchants of Borås were among those who complained. In 1766 the citizens of Borås petitioned the Board of Customs and the Board of Commerce for excise duty to be levied in Borås on all illegal house-to-house peddling carried on by the countryfolk of the districts of Ås, Gäsene, Marks and Vedens. The authorities' promise to approve this petition led to a bitter conflict between the countryfolk and the citizens of Borås. The countryfolk were victorious, and the monopoly on trading that Borås had enjoyed was withdrawn in 1776.[23]

Notwithstanding the authorities' support of town-based manufacture and the sceptical attitude towards peasant handicrafts, the latter was hardly discouraged in practice. On this point the 'town economic policy' was ambiguous. On the one hand, there was too much 'peasant meddling' in occupations that were reserved for the townfolk – in particular the various handicrafts. On the other hand, there were areas in some parts of the country where more handicraft production, at least of a certain kind, was evidently to be encouraged, examples being the textile districts of Sjuhärad, Hälsingland and Ångermanland mentioned above. Among the measures the government introduced to stimulate handicraft production was an incentive scheme in which the producers had the quality of their cloth valued and rewarded accordingly. At the same time, special spinning schools were set up, such as those opened in Nätra and Själevad in Ångermanland in 1741 at the instigation of Stephen Bennet, a Scotsman, who was also appointed director of the Flors linen manufactory.[24] The efforts on behalf of this county made by Per Abraham Örnsköld, the County Governor, are widely acknowledged.

Örnsjöld introduced a comprehensive system of incentives to encourage more spinning. They included three silver-gilt jugs donated by the Manufactory Office to be awarded to deserving spinsters.[25] But it should be noted that these initiatives were for spinning alone, and were thus not a sign of any wholehearted support of peasant handicrafts. As with the laws that governed the mining regions, the authorities wanted the rural producers to supply the input goods – spun flax – and the weaving and processing of the fabrics was to be done in the town in special centralised factories or shops. The intention was clearly to encourage special spinning districts to develop along the lines of the mining system's blast furnace districts with their supplies of pig iron. The development of these spinning districts became an important feature of the manufacturing policy of the time. In the Age of Freedom and later, the preparation of the raw material (wool and linen) from these spinning districts was essential to the town-based textile industry.

The industrialisation of traditional crafts

The 1720 legislation on guilds codified the pre-industrial crafts in their traditional form. Under this legislation, guilds were to be formed in all towns which had at least three masters of a craft. In the guilds there was a strict division between masters, journeymen and apprentices. Under the new guild system the journeyman was allowed to marry, but he had to refrain from all the abuses that had previously been so common, such as not working on Mondays, general 'strutting about' during working hours and 'copious feasting'. The guilds maintained their hold on small-scale craft work through the eighteenth century, not only in the small towns, but also in larger towns, including the city of Stockholm.[26] The guilds' exclusive right to forbid people to set up a business outside their control was often criticised. Many nobles, for example, said they should be entitled to employ their own craftsmen. Others felt that the power of the guilds inhibited the development of industries. But the guilds were strong, and they had a great deal of political power. For example, the trial project started in 1724, allowing so-called free masters to establish themselves outside the guilds, had to be abandoned after only seven years.

The nature of craft production had not changed by 1820. Cobblers and tailors, followed by tanners and carpenters, were still the most common craft occupations. The number of journeymen and apprentices per master was still very low. By no means all the accredited masters had their own journeymen and apprentices: many of them worked alone. The number of crafts in a town varied, by and large with the size of the town. On the other hand, there was a higher percentage of craftsmen in the populations of smaller towns than in the larger towns and cities.[27] It was also more common for craftsmen in small towns to be dependent on the rural areas for their markets.

This picture remained largely unchanged until the mid-nineteenth century. True, the crafts expanded, with the number of craftsmen doubling from about 15,000 to 30,000 in the hundred years from 1750. Growth was particularly marked from 1750 to 1780 and from 1810 to 1845. In the first of these periods the number of journeymen and apprentices increased at more or less the same rate. This meant that they continued with small-scale production. Then, after 1810, the pattern of expansion changed, with the number of journeymen remaining largely constant while the number of apprentices gradually increased. In 1810 there was an average of 1.5 apprentices per workshop, while thirty years later the figure was 2.1.[28]

However, the expansion of craft production was not uniform, either geographically or over time. From 1750 to 1780 crafts in the larger towns stagnated and even lost ground (for example in Stockholm). This decline in Stockholm is partly a reflection of the difficulties the city experienced in maintaining its population level in the Age of Freedom and the Gustavian period. The mortality rate was so high that even the relatively large migration to the city from the countryside failed to maintain the population level.[29] To some extent the decline in the number of craftsmen was also due to an important structural change, namely the emergence of an industrial sector which was separate from the crafts. In some trades – most notably textiles – a growing number of workers were employed in the manufacturing segment, which was quite detached from the merchant and craft guilds. We shall return to this later.

Instead, the most marked expansion between 1750 and 1780 was in crafts based in the country towns, particularly in the occupations that produced goods to be sold in the rural areas. While agricultural expansion and transformation generated a great demand for tanners, wainwrights, carders and dyers, the garment-producing crafts declined in the face of growing competition from both the peasants' craft production and the manufactories in the cities.

After the period of stagnation between 1780 and 1810 there was another resurgence in the crafts. However, the expansion was confined to the larger towns, and the growth rate in the smaller towns was far more modest. The marked decline in Stockholm was reversed from 1820 onwards. Here, too, the highest growth rate was not in the occupations that directly supplied the rural communities; instead, the town-based crafts increasingly came to supply the towns' own needs. Growth was seen in occupations that were related to the intensive wave of building that was a characteristic feature of life in small towns in this period: bricklayers, carpenters, tiled stove builders, and painters. The crafts that supplied broad categories of the population with necessities also grew: tailors, cobblers, joiners and cabinetmakers. The number of employees per master-craftsman also rose in these occupations.

In general, the number of journeymen and apprentices per workshop rose from the beginning of the nineteenth century. There does not usually appear to have been any corresponding increase in income differences between different master-craftsmen. At least, in the case of crafts in the city of Malmö, Lars Edgren arrives at something close to the opposite conclusion. There

Figure 2.4 Craftsmen in large-scale production in Sweden's growing towns. Manufacture of glazed clay pipes for Norrköping's water mains. A pipe factory in Höganäs, 1890s. NMA.

were significant differences in the number of workers as early as the mid-eighteenth century, and in the subsequent period the income gap between craftsmen appears to have narrowed.[30] During this period it is hard to find any category of worker emerging as distinct from the craft collective in general, i.e. wealthy craftsmen who employed a large number of workers and who in time became factory owners and important industrialists. Instead, this period was notable for its continuity. It is likely that the social environment that shaped the consciousness of the craft groups – formalised in the guilds and in the different customs and traditions peculiar to the crafts – discouraged strategies and behaviour of this kind. Old traditions and standards undoubtedly played a decisive part here.

In light of the above, a closer study of Eskilstuna, a place where guilds were dissolved and banned at an early stage, is of particular interest. Since 1660, when Reinhold Rademacher opened his business in this town, Eskilstuna was known for its specialisation in the fine-working of weapons, knives, locks and implements. To encourage the improvement of these crafts, Eskilstuna was designated a staple (entrepôt) town on the English pattern (e.g. Birmingham) in 1771, which gave every metal craftsman the right to establish himself in the town. The regulations also barred guilds and encouraged free competition. The result was a sharp rise in production in the first half of the nineteenth century and relative differences in expansion between different metalworkers. Some forges turned into factories of a kind, and employed large numbers of people. In several cases the career path that a simple blacksmith followed resulted in the foundation of what was to become an important industrial complex after the mid-nineteenth century. Thus we

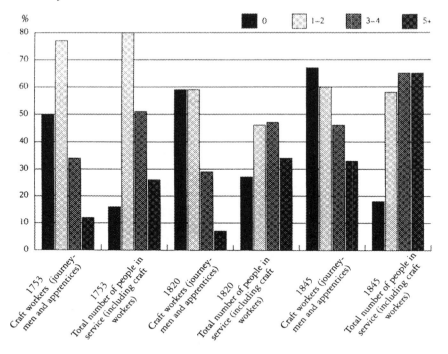

Figure 2.5　Size of craft workshops in Malmö 1753, 1820 and 1845. Bricklayers and carpenters
　　not included.
Source: L. Edgren, *Apprentice, Journeyman and Master*, Lund 1987, p. 123.

can see a clear process of proletarisation in Eskilstuna. In the large craft
organisations, which were soon transformed into mechanised factories,
journeymen and apprentices became forge workers and, instead of following
the tradition of living with 'their' masters, they set up their own households.[31]

This is a progression that has no real equivalent in the guild-dominated
world of crafts, where the system of apprentices living with their masters
continued for many years. In the mid-1880s, for example, the craft workers
of Malmö were remarkably young, their average age being just over twenty.
The status of journeyman, which was held for a limited time, served as a step
on the way to qualifying as a master-craftsman, or to starting some other
form of work. Most of them still lived in the traditional way, and did not
form a clearly defined working class. This, of course, is not to say that there
were not master-craftsmen in Malmö who employed people: in 1845 we find
a tailor called Ekström with twelve craft workers, or Karna Dalman, the
carpenter's widow, who employed no less than forty-three craft workers.[32] But
this latter was the exception that confirms the rule of continued small-scale
activities and a low level of differentiation.

The manufactories

'Manufactory' is yet another term that may be confusing. It is sometimes used to mean a centralised production organisation as distinct from the decentralised putting-out system. It may also be used as a financial term for the complex of rules that came into effect in the eighteenth century: the special manufactory legislation. In this last sense, the physical production organisation has nothing to do with the 'manufactory' of the first sense, that is to say, the way in which we shall use this term.

The origins of the manufactory legislation may be traced to the strong interest of the authorities in establishing profitable industrial manufacturing – mainly to replace the import of foreign textile goods or other consumer goods (often luxury ones). The prevailing view was that this kind of centralised production should preferably be located in the towns. Following the example of other countries, the aim was to set up centralised production units. The idea of obtaining longer production runs, achieved by a greater division of labour and by using workers housed in 'tenements', had its advocates in Sweden too.

These were the circumstances in which special legislation on manufacturing was introduced at the end of the seventeenth century. The Crown had already approved assistance and concessions for the establishment of copper and brass manufactories, for example when Reinhold Rademacher started his metal-working manufactory in Eskilstuna. To qualify for the exclusive privileges, Rademacher had to move his manufactory from Livonia, which was then

Figure 2.6 The workshop of a Rademacher smithy. Oil painting by Olof Hermelin, 1887. NMA.

Swedish territory. There was no other general policy of assistance at the time. It was not until 1668 that a special manufacturing policy began to be pursued in the form of the so-called craft house privileges, which encouraged the establishment of special craft goods enterprises in the towns. Entrepreneurs who founded such 'houses' were exempt from tax and qualified for other relief. They were entitled to organise their businesses without intervention from the guilds. This meant that the manufactories had considerable authority over their workers. One of the earliest manufactories, the Barnhuset (Children's Home) in Stockholm will serve as an example. Its first director, the architect Jean de la Vallée, was also the sponsor for all the new legislation on the manufactories. Next to premises for spinning and weaving woollen cloth at the Klara lake was added a children's home, where orphans and destitute children were 'in fear of God and in discipline and honour, to be taught reading, writing and arithmetic, and be maintained there'. According to the same source, the craft houses were 'to be both a house of correction and a spinning factory, in which bad, mischievous and roguish people, both male and female, may be shut in and work for their food'.[33] In light of this, it is perhaps not surprising that the first centralised manufactories – both in Sweden and in the rest of Europe – came to be regarded as virtual prisons.

Thus, in the following decades, general measures came into force designed to support something that was called the manufactory industry. These included protectionist measures in the form of the tariffs of 1667, special regulations banning the import of silk (in 1688, 1690, 1693, 1695, etc.), tax exemption, workers' exemption from military service, contracts as government suppliers, government regulation and inspection, and last but by no means least important here, the right to sell goods, both wholesale and retail, in the manufactory's home town and in entrepôt markets all over the country.[34]

However, this manufactory policy had no real impact until the 1720s. In 1722 a lower court (Market Court) was set up for the manufactories. Some years later the Parliament of 1726–7 set up the so-called rural assistance fund to award government loans to the manufactories. On this basis, a government loan bank was established as a commercial bank for the manufactories, which was to operate for almost 150 years and whose importance for the process of industrialisation should not be underestimated. The culmination of the manufactory policy was the '1739 Market Regulation and General Factory Act for all Manufacturers of Silk, Wool and Linen, and Craftsmen and Others not included under the Guild Resolution'. This resolution was in effect, at least on paper, until 1846, when it was repealed. According to this resolution the Market Court was to monitor in detail the manufacturing industry and its workers and rule in disputes between manufacturers and workers. This court was also to ensure that all goods were marked. As was the case with the privileges of 1668, the position of manufactory owner was an opportunity to evade the draconian rules that governed the crafts. They were not limited by the guild rules and could thus employ as many people as they wished and had extensive trading rights.

There has been much debate about the impact of the manufactory policy on industrial development. Eli Heckscher's view was that the policy of assistance caused manufacturing to flourish rapidly in the Age of Freedom, particularly in Stockholm. But when the crisis years of the 1760s and the austerity policy of the Caps Party cut back on support, the manufactories stagnated. Heckscher's processing of the statistics on manufacturing showed that the number of manufactories, weaving looms and workers fell – the manufactory industry was quite simply a typical hothouse plant that could not survive on its own. In the debate that followed Heckscher's work, Per Nyström and Olle Krantz were notable for their dissenting views. They were probably right in contradicting Heckscher, maintaining that the manufacturing industry was not a hothouse plant and could very well have survived unaided. Moreover, this sector, or at least parts of it, lived on despite the reduction in assistance after the 1760s. It is true that manufacturing was hit hard by the general economic downswing of the 1760s and 1770s but, according to Nyström and Krantz, it gradually recovered. It was mostly the weakest entities that failed to survive the crisis years. This is supported not least by the evident rise in production per worker and loom after the testing years of the industrial crisis of the 1760s.[35]

Textiles were without doubt the most important of the manufactory industries. This sector answered for over 50 per cent of total production value throughout the whole period up to the mid-nineteenth century, and it was never less than 65 per cent in the eighteenth century.[36] Wool manufacturing was the biggest industry in this sector, divided into the manufacture of carded wool or combed wool fabrics. The largest single manufactory in Stockholm was the Barnängen weaving manufactory on the banks of Hammarby lake in Södermalm with its production (to government order) of sailcloth, tent canvas and other linen fabrics. According to the Market Court figures, this manufactory employed about 1,300 workers in 1745.[37] In addition to these large enterprises in the capital there were a number of other manufactories in the rural areas, among them tobacco-mills, sugar-mills, manufactories for leather-working, metal manufactories and glassworks, paper-mills and china works. At the beginning of the 1760s this sector was at its height, with the number of workers totalling between 16,000 and 17,000 according to the Market Court records. The number of workers then fell rapidly, there being well under 10,000 by 1820, rising to around 17,000 in 1846.

Throughout the whole of this period the most important manufactory town was Stockholm, followed by Norrköping and Gothenburg. In 1760 there were roughly 10,000 manufactory workers in Stockholm, 2,000 in Norrköping and some 400 in Gothenburg. However, the most famous manufactory was in Alingsås, where Jonas Alströmer, the man who introduced potatoes into Sweden, had a large textiles manufactory in the 1720s,

Figure 2.7   Painted door lintel 1768–1834 at the home of Rudolf Stenberg, silk manufacturer of Stockholm. Oil painting. NMA.

and also embarked on a number of rather exotic enterprises, including tobacco cultivation. As was so easy for the critics of the manufactory policy to point out, Alingsås was really a hothouse plant that would never have survived without massive government support. For a few short decades, however, the manufactory works and the town flourished – according to Heckscher, the town of Alingsås was seen as nothing more than an appendage to the manufactory – and it went into severe decline before the 1760s. Other well-known manufactories such as the above-mentioned Barnängens clothing manufactory in Stockholm (linen etc.), the Ullanderska factory in Norrköping (wool), Hans Coopmans in Gothenburg (wool), Utenhoffs silk manufactory in Stockholm, the Eskilstuna steelworks, Rörstrands china factory, Hegardts garment manufactory in Stockholm, the Stockholm Marieberg manufactory (china), and Flor in Hälsingland (linen) were more viable and vigorous enterprises.

There was an interesting shift in the geography of the manufactory industries in the nineteenth century. As we have already seen, there was a sharp upswing in manufactory production after the Napoleonic Wars, particularly in wool production, which dominated this sector. But while production in Norrköping, for example, increased by as much as 460 per cent from 1816 to 1845, it *fell* by 60 per cent in Stockholm. The reason for the sharp decline in wool production in Stockholm and the fall in the number of workers and production value are complicated. The explanation can scarcely be that Norrköping managed to out-compete Stockholm, because, for example, Stockholm had higher relative labour costs. In all important respects the two towns do not appear to have competed in the same markets. The success of Norrköping was rather because it was able to meet the growing demand from the rural areas, initially for fine quality goods and later for ordinary goods. Stockholm was far from successful in taking advantage of this new demand. Stockholm's market consisted largely of its own population, which stagnated – at least until the 1820s. To this market was added the substantial government orders, particularly from the army. But these orders also slowly diminished during this period, which partly explains Stockholm's decline. Instead of entering into serious competition with the expanding industry of Norrköping – or rural protoindustry – Stockholm's industries began to produce more expensive fabrics in new qualities (drapery and cashmere) in the 1840s, which, however, failed to compensate for the overall decline on the demand side.[38]

The authorities regarded the policy of assistance primarily as a means of encouraging more centralised production. However, this does not mean that all 'manufactories' to be found in the Market Court records were centralised industrialised plants. Some of the larger manufactories – the Barnängen linen-weaving shop is a good example – could clearly be classed as centralised manufacture. Most of the production was situated in large workshops manned by a large number of workers. Barnängen was also a complete factory inasmuch as most of the specialist workers needed to produce the linen fabrics were to be found in the manufactory. The same applied, for example, to Lorenz Pauli's garment manufactory in Södermalm in Stockholm. In addition to spinsters and weavers there were also wool workers (scrubbers, sorters, etc.) and other workers such as dyers and cutters who processed the cloth.[39] There were also far smaller plants in the manufactory sector, such as the weaving shops that produced nothing but cloth for garments, in which the total number of employees was far smaller – perhaps four or five weavers and a few assistants. Most of these garment shops concentrated on certain parts of the manufacturing process, especially weaving. Under this heading there were, at least in the Stockholm wool industry, a number of manufacturers who were in fact pure craftsmen who worked for themselves, assisted by one or more members of their family. Although they were actually craft weavers, they were recorded as manufacturers in the statistics. At least some of the smaller garment-weaving shops and clothing craftsmen had established connections either with a merchant or with larger manufactories. Sometimes this relationship took the form of a putting-out system. A kind of 'kauf' system was, however, more common, in which the manufacturers bought semi-finished goods and sold on the finished products to different merchants or larger producers.

Detailed reports on the number of workers employed in the manufactories, the number of looms, the production volumes and production figures were submitted to the Market Courts. But it is clear that a significant percentage of the labour force was never included in the statistics. In addition to the formally employed manufactory workers – perhaps 15,000 in the 1780s – there may have been a further 5,000 people working at home for the manufactories. This was especially true of weaving, but also of the pre-manufacturing and finishing work that was not done at the garment-weaving shops.[40] To this figure must be added the labour force in the spinning districts. We have already mentioned the efforts of the authorities during the Age of Freedom to set up these rural spinning districts. These came to act as subcontractors to, for example, the major clothing manu-factories in Stockholm at the end of the eighteenth century.

The nature of the manufactory as an enterprise was complex and varied. The degree of centralisation naturally also varied from one type of manu-facture to the next. But there were only a small number of the centralised craft-based factories that the literature describes as typical of the manu-facturing sector. Instead, there were many small-scale entities in which a significant proportion of the workforce were homeworkers, usually women. Stockholm may therefore be described as a 'bazaar economy' of small enter-prises with intricate buying and selling relationships with one another.[41]

The 1850s: the first industrial expansion

As discussed earlier, the agricultural revolution and the growth of the agricultural sector created the conditions for an increase in demand and an expanding domestic market. Until the mid-nineteenth century the existing production structure was able to meet the higher demand. There is no doubt that household handicraft production played an important part in supplying the population with various consumer and utility goods, including clothing, agricultural implements, etc. But the town-based manufactory sector played an important and increasingly prominent part here as well. We have, for example, mentioned above the rapid expansion of Norrköping as a wool town. At the same time, crafts expanded in the towns. The reason was the growing rural demand together with the demand from the towns' own inhabitants, as their numbers increased from the 1820s onwards.

The expansion of the textile industry in particular, was undoubtedly fuelled by the rise in incomes in the agricultural sector. Consumption of textile goods increased steadily from 1820 until the 1860s. It was during this period that cotton fabrics became widely popular. This consumption was not accompanied by falling prices for cloth, which suggests that the increase in demand was *either* because incomes rose *or* because a higher percentage of people's incomes was spent on fabrics and clothes. Because we can say with confidence that income rose, the first alternative is the most likely one. But it is also clear that the demand for different qualities of fabric changed. In the 1830s the sharpest increase in production was of fine quality fabrics, while the reverse is true in the 1850s. Lennart Schön interpreted the growing demand of the first period as being largely attributable to the upper classes in the rural areas and in the towns, namely the prosperous peasants and burghers. In the 1850s, however, demand was led by the lower classes.[42] Until the 1850s, small-scale handicraft production and the manufactories

Figure 2.8 Cotton-mill in Torshag outside Norrköping, built in 1846 to drawings by Andrew Malcolm, a Scotsman, and Carl Teodor Malm, a town architect in Norrköping. From D. H. Bagge, *Notes on Sweden's Cotton Mills Gathered During a Long Life* (1889).

were able to keep pace with the rise in demand. But it proved impossible to keep pace with the rising demand for cheap mass-produced fabrics, particularly cotton.

It is also around 1850 that we can see the first signs of more large-scale centralised production. As the manufactories gradually fell into disfavour, the Board of Commerce began, from the early nineteenth century, to differ between 'handicraft', on the one hand, and what were called 'factories', on the other. As with the old manufactories, the factories were not part of the craft guild system. The term 'factory' was first used to mean production plants, both in towns and rural areas, such as engineering works, sawmills, sugar-mills, paper-mills, match factories and printers. As time passed, factories in other sectors – textile factories, metalworking shops, etc. – came to be included in this term. By definition, the factory was a larger plant that was not part of the craft sector – and was outside the jurisdiction of the Market Court. This indicated that the factories were located in rural areas. However, as time passed, every plant above a certain size was designated, in the fiscal sense, as a 'factory'. Of course, this did not mean that these 'factories' were not still relatively small operations as late as the mid-nineteenth century. According to the Board of Commerce statistics, in 1835 there were 2,037 'factories' in Sweden with a total of 14,925 workers. After this time both the number of factories and workers increased. According to the average figures, the number of workers per workplace rose very slowly. Although there were many exceptions, we cannot say there was a real breakthrough of centralised large-scale industry before the 1870s.

A sector that deviated somewhat from this pattern was the textile industry – which in Sweden, as elsewhere, was the first mass-production industry. In Norrköping, for example, as early as 1845 there were close to 100 garment factories which employed about 3,000 workers, mainly in weaving wool. A number of large cotton-mills had already ben founded in the 1830s: Rydboholm, Jonsered, Näs, Strömma near Karlshamn in Blekinge, etc. In the 1850s and 1860s, there was strong expansion in large-scale factory-based cotton weaving, not least in Norrköping, where structural change had brought on a crisis in the wool industry in the 1840s. This crisis caused numerous factory closures and widespread unemployment which generated serious social unrest. The wool industry was gradually replaced by a larger-scale cotton industry which combined spinning and weaving. The Norrköping Cotton Mill, founded in 1847, was from the middle of the 1850s an example of this kind of modern, integrated factory. It had 165 workers (half of them children) employed in spinning, and 400 people working at weaving and after-treatment.[43]

The textile industry differed from the general pattern in another respect. Beginning in the 1830s, some mechanisation was introduced, initially in the large cotton-mills. Modern mechanical spinning-frames, mostly driven by water power, began to come into use. This technology came almost exclusively from England. The Rydboholm Mill employed Charles Hill, an English master-weaver who later helped to build up cotton-mills in both Norrköping and Alingsås.[44] Mechanical looms were introduced in Norrköping in the 1850s, for example at Norrköping Cotton Mill (later Bergs AB), and in Holmens Mill, which was one of the largest of its time. The workforce in these new, mechanised mills was largely female. Child labour was also used. Water was still the main power source in the 1850s and 1860s. Steam had begun to come into use, but mainly to heat the factory buildings.

Outside the textile industries, the number of 'factories' also increased in the mid-nineteenth century. A mechanical engineering industry had been established in Sweden even earlier. There were some workshops in Stockholm, among them Bergsunds, Ludwigsbergs and Bolinders works, and also the Motala works, Munktells (Eskilstuna) Kockums (Malmö) Keilers (Gothenburg) and the engineering works in Norrköping and Nyköping. More engineering works were opened in the mid-nineteenth century, including Köpings Engineering Works, Atlas in Stockholm and Nydqvist & Holm in Trollhättan. A notable feature of these early engineering works was the number and variety of occupations involved. Almost every imaginable product was made to order. Munktells, for example, made agricultural implements, machine tools and dredgers – as well as the cupola for the famous Gustavianum building in Uppsala! A foundry was often added to these engineering works, for casting machine parts etc. At Bolinders, for example, cast-iron stove production became one of the main activities.

Figure 2.9 Turning workshops at the old Gothenburg shipyard. From *Sveriges industriella etablissemanger 1870–76*. KB.

Unlike the textile industry, most of the workers in these engineering works were men. A remarkable number of them were highly specialised and skilled workers who had been trained in a craft, either in engineering works or rural smithies. They employed a varying number of assistants to help them, many of them recruited from the countryside or the poorer urban population. Again, unlike the textile industry, little enough of the production process was mechanised until the 1870s, although it is true that modern machines, particularly lathes for steelworking, were installed at some of the larger workshops, for example at the Motala Works where, as in the textile industry, both technology, special techniques and key workers were imported from England.[45] Before the 1870s the most common power source in these workshops was water power, fed to the machines by belts. But most of the work was entirely manual. The works were made up of a number of separate workshops – smithy, foundry, plate works, carpenter's shop – where the work was carried out with simple traditional tools.

From the 1830s onwards we may note that factory-based operations grew in other sectors as well, not least in the consumer goods sector, such as sugar-mills, paper-mills and printing works. Again, we may see here the consequences of a growing demand generated by an expanding agricultural sector. There was also growth in wood products, and the sawmills prospered in the mid-nineteenth century. As with so many other branches of industry, the sawmills began as a purely rural phenomenon. Everywhere in the forestry and the mixed forestry and agricultural communities of south and mid-Sweden there were small, often seasonal, peasant sawmills. These were simple mills and the work was done manually or with the help of water power. But a far-reaching process of change began in the 1850s. Along the Norrland coast, a number of large exporting sawmills grew up equipped with band-saws of a completely new design and capacity, usually steam-powered. The sawmill coast of Norrland experienced something akin to a 'Klondike boom', to use Heckscher's expression, in the 1850s. We shall return later in this book to this export-led process of industrialisation and its importance and implications. However, when it comes to the expansion of the sawmills in the 1850s, we must emphasise that it was also fuelled by domestic demand. More intensive building in the towns and rural areas caused a sharp rise in demand for building materials such as timber and board.

The industry that had traditionally supplied the population with non-agrarian goods was on the brink of sweeping organisational change in the mid-nineteenth century. The rapid growth in demand had outstripped the old production capacity. In this respect the 1850s were, without doubt, a dividing line between the old order and the new, and the relative stagnation of the 1860s may be seen as a breathing-space. In the next decade, the 1870s, industrial development was poised for explosive expansion.

Figure 2.10 The Jönköping match factory with its proudly smoking chimneys. From *Sveriges industriella etablissemanger 1870–76.* KB.

3 Regulation, deregulation and adjustment

The state that entered the eighteenth century after the age of 'great power policy' and the end of the absolute power of the monarch was still traditional in nature. To make its mark in the troubled Europe of the time, a nation needed a broad tax base and an effective tax system. The government's interest was still largely focused on fiscal matters. This is the point of departure for the political ideology of the eighteenth century, cameralism, to which great importance was attached in countries such as Sweden, Prussia, Denmark and Austria. The word cameralism derives from the Latin 'camera', the sovereign's chamber, i.e. the treasure chamber. The most important feature of cameralism is that its main purpose is to enhance the power of the state. This requires a sound economy capable of generating a surplus of precious metals, while supporting a growing population. To this end, it was thought that privileges should be granted to agriculture and commerce. For the same reason, the country must also process its own raw materials in factories, either to replace foreign imports or to export and thus acquire precious metals. There could be some conflict of goals here. If taxes and charges were raised too high, there was a risk of agricultural, industrial and commercial stagnation.

This was the dilemma which took up much of the debate on Sweden's economy in the eighteenth century. There were many who maintained that support must be given to export trade and modern manufacture, even if it was at the expense of other sectors such as agriculture and the crafts. The 'town economic policy' that dominated in earlier centuries could be a feature here. On the other hand, it was widely believed that support of the manufactories, for example, should not be allowed to go too far. Excessively severe taxation and regulation could have the opposite of the desired effect. Some observers went as far as to criticise, at the theoretical level, the limitations that the town economic policy placed on trade and commerce. Among these observers was Anders Chydenius, the radical priest from Österbotten, who even wanted to see the regulation on live-in workers lifted to ease the restrictions on the labour market. Another influential 'liberal' critic of the entire complex of rules and regulations, such as the limits on rural trading, was Anders Nordencrantz, the well-known debater. He was clearly inspired

Figure 3.1 Left: Anders Nordencrantz (1697–1722). Engraving after a portrait by P. Kraft. KB; Right: Anders Chydenius (1729–1803). Copperplate engraving by J.F. Martin. KB.

by ideas of natural law, and referred to Hume, Mandeville and Helvetius in his voluminous polemic writings. Nordencrantz and Carl-Gustav Scheffer, the argumentative politician and royalist who had absorbed the modern pro-agriculturist ideas in Paris, where he was in close contact with important physiocrats such as Mirabeau and Quesnay, were both advocates of the principle of 'craft freedom'. Nordencrantz wrote with irony about guild restrictions and the current 'craft system' under which the authorities decided on the number of people allowed to practise their trade in each sector. Would it not be just as good, he wondered, 'to establish in law, under the supervision and control of government officers, how much each and every person should eat and drink in a day or a year'.[1]

However, many thought it enough to state that agriculture must not be neglected or subjected to excessive taxes. In the lively debate carried on throughout the 1750s and 1760s, which came to be known as the 'controversy over industrial precedence', there were many who spoke in support of agriculture. Carl Leuhusen, a champion of agricultural interests, said that agriculture was the only 'art' that generated 'new materials for the needs of mankind'.

Thus, as the eighteenth century passed, the understanding grew that a state which only looked to its own interests and was driven by fiscal motives could very easily work against its own interests. For this reason, benefit to the state became interwoven with another objective: the general improvement and expansion of the economy. Accordingly, the principle of the

Swedish cameral government of the eighteenth century was 'the prosperity of the people and the honour of the state'.

The idea that the welfare of the population could coincide with the national interest was new. But the state of the eighteenth century was still largely a product of its past. The 'town economic policy' was still dominant – a theme that grew stronger in the first decades of the Age of Freedom. Policies continued to be structured on the basis of the estates of the realm, examples being the ban on rural trade and on metalworking in the mining districts. But policy was not uniform or dogmatic; in practice it often reflected traditional boundaries. While there was still faith in the old policy of regulation, there was also an ambition to prepare for new forces to come into play. The future clearly lay in the development of a modern industrial sector that was supplied with capital from a capitalist sector. Technical and organisational innovations were encouraged. At times, this view meant that the current system of regulations had to be set aside, which caused protests from both craftsmen and town burghers and others who benefited from strict compliance with the policy of regulation.

In the eighteenth century, Sweden's government was still 'porous' in the sense that it was susceptible to outside influence, and this placed clear limits on political action. There was a high degree of autonomy at the different levels of the bureaucratic-administrative apparatus, which made it difficult for central government to have regulations put into effect. Pursuing a given economic policy required more than edicts issued 'from above'. It is therefore misleading to speak of a coherent 'economic policy' while this autonomy existed. Despite the efforts made in the seventeenth century to increase centralisation, there was still a wide gap between what was decided by Council and Parliament in Stockholm and the actual exercise of power at the local level. True, compared with many other nations Sweden was unusually centralised. Yet, as Per Frohnert maintains, it was still a 'uniform state with particularistic features at the local level'.[2] There was still insufficient control over local officials and 'particularisation of the estates of the realm' was still widespread. Sweden was still far from the tightly-regulated, disciplined and powerful bureaucracy which Max Weber sees as the hallmark of the modern Western state.

Mercantilism in Sweden

The knowledge that the power of the nation derived from a large population and a strong economic base led the power-holders and economic–political thinkers of seventeenth- and eighteenth-century Europe to advocate industrialisation and import substitution. This 'policy', which in view of the porosity of the state was impossible to implement consistently, was usually called 'mercantile'. Holland was often taken as an example in support of this kind of policy. This little republic had gained wealth and considerable political power from its trade and industry. Despite its insignificant size and inadequate agricultural sector, it supported a large and prosperous population. This was an example to be followed.

In England and other countries the study of this upstart neighbour led to more economic nationalism. High protective tariffs were introduced to favour England's domestic industries. Instead of exporting raw materials, they were to be processed in the country, either for domestic consumption or for export. From time to time, prohibitions were even introduced on the export of selected key goods, including precious metals and cereals. But it is hardly possible to sustain bans of this kind, and the ban on exporting precious metals, for example, was lifted in 1660. Critics of this prohibition – including the well-known mercantilist Thomas Mun (in his pamphlet, *England's Treasure by Forraign Trade*, published in 1664 but written over thirty years earlier) – maintained, for example, that some export of precious metals was essential in order to buy goods from countries that wanted not goods but money in return. Otherwise it would be impossible to import sought-after silk and other exotic products from India, which could then be re-exported at a net profit to England or, even better, be processed in the country (making, for example, silk garments from raw silk). With the republic of Holland in mind, England introduced, in the Navigation Acts of 1651 and 1662, a nationalistic shipping policy that banned the export of all goods from England to any country other than the English colonies. The best solution was to manufacture and refine as much as possible at home. Only the export of finished manufactured goods would be entirely exempt from duties (logically one must, however, be prepared for one's trading partners to levy duties on these goods). This would create secure employment and prosperity. A country with the largest possible industrial sector – and with the greatest possible added value in exports – was a country with military and political might.

These ideas were by no means unique to England – they are to be found in contemporaneous debates in France, Spain, Italy (Tuscany), Austria and other countries. Neither were these ideas entirely new in the seventeenth century. The ban on the export of raw materials (including precious metals) was an enduring political dogma: in England the long-lived Statute of Employment was introduced, under which foreign merchants were obliged to spend their hard-earned English money in England. Yet it was in the seventeenth century that this policy first became widely applied. It should be emphasised that this was often against the advice of many economic writers, who warned against too much protectionism and government intervention in the economy.

As noted earlier, the policy of import tariffs took a more protectionist direction in Sweden in the seventeenth century. At the same time, a policy was introduced that aimed to support domestic manufacture. This policy was widely applied after the Treaty of Nystad of 1721. Notwithstanding all talk of the opposite, political thinking in the Age of Freedom was permeated by a strong desire for military revenge. Sweden had been forced into ignominious retreat from its position as a great power in the Baltic region. The country was now threatened by the emerging Russian Empire and by new powers such as Brandenberg-Prussia. There was broad agreement that a return to the status of a great power would require rapid population growth. As in Holland, this could only happen if industry and manufacturing expanded. Sweden, like the other Western European countries, had to become more self-sufficient and replace the import of industrial goods (such as textiles) with domestic products. But it was widely agreed that agriculture could only expand if helped by growing demand from an expanding urban industrial sector.

However, as we have seen, there was lively debate about the 'controversy over industrial precedence'. Particularly under the government of the Hats Party from the 1720s until their defeat in the Riksdag of 1765/6, an intensified policy of industrialisation was advocated. Without doubt these ambitions were hampered by the poor state of government finances and with the problems that accompanied the government's generosity and its inadequacy in enforcing its regulations. We can hardly say that a modern industrial sector was established in the eighteenth century. But government efforts still laid the foundations for such a sector. Perhaps of even greater importance was the considerable interest that focused on the country's own resources and their use. According to the 'utilistic' ideas of the eighteenth century (Sten Lindroth), mineral ores should be prospected, new cereal crops introduced, plants refined, new technology and inventions encouraged and machines introduced – all to improve the country's industries.

Manufacture, excise duties and shipping policy

A number of regulations were introduced in the Age of Freedom aimed at securing growth in domestic industrial production. The Riksdag of 1723 issued an Instruction with the following wording. 'The Estates of the Realm have found that the prosperity, welfare and improvement of the country requires the import of foreign goods to be reduced by means of a sound domestic economy and, by founding plantations and other good establishments, the increase and expansion of domestic production and manufacture to maintain balance.'[3] The situation was, in fact, serious, according to Emanuel Swedenborg, a prominent metallurgist and debater. The accounts he submitted to the Diet of the Estates in 1723 showed that imports were substantially higher than exports, 'smuggling not included'. To eliminate the 'deficit', the Diet swiftly decided to examine the matter of extending religious freedom with a view to attracting skilled and experienced labour to Sweden. The possibility of starting more garment factories in Stockholm was also discussed. Since yarn was in short supply it was also suggested that a spinning- and carding-mill should be set up on the island of Långholmen, where beggars, 'loose women' and the lawless were to carry out forced labour.[4]

The debate at the 1722/3 Riksdag started the debate on the necessity of pursuing an economic policy that aimed to replace imports. This policy, which would be in effect throughout the entire Age of Freedom, would have a number of practical consequences.

A concrete measure already introduced in 1724 was the Commodity Act (*produktplakat*). Its origins lay in the Proclamation on the so-called 'full and half' exemption from customs duty for Swedish shipping of the seventeenth century (the Customs Resolution of 1645), intended to promote Swedish shipping and Swedish shipbuilding. This Act, which was modelled on the English Navigation Acts, barred foreign ships from carrying any cargo to Sweden other than products of the ship's own country. This measure was, of course, aimed chiefly at the Dutch, who were the main carriers of exports and imports to and from Sweden. The Act was also expected to promote Swedish shipping and shipbuilding. A profitable trade in salt and other essentials was expected to develop with the Mediterranean ports. Finally, the larger number of vessels could also be swiftly armed in time of war. This had been an express goal of the excise duties introduced in 1645: full exemption from duty was only granted to vessels armed and equipped for war, while other Swedish vessels were entitled to only 50 per cent exemption.

The Commodity Act was criticised from the outset. Its critics (among them Anders Chydenius and Lars Salvius) said that this ban put up the price of imports such as salt and brought down the demand for Swedish goods, particularly iron. Because the Dutch and the English were barred from trading with Sweden they were less interested in putting in to Swedish ports

Figure 3.2 Left: Professor Carl Linnaeus, Uppsala. Aquatint by J.E. Rehn, 1747. UUB; Right: Emanuel Swedenborg. Copper etching by J. F. Martin. KB.

and carrying Swedish iron. Whatever the case may be, they paid less than before for Swedish iron, and shipping costs rose.[5] Yet the Commodity Act proved to be long-lived. It was not fully repealed until 1857, when all differences in duties between Swedish and foreign vessels were abolished – although they had in practice ceased to be applied far earlier.[6]

As early as the 1720s, a policy was introduced to support the manufactories, as we have already discussed. The alleged balance of trade deficit was to be remedied by having the citizenry 'renounce their unpatriotic love of foreign goods'. For the so-called manufactory policy of the Age of Freedom, the 1727/8 Riksdag was an important step forward. It was at this Riksdag that the Board of Commerce managed to persuade the Diet of the Estates to introduce a special 'discount rate for manufactories', the main purpose being to supply the manufactories with working capital. Government involvement was for the usual, well-known reason: 'all useful manufactories fail and are destroyed soon after they are started unless they are assisted in time by public funding and given the kind of benefits and privileges that could eliminate the difficulties they face'.[7] A letter dated 3 July 1727 also issued the letter patent for Alingsås which would later attract so much criticism. Jonas Alströmer, who owned the Alingsås works, had considerable privileges conferred upon him. He was given his own jurisdiction and official powers, special treatment in the matter of debt claims, financial assistance to introduce costly foreign machines, assistance in establishing his tobacco plantation and exclusive monopolies, including that on the manufacture of belt-driven weaving-mills. From 1724 a number of royal letters patent were issued which granted various privileges to encourage the establishment of different manufactories and factories. The assistance extended to the tobacco plantation mentioned above as well as to the cultivation of hops, to wool factories, linen-weaving-mills, paper-mills, marble works, china works, glassworks and other enterprises. All these manufactories were to be supported by means of high duties and an import ban, cash assistance, and in several cases an exclusive monopoly on sales for periods of up to twenty years.[8]

The Riksdag of 1738 underscored the necessity of further extending the manufactory policy. This Riksdag also saw the final period of power by the Hats Party. The argument in favour of increasing support of the manufactories was, once again, an alleged 'underweight' or deficit in the balance of trade. From 1734 to 1736 the Board of Commerce figures show an annual export of 22.5 million copper daler (kmt) while imports totalled 24.5 million daler (kmt). Cereal imports were worth 7 million daler kmt, tobacco answered for 2 million daler kmt, dry goods for 2.5, salt for 1 and diverse manufactured goods for 4 million daler kmt.[9] It was particularly this last item that the manufactory policy aimed to eliminate. And it is against this background that a number of measures were forced through the Riksdag. Further restrictions were now introduced on, for example, foreign silk and wool products, and Sweden's manufactory products were exempted from the

Figure 3.3 The manufacturer Jonas Alströmer (1685–1761), who is credited with introducing the potato to Sweden. He became very influential, and was granted special privileges. KB.

lower excise duty, i.e. the duty normally levied on all domestic trade. With the same intention, strict measures were introduced to counter foreign smuggling and, as we have already seen, a special Market Resolution, manufactory legislation and a Manufactory Office were introduced. Lastly, a factory fund was set up which became active in 1739.

The manufactory policy reached its peak in the 1740s and 1750s. Its centre of power was the Manufactory Office (*Manufakturkontoret*) under the leadership of its untiring Commissioner, Eric Salander. Just over a hundred years later J.W. Arnberg, professor of economics and head of the Bank of Sweden (*Riksbanken*), described the multifaceted activities of this Office in the 1740s:

> Until the Riksdag of 1746 the Manufactory Office worked diligently, using its best judgement to stabilise and expand this sector. 'Swedish cotton' was consolidated and expanded, mulberry trees were imported from America and planted, Linné was commissioned to study plants that were of use to industry in our flora, particularly different dyeing grasses. Burdock was planted in the Kalmar area, commissioners despatched to establish direct trade links with Poland for the wool trade, with Italy for the silk trade and to recruit silk workers, and in general to study work methods. Spinning schools were set up in Värmland, Dalarna, Närke

and other regions where wool was in good supply, and premiums and advance payments given to master-craftsmen who taught young Swedish people etc.[10]

As already mentioned, the liberal privileges and the policy of assistance attracted more and more criticism, particularly in the 1760s. The critics claimed that many of the investments were not serious in nature and that the system was a serious waste of public funds. Accusations were made of corruption, particularly from the Caps Party. The crisis of the 1760s, combined with the Caps Party's return to power, also stopped the generous distribution of benefits. The government coffers were empty and the current policy of deflation resulted in numerous bankruptcies, not least in the manufactory sector.

We have already noted that the manufactory policy went hand in hand with the introduction of *tariffs, export premiums* and *import prohibitions*. In the first years of the Age of Freedom the relatively 'moderate' (Heckscher) tariff of 1719 was levied. However, as time passed, stricter measures were introduced with the aim of preventing the import of selected strategic goods. But it was, above all, the tariff of 1739 that targeted on a broad front the import of foreign manufactured goods. The higher duty had to be levied on both export and import goods, but it had to be selective, levying more duty on more finished import goods and less finished export goods. Thus the export of processed manufactured products would be favoured, as would the import of foreign raw materials (and raw materials for the manufactories).

When it came to the impact of this policy, however, other measures were probably more effective, particularly the numerous prohibitions on exports. It is true that export premiums were introduced from time to time throughout the Age of Freedom as a way of stimulating the export of manufactured goods – but the effect of these measures could hardly be said to be very significant. By contrast, the bans on imports introduced after the 1738/9 Riksdag came to have important consequences. A large number of products were banned, this protection initially extending to the textile and garment industry, with much of its production protected from foreign competition. A curious example of this protectionist policy was the introduction of the so-called Swedish dress. The Swedish nobility were forbidden to wear clothing of foreign origin on formal occasions. Special formal attire was to be worn instead, which was, of course, made in Sweden. The import of a number of other products was also banned, including silk screens, tobacco leaf, bottle glass, bricks, glassware and iron. Despite the good intentions of these bans, their effects were probably mostly negative, i.e. barring the import of certain kinds of manufactured goods generated a shortage of goods, which led to smuggling and higher prices. To some extent it may also have resulted in import substitution, i.e. foreign goods being replaced by goods manufactured in Sweden. If so, this could have been true of some garment manufacture, but hardly of Swedish tobacco, china or the like, which could not compete with foreign goods either on price or quality.

This strongly prohibitive policy of excise duties and import bans was relaxed somewhat in the reign of Gustav III. In 1776 some thirty import prohibitions were lifted and under Johan Liljencrantz, Gustav III's minister of finance, the introduction of free ports, notably on the island of Gotland and in Marstrand, was discussed. But these activities met with little success and had to be abandoned after some years. At the time of the Napoleonic Wars, Sweden returned to a stricter protectionist policy, expressed, for example, in the tariffs imposed in 1799 and 1816, which brought dramatic increases in import duties. The tariff of 1816 targeted agricultural goods in particular, causing Arthur Montgomery, the economics historian, to say that the programme of tariffs was reactionary and of greatest benefit to 'agricultural interests'.[11] A range of import bans was also introduced, 300 in all, in 1816, the most important relating to mining, textile products, yarn, fabrics, sweetmeats and cane sugar, prototypes and implements. On the other hand, a number of export duties were reduced – but some fifty export prohibitions were also issued, most of them on raw materials and semi-finished goods such as ore, pig iron, crude copper, untreated hides, leather, etc., that it was thought should be processed in Sweden.[12] These prohibitive measures were, it is true, relaxed to some extent in the decades that followed. But no more liberal foreign trade policy was applied before the Gripenstedt reforms at the end of the century. In 1850 the bans on the export and import of pig iron were still in place, as were the bans on ore exports and bar iron imports. This latter also applied to various textile goods (particularly fabrics) and manufactured goods.[13]

A full picture of the 'mercantile' policy of the eighteenth century must also emphasise the advance of what we have called the *town economic policy*. In the Age of Freedom, and for many years after, the restrictions on domestic and foreign trade remained in force. The ban on rural trade and the levy of the lower excise duty on domestic trading applied to the former, while the staple town (entrepôt) system and the compulsory routing of all merchandise for export to the Baltic region through Stockholm placed serious limitations on the traffic in export goods. At the same time as the Commodity Act was passed in 1724, the exclusive right of the city of Stockholm and the other larger towns in Sweden to export trade was further strengthened. But this exclusive right was withdrawn in 1765, when a number of towns in the province of Norrland and in Finland were empowered to conduct their own export trade. The system as a whole was finally discontinued in 1812, when all towns were given the right to receive foreign shipping.[14] As we have seen, many of the other restrictions on domestic trade were also gradually suspended, not least through the relaxation of the ban on rural trade.

At the same time, most of the limits on trade discussed above continued to be enforced. In the rural areas, the ban on rural trade and certain kinds of handicrafts was, once again, a severe limitation. In the towns, the guilds still exercised their old power over the crafts. In the same way, the complex of privileges conferred on the manufactories severely limited competition. The manufactories, which were the real favourites in the Age of Freedom, were protected from exposure to any real competition. The manufactory director, Eric Salander, in particular, along with other supporters of the policy on manufactories, was generally sceptical about competition. Johan Låstbohm of Uppsala, then a reader in economics at Uppsala, asked why something should be done 'crookedly' when a straight line could be taken. He wrote: 'It is imprudent and in conflict with the rights of society to allow our industries to find their own level; rather, the population should, through wise contrivance, be deterred from harming themselves and others'.[15] Why allow primitive competition to determine the number of master-craftsmen or producers there should be in a given trade? Surely it would be better to have the authorities determine the number of producers in a civilised manner by applying a general plan. The first professor of economics in Uppsala, Anders Berch, was an enthusiastic supporter of this kind of economic management. In a speech to the students of Uppsala in 1749, published under the telling title, 'Address on the Proportioning of Students Required for the Vacant Positions in the Country', he proposed the principle that the authorities should be allowed to determine the precise number of students in different disciplines in a comprehensive plan which detailed the number of clergymen, pharmacists and so on, that the community needed.

At least from the manufactory sector it was said that the rural trade in peasant household craft products was a disruptive factor in the process of introducing modern manufactories and factories. And, as we have seen, the manufactory interests had some success in turning policy against homecrafts. In a 1745 publication, the Manufactory Office says the following (and we may sense the pen of Salander at work here).

> Home weaving is of as little benefit to the general public as it is to the individual. For the former, it disturbs both the natural order of movement between town and country, and also the division of the occupations of the inhabitants, since the latter only manufacture a poor article at high cost. The changes in our economy are now so great that the burgher ploughs and sows, the peasant weaves and trades, households dabble in the manufacturer's trade, and thus each brings the other's activities into disrepute, from which it follows that the towns become impoverished and the countryside ill-used.[16]

Liberalism in Sweden

The form of government that emerged after the demise of absolutism – which was ratified in the Constitution of 1770 – aimed to limit the power of the monarch. From the European debate of the time, coloured by ideas of natural law, came the idea that the power of government derived from a pact between rulers and their subjects. The monarch was to be 'exalted', and the will of the people as expressed in the pact was to be interpreted by the estates of the realm. Accordingly, the new constitution gave the Estates a strong position. The fathers of the constitution, especially David Silvius, would have liked to build a balance of power into the new constitution. In fact, it produced a form of government which gave the estates of the realm virtually absolute powers. Despite the fall of absolutism the 'principle of government supremacy' inherited from the seventeenth century continued to be held. 'The supreme power of the monarch was transferred to what gradually became the equally powerful Diet of the Estates', writes Einar Ekegård.[17] In accordance with the ideas of the great Pufendorf, it was emphasised that the state was a sensible entity, while the subjects needed to be governed – this was the main thinking underlying the 'pact'. Neither was the government particularly democratic in other respects. Representation was still through the old Diet of the Estates in which the nobility and the clergy, despite the small percentages of the population they represented, had two of the four votes on a Bill, for example. In some matters, such as foreign policy, the peasant estate was even refused a hearing. One of the major advances in the constitution of the Age of Freedom was the liberal attitude embodied in the regulations on the freedom of the press – especially the regulation of 1676 – and the opportunities it afforded to carry on a relatively open political debate. This freedom was expressed in several ways, including a torrent of pamphlets, books and other publications. The debate, during the troubled decade of the 1760s, when the Hats Party fell, was particularly lively. Heckscher calculated that in 1761 and 1762 a total of 364 pamphlets were published, most of them addressing the subject of economics. The end came with the restrictions on the freedom of the press that Gustav III introduced in 1774, and the flood of pamphlets began to abate.

The economic debate of the Age of Freedom was on topical themes such as the manufactory policy, 'the conflict over industrial precedence', the Baltic trade restrictions described earlier, and the general regulation of economic life. In the course of the debate a group emerged that fought tooth and nail in defence of prohibitive legislation. This line was particularly well represented among the instigators and devotees of the manufactory policy. Also, Anders Berch, the first occupant of the chair of 'Oeconomiae, jurisprudentia et commercium' in Uppsala, supported this view. His textbook on economics, 'An Introduction to General Economy' (*Inledning til Almänna Hushålningen*), published in 1747, the only one of its kind until the 1820s, also leant strongly towards authoritarianism. Without doubt this book had its roots in the state supremacy policy of the time, mixed with the enlightened 'utilism' of Christian von Wolf, the German, that was the most fashionable philosophy during the early years of the Age of Freedom. These sources praised the benefits of regulation, while the risks of too much competition, polyopoly, were emphasised. Even monopolies were harmful and, in fact, an effect of 'polyopoly'. It would therefore be better to choose a third way that underscored the overall responsibility of central government – 'propoly'.

Another line of debate was critical of all or some parts of the current policy (pursued by the Hats Party). As early as the 1720s, Christopher Polhem, the inventor and dilettante, recommended more freedom of trade, using the slogan 'monopoly is as harmful to a nation as gangrene is to the body'. His main criticism was of the system of staple towns and inland towns (*uppstäder*) which gave a monopoly to the former. This critical view was then refined by people such as Lars Salvius, a well-known Stockholm book printer, in his periodical, 'Reflections on the Swedish Economy' (*Tanckar öfver den swenska Oeconomien*) of 1738.[18] Such critics, who included in their number the famous Emanuel Swedenborg, could always be attacked for representing a special interest, namely the efforts of the ironworkers to assert their independence of the 'Skeppsbro nobility' of Stockholm. But from the 1750s onwards a more theoretical criticism of the government's policy began to emerge. As already mentioned, this criticism was set out in pamphlets such as the 'controversy over industrial precedence' or 'the battle of the Swedish factories', where Salander, the Manufactory Commissioner, or J. F. Kryger, the writer, supported the government but were attacked by people such as Carl Leuhusen, Anders Nordencrantz and Anders Chydenius. In his writings in the 1760s Chydenius in particular took up the theoretical aspects of the criticism of the current regulations. In a comprehensive document, 'To the Honourable Estates of the Realm Gathered at the Riksdag of 1760 . . .' (1759), Nordencrantz acted as spokesman for a liberal view that was in line with the Scottish and French enlightenment's most advanced thinking. Similarly, Chydenius emphasised in 'The National Gain' of 1765 that the economy worked best if people were allowed to produce and trade as they themselves wished.

These advanced ideas attracted a great deal of attention and undoubtedly had the long-term effect of relaxing the regulatory economy that ensued towards the end of the eighteenth century. There was no question of a complete reversal of this policy. The very cautious attitude the Swedish economic writers adopted towards Adam Smith is typical of this thinking. On the one hand, for example, Lars Gabriel Rabenius, a professor in Uppsala, in his textbook of economics – which replaced Berch's now hopelessly outdated text – was prepared to recognise the superiority of the 'Smith system' over the other theoretical systems, the mercantile and the physiocratic. But he took as his starting point the emphasis Smith gave to the prosperity that work and production generated. He was far more doubtful about laissez-faire ideas.

More sophisticated liberal thinking was not widespread until the midnineteenth century. This is true not least of the academic economists who, with few exceptions, were unsympathetic towards radical liberalism. Yet the community was inspired by the free trade movement in England, for example, and the repeal of the Corn Laws in 1846 caused vigorous debate.

However, it was less Richard Cobden and more the harmony economics school of the Frenchman Frédéric Bastiat which was the most important source of inspiration for liberal critics such as J. A. Gripenstedt, the minister of finance (to whom we shall return later). For educated economists the real breakthrough did not come until after the National Economics Association was founded in 1877. At this time, the principle of free trade had established its strongest political foothold; since 1865 Sweden had been part of the Western European free trade system. But by the end of the 1870s more protectionism was once again called for. Paradoxically, the success of theoretical economic liberalism was almost parallel with its virtual demise in politics.[19]

Generally speaking, it was difficult for liberal ideas to have any impact in Sweden. There was a change in direction, but it was very slow in coming, and by no means comprehensive. The period of absolutism (1772–1809) was, it is true, replaced by a new constitution that reintroduced limits on the power of the monarch and granted more power to the estates of the realm. The Constitution of 1809 also granted broad freedom of the press and freedom of speech. Karl XIV Johan, the new monarch, pursued a conservative policy, but some of the Riksdags were characterised by their liberal reformism – especially those of 1823 and 1840, where a more liberal opposition made its voice heard. The Riksdag of 1840, in particular, paved the way for many of the important reforms that in time proved to be of great importance, not least for continued economic expansion. But there were many setbacks. And after 1848 politics returned to a more cautious and conservative line. With considerable difficulty, Louis De Geer, the prime minister, managed to force through the dissolution of the Diet of the Estates and introduce a bicameral Riksdag in 1866. The conservative Agrarian Party had a very strong position in this new Riksdag. It was not prepared to make any revolutionary changes. Change was also cautious and slow in the sphere of economic policy. There were no real departures from the earlier policy of protectionism and the numerous import and export bans put into effect before the mid-1850s. Then, almost as a coup, Gripenstedt managed to bring Sweden into the Western European free trade system by means of the 1865 Treaty of Paris. As Rabenius, the professor of economics, emphasises, the policy throughout this period was relaxed restrictions and more freedom, but achieved through due process.

Deregulation or readjustment

Notwithstanding the cautious retreat of the old system, it is clear that the first half of the nineteenth century was a period of important institutional change. As has been emphasised above, the complex of social and political institutions formed a framework for the economy. This framework had a decisive effect on the way the economy performed. We have already seen how the economic expansion of the eighteenth century and the early nineteenth century was a break with the low-yield agrarian economy that had dominated up to that time. A number of institutions were added to the old economic order, which now had to be either abolished or modified to allow the economy to grow. A smoothly functioning industrial economy requires, for example, markets that operate well, a stable currency, improved communications, a functioning credit system, clear 'rules of the game' from the government that allow long-term assessments and risk, and broader and deeper education. The need for functioning markets also requires private ownership rights and private contracts to be respected, and protection from competition in the form of patent and brand-name rights to be in effect. In general, a modern industrial economy must offer protection against total competition to the entrepreneurs who operate in the market. A totally free market is hardly a desirable situation. To 'tame' the market, modern business forms, including the joint-stock company, gradually came into use and the government also introduced special measures.

Far from leading to the dismantling of the system of government intervention, the inception of the modern industrial economy was accompanied by a great deal of government involvement. Without this institutional structure, the industrial society that emerged in Western Europe, beginning in the nineteenth century, would not have been possible. It is also quite wrong to claim that the future role of the government would be purely supervisory, that the government would become a 'night-watchman state'. Instead, the interventionist role of the state intensified. The government constantly acted to control and regulate the market, moderate competition, create competitive advantages over other countries, promote growth, and regulate the disputes in distribution policy that threatened long-term economic stability and calculability. This is by no means unique, as is often assumed, to the 'welfare capitalism' of the twentieth century. In fact this government interventionism is intimately linked to the emergence of the industrial society.

It is difficult to find any uniform measurement of the public sector's percentage of the economy in a country like Sweden. In any case, the figures calculated for direct government expenditure do not suggest any decline in government undertakings. On the other hand, a change may be discerned in the nineteenth century from military to civil commitments. In Sweden, this was characterised by the long periods of peace that followed the Norwegian war operations of 1814. The figures, at least, do not give any basis for regarding Sweden as a 'night-watchman state'. Instead, a feature of the first half of the nineteenth century was the relatively swift pace at which the institutional changes were introduced that created the conditions for Sweden's industrial development in the second half of the century.

The most spectacular change was the introduction of *free trade*. This change, which took time, began with the dissolution of the guild system in 1846 and the enactment of the Free Trade Resolution of 1864, which had the following preamble: 'Swedish men or women are . . . entitled to carry on trade or factory enterprises, handicrafts or other processing, in town or country; to export to or import from a foreign place and transport goods between foreign places.'[20] As we have seen, the so-called lower excise duty had been withdrawn earlier, the provisions of the Commodity Act relaxed and the system of staple towns introduced. The ban on land purchase had also become less strict. The Resolution of 1846 also gave women better rights to pursue a trade on the same terms as men. The 1845 decision on equal inheritance rights was another move in the same direction. Thus the 1846 Resolution appears to have cleared away at a stroke the remnants of the earlier more restrictive legislation, including the limits on married women's rights to start and run businesses. But reading the fine print of this legislation leads one to conclude that it did not introduce absolute freedom of trade. Some restrictions were still in effect, including provisions on freedom from debt and the payment of taxes. As we shall see later, a number of other important limitations were to be introduced soon enough.

As was the case with crafts, after 1846 other special legislation that had placed limits on certain sectors was also gradually discarded. As we have seen, the specific legislation governing the manufactories gradually fell into disuse. The restrictions on the manufacture of pig iron were also lifted in 1835, which removed the old limits on production. Some years later, in 1846, all mining legislation went the same way.

Of special importance for long-term economic stability – and thus calculability – were the changes that took place in the field of *currency*. The period immediately after 1815 was one of considerable unrest in this area, which was expressed in a number of ways including rapid changes in prices and strong fluctuations in exchange rates. A high percentage of the money stock was in the form of notes that could not be redeemed. The Riksdag of 1830 decided on a devaluation, and four years later a silver coin standard was introduced. This was clearly a very successful move. The decision to put Swedish currency on a silver standard created price stability and fixed exchange rates with other countries until 1873, when Sweden's silver coinage was replaced with gold. If the system of irredeemable notes had continued, a modern-style *Riksbank* (Bank of Sweden) would have been needed. But at that time neither the Bank of Sweden nor any other central bank could take on a task of this kind. The most important function of the 'Bank of the Estates of the Realm' was still to lend money, thus competing with the private lending banks that were set up as time passed. Until 1903 the Bank of Sweden did not even have a monopoly on issuing banknotes. To control the exchange rates it would at least have needed the power to regulate the interest rate. This was, however, not an option – prior to 1864 interest was set at no less than 4 and no more than 6 per cent. Any interest rates outside these limits were considered usurious, and therefore prohibited. After 1834, with the help of the metal coin standard, exchange rates were regulated through the import and export of silver (and later gold). Any drastic worsening of exchange rates under this system resulted in a dramatic

Figure 3.4 The dissolution of the guilds and the 1864 Resolution on Freedom of Trade extended women's rights to run businesses. Advertisement from *Ny illustrerad tidning* 1868. KB.

shortage of liquidity, the so-called strangulation system. Yet by all accounts the silver and gold standard was a system that worked well for Sweden in this period. Many people have even claimed that this stable international system was one of the main reasons underlying the general rapid rate of economic growth in Europe in the second half of the nineteenth century. If this is the case, it was true of Sweden as well.

In pace with the efforts to build institutions that were better suited to an expanding industrial economy, a number of *administrative changes* were also introduced to make centralism in the public sector stronger and more effective. The 'departmental reform', which after a debate lasting several years was finally adopted in 1840, was particularly important here. Its purpose was to give cabinet ministers more influence in their respective policy areas and to bring more professionalism to government administration. Under this reform, seven government departments were established, each headed by a cabinet minister, and a further three cabinet ministers without portfolio were appointed. At the same time, the formerly very powerful position of secretary of state was abolished, which, above all, made the government stronger in relation to the power of the monarch. In time, this system created an administrative apparatus for implementing the numerous reforms that were to be introduced in rapid succession.

An area in which the reformed and more effective state, with its new, pro-active profile, really had to prove its mettle was *communications*. A number of new government initiatives were taken here. The Royal Mail was expanded and made more efficient; of particular importance was the decision taken by the 1853/4 Riksdag to introduce the postage stamp. To pave the way for a modern telegraph network – the first cable was laid between Stockholm and Uppsala in 1843 – a government telegraph office was set up. The government was an important actor in extending Sweden's railroad network. From the 1850s, the railroads became the dominant political issue. Pressure was brought to bear in the rural areas to speed the extension of the railroads. At an early stage the government took a number of important initiatives in this matter. The first line, between Örebro and Hult on the shores of Lake Vänern, was designed by Count Adolf Eugen von Rosen, who had worked closely with John Ericsson in England. Von Rosen managed to persuade the Riksdag of 1847/8 to issue interest rate guarantees for this project. Despite this, he failed to raise enough capital for his railroad, which brought to a head the question of financing Sweden's future railroad network. A commission of inquiry was appointed, which proposed that the state should build and run a number of main lines to which smaller, privately-run lines could be connected. When von Rosen then applied to build several large railroad lines in Sweden in co-operation with a British consortium, he was met with an outright refusal. An 1853 Bill which was strongly supported by *inter alia* Gripenstedt, the champion of free trade, stated unequivocally that 'no railway lines should be planned or built in Sweden without the government's immediate involvement, and at its expense'.[21] This was the government policy that was applied thereafter.

Figure 3.5 The 'Trollhättan' locomotive, the first manufactured at the Trollhättan mekaniska verkstad, shown at the Paris World Exhibition in 1878, and 'of the most excellent quality' according to the Engineers' Association. That 134 locomotives were ordered by the Swedish government, and 304 by private Swedish railway companies, was the proud claim published in *Svenska industriella verk och anläggningar 1896.* KB.

To finance the costly expansion of the railroad network, the government raised large debenture loans, many of them from abroad. Thus in the second half of the nineteenth century, German banking institutes (in Hamburg) in particular, and, increasingly, the French banks, made a long-term contribution to the supply of capital to Sweden's public sector. This borrowing, most of which was for the expansion of the railroads, telegraph communications and other infrastructure, accelerated the growth of the national debt, which totalled just over SEK600 million in 1914. The national debt soon became so large that it attracted a great deal of contemporary criticism, especially from C. A. Agardh, the professor of economics and botanist from Lund, who condemned the policy in strong terms. Domestic borrowing may have been good, since it led to greater savings and greater national wealth. But if foreign loans were raised, 'all the small expenditures on pleasures that are exempt from Swedish tax, then pay interest abroad, to generate pleasures for the foreigners; and the bottle of champagne that the Swede may not drink is now drunk in Hamburg'.[22] However, all in all, these debenture loans – which were matched by private loans – substantially increased Sweden's capital supply during its period of industrial expansion. Loans were raised for productive investment, particularly in the railroads. And especially as many of these loans disappeared in the turbulence of World War I, they were very good business for Sweden.

In addition to the above we should mention here a number of other important reforms in different areas which also helped promote the conditions for economic growth and the transformation of Swedish society. There was very little investment in *higher education*. On the other hand, in the long term the introduction of the Education Act of 1842 did much to raise the level of education of the population. Without doubt, better basic education was an important prerequisite for the emergence of a modern industrial society. A new *Bank Act* was passed in 1864 which allowed permanent commercial banks to be established. Before this, letters patent (*oktrojer*) for private banking had been issued for limited periods only, ten years for example. With this Act a new government Bank Inspectorate was founded in 1871. In general, the government – as we shall soon see – was involved in every aspect of establishing a modern commercial banking industry. Following the crisis of 1867, for example, the government intervened to save banks that were on the brink of insolvency.[23] In 1861 a government mortgage bank was founded to co-ordinate the borrowings of the local credit associations. In general, the importance of the government's initiatives in creating a better credit system should be emphasised. The reform of the Bank of Sweden to create a proper central bank was, however, not initiated in the period we are dealing with here.

However, the list of government initiatives in this period is still incomplete. The new *Companies Act* of 1848, with its statutory limitations on financial responsibility had, of course, considerable impact on industry and commerce in the longer term. The new *Local Government Act* was another

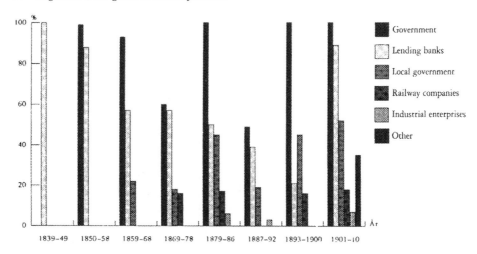

Figure 3.6 The percentage of Sweden's borrowings that originated abroad, by borrower 1835–1910.

Source: L. Schön, 'Capital Imports, the Credit Market and Industry 1850–1910', in E. Dahmén (ed.), *Borrowing and Development. The National Debt Office 1789–1989*, Stockholm 1989, p. 245.

important reform, which created more effective and probably more cost-effective local-level administration. The new municipalities were based on the principle of autonomy and were empowered to levy their own taxes. They would be responsible hereafter for social facilities such as schools and the care of the sick and poor. The responsibility of the parishes for the poor had also been embodied in the 1847 legislation on poor relief, which stated that no local authority had the right to refuse to accommodate people without means. The withdrawal of the old regulations on *laga försvar* (a regulation which stated that everybody who did not own an estate or was not a burgher must be employed by someone) in 1885, led to a considerable increase in the mobility of labour. In this context, the withdrawal of compulsory travel passes, both foreign and domestic, in 1860 was also important. Before that time, anyone who wanted to travel within the country or abroad was obliged to apply to the County Board for permission. This restriction was now lifted – in all certainty to the lasting benefit of communications, trade and a more mobile labour market. Compulsory passports for foreign travel were reintroduced in 1917.

The Gripenstedt system

On the subject of protectionism, a cornerstone of earlier 'mercantile' policy, we have already said that there was no theoretical support of free trade until the 1850s. In 1850 the export and import bans were still in effect on a number of key products. But in the 1853/4 Riksdag the liberal opposition made considerable advances. A number of export and import prohibitions were lifted and excise duties were cut on over 200 articles.[24] Towards the end of the 1850s, however, protectionism gained ground in Sweden once again. For example, the Tariffs Bill of 1857 did nothing to encourage free trade. Many members of parliament even moved so far towards protectionism in the 1859/60 Riksdag that they called for a more comprehensive bar on imports. The negative balance of payments after the crisis of 1857 had considerable influence on public opinion in this matter.[25]

Despite constant objections from the liberal opposition, the basic attitude that prohibition was a necessary means to achieve desirable industrial growth prevailed. The supply position and the need to increase government revenues also played an important part. This was still the case at the 1860 Riksdag, when opinion swung in favour of stricter protectionism. Shortly after, however, from 1865 and for two brief decades, Sweden became a member of the international free trade system that emerged along the lines of the Cobden Treaty between Britain and France in 1860. As already indicated, Sweden became a member in a period of great political turmoil. It was, above all, the considerable authority of J. A. Gripenstedt, the minister of finance, that made it possible for Sweden to join this system. We should devote some space to this man, whose importance for the 'deregulations' of the nineteenth century cannot be overstated. Johan August Gripenstedt was born in 1813 and died in 1874. He made his political debut in the Riksdag of 1840, and from the year of the revolution, 1848, until the dissolution of the Diet of the Estates in 1866 he was a member of the government, most of the time as minister of finance. He had been captivated early on by liberal ideas and, as his biographer Olle Gasslander clearly states, he was strongly influenced by Bastiat, the French economist and advocate of free trade. But Gripenstedt was not a doctrinaire liberal in political matters. He often infuriated the liberal paper *Aftonbladet* and radical liberals, including Lars Johan Hierta, with his constant compromising. But there were also strong forces that he had to consider: first, his conservative government colleagues, and then two monarchs (Karl XIV Johan and then Oscar I) who, at least according to Gripenstedt himself, had evident political ambitions. King Oscar, for example, clearly saw Napoleon III as a shining example. In private, Gripenstedt was a wealthy man, not least through his marriage to Eva Anckarsvärd. He moved in highly conservative business circles, and was a personal friend of André Oscar Wallenberg.

The 'Gripenstedt system', which exemplified the reforms we have described above, was applied mainly in the 1850s and 1860s. Gripenstedt himself was behind both the 1865 Free Trade Treaty and the government railways policy, the reforms in banking (where it was clear that he co-operated with A.O. Wallenberg), the removal of restrictive trade practices in 1864 and the abolition of compulsory passports some years earlier. In the 1850s he had already taken a definite stand in favour of establishing a

Figure 3.7 Left: André Oscar Wallenberg (1816–86). *Ny illustrerad tidning* 1875. KB; Right: J. A. Gripenstedt (1813–74). KB.

number of private banks. In 1853 he was involved in granting the concession for the founding of Stockholm's Enskilda Banken – André Oscar Wallenberg's bank – which paved the way for the 1864 Bank Act. There was also the initiative he took in decimalising the coinage, before which there were 48 skillings to a riksdal and 12 runestycke to a skilling. After 1855 the system of 100 öre to a riksdal was applied. Thus Gripenstedt's reforms reached far into the future. In many ways he came to personify the deregulation and liberalisation that took place in Sweden in the middle of the nineteenth century.

Yet there is some duality about the Gripenstedt system, and this is also true of Gripenstedt himself. On the one hand, he worked assiduously to introduce liberal reforms, not least the freedom of trade. At times he could be almost doctrinaire in this respect. Freedom of trade, he wrote in 1851, 'is based on one of the conditions on which all human progress rests'.[26] But, on the other hand, he did not hesitate to assert the importance of the role government can and should play in economic developments. This was particularly true of the debate in the early 1850s on a government or private network of main railway lines. Gripenstedt was without doubt the 'foremost advocate of a policy of government railways since the 1850s'.[27] In a speech to the House of Nobility (*Riddarhuset*) in 1853, he stated very firmly that in society 'there were some duties which, due to their nature, never can nor should be separated from government'.[28] What is interesting about this statement is that it was made at the time when Gripenstedt was most deeply committed to promoting free trade.

But there are examples other than the railways. His actions in connection with the economic crisis of 1857 also speak for themselves. In the autumn of that year, Sweden was hit by the general crisis that spread after the end of the Crimean War. This crisis took the form of a rapid deterioration in the current account of the balance of payments, accompanied by a shortage of liquid funds. The commercial banks in particular found themselves in serious difficulties. As we have seen, liquidation was an item on the agenda of several of these banks. At first, Gripenstedt supported a non-interventionist line but then changed sides. First, he saved Skånes Enskilda Bank from liquidation by offering a loan of 500,000 riksdaler – brokered by A. O. Wallenberg. In the middle of December 1857 he then put forward a proposal that the Riksdag should raise a foreign 'crisis loan' to pass on to 'needy sectors'.[29] He defended his interventionist line to the House of Nobility by saying that no-one 'can with a clear conscience leave the country's various industries to their fate'.[30] Once again, Gripenstedt showed in practice that his 'system' was in fact 'pragmatic, nationalistic liberalism that recognised both market forces and government responsibilities'.[31] This was symptomatic of the whole complex of reforms that was begun early in the nineteenth century but which culminated during Gripenstedt's time as minister of finance. This complex of reforms demonstrated, first, that institutional reform was essential to create the conditions for continued economic growth and industrialisation. Second, Gripenstedt's pragmatism was quite simply a recognition that the state would continue to have an important role to play. To set the institutional framework and then retire from the scene was far from the part the state would come to play in the future work of building the country's industrial structure.

Figure 3.8 The telephone in Stockholm. The exchange at the Central Station. Drawing by Victor Andrén. *Ny illustrerad tidning* 1881. KB.

4   A transformed élite

Alongside the simple agrarian-based market economy, a different socio-economic system emerged: capitalism. Until the nineteenth century this system was generally based largely on foreign trade and private banking. It was, moreover, an activity controlled by a very small number of people concentrated in the major cities: export merchants, bill-brokers, bankers and providers of working capital (credits) in the putting-out system. A large number of people, however, were affected indirectly by their activities. These were the farmers, smallholders and labourers who spun and wove at home in their cottages for the merchant-employers. They were people who had, in various ways, been brought into a growing international trade sector. As Eric Wolff, the anthropologist and historian, had pointed out, there were hardly any people or continents that were not affected by capitalism's hungry search for desirable goods and markets – not infrequently by means of expropriation, theft and colonialist violence. But for a long time this commercial capitalism failed to make any real inroads into the household-based market economy. Most people were therefore only indirectly affected by export-based capitalism, although this did not prevent large numbers in the proto-industrial regions becoming directly dependent on this capitalism for their livelihoods.

The impact of this activity, so long of only peripheral importance, should be brought to the fore when discussing capitalism in Sweden. It is true that Sweden became part of an expanding international division of labour in the seventeenth century. The part formerly played by the Hanseatic League was taken over by Holland, and later by Britain. A series of credit relationships linked Sweden's mines and ironworks to a growing international economy. These links were strengthened and developed in the eighteenth and early nineteenth centuries. In addition to the mining and iron industry and its bar iron production, other sectors, especially the wood and wood products sector, became increasingly dependent on the international economy. Yet the older-style economy still dominated at the beginning of the nineteenth century. Large-scale export trading to maximise profits was an enterprise pursued by a very small number of people. It was even more unusual for these few people to be running large-scale production units from which they exported.

The social élite

Almost all societies have had their élite strata. Common to all these élite groups is that they have enjoyed greater influence than their numbers justify. Many societies have also had more than one strong élite that have competed with each other for power and influence. Attention has often been drawn to the existence of competing oligarchies in Western European societies in the early-modern epoch. According to the prevailing view of the time, there was in this period a 'modern' élite of export traders and capitalists who competed for power and influence with an 'old' élite of landowners and/or the civil or military nobility that had been absorbed into the bureaucracy. This interpretation is certainly accurate in some respects. But an alternative view has emerged in recent times. Network studies and other research into the early-modern élite have shown a considerable overlap between these two élite groups. In seventeenth-century Sweden, for example, many new nobles were prominent merchants and 'capitalists'. Similarly, it was not unusual in the eighteenth century for wealthy businessmen to become major landowners; one example being the Arfwedson merchant family who in the eighteenth century acquired with their trading profits property which included the manors of Harboholm, Berga and Broby in Uppland. A social historian noted the following about conditions in general in Western Europe: 'Despite the frequent short-term tensions between the townspeople in the cities of the continent and the old aristocracy, in the course of three or at most four generations the members of successful burgher families were assimilated into the landowning aristocracy.'[1]

Thus the 'new' and the 'old' élites became intertwined. Very often they were the same people or, to be more precise, people who belonged to the same network of family or other connections. Individuals in these networks might, of course, have different interests to safeguard. But apart from conflicts of that kind – which varied in severity from place to place – it is the way they complemented one another that is noteworthy. It is difficult to arrive at a definition of an 'élite'. *One* important criterion of an élite, however, is probably that they are able to develop stable networks through which they gain social advancement. The élite should preferably also develop its own socio-cultural characteristics (or 'life-forms'), to use the terminology of present-day sociology.

In this sense it is, however, difficult to identify a 'capitalist' or even an 'upper-class' stratum – to use Tom Söderberg's term – in Sweden as separate from the other economic and political élites. In the eighteenth century and well into the nineteenth century, this 'upper class' consisted of senior government officials, military officers, ironworks and mill owners, export traders and landowners. Nobles were also included in this group, although as time passed their numbers fell.[2] By definition, they cannot, of course, be defined as 'upper class', since according to the division of the population into the estates of the realm they were classed as 'nobility'. But in both their

Figure 4.1 John Jennings, the merchant (1729–73) (right) and his brother Frans and his wife. Together with his brother-in-law Robert Finlay, John Jennings founded a large complex of manufacturing estates which included the Gimo and Skebo works in Roslagen and Robertsfors in Västerbotten. After a portrait by Alexander Roslin 1769. KB.

economic and political functions and their lifestyles, these two groups are very similar.

Against this background it is hardly appropriate to use the old classification of the four estates in an attempt to understand the roles played by different social groups in the economic transformation of Sweden in the eighteenth and nineteenth centuries. As with the nobility and the 'bourgeois' and agricultural occupations, the category of 'burgher' could include anyone from the master-craftsmen, shopkeepers and impoverished hawkers of the towns, to the cream of the exporting merchants and the ironworks, foundry and sawmill owners, who quite clearly lived in a different social world. The term 'class' has therefore been introduced as an alternative to the classification of the four estates. But this term, rooted as it is in Marxism, may be misleading, at least if it is related solely to the ownership of the means of production. From this viewpoint the main characteristic of the bourgeoisie is that they own the means of production and employ labour. But the difference between the small-town craftsman who employs a few workers and the powerful owner of a mine, foundry, ironworks or sawmill, is still very great. They are quite clearly people with different economic and social functions. And where do we place the powerful export merchants? It is true that they only employed a small number of workers, but they should be counted among the foremost 'capitalists' before the industrial revolution.

Clearly, reconstructing the social networks as they existed tells us more about the roles the different groupings played in the economy. In light of this, we should speak here of an economic élite connected to a capitalist sector that was based on international trade. We should emphasise that this economic élite was closely connected with other élite groups, such as the political–military and bureaucratic constellations and the great landowners. Various kinds of social connections were forged between these groups. We need take only one example here: the ownership grouping behind Sweden's first large-scale joint-stock bank, the *Skandinaviska kredit aktiebolaget*, founded in 1863. Several of the principal investors may have been from the 'middle class', such as André Oscar Wallenberg, the bishop's son from Linköping who had pursued a career as a naval officer, but otherwise we see here the absolute cream of Sweden's financial and political élite. In the so-called Stockholm group (there was also a Gothenburg group) we find Holm and Cervin, the private bankers; Åkerman, president of the Swedish Board of Trade; the County Governors Bildt, Lagerbjelke, af Ugglas and Sparre (these last three were also prominent politicians in the forefront of different Conservative factions in the House of Nobility (*Riddarhuset*), and the former minister of war, Nils Gyldenstolpe, who was well known as a founder of banks.[3]

The great merchant houses

An obvious starting point in attempting to identify a special élite of wealthy capitalists in the eighteenth and early nineteenth centuries is the great merchant houses of Stockholm and Gothenburg. As we have seen in an earlier chapter, these houses had close connections with the country's mines, ironworks and mills. Kurt Samuelsson is overstating the case when he says that the merchant houses were 'the only really dynamic factor in the Swedish economy'.[4] In fact, Sweden underwent a period of great transformation, mainly in agriculture. Yet it is in the merchant houses, and only there, that we can find traces of any large-scale domestic capitalist activity during this period.

The expansion of the merchant houses must be seen against the background of the growth of foreign trade in the eighteenth and early nineteenth centuries. We have no clear picture of the extent of this trade, not least because the high customs duties encouraged hidden trade and smuggling. But a study of the official figures for some of the most important commodities exported through the staple towns – iron and steel, pitch and tar, sawn timber and salted herring – shows that their export, calculated in tons, doubled from the 1740s to the turn of the century.[5] The first half of the nineteenth century also saw a sharp increase in these exports. As in earlier centuries, Stockholm was by far the most important export port in the mid-1700s, answering for perhaps half of the total tonnage exported. However, Stockholm's foreign trade was no greater in 1800 than it had been fifty years earlier. Instead, it was the port of Gothenburg that expanded rapidly. In the same period the quantity of goods shipped out of Gothenburg increased more than threefold.[6] The relative importance of different export goods also changed. While iron exports increased little, there was substantial growth in exports of forest products (sawn timber, pitch and tar). Large quantities of salt herring were exported from the 1760s onwards. The most significant change in imports was the fall in the import of cereals. Imports of base goods such as salt continued to be important, but it was the import of foreign industrial and manufactured goods that increased – despite the protectionist policy of the time! From the middle of the eighteenth century, England won a larger share of the export trade while Holland lost ground. The Baltic ports continued to play an important part in both the export and import trade. Against this background a number of merchant houses, carrying on a substantial export and import trade, grew up in Stockholm in the Age of Freedom. The foremost of these houses included the Grillska Company, the brothers Abraham and Jacob Arfwedson, Jennings & Co., the Plomgren Company (the brothers Thomas and Anders Plomgren), Charles & William Tottie (after 1771, Tottie & Arfwedson), Gustaf Kierman, Alnoor & Issendorff, J. D. Wahrendorff, De Ron, Koschell, J. C. Pauli, Hebbe and others. The people who headed these enterprises were known collectively as 'the Skeppsbro nobility'. As this list of names suggests, most of these 'nobles' were immigrants. A typical example is the Grillska Company, which was founded at the beginning of the eighteenth century by the brothers Abraham and Carlos Grill, whose father was Italian. The Tottie family were descended from a tobacco factory owner who immigrated from Scotland in 1688; the Jennings Company was founded by Frans Jennings, an Irishman who moved to Sweden in 1754; the Wahrendorff Company was founded in the 1750s by Joachim Daniel Wahrendorff, a German; and the Hebbe business can be traced back to Christian Hebbe the elder, who came to Sweden around 1710. Both Jewish and Scottish people were well represented among the foreign owners of merchant houses.[7] Then came the enterprises owned by Swedes: Plomgrens, Westerbergs, Bohmans, Hassel & Gjörges, etc.

The most common business structure was a kind of trading company formed by a small number of people, often from the same family. This type of company was a relatively recent phenomenon that did not become widespread in Western Europe until the seventeenth century. Its predecessors were the trading associations, well-known examples being the 'chartered companies' such as the Merchant Adventurers or, earlier, the East India Company in seventeenth-century England. The trading associations were normally formed by a number of private merchants who fitted out their own ships but who sailed together for protection and to deny others the use of the

Figure 4.2 Exports of sawn timber, pitch and tar grew in the second half of the eighteenth century. The picture shows tar-making in Österbotten. Etching by J. H. Seeliger after A. Dahlström in C. F. Mennander and E. Juuelius, *Tiärtillwärkningen i Österbotn* (1747). KB.

profitable trade routes. The more modern joint-stock company had a different structure (as it has today). They were not very different from the present-day companies based on capital association. Unlike the modern joint-stock company, however, the partners in the trading company carried joint responsibility, and were obliged to commit their entire personal fortunes if the business became insolvent. The parties were also jointly and severally responsible. However small their own investments might be, they were liable to support the company if it got into difficulties. As a result, there were seldom more than two owners – as Kurt Samuelsson writes, it was probably 'the exception for anyone to want to commit themselves in this way without being able to have active control of the business'.[8] This in its turn was certainly one of the main reasons why so few of these merchant houses lasted very long. The most important exception to this rule was one of the largest businesses, Tottie & Arfwedson, which traded for well over a century, closing in 1867. But as a rule, this form of company was not suited to the development of stable and durable enterprises. The ties between these firms and their owners were strong. There was no clear dividing line between business and personal relationships. When the main proprietor of the business died or found himself in difficulties, the company often had to close down. An example is the once-powerful Grillska Company, which lost all of its earlier status on the death of Claes Grill in 1767. There were also numerous bankruptcies, particularly during the trade and monetary crisis of the 1760s when, for example, Jennings & Finlay, Kierman, Petersen & Bedoire, and Lefbure all became insolvent.[9]

Although the merchant houses of Stockholm carried on a wide range of business, their principal activity was trading in general goods. These houses were important both as importers and exporters. From 1750 to 1820 the number of exporters from Stockholm remained fairly constant at around 140 to 160, while the number of importers was much higher at between about 420 and 480. Among these there was an élite of about twenty firms. From 1750 to 1820 between 60 and 70 per cent of Stockholm's exports and around one third of its imports were in the hands of about ten companies.[10] At least until the middle of the nineteenth century, this group does not appear to have become any more concentrated, nor was there even any tendency for the larger businesses to force the smaller ones to the wall. Instead, there was vigorous competition, particularly in imports. Neither can any consistent form of specialisation be discerned among the exporting and importing companies. Samuelsson, for example, maintains that the multiplicity of their activities was due to 'some residual system of payment-in-kind in international trading'.[11] If this was the case, an exporter would be compelled to accept payment for his cargo in goods, but it is hard to say how common this arrangement was. The widespread use of exchange bills after the middle of the eighteenth century, however, suggests that payment-in-kind had outlived its usefulness by that time, if it ever had actually been in common use. This theory is also contradicted by the fact that the great export merchants clearly attempted to sell abroad more than they bought, and payment-in-kind was therefore far from an ideal arrangement.

The most important of the goods imported by the merchant houses were cereals, salt, sugar, tobacco and textiles. There was some division of labour in cereal imports. Some firms were particularly active in this trade, one being the Wahrendorff Company, whose import of cereals in some of the peak years reached 90 per cent of the total import trade. Some of the other larger businesses, Grill, Jennings, Kierman and Tottie, for example, imported virtually no cereals, concentrating instead on other goods such as salt, sugar, tobacco and textiles. Cereal was usually brought from the Baltic region, while salt came from Portugal and the Mediterranean ports. The other goods were usually imported from Holland, England and France.[12] This was true at least of the period after 1750, when the earlier strong dependence on foreign direct trade (mainly with Holland) was also replaced by an increase in imports through the Swedish merchant houses. We should, however, keep in mind the strong foreign representation in the 'Skeppsbro nobility' and, no less important, the fact that a large proportion of the goods were still shipped in foreign vessels.

Pig iron was by far the most important of Sweden's exports. Iron was easily the biggest export of the firms of Grill, Jennings, Lefbure, Kiermans, Tottie and Wennerqvist. In the 1750s and 1760s, in particular, Jennings & Finlay were the biggest exporters of iron, while from 1772 the leading position was taken by Tottie & Arfwedson. After iron the most important exports were copper, tar and sawn timber. Tottie & Arfwedson were very active in the trade of tar and sawn timber. Much of the export trade was to the Baltic towns and to Holland and England. Here, however, there were major differences between the companies. Both Jennings & Finlays and Tottie & Arfwedsons exported mainly to England, while Grills exported to Holland, and Wahrendorffs to the German ports.[13] The original nationality of the owners undoubtedly had a great deal to do with their choice of export ports. In general, we should assume that our merchant houses were (albeit secondary) nodes in the changing international network of trade policy and financial relationships of the times.

Gothenburg

The second half of the eighteenth century saw an explosive increase in Gothenburg's foreign trade. This port was, of course, very favourably located for trade with both Holland and Britain, and, as we have seen, it was particularly the relations with Britain that gained in importance after 1750. Large quantities of cloth and woven fabrics, salt, sugar, tobacco and tea were brought into the country through Gothenburg, although the sporadic import prohibitions at times prevented the import of finished manufactured goods. In their place came a relatively large import trade in raw materials for textile manufacture, especially flax seed, hemp and raw silk and, some years into the nineteenth century, cotton. At the beginning of the nineteenth century large quantities of salt herring were imported after the 'herring run' came to an end. On the other hand, exports were concentrated on a number of key goods, with iron as the most important throughout this period, mostly bar iron, but also bolt iron, strip iron, boilerplate, nails, etc. But the export of sawn timber and herring was, at least at times, very considerable. Towards the end of the eighteenth century there was some 'warehouse trading'. This was the re-export to the German Baltic ports or to Russia of imported salt, wine, sugar, spices, spirits, etc.[14] As with Stockholm, this lively foreign trade was the foundation on which a number of important export companies were built. The leading Gothenburg merchant in the mid-eighteenth century was undoubtedly Niclas Sahlgren (1701–76). As well as a large trading business, he owned several manors and estates (among them Östad, Koberg, Dal, and Gåsvadeholm). On his death he left an almost unparalleled fortune of 4,159,498 silver dalers. He had a close business and personal relationship with his neighbour in Alingsås, Johan Jonas Alströmer, who had benefited so much from the manufactory policy. Another important Gothenburg company of some decades later was Nils Arfwidsson & Sons. In addition to its trading activities, this enterprise owned many ships and was also part-owner of a large shipping company. As with Stockholm, these trading capitalists were involved in a wide range of business activities. Both in Gothenburg and Stockholm this also involved close contact with the manufactories; the merchant houses acted as exporters, organisers of domestic manufacture (the putting-out system), and were sometimes the owners of manufactories or ironworks. But their main business continued to be exports and imports.

The most spectacular feature of the export and import trade based on Gothenburg – and perhaps of Swedish trade capitalism as a whole in the eighteenth century – was the East India Company. This company, founded in 1731, was granted a monopoly on all Swedish trade east of the Cape of Good Hope. The Swedish East India Company, which operated until 1813, was not an exclusively Gothenburg-based operation. The business itself was run in Gothenburg, but the partners were merchants from both Stockholm and Gothenburg. The Scots were also strongly represented from the outset. Colin Campbell, who had earlier been a partner in the English–Dutch Ostende Company, was the Swedish company's main shareholder in its first years. In the middle of the eighteenth century the Scotsmen Robert Finlay and William Chalmers, both operating from Gothenburg, also had major holdings in the company. But Swedish holdings grew as time passed. The Board had a number of directors recruited from the merchant aristocracy. In 1753 the directors were Colin Campbell and Niclas Sahlgren, both of Gothenburg, and Anders Lagerström, Head of the Board of Commerce, Anders Plomgren, the merchant, two members of the merchant family of Grill, and Jacob von Utfall, the merchant.

To found enterprises for trade outside Europe was highly fashionable during this period. In addition to the East India Company, a Levant Company (Letter

Figure 4.3 Gothenburg at the end of the nineteenth century with stora Hamnkanalen (the harbour canal), Norra Hamngatan and Södra Hamngatan etc. View to the east from Lilla torget. Watercolour, signed J. F. Weinberg 1794. Gothenburgs stadsmuseum.

Patent 1738) and a West Indian Company (1745) were also set up. Later, a West Africa Company and a Greenland Company (whaling) were founded, and as late as 1815 a company for re-export trading across the Baltic. The main purpose of the East India Company was to import colonial goods from China and other parts of south-east Asia for re-export or processing in Sweden. The East India Company was very much a product of its time and of the prevailing ideas about the benefits of higher export revenues and increasing added value. This explains the large numbers of people from government offices who sat on the Board of the East India Company, and the considerable interest the government took in the Company.

Granting a charter (which was only valid for a limited time) was, however, not without controversy. The export of precious metals was viewed with suspicion, a remnant of earlier ideas, and the export of Swedish goods to the Far East was hardly feasible. Another controversial issue was that imports, of silk cloth for example, could out-compete domestic Swedish manufacture. Against this background, the first years of the Swedish East India Company were described as follows by a more or less contemporary observer. One may suspect that the large profits which the Company generated might finally have brushed aside all objections.

Many objections were voiced in the Riksdag, and many who opposed this trade were genuinely convinced that it would do our Mother Country more harm than good. However, its defendants, led by H. König, minister of trade, were victorious, and on June 14th, 1731, the King issued a Letter Patent for an East India Company. The first ship sailed from Gothenburg in February 1732 with one of the Company's directors, Mr. Colin Campbell, on board to bring order to the trade. The ship sailed to Canton, returning in August 1733, and in 1734 the associated parties received in two payments a profit of 75 per cent. This encouraged them to continue the trade, notwithstanding the misadventures that occurred, including the obstacles the English tried to place in the path of Swedish East India trade, going so far as to plunder the Swedish factory that was built in Porto Novo on the Coromandel coast and remove all the effects.[15]

In its lifetime of rather more than eighty years, the East India Company undertook 132 expeditions, 124 of which had Canton as their destination. Large quantities of colonial goods, particularly tea (a regular quantity of seventeen tons a year, according to Heckscher), raw silk, china and other goods were shipped to Sweden. This import speeded the evolution of a modern and clearly consumption-oriented culture among the wealthier classes. But a large percentage of these imported goods were, as was the intention, re-exported at a good profit; Heckscher writes that 'merchants from many countries gathered' for the Company's auctions in Gothenburg.[16]

A far more prosaic phenomenon was the export of considerable quantities of salted herring and fish train oil following the rich catches of herring along the west coast of Sweden after 1750. It is likely that this export, most of

Figure 4.4 Herring and train oil were important export products at the end of the eighteenth century. Herring fishing at Fjällbacka, 1878. Drawing on wood by J. Hägg. *Ny illustrerad tidning* 1878. KB.

which went to the Baltic ports (Danzig, Riga, etc.) including Denmark – was more important in total than the East India Company's re-exported goods. After disappearing from Swedish coastal waters during the Great Nordic War – the fish being 'frightened by the disturbances and clamour of war' according to one source[17] – there were record catches after 1747. Certain prominent Gothenburg merchants were noted for their exploitation of this capricious natural resource. In the bays round the coast of Bohus county, heavy investments were made in plants for curing herring and rendering fish train oil. In 1787 we find a total of 336 herring curing plants in the Bohus skerries, the largest being owned by Gothenburg merchants. In the 1780s and 1790s catches were at their peak, and the value of fish train oil and herring exports was only exceeded by iron exports. At the beginning of the nineteenth century, however, the herring run was over and most of the salting and rendering plants were closed down.[18]

Mining and ironworking

In addition to their role as exporters, the merchant houses came to fulfil an important function as suppliers of capital to Sweden's mines and ironworks. In the eighteenth century several of the great merchant houses – we have already mentioned Jennings & Finlay and Tottie & Arfwedson – also financed the sale of bar iron. The most common system was for bills of exchange to be issued when the goods were delivered and before the consignments were sold on by the merchant house. But in many cases the large Stockholm companies also financed the production costs with advances, '*förlag*', in the form of money or payment-in-kind to the ironworks. This credit was then repaid with consignments of iron. However, the debit and credit side often failed to balance, and the ironworks would often find themselves in debt to the exporting merchants. In any event, the merchant houses came to supply a substantial proportion of the ironworks' need of working capital. In some cases they even lent money for investments in fixed plant and machinery and they even took over the ownership of ironworks in some areas, although this was less common; supplying capital in the form of an annual debenture loan was the usual method.

In the eighteenth and early nineteenth century, export sales of bar iron and other iron goods increased, fairly rapidly at times. Yet it is clear that this growth was not as swift as timber and wood products, for example. Income from bar iron exports therefore fell as a percentage of total export income. That is probably what lies behind the notion that the iron industry as a whole stagnated in the second half of the eighteenth century and the beginning of the following century. This stagnation is generally attributed to the restrictive policy in effect until 1846 that aimed to limit bar iron production (and prevent the export of pig iron). However, some of these restrictions were relaxed during this period. In 1836 production was allowed to increase from about 50,000 tons to 68,628 tons, and up to 1846, when the restrictions were lifted entirely, the statutory upper limit for iron manufacture had been raised to 93,544 tons![19] One motive for these restrictions was said to be the assumption that the forests would be depleted and charcoal be in short supply if output were not limited – although many have suspected a kind of monopolistic thinking behind these restrictions. Curbing the output of bar iron would keep demand and prices high.[20] This was undoubtedly one of the main ideas behind the foundation of the Iron Bureau (*Jernkontoret*) in 1747 for the official purpose of safeguarding the interests of the Swedish ironworks and to act as a lending bank for this industry. Whatever the purpose of the restrictions may have been, it is quite clear that they caused Swedish iron to lose market share and opened the door for other countries, Russia in particular, which rapidly increased their share of iron exports. As already mentioned, in the eighteenth century England was by far the biggest market for exports of Swedish bar iron, and the English market continued to grow through the first half of the nineteenth century. During this period, much of Sweden's bar iron exports were shipped through Hull to the rapidly expanding iron and steel industry centred on Sheffield.[21]

We can see how the concentration of ironworks in the Kopparbergs, Örebro and Värmland counties intensified during this period. The ironworks of Uppland, on the other hand, lost ground in relative terms, although some of the largest works are still located in this county. But many of the larger foundries also grew up in other areas. In 1844, for example, we find several large foundries in Värmland, the most important being the Uddeholms iron-works. Or, in the county of Örebro, mainly in Hellefors, and the important Fagerstabruk complex which had been built up in a few decades by von Stockenström, the well-known ironmaster.

Apart from Stockholm and Gothenburg, only Gävle sold a significant quantity of iron for export. In the second half of the eighteenth century it was common for over 200 ironworks to deliver their products through Stockholm. The ironworks of Västmanland dominated here, both numeric-ally and in tonnage delivered. There were far fewer ironworks in Uppland that delivered iron to the capital, but these works were bigger and therefore came in second place in tonnage delivered.[22] The ironworks of Dalarna also grew in importance in the early nineteenth century. In the eighteenth and early nineteenth century the greater part of the iron that passed through Gothenburg was from the ironworks of Värmland, most of which were, as already mentioned, small. But as we have seen, there were also a number of relatively large ironworks supplying bar iron to the merchant houses of Gothenburg.

A fairly large number of iron foundries were subordinated to the most powerful merchant houses. In 1777, for example, twenty-five ironworks with an aggregate annual production of 4,900 tons were linked to Tottie & Arfwedson as their agent, a number that had grown to forty-two by 1813, with a total production of 8,900 tons. Similarly, in 1777, a total of eighteen ironworks were linked to the important firm of Bohman, Hassel & Gjörges, producing 2,400 tons of iron. In this case the number of foundries had fallen to nine by 1813, and the tonnage to 420. But that year was obviously an extremely poor one. In the previous year thirty-seven ironworks had supplied 4,900 tons. [23]

There were no sweeping changes in the production methods and organisation of the pig ironworks until close to the middle of the nineteenth century. The first major phase of transformation was already over. True, exports increased in the decades that followed, but the number of ironworks remained constant and production grew slowly. While pig iron production, from which bar iron was made, had remained steady at around 60,000 tons a year in the second half of the eighteenth century, between 1815 and 1820 it rose to about 80,000 tons. About 95,000 tons a year were produced in the 1820s and by the mid-1840s it had risen to 130,000 tons. [24]

Thus, despite all the talk of stagnation, production doubled in fifty years. At least one evident reason for this is the gradual improvement in productivity; although production rose, the number of blast furnaces hardly increased. In the first decade of the nineteenth century average production

Table 4.1 Swedish iron production 1844

County	Pig iron production		Bar iron production		Iron hardware production
	Number of blast-furnaces	Production in tons	Number of forges	Production in tons	Production in tons
Norrbottens	3	532	24	588	37
Västerbottens	1	460	17	947	78
Västernorrlands	5	2,679	84	4,664	330
Gävleborgs: H	8	5,697	63	4,900	55
Gävleborgs: G	15	7,332	101	6,959	194
Uppsala	7	5,302	29	3,128	108
Stockholms	3	2,591	19	1,757	152
Kopparbergs	46	30,263	178	11,493	1,514
Västmanlands	13	5,288	130	9,334	666
Örebro	55	27,911	169	11,097	2,242
Värmlands	26	14,919	259	15,910	3,000
Södermanland	5	4,180	46	2,170	1,140
Östergötlands	2	1,662	78	4,035	1,035
Skaraborgs	0		24	1,260	93
Älvsborgs	1	177	39	3,050	1,250
Kalmar	8	3,021	34	1,510	177
Jönköpings	12	2,884	35	1,572	232
Kronobergs	8	1,697	22	951	288
Total	219	116,660	1,362	85,555	11,721

Source: A. Attman, *Fagerstabrukens historia*, II, Uppsala 1958, pp. 46–7.

per blast furnace was about three tons per smelting day. By the end of the 1840s the figure was about four tons.[25] There were no dramatic improvements in technology to account for this increase in production. In the three first decades of the nineteenth century, however, a number of experiments to improve the technical methods used were carried out under the auspices of the Iron Bureau. These experiments were on improved carbonisation, pig-iron smelting, casting, puddling, crucible steel production, etc. They were of at least some benefit to the iron industry. The most important improvements were the reduction in charcoal consumption at the various stages of the iron production process, and the higher and more consistent quality.[26] Another important innovation was the introduction of hot-air blowers in blast furnaces and forging hearths, the first being those at the Brefvens, Ankarsrums and Högfors ironworks around 1830. At about the same time, better roasting methods evolved, and an improved blast furnace design that could take larger capacities (1840s) was introduced. But, by and large, it is likely that the increase in production resulted from improvements in organisation and skills, better raw material processing, etc., as well as a number of technical improvements of a more mundane nature that may have appeared to be insignificant but, when taken together, resulted in higher productivity.

The same applies to the final product for which pig iron was produced: bar iron. We find no great technical advances here either. At the beginning of the nineteenth century total production was about 90 per cent so-called German iron and 10 per cent Walloon iron. Here, too, the introduction of improved blasting methods played a major part in increasing production, particularly towards the end of this period. The most important improvements were to the bellows, and the modern 'hot air machines' that began to be introduced in the 1840s.[27] There were also, perhaps equally important, minor changes of the kind mentioned above that were attributable to improved skills etc. Together, these changes resulted in a higher and more consistent quality of bar iron.

However, it is likely that the most important factor in the improvement of the iron industry in this period was the administrative management and ownership of the ironworks. Ownership and operation of the ironworks was still decentralised in the mid-eighteenth century. Artur Attman, for example, tells us that 'the ironworks were largely independent production units'.[28] But from the 1840s onwards, groups of ironworks became more common. Powerful owners began to emerge who wanted to create efficient and profitable enterprises. Such demands also gave rise to the extensive structural transformation and the 'death of the ironworks' which the industry faced a couple of decades later, from the 1860s onwards. Initially, these 'combines' of ironworks were nothing more than a group of several ironworks coming under a single owner. But as time passed, more interest was shown in at least some measure of co-ordination. Initially, the focus was on the arrangements for financing the operation and for disposing of the product. In the long term, however, interest

Figure 4.5 Domnarvets Ironworks by the Dalälven. Woodcut. *Ny illustrerad tidning* 1884 KB.

Figure 4.6 New machines at the ironworks. Crucible steel is poured into ingot moulds at Österby crucible steel works. From A. Attman, *Fagerstabrukens historia* (1958).

extended to production conditions, including the first signs of specialisation. They were, it is true, still dependent on the larger merchant houses at this time, but it is clear that several of the complexes of ironworks began to have ownership structures, either as companies or family businesses, that soon wanted to extend their influence to the field of export sales. As early as the 1840s the Uddeholm Company, for example, began to sell direct to its English customers. Several of the merchant houses then began to act as agents, commissioned by the ironworks to sell iron. Even the powerful Stockholm merchant house of Tottie & Arfwedson became involved, handling the practical sides of the export of Dannemora iron to England, for example, with the contract negotiated between the owner of the ironworks (P. A. Tamm) and the customer.[29] The following are examples of these groupings of ironworks: Uddeholmsverken (twelve ironworks), owned by a separate company with several owners, Fagerstabruken (six ironworks) under von Stockenström, Stora Kopparbergs mining district (eight ironworks), which was also a private company, and Carl De Geer's group of Dannemora works (six ironworks). Other prominent owners who attempted to improve co-ordination between their ironworks included Tamm (Österby, Söderfors, Hedviksfors, Strömbacka), Nordin (Forsbacka, Karmansbro), Petré (Hofors and some neighbouring ironworks), Tersmeden (Ramnäs, Larsbo), and others.[30]

Exports of wood products

As late as the middle of the nineteenth century, Sweden's iron production was the only real export industry with strong capitalist features. But other industries gradually began to concentrate on exports. Examples include the products of the intensive herring fishing industry or the increased sale of oats from the expanding agricultural sector. But the export of wood and wood products, particularly tar and pitch, and later sawn timber, also increased. The export of sawn timber in particular rose dramatically in the economic upswing of the 1850s.

Wood product exports were limited, at least in the eighteenth century, by the restrictions that, among other things, preserved the forests for the ironworks. There was no general bar on the export of these goods until after 1723. But excise duties were high at times, and were not significantly reduced until after 1818.[31] In the eighteenth century the most important markets for sawn timber exported from Stockholm were the Mediterranean ports and Portugal. Most exports from Gothenburg went to Britain. In the nineteenth century the greatest rise in demand was also from Western Europe, especially from England. Exports rose sharply from 1806 to 1814, when the Commodity Act was temporarily suspended and the English ban resulted in a strong demand for products from more 'friendly' nations. Exports rose even more when England introduced free trade in the 1840s. As with iron, exports of both sawn timber and tar were handled by the great merchant houses, foremost in Stockholm, Gothenburg and Gävle.

Figure 4.7 A small water-powered sawmill. Aspa sawmill at the end of the eighteenth century. Watercolour by Elias Martin. KB.

Production units were, by and large, still very small and spread fairly evenly throughout the country. Until the 1840s the small sawmills were driven by water power and had simple saw gates, and most of them could be described as seasonal producers for the market.[32] However, even in the eighteenth century there was a distinction between sawmill production for household needs and production for the market. Towards the end of the eighteenth century there were, for example, a number of large commercial sawmills along the southern coast of Norrland. In 1796 there were thirty-six sawmills in Hälsingland and 151 sawmills for local domestic needs. In the same year we find thirty-six sawmills in Gästrikland producing for the market and fifty-seven mills producing for local needs.[33] Thus the sawmill industry in the coastal parishes of southern Norrland and elsewhere was fairly substantial. Most sawn timber was probably sold on the domestic market, but some was certainly exported. Almost all of the small sawmills for local needs, but some of the larger commercial mills as well, were owned and operated by peasants as a sideline. However, even at an early stage, many of the commercial sawmills were owned by merchants from the towns of Norrland, for example. Writing about these towns in the early nineteenth century, Maurits Nyström has noted that: 'Merchant capital has made its mark on what was formerly a peasant-controlled industry'.[34] The trading burghers of the towns and people who formed the vague category of 'people of standing in the rural areas', such as justices and assizes judges, thus began to invest in the sawmill industry by providing working capital. It was not uncommon, even in the first two decades of the nineteenth century, to find that the burghers of Stockholm had substantial holdings in large sawmills in northern Norrland. Local merchants were more often part-owners of the sawmills further to the south. Finally, a growing number of ironworks owners had holdings in sawmills, particularly in the villages where their ironworks were located. This meant, for example, that the ironmasters of Hälsingland soon had substantial holdings in the commercial sawmills of that county.[35] Despite this, the sawmills continued to be a secondary occupation. Most of their labour was still employed on a seasonal basis. At some of the larger sawmills such as the Mo sawmill there were, however, some labourers, bookkeepers, inspectors and saw-fitters employed on a full-time basis as early as the beginning of the nineteenth century.[36]

The 1850s saw a breakthrough for a more large-scale sawmill industry, partly on the initiative of the great merchant houses that had exported wood and wood products. In several cases international capital was involved here. The new joint-stock company form of organisation was now in more frequent use in establishing large, exporting sawmills that also had steam power installed to drive the modern saws. Most of these new mills were set up along the coast of Norrland. We shall describe later in this book the development of this industry after the 1850s. It is enough here to highlight the growing capitalist aspect of this sector from the 1840s onwards.

In the eighteenth century tar and pitch still generated more revenues from export than sawn timber. Despite the restrictions on exports, there was in this century a very strong increase in tar exports. From the 1730s until around 1800, exports increased threefold, to reach about 140,000 barrels a year from 1801 to 1808. Holland and the Baltic ports had long been important destinations for these products. In the eighteenth century, however, Britain gradually became a more important export customer, particularly during the Napoleonic Wars. Stockholm was by far the most important export port for tar, with Fredrikshamn in Finland in second place until 1809.[37]

Credit and financing

At least until the 1860s, the great merchant houses of Stockholm and Gothenburg were the link between Sweden and an expanding international economy. We have already discussed their role as a source of capital for the ironworks and sawmills and also described the way in which these merchant houses were involved in the expanding export trade of sawn timber from upper Norrland. There were also clear financial links between the smaller merchants in the country towns, in southern Norrland for example, and the larger trading companies in Stockholm. A number of the capital's great trading houses worked on commission from their smaller rural counterparts. Neither was it unusual for the powerful trading companies to provide the smaller merchant houses with a large part of their working capital. In general, perhaps the most important task of the trading companies was to provide circulating working capital to different industries. There were, of course, fixed capital investments, for example in building herring salting factories or commercial sawmills. But in the period we are addressing here, this was still the exception. Larger-scale capital investment in production is to be found more in the second half of the nineteenth century.

One of the most important prerequisites for the emergence of a modern industrial sector in Sweden was the involvement of foreign capitalists in production. If this had been only sporadic up to this time, it was largely due to the unsophisticated system of credit that was still in use. Until the end of the 1850s there were, in principle, no modern commercial banks that were either able or willing to make capital available to start or expand industrial enterprises. Instead, the main sources of private credit were the merchant houses and a number of private bankers. The former were largely involved in providing enterprises with essential working capital over the year, while the latter were very reluctant to risk their capital over a longer term. Apart from simple cash loans, borrowing was arranged in the form of promissory notes against real property, often for a period of six months. As an example of this 'individualistic capitalist active in the traditional system', the name of Agathon Wallenberg may be mentioned, brother of the better-known André Oscar Wallenberg, to whom we shall return below.[38]

Credit was available from a number of other institutions. We have already seen that the Bank of Sweden arranged loans for the ironworks and other enterprises in the seventeenth century. But most of its activities were limited to consumption loans issued against a mortgage on property. The Manufactory Fund was another important source of credit. But, as mentioned above, this fund was involved almost exclusively in financing day-to-day operations and not in long-term investments. Finally, mention should be made of the numerous agricultural credit institutes that sprang up after the 1820s. As Rolf Adamsson shows, it is wrong to believe that the sole purpose of these institutes was to lend money to the agricultural sector. They probably also played an important part in providing the ironworks and sawmills with more long-term loans.[39] As we have seen, these banks in their turn borrowed abroad, thus making an active contribution to increasing the supply of capital to the benefit of both the agricultural sector and the burgeoning industrial sector.

Towards the end of the 1850s, a more modern type of commercial bank also appeared. Their only true predecessors were the small number of private lending banks that arranged short-term credit against a guarantee or security. These commercial banks included the *Göteborgs diskontokompani* (founded in 1802), the *Malmö diskont* (1803) and the *Göta kanals diskont* (1810). All these banks had to close in 1817.[40] Half a century later, the Stockholm Enskilda Bank (SEB) opened as the first of the private commercial banks with a broader range of activities. Behind this bank was André Oscar

Figure 4.8 The Stockholm Enskilda Bank in Lilla Nygatan, ca. 1870.
Photo: Johannes Jaeger. SSM.

Wallenberg, a former naval officer and 'private capitalist', who ran a
steamboat company and traded in promissory notes either himself or in close
co-operation with the Lovén & Co. trading company. By the end of the
1850s he was known as the 'bank-maker' *par excellence*, having opened
branches of his bank in Sundsvall and Härnosand (1855) and founded the
Stockholm Enskilda Bank in 1856. An innovation of the SEB was that it did
not obtain its capital by issuing notes. Instead, it raised capital by borrowing
from private customers against interest and by selling bonds that drew on
the capital reserve fund which the government obliged new private banks to
set up in order to secure the interests of the general public. This use of the
capital reserve fund may not have been against the letter of the law, but it
was certainly against the spirit of the law. In his efforts to establish a
commercial banking operation in a new area, A. O. Wallenberg more than
once had to cross the boundary of what was generally considered to be honest
and proper. To give an example, the regulation limiting interest rates to not
more than 5.7 per cent (6 per cent after 1861) was still in force. Wallenberg
found an ingenious solution to the problem of adjusting interest to reflect
the supply and demand of money by adding or subtracting certain administrative charges in his dealings. In time, however, most of the institutional
obstacles were overcome, not least through the close co-operation that

developed between Wallenberg, the 'capitalist', and J. A. Gripendstedt, the minister of finance. Their co-operation undoubtedly laid the foundations of the modern banking legislation that came into effect in the 1860s.

An important aspect of the commercial bank programme which A. O. Wallenberg introduced was the use of new 'lubrication' for the banking machinery such as bank credits, checking accounts and cashiers' cheques to facilitate short-term capital movement. In practice the SEB came to act for several decades as a central exchange for the rural banks, a function that was later taken over by the Bank of Sweden. The rural banks thus kept funds in the SEB that could be used for clearing or in the event of a sudden shortage of liquid funds. The functions that were taken on by the SEB were of particular importance to the economy as a whole. They certainly increased the mobility of capital while bringing down the transaction costs of money circulation. Suddenly, reserves of money and fortunes that had previously lain idle could be put to use in business.[41]

But the SEB also came to have real importance as a provider of more long-term credit. Although vigorously opposing the establishment of the *Skandinaviska kreditbolaget* joint-stock bank, which was intended to be the Swedish counterpart of the French Crédit Mobilier bank and deal mainly in direct investments in industry, Wallenberg had nothing in principle against stronger links with industry. Without doubt he saw the transfer from trade capitalism to industrial capitalism as a necessary step. His objections were rather that the majority of the banks' owners would be foreign. It is also possible that A. O. Wallenberg did not want to have too many competitors. Already by the mid-1860s, long-term so-called working capital credits had tied a number of companies to his bank, among them the Gellivara Aktiebolag, Leijonströms Sågverksinteressenter, Härnösands Ångsågs AB, Holm & Graninge Bruksbolag, Sörfors Bruksinteressenter, Norra Hälsinglands Trävarubolag, Siljansfors Bruksbolag, Hällefors Bruksinteressenter, Westerås Minuteringsbolag, Liljeholmens Vinfabrik AB, Stockholms Knappfabriks Bolag, Jönkopings Tändstlcksfabriks AB, Uddeholmsverken, and Motala Mekaniska Verkstad.[42] We shall return later to the matter of industrial financing in the nineteenth century. It is important to note here, however, that much larger industrial financing was a significant part of A. O. Wallenberg's commercial banking programme. As he said in 1856:

> The industrial life and the spirit of industry that characterises our times, and of which our country carries the most unmistakable stamp, is and must be accompanied by a strong demand for working capital. This demand, which generates a high rate of interest, particularly in countries where capital formation is slow, can only be satisfied by an appropriate arrangement of credit, that powerful lever for industry, and which, even if it neither can nor should be used wholly to replace capital, is today in most cases almost as indispensable for the utilisation of those assets which in its absence will continue to lie idle.[43]

Large-scale business dealings

The word capitalist first became widely used in the Swedish vocabulary around 1840. It described people like the Wallenberg brothers, who carried on a business in promissory notes, or those who dealt generally in large-scale financial transactions. In the eighteenth century these 'monetary transactions' were effected with the help of bills of exchange. We know a great deal about the merchant Peter Westman's large-scale speculative dealings in the 1730s and 1740s.[44] Westman carried on a business in bills of exchange with numerous merchant houses in London, Amsterdam, Hamburg and elsewhere in Western Europe. His dealings were sometimes, but by no means always, rooted in genuine goods transactions. The consignments of goods to which the bills referred often did not exist, or at least they never left the ports. This is an example of large-scale speculation. And Westman was certainly not alone in carrying on such business, although his dealings were unusually spectacular.

What we regard today as speculation was an important occupation for the capitalists of the eighteenth century and the early nineteenth century, not infrequently using public funds and institutions. Speculation of this kind was roundly condemned in the 1760s when the Caps Party came to power. In the 1765/6 Riksdag the government's so-called Exchange Bill Office, which was set up in 1747 under the leadership of the great merchant and Stockholm mayor, Gustaf Kierman, was severely criticised for deliberately forcing up the exchange rates for its own gain. This office had been set up to improve, i.e. force down, Swedish exchange rates through its dealings in bills of exchange. Soon, an 'Exchange Bill Party' was formed, which included in its membership prominent politicians from both within and outside the Banco Deputation and the cream of the export merchants allied with the Iron Bureau. Rising inflation, expressed in rising exchange rates and a fall in the value of Swedish currency in Hamburg and Amsterdam, gave the merchants an opportunity to 'buy cheap and sell dear'. The amount the bills could be redeemed for, by the ironmaster in Dalarna for example, fell constantly in relative terms. The merchant and the politician – often one and the same person – were able to pocket the difference. The most bitter critic of this system was Anders Nordencrantz, who from the 1760s became well known for his liberal economic ideas. In 1767 he said, 'a few people in Sweden have ... with bank loans on exports and ironworks property, and speculative dealings since 1755 intended by the misuse of these loans to govern the whole of Sweden, while concealing under various pretexts their activities and intentions from the high and the low, to gain the entire nation under various pretexts'.[45] This author's 'wild diatribes' (Heckscher) against this speculative trade did not, however, rest purely on principle. When he is particularly critical of the firm of Jennings & Finlay, it is for purely private financial motives. As early as 1756 he had already sold a number of ironworks in Roslagen to this company. The purchase price – 'under various pretexts', one must assume – had, however, not been paid until 1763. During this time the company had made impressive gains from inflation. Otherwise, it was mainly Kierman, the mayor, who found himself in the midst of controversy. He was accused of enlisting the help of the Exchange Bill Office to purchase ironworks at low prices for personal profit. A court later ordered him, together with a few others, to pay a sum of six million dalers of silver coin – and he was punished by a furious crowd which pelted his home in Munkbrogatan with stones. As Heckscher mentions, the generous issue of banknotes was the main cause of inflation and the rise in the exchange rate, and not this speculation in itself. But this is not to say that private interests could not make substantial profits from such trans- actions, as the case of Anders Nordencrantz, for example, illustrates so well. We cannot entirely ignore the suspicion that this policy of freely issuing banknotes could have stemmed from 'ubiquitous selfishness and poor judgement'. The political structure in the Age of Freedom, with its powerful lobbies and special interests, actually served to ensure that the distinction between private and public interests became vague.

Opportunities for people to line their pockets were not limited to the Age of Freedom. The following period also offered great opportunities for people to feather their own nests. Despite the devaluation of 1776, the temporary introduction of the silver standard in 1776–89, the withdrawal of banknotes, a restrictive lending policy from the Bank and the general deflationary policy pursued by the Caps Party into the first years of the reign of Gustav III, prices continued to rise. Exchange rates would, in theory, continue to fluctuate until the great reform of 1834. The situation became particularly precarious in the war years around 1790 and again in 1808 and 1809. As Bertil Dahlström has described, Eric Ruth, the minister of finance, spared no pains to finance the Russian campaign of 1789. He raised loans both at home and abroad and instructed the newly founded National Debt Office to issue credit notes or so-called national debt notes. In this atmosphere of constant turbulence in monetary matters there were undoubtedly opportunities for anyone inclined to take advantage of them.[46]

This was also true of the dealings undertaken by the government, as dubious as they were daring, more or less continuously from the Age of Freedom onwards. For example, in 1789 the National Debt Office Commis- sioners raised substantial loans – 8 million lire – from De la Rue et fils in Genoa and from the King of Prussia (1.1 million Riksdaler). These borrow- ings were to settle short-term liabilities incurred by the 'hard-pressed merchant houses abroad' (Hasselgren in Amsterdam, Averhoff in Hamburg, Tourton & Rawel in Hamburg, Le Lui in Paris and others), 'who have provided the Swedish Crown with advances in the form of promissory notes of some months' duration'.[47] Similarly, Gustav IV Adolf's unsuccessful German war was partly financed with promissory notes issued on Hamburg banking houses.[48] Yet another example was the promissory note dealings in the reign of Karl XIV Johan. From the early 1820s, Skogman, the minister of finance, attempted to stabilise the uneasy exchange rates by means of transactions in foreign promissory notes. A special representative in Hamburg, the wealthy banking firm of Westphalen & Rist, were used for this purpose.[49] But major losses were incurred and large sums had to be borrowed, in one case with the Swedish colony of Saint Barthélemy as security.[50] Finally, we can hardly overlook the hazardous dealings of 1825–6 which have come to be known as the 'ship business'. The purpose of this business was to repay short-term liabilities of the kind described above. We have the following detailed description of the course of events from the pen of Per G. Andreén.

> The decisions were taken after several years of negotiations. In the autumn of 1823 a representative of the revolutionary government in Colombia had presented a petition to purchase warships from Sweden. Rudolf Cederström, Admiral of the Fleet and a cabinet minister, drafted a memorandum on the subject. A year later Colombia submitted a more detailed request, for the purchase of a ship of the line and a frigate. The Swedish government was positively disposed towards the business. Through the agency of Goldschmitt & Co. in London and Michaelsson & Benedicks in Stockholm, a preliminary agreement was apparently drawn up in December 1824. All preparations were completed in the spring of 1825. On March 8th and April 19th a ship of the line and a frigate were sold to Colombia for, respectively, 171 rdb and 19,000 p st. A second ship of the line and two more frigates were sold to Mexico on May 31st for a total sum of 361,500 rdb. This business, in which the above-mentioned merchant houses acted as intermediaries, was made to appear to be trade transactions. In reality these South American governments were, of course, to use the vessels in the war with Spain. The Colombian business was completed according to plan, but in the Mexican trans-action Russia was required to act as intermediary, and the substantial gain with which the government had counted thus became a consider-able loss.[51]

This 'business' was more than just a piquant example of the interplay between commerce and politics in this period. First, it demonstrates the close links between private interests and the government, particularly with regard to government attempts to stabilise the currency. Second, as with our earlier examples, this shows the extent of Sweden's involvement in the world of international finance. As mentioned above, a great part of Sweden's foreign trade was financed by exchange bills issued by large foreign trading and banking companies in Hamburg, London and Amsterdam. Hamburg became the most important city in this respect, particularly after 1800.[52] A number of important foreign banking firms were closely connected with Swedish merchant houses, particularly Tottie & Arfwedson, whose letters of credit were 'Sweden's most secure means of payment abroad'.[53] This was also the way in which Gustav III was able to finance his famous journey to Italy – with a letter of credit from this company in his pocket to the value of 100,000 rdr, which was redeemed as the journey progressed.

The provision of foreign capital was, however, largely limited to the merchant houses (and the Crown) – at least until the middle of the nineteenth century – and thus very little long-term capital was provided from foreign sources. But the very fact that the trading houses and the Crown were dependent on short-term working capital from abroad made Swedish industry and commerce extremely sensitive to economic fluctuations. In the next chapter we shall describe in more detail how Sweden became enmeshed in the international economic cycle from the nineteenth century onwards. But it may be said here that when the merchants of Hamburg, for example, withdrew their credit, Swedish merchants, ironworks, papermills and sawmills, farmers who had amassed debts, and even the most insignificant shopkeeper in every corner of the country, found themselves in immediate difficulties.[54] To this was added the Swedish government's convoluted international business dealings. As we have seen, people were at the mercy of foreign banks, even for short-term funding. On several occasions, promissory note transactions and borrowings led to acute crises in which unconventional methods had to be used – even committing Swedish colonies as security and selling ships to revolutionary governments! There was also the more long-term increase in the government debt, particularly after the 1840s, through the large debenture loans extended to the railroads and other infrastructure. Clearly, Sweden was being drawn into the international economy, and events then moved swiftly.

Figure 4.9 A bank acceptance from the eighteenth century for Uhrfors Ironworks in Riksens ständers bank. KB.

5   Industrial transformation

The prevailing view of history has the 'industrial revolution' as a clearly defined period of transition from the old to the new and the replacement of the old agrarian society with a modern industrial society. There is, in contrast, no such general agreement on the matter of how the term 'industrial revolution' is to be understood. The question is whether this term refers to (1) rapid growth in the economy as a whole, (2) a sharp increase in the industrial sector's share of the economy or, (3) important organisational changes in production, finance and distribution in the industrial sector. Of course, changes in all these three areas may occur simultaneously, but this is by no means always the case. To give an example, the relatively modest overall growth figures for Britain in the period formerly known as the 'industrial revolution' (1750–1850) has in recent years brought into question the whole concept of industrial revolution. Further, many researchers have questioned the theory of a sweeping process of change, pointing instead to the gradual organisational changes that brought about greater centralisation of production and distribution (the 'factory'). Yet it has been admitted that the low average growth rate does not necessarily mean that growth was not impressive, nor that important organisational changes did not take place in particular sectors – nor that there was considerable pressure for transition which resulted in a great deal of geographical relocation in industry and other sectors.[1]

In the case of Sweden, however, it seems reasonable to use the term 'industrial transformation' to define the period from the mid-nineteenth century until the First World War. Here, we can establish with certainty *both* an accelerating average growth rate, a substantial increase in the industrial sector's share of the economy, *and* important organisational changes in the industrial sector.

Growth and structural transformation

We can see how the agricultural sector's share of the economy diminished from the mid-nineteenth century. The figures indicate the same trend for both the agricultural sector's percentage of the population in work and this sector's share of the gross national product (GNP). That the percentage of the labour force employed in agriculture, despite a steady fall in the population, is greater than the agricultural sector's percentage of GNP only shows that GNP per capita is less in agriculture than in industry. This means that the movement of labour from agriculture to industry generates a *transfer gain*. The growth in the period from the mid-nineteenth century is actually largely a result of the labour force moving from agriculture to industry. As Table 5.1 shows, the annual increase in GNP rises from just on 2 per cent from 1860 to 1890 to about 3.5 per cent after 1890. Growth is then constant at this level for many years, including the crisis years of the 1920s and 1930s. This table also shows that this growth rate, high even in an international comparison, is largely attributable to an expanding industrial sector.

Growth is constantly higher in industry than in other sectors, and was particularly high from 1891 to 1915. Sweden clearly experienced an industrial revolution in which rapid industrial growth and transformation laid the foundations for the prosperity of the twentieth century.

It follows from the above discussion on the reasons for growth that this economic expansion should be seen primarily as a result of an increase in the input of production factors. By providing more capital, labour, land and technical and organisational improvements that increase productivity, growth increases in, for example, the industrial sector. Various measurements using the so-called production function indicate that a higher input of real capital (buildings, machinery, etc.) was a particularly important factor at the end of the nineteenth century, but the role of real capital appears to have weakened in the twentieth century. Instead, it is the so-called black box factor that comes to the fore in the twentieth century. As we have seen above, the black box factor is in fact a residue – what remains after capital and labour inputs have been calculated. We do not know very much about what this 'residue' is made up of. It is usually assumed to be a measurement of the importance of the kind of technological and organisational innovations that improve productivity.

Table 5.1 Production growth by sector, 1861–1965. Annual percentage increase

Sector	Year			
	1861–90	*1891–1915*	*1921–40*	*1946–65*
Agriculture etc.	1.7	1.8	1.1	1.9
Industry and crafts	2.7	6.1	5.4	5.6
Building	2.9	3.3	3.6	5
Communications	6.2	4.8	3.8	3.5
Trade	2.3	3.6	2.7	3
Public services	3.4	2.9	3.6	4.1
Housing	1.4	2.1	2.8	3.7
Gross domestic product	2.3	3.6	3.5	4.3

Source: Y. Åberg, *Produktion och produktivitet in Sverige 1861–1965*, Uppsala 1969, p. 17.

As we have noted, some of the growth may be seen in terms of the economy as a whole, as an effect of the transfer gains that occur when people move from agriculture to industry. According to Yngve Åberg's econometrical calculations, 14 per cent of growth from 1871 to 1890 is attributable to this gain, 19 per cent from 1891 to 1915 and as much as 25 per cent of growth from 1921 to 1940.[2] Similar transfer gains may also occur when labour moves from industrial sectors with a lower production value per employee to sectors with a higher production value. If the relative share of production and employees increase in the higher production value sectors, there is an 'automatic' rise in per capita production. It is difficult to make an exact calculation of transfer gains when people move from, for example, low-productive to high-productive industrial sectors. But there is no doubt at all that such movements must improve the average growth figure for industry as a whole.

Our argument thus far suggests that industrial transformation cannot be seen solely as the expansion of industry as a whole. The average figures conceal major structural changes both between and within industrial sectors. To arrive at a concrete picture of industrial expansion we must therefore consider the dynamic that developed at the sectorial level – or even within industrial sectors. What exactly were the conditions at the micro level for this growth and sweeping transformation?

The preconditions for industrial transformation

The underlying causes of the industrial revolution have been discussed in the international literature since the nineteenth century. The idea that this transformation was engendered by the introduction of any single pioneering innovation such as steam power has long since been dropped from more serious debates. Generally speaking, the explanatory technical factors have been pushed more into the background with the passage of time. This change is largely due to a better understanding that the first phase of the industrial revolution was in small-scale production and used fairly rudimentary technology. As British researchers such as Sir John Clapham and Phyllis Deane have emphasised, in Britain it was often not until *after* centralised factories had been established that mechanised production and a new power source, steam, were introduced.[3] Not even in the textile industry, normally the classic example of the importance of technology, can any clear links be established between the founding of factories and any pioneering technical innovation. The dominant technology, the oft-quoted 'spinning jennies', for example, were so small in scale that they could easily be installed in the little cottages of home workers. Thus the factory system derived in part from factors other than what economists call technological indivisibility, i.e. that modern technology presupposed centralised factories. This connection was, of course, a factor, particularly for the various process industries (where, however, the greatest period of expansion was some time after the industrial revolution), but it can by no means be generalised. It should also be added that in the leading industrial countries, the consumer industries, especially the textile industry, were at the forefront of industrial advance. Thus the capital goods industry followed the process industry in industrial transformation.[4] We discuss below how true this was in Sweden.

In the international debate, explanatory factors other than technology have come to the fore, especially the part played by demand, which has been strongly accentuated in relation to the great expansion of the British textile industry in the second half of the eighteenth century. It appears to be beyond any doubt that an increase in demand, both from an expanding domestic market and the export market (particularly the colonies), was the main reason for the rapid increase in the supply of textile goods at that time – and that triggered important organisational changes in the traditional textile industry. This increase in demand initially led to an expansion of the existing protoindustry. But there was clearly not enough potential for expansion within the limits of protoindustry. For a merchant-employer running a putting-out system with a full order book, the temptation to centralise production must have finally proved irresistible. The putting-out system did not allow him any control of the work itself or of production. The upswing in demand required supply to be more reliable. It also meant that quality had to be improved. Similarly, the costs of supervision and other factors that come under the heading of transaction costs rose in pace with the increase in supply. All this led to a search for new ways of organising production. Proximity to the customer and the ability to respond swiftly to new signals from the market were further arguments for more centralised production.

In the modern type of enterprise that gradually emerged in the nineteenth century, production and marketing were integrated in a single organisation. As we have seen, these functions were clearly separate before that time. The purpose of centralisation was to give the business more direct control of production and sales, but also of strategic input, exclusive market channels, skilled labour and, not least, new intangible capital in the form of new, attractive goods that could find a market. This 'programme' also aimed to gain a stronger hold on the workers on the factory floor. It was hoped that the greater potential for supervision a factory offered would improve both workers' timekeeping and performance, and also product quality. The prime aim of the modern, centralised industrial enterprise that emerged in the nineteenth century was to gain better control of both production and marketing processes.

When it comes to the industrial transformation in Sweden, we should, in light of the above, highlight four important factors that drove up demand, or created the conditions for translating growing demand into higher production, and which in the long term laid the foundations for both growth and structural transformation: the international environment, the expanding domestic market, the once so prevalent cottage-based handicraft production, and the supply of capital.

The international environment

The earlier, more broad-based economic-historical works often emphasise the importance of foreign demand in Sweden's industrial transformation. Lennart Jörberg, for example, says the following: 'Until the 1870s Sweden's industrial development was largely an adjustment to events beyond its borders and to a lesser degree an independent economic expansion'.[5] An example often quoted in this context is the very sharp rise in sawn timber exports that began in the 1850s. As with the parallel rapid increase in demand for iron and steel, this rise could be seen as the result of the swift pace of industrial advance in Europe, and particularly in Britain, which was the most important single export market for Swedish wood and iron. Following an earlier period of intense expansion in the consumer goods sector in Britain, growth in the capital goods industry now began to accelerate. This generated a need for more raw materials and input goods such as iron, steel, sawn timber, lumber, iron ore and wood and paper pulp. The free trade policy that Britain began to apply with the repeal of the tariffs on cereals in 1846 helped speed this development. The removal of excise duties played an important part in increasing demand for goods of the kind that Sweden could produce.

These observations are certainly largely accurate. A clear indication of the importance of exports for early industrialisation in Sweden was that the export sectors came to answer for a substantial share of aggregate industrial production in the second half of the nineteenth century. Unlike Britain, for example, where pure consumer goods industries such as textiles played a major part in the early stages of industrialisation, in Sweden export industries such as the sawmills, the iron and steelworks and the mines were more important in the early stages.[6] But it should be noted that the textile industry in England, unlike its Swedish counterpart, was an important export industry right up to the inter-war years. Similarly, there was considerable domestic demand in Sweden for the products of both its sawmills and ironworks. It is generally true that exports were helped along by an expanding domestic market, as we shall soon see.

These viewpoints do not, of course, mean that the rapid industrialisation in Sweden's international environment was not a factor of central importance in Sweden's own industrial transformation. Sweden's favourable export position was strengthened by at least two significant factors. First, at least until the turn of the century, Sweden had few competitors in its export of certain strategic goods. As we have already seen, Sweden's iron and wood products had long been fairly important. For many decades the country had also been well-integrated with the countries of Western Europe through its export sector. Sweden also had an efficient infrastructure and a government that strongly favoured the export sector. Sweden could offer lower prices for iron, ore and wood products than the more developed industrial countries that were its competitors. Unlike its future competitors such as Finland and

Russia, Sweden was close to the main trading routes. If these countries were to develop their export trade, they would have to make considerable investments in infrastructure, a process which could only be carried out in gradual stages.

Second, the relative increase in the prices of Sweden's export products also favoured Sweden's expansion. There was a clear improvement in Sweden's terms-of-trade in the second half of the nineteenth century. In marked contrast to much of the twentieth century, the price of raw materials such as wood, iron and ore rose faster than the prices of many finished goods (which fell in price in the 1870s and 1880s). Sweden was fortunate to become industrialised as part of an international environment that was extremely favourable to the country.

Sweden's international dependence continued into the twentieth century and even increased. It is generally true that from a comparative perspective Sweden's dependence on exports and imports was unusually strong. As we shall discuss later, one effect of this was that Sweden's economy became highly sensitive to the international economic cycle. Although Sweden's various trading partners have varied in importance over time, it is still clear that Sweden's closest Western European neighbours maintained their dominant position.

The domestic market

Domestic factors also favoured Sweden's industrial transformation. The rapid rise in incomes, particularly in agriculture, generated a growing demand for both consumer goods such as textile products, and also capital goods (particularly for the agricultural sector). An accelerating rate of investment and production caused both consumption and savings to rise in the agricultural sector. It is often maintained that the increase in productivity in agriculture released a higher percentage of the labour force from this sector. And, as we have seen, the agricultural sector's percentage of the labour force did fall in the second half of the nineteenth century. But it was not until some time into the twentieth century that the number of employees in agriculture with secondary livelihoods fell in absolute terms. Until that time, agricultural employment increased in line with employment in the industrial sector, albeit at an ever-slower rate.

The fact that the agricultural sector was able to absorb more people at the same time as industry expanded showed that the sharp rise in population in the nineteenth century did *not* lead to mass poverty and destitution. On the contrary, there was a rapid overall upswing in incomes which in its turn accelerated the expansion of the domestic market. However, this vital fact has not always been acknowledged. Instead, it was accepted that there was overpopulation in this period, and agricultural workers were marginalised. In line with this analysis, the theory has been persistently advanced that large-scale emigration to America, totalling about half a million people up to the

Figure 5.1 About a million Swedes emigrated to America. 'The farewell sermon for emigrants on their departure from Gothenburg, May 1869.' Drawn 'from nature' by A.G. Hafström. *Ny illustrerad tidning* 1869. KB.

Figure 5.2 The rail-laying team on the Åby-Koler line, the northern main line through upper Norrland in 1893. Photograph collection, the Swedish Railroad Museum, Gävle.

beginning of the First World War, saved Sweden from widespread poverty and starvation. This theory is an example of a contra-factual hypothesis to which it is impossible to obtain an answer. But we can say that the wave of emigration was not an unmixed blessing. At the beginning of the twentieth century there were many who said that the emigration wave was more a loss of labour and demand. In this light, the hypothesis that the emigrants should instead have been able to find places in a rapidly expanding agricultural sector or in industry, which would then have grown even faster, should be given serious consideration. A number of researchers have pointed out in this context that it was more the domestic market – at least until the 1890s – that was the limiting factor for industrial growth in Sweden.[7]

A clear indication of the substantial surplus labour demand – from both agriculture and industry – was the rise in real wages during this period, a time that is usually referred to as Sweden's industrial transformation. Although it is true that in the 1820s, 1830s and 1840s real wages fell, for day labourers in agriculture, for example, the opposite was true in the 1850s and again from 1870 to 1914.[8] Further, higher real wages also meant that demand for the products of the domestic consumer goods industry could also increase.

Apart from the increase in incomes generated by agriculture, the expansion of the industrial sector also contributed to the rapid growth in domestic demand for both consumer and capital goods. This increase in demand was evident as early as the 1870s, a period of considerable expansion, particularly in the engineering industry, which was at the time still strongly oriented towards the domestic market. But the consumer goods industry, especially the food industry, also expanded during this period. It should, however, be emphasised that the strongest growth in the 1870s was in the export industries.[9] Finally, we must also draw attention to the rise in incomes that resulted from government borrowings abroad for, among other things, building the railroad network and other infrastructure. As Hans Modig has pointed out, it is easy to attach too much importance to the railroads in the generation of a direct increase in demand for rails, timber and engineering products, for example. But in the 1870s, demand from the railroads actually answered for as much as 10 per cent of the entire production of the engineering sector.[10] There were also various indirect income effects such as railroad workers' wages, land acquisition, etc. Even more important were the income effects of falling transport costs and the greater availability of goods. These effects are, of course, difficult to compute, but were undoubtedly substantial.

Early protoindustry

The household-based craft industries and protoindustries that were once so widespread now made several important contributions to the development of industry. We have already indicated that protoindustry, together with agriculture, led to higher incomes, which in turn speeded industrial expansion. In all likelihood it also made a considerable contribution to the expansion of the export industry after 1850. Even before 1850 at least some of the trade in domestic wood products was for export. The former homecraft industries made numerous contributions to the continued expansion of industry at the end of the nineteenth century. First, these crafts produced skilled workers who were a strategic growth factor, at least in some sectors. This was true of the engineering industry, for example, which for many years to come was characterised by the multiplicity of its skills and the high standards of craft skills required. Studies of labour recruitment in the engineering industry in the nineteenth century show that a substantial proportion of the skilled workers in this sector came from one of the earlier manufactories, ironworks or protoindustries. But this was certainly also true of other industries such as the early sawmills, textiles and others. At the same time, the progression from an exclusively home-based craft industry environment to a factory environment sometimes caused the workers real difficulties. It could at times even be difficult to recruit skilled labour to the new factories. These workers, proud as they were of their skills, often resisted as long as possible entry into employment in the clattering 'treadmills' that horrified the famous nineteenth-century Swedish author Viktor Rydberg and many others. Further, the 'knowledge in practice' these skilled workers possessed was not suited to the needs of modern industry, and this helps to explain the numerous complaints from the owners of the larger engineering works about the shortage of skilled workers. There was also general complaint about the working habits of workers in the homecraft industries. Inherited traditional skills were closely linked to a 'troublesome' culture, the elimination of which the modern industrialists saw as essential to continued industrial growth.[11]

Second, early protoindustry contributed to the expansion of the simple market economy that already existed in the household-based economy. The increase in the division of labour brought about by homecraft production for the market created new markets and new market contacts. An important feature was the emergence of a market culture that tempted people to buy and sell more. To be attuned and willing to respond to the market's signals is not natural behaviour; it has to be learnt. There is abundant evidence, particularly from the boom years of the 1850s, of the way country folk succumbed to the temptations of the market economy. The following is a description from 1855 of conditions in a parish in Småland.

> When the sons of the peasantry are often sent on journeys to Gothenburg and the coastal towns of Skåne and Halland to sell butter, wax, tallow and game, they become familiar with the dress habits of distant provinces and their more educated taste for luxury. – One may often see a peasant's son wearing a topcoat and smoking a cigar standing beside his father who is dressed in short leather trousers and a hooked, long-skirted coat.[12]

There were other obvious effects of the growth of homecraft production, one being the expansion of the transport and communications networks in the first half of the nineteenth century. In 1806 Baltzar von Platen gave as a reason for building the Göta canal that mining, agriculture and other industries would benefit from 'a navigation way through the country'.[13] The same argument was put forward for the earlier plans to build railroads in the country. The efforts made before 1860 to bring into being a modern commercial banking system in Sweden may also be seen in this light. The founding of the Stockholm Enskilda Bank in 1856 by André Oscar Wallenberg, one purpose of which was to provide the provincial banks with credit, was based on the existence of a rapidly growing protoindustry. Neither can we ignore the lending of the mortgage banks and 'discounting banks' which, directly or indirectly, benefited the earlier homecraft industries. The modern credit system that gradually evolved was built at least in part on these foundations. Finally, we should also consider that an important part of the 'liberal' reforms, from the legislation on freedom of trade in 1846 to Gripenstedt's reforms in the 1860s, came about in an environment that was still dominated by protoindustry. To a not insignificant degree, these reforms were carried forward by an opinion, particularly in the estate of the peasants, that saw these reforms as an opportunity for expansion.

Capital supply

Finally, let us examine the role of capital supply. Industrial expansion requires investments in the form of operating capital, and particularly as an increase in material capital investments. New plants must be built, often on a larger scale than before. This kind of capital formation may, in theory, have two sources. First, an established enterprise such as a small-scale craft business may set aside some of its profits to invest later. The importance of a business ploughing back its own profits must not be underestimated. In the case of Britain, for example, it has been said that this was the foundation of most of its industrial expansion during the industrial revolution. The backbone of expansion was small and medium-sized companies that required only a modest amount of capital in the form of buildings and machinery.[14] The second method of capital supply was to look elsewhere for investment capital – to banks, private investors and the like.

We have already discussed the importance of the limited ability of the credit institutions of the time to supply Sweden's expanding industry with investment capital. Before the mid-nineteenth century, Swedish capitalism was carried forward by the merchant houses in the largest towns and cities. Here, there was a substantial amount of accumulated capital that could be used, for example, to build up new factories or extend old ones. But the main role of the trading houses was still to provide ironworks and other enterprises with working capital. Their ownership of, or direct investment in, industry was still fairly limited. This, however, did not prevent a gradual move towards more interventionism, starting as early as the beginning of the nineteenth century. This occurred not least with the profitable sawmills, but in other industries as well, including the ironworks.

Earlier literature often highlights the role of foreign capital after 1850, particularly with regard to the large number of new businesses established at this time. The large amount of Scottish and German capital, for example, invested in modern steam-powered sawmills from the 1850s onwards, particularly in the Sundsvall area, is cited in this context. But although these sources of foreign capital must not be underestimated, domestic capital was still more important. According to Torsten Gårdlund's study of industrial financing in Sweden from 1830 to 1913, at the beginning of the nineteenth century industrial enterprises obtained 'their foreign capital from the bond market, the merchant houses and to some extent from the government's credit institute'.[15] Gårdlund emphasises the overall importance of the merchant houses in this first period of industrialisation. They lent money directly to industrial companies – or through the extensive bond market, which was otherwise dominated by individual savers in commerce, agriculture or government administration. Figure 5.3 shows the importance of government credit institutes such as the Bank of Sweden and the so-called government 'discount' banks which served the manufactories. It was not until the late nineteenth century that other forms of borrowing, mainly bond

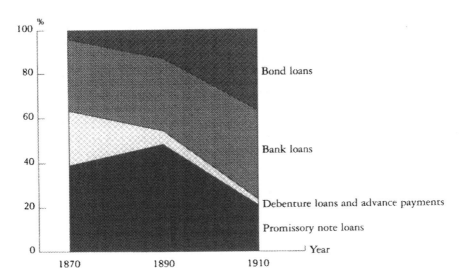

Figure 5.3 Swedish industrial financing, 1870–1910.
Percentage change by type of borrowing.

Source: T. Gårdlund, *Svensk industrifinansiering under genombrottskedet 1830–1913*, Stockholm 1947, p. 161.

loans, came into the picture. Lending by the commercial banks also became more important after the mid-nineteenth century.

In Torsten Gårdlund's view, only a small proportion of the capital came from agriculture. However, the actors in the bond market included representatives of the agrarian sector. It is also possible that Gårdlund's selection of mostly large companies – for which the accounts are still available – resulted in the importance of this sector for capital supply in Sweden's period of industrial transformation being underestimated. Many small companies probably obtained their start-up capital from the agricultural sector. Neither can we overlook the fact that some of the money lent by the mortgage banks was used to establish small rural companies that were closely linked to agricultural enterprise.

Sectors and companies in the industrial transformation

The 1850s are perhaps best known as a period of transformation for the *sawmill industry*. In 1842 the last obstacles to the right to establish and operate sawmills had been removed and they were no longer limited by the needs of agriculture and the threat of forest depletion. It is difficult to say anything definite about the importance of these regulations. But according to Arthur Montgomery, they were largely a 'dead letter', i.e. restrictions that were not applied in practice.[16] Of greater importance to the rapid expansion of the sawmill industry in the 1850s was the sharp upswing in foreign demand for sawn timber, beams and posts. Barely 200,000 cubic metres of board was exported in the 1830s. Towards the end of the 1850s exports had more than tripled and would increase a further threefold by the 1870s.[17]

To confirm the view of the 1850s as a 'breakthrough period', an important technical innovation was installed in the exporting sawmills in the province of Norrland in that decade. This was the steam engine. However, until the 1870s these engines were of limited capacity. They could rarely power more than four log frames. This example of an as-yet-undeveloped technology was presumably the main reason why water-driven sawmills continued to dominate, at least until this period. But from the 1870s steam power became more widespread. At the same time, many of the smaller exporting steam sawmills were forced out of business. The process of concentration put the larger steam-powered sawmills in a dominant position. The new steam sawmill at Ljusne, for example, which in 1881 replaced an older water-driven mill, had sixteen log frames. The Skutskär mill, established in 1886, had twenty-one frames and when it opened in 1897 the Korsnäs sawmill had thirty.[18] The process of concentration was accompanied by changes in the arrangements for financing the sawmill industry. In the 1880s the joint-stock company became a common form of organisation in the sawmill industry, and at the same time the influence of the commercial banks grew while the merchant houses lost some ground. According to Ernst Söderlund,

Figure 5.4 The new steam-powered sawmill at Härnösand. *Ny Illustrerad tidning*, May 1861. KB.

Figure 5.5 Child labour was common in Swedish industry, particularly in the sawmills, at the end of the nineteenth century. A ten-hour working day was the rule, even for minors, and they sometimes worked twelve or fourteen hours. The picture shows so-called marking-boys at the Sund sawmill north of Sundsvall, in the 1890s. SCA, Merlo Archives.

this led to more stability. Before this time, there had been much wild speculation in this sector, not least in western Norrland.[19]

As part of this transformation, many sawmills were moved. Most of the large exporting sawmills were relocated to the coast. As they were no longer dependent on water power, these mills could be positioned along the coast. If nothing else, this gave substantial savings in transport costs. Before the 1850s it was undoubtedly the low transport costs that had made Norway such an attractive exporter of sawn wood products. But when a growing shortage of raw materials caused the price of Norwegian sawn board to rise, interest shifted to the east. It was, not least, against this background that western Norrland and the Sundsvall area in particular became a Klondike for a rapidly expanding sawmill industry. Large numbers of workers moved to the sawmill towns and districts of the region. They came from different parts of the country, but it was not uncommon for labour to be recruited from the surrounding villages. Many of the local workers had formerly combined small-scale farming with seasonal work at one of the water-powered saw-mills. More of these workers now became permanent sawmill employees.[20]

The investments made in saw frames, steam engines and permanent installations at the mills were only the tip of the iceberg. Large-scale timber sawing also required a supply of the raw material and cheap transport to the coast. Both these factors were major problems for the early sawmill industry, and they required a great deal of capital investment. At first, the forest and forestry enterprises were largely dependent on the amount of forest the forest-owning peasants felled. Throughout the nineteenth century these peasants had acquired ownership of large areas of forest through the Enclosure Act. Partitioning was part of the general process of land consolidation of the nineteenth century, under which large areas of common forest land came under the ownership of freehold farmers or the Crown. In the sparsely populated province of Norrland a single farm could be allocated huge areas of forest. As long as this forest was not felled, perhaps because it was located in a remote area and/or the timber could not be transported, it was a largely worthless asset. But this changed swiftly with the advance of the sawmill industry.

The sawmills' main alternative strategy to gain access to more timber was to try to buy more forest for themselves. There were obvious benefits for sawmill owners who controlled their own reserves of timber: it is likely that cost savings was one. But it was probably also impossible for the sawmill to secure adequate supplies of raw timber without access to their own forests which they could fell themselves. In light of this it is perhaps not difficult to understand why the forest companies seemed so eager to acquire forest holdings. There are many stories of how peasants were cheated out of large forest tracts by cunning sawmill owners, a phenomenon that came to be known as 'baggböleri', after the small district outside Umeå which came to typify these (dubious) transactions. The truth is that if the sawmills had not owned more forests, it is unlikely that large-scale felling would have taken

Figure 5.6 The log-driving waterways were extended to take timber from the inland forests to the coastal sawmills. The picture shows so-called downstream log-jam breakers, probably at the turn of the century. From *Uppfinningarnas bok (1907–9)*.

place. The forests could only be exploited if large investments were made in transport, and this required large amounts of capital, which neither individual farmers nor the village community associations could raise. However, by no means all sawmills found that owning their own forests obviated the need to buy timber. In the 1880s, Hudiksvalls Trävaruaktiebolag, for example, even increased the percentage of timber it bought.[21]

The other disruptive bottleneck was transport from the interior. Floating was the most common solution to this problem. But floating required substantial initial investment to clear waterways, build dams to bypass unnavigable waterfalls, etc. It is clear that large sums were invested in these projects in the second half of the nineteenth century. Gustaf Utterström, who wrote the history of Hudiksvall Trävaruaktiebolag, says that he was 'struck by the size of the annual investment in clearing waterways and floating channels, on floating logs and the entire transport chain.'[22] It was, of course, mainly the larger sawmills that had the resources and opportunity to undertake expenditure of this magnitude. Sometimes the sawmills joined forces to build log floating channels. One example was Hudiksvalls Trävaruaktiebolag which in the 1880s extended the waterways of western Hälsingland as a joint venture with the Marma, Sandarne and Bergviks companies.

Compared with industry as a whole, the 1870s represented a golden age for the sawmills. In this decade, they answered for just over 40 per cent of Sweden's total export value, after which there was a gradual decline. This, however, was not a drastic general depression. On the contrary, export sales rose in this sector, and the size of the workforce grew. At the same time, production became more concentrated on a smaller number of large exporting sawmills. The large number of small and medium-sized sawmills spread throughout the country that both supplied the domestic market and produced for export should also be mentioned here. These mills also experienced a sharp upswing in demand as part of the general industrial expansion and as a result of the disastrous fires that raged through towns in the nineteenth century, reducing Gävle, for example, to ashes in 1869, and destroying Sundsvall in 1888.

The sawmills of Norrland came to be so strongly associated with the industrial revolution mainly because they were run as large-scale industries. The large sawmills, with their impressive steam engines and efficient log frames which produced finished board at high speed, came to epitomise modern factory production. The rapid influx of workers and the shanty towns that sprang up around the sawmills invite comparison with the early textile industry in England.

Another industry that is undoubtedly part of the industrial revolution but was not so obviously large-scale in nature is *engineering*. As we have seen, this industry gradually grew up in the towns from the beginning of the nineteenth century (see Chapter 2). But the expansion of the engineering industry was most noticeable in the 1870s, a time when many new engineering works were built, the factories increased in size and the number of workers employed shot up. The driving force that powered this expansion was the domestic market, not least the demand from the expanding agricultural sector. In the 1890s, and especially at the turn of the century,

Figure 5.7 One of the workshops at Aktiebolaget L.M. Ericsson & Co. in Stockholm – 'the world's biggest factory for the manufacture of telephones' – at the beginning of the century. From *Uppfinningarnas bok* (1907–9).

there was a vigorous upswing in export sales. In 1896 some 20 per cent of the engineering sector's total output value was exports. By 1912 this figure was close to 42 per cent.[23] But export sales were spread unevenly between different enterprises in this sector. Most exports were from the 'inventors' industries' that based their operations on innovations and inventions. The most important of these were the Stockholm-based L.M. Ericsson (telephones) AGA (gas lighthouses), Separator (milk separators) and Nya AB Atlas, later Atlas Copco (drilling and mining equipment) and the Göteborg-based firm of SKF (ball-bearings). These were quite specialised companies with access to a large and growing export market.

Most of the engineering sector was, however, made up of enterprises that were typically involved in many and varied activities. This was particularly true of the country's numerous small businesses, but also of many larger companies, such as Bolinders in Stockholm, which manufactured log gates for the sawmills of Norrland as well as cast-iron stoves and machine tools. There was also Munktells of Eskilstuna, which manufactured a wide range of products, mainly agricultural machinery such as threshing machines, but also steam engines, machine tools, dredging machines, bridges (!) and, increasingly from the turn of the century, diesel engines. Large engineering works like Bolinders and Munktells, which employed hundreds of workers at the turn of the century, were also commissioned to do special work for individual customers, and they even carried out repair work. At the beginning of the twentieth century, enterprises like these also began to increase their export sales, at least in the Russian market, a very important outlet for Sweden's engineering industry right up to the beginning of the First World War, after which it dwindled to almost nothing. In 1913 sales in this market amounted to as much as 31 per cent of the engineering sector's export sales.[24]

The wide variety of work done, the low level of specialisation and the large number of small enterprises give the impression of an engineering industry that changed very gradually over time. The variety of the work continued to require skilled workers, including smiths, foundrymen and sheet-metal workers. Short production runs and few attempts to standardise made mechanisation a slow process. It also meant that many of the skilled workers had to be recruited from the ironworks, the craft industries and the formerly widespread metal crafts. It was not until the beginning of the twentieth century that specialised engineering works began to appear, which paved the way for a greater division of labour and more 'scientific work management' on the Taylorist pattern. However, experiments in this direction, which included the use of time-clocks, time and motion studies and work supervised by trained engineers instead of skilled craftsmen, hardly emerged on a significant scale until the inter-war years. As a result, companies continued to carry out a wide range of work, and were therefore very dependent on their skilled workers.[25] Thus the development of the mechanical engineering industry was characterised by continuity and very

Figure 5.8 The Lägerholm lighthouse. The first large-scale automatic AGA lighthouse. From *Svenska industriella verk och anläggningar* (Yearbook 10).

gradual change. The wide range of skills required, combined with the difficulties in mechanising many of the work operations, made it difficult to compete by expanding the enterprise, capitalising on the economies of scale and bringing down unit costs. This option was open only for simple kinds of mass production. The engineering companies had to compete by developing new products, gaining control of strategic raw materials, assembling a skilled workforce and establishing exclusive market outlets. Much work was done to develop the commercial side of the business operation and to evolve unique products that could carry the company's trade name. To give an example, the contacts made between the well-known Öberg file factory in Eskilstuna and Gustaf Ekman at the Lesjöfors works had a decisive effect on the successful growth of the former company. From 1835 Ekman was a pioneer in high-grade steel manufacture for the mechanical engineering industry. Not until C.O. Öberg contracted Ekman as his (exclusive) supplier of special steel did his business grow rapidly.[26]

By contrast, a sector where the economy of scale had an important, albeit limited, effect was *iron and steel*. Most of the stimulus for change in this sector came from outside the industry. This was Sweden's traditional export sector, which sold large quantities of bar iron, particularly to Britain. Towards the end of the eighteenth century the puddling process was introduced in the British iron industry. The use of coke in the hearths produced an acceptable grade of iron far cheaper than in the Swedish charcoal, German and Walloon forges. Furthermore, in the modern British plants, roller-mills gradually replaced the costly hammer-forging process.

Figure 5.9 The successful Nordiska Kullager Aktiebolaget in Gothenburg was a company typical of its time. The *Svenska industriella verk och anläggningar 1910* says of the new Hisinge section, powered by electricity from Trollhättan, that 'all the workshop premises are equipped . . . with consideration given to modern standards and good overall work supervision.'

Without doubt, this competitive cost edge made considerable inroads into the demand for Swedish iron. At the same time this fall in demand from Britain in the early nineteenth century was almost completely balanced by higher demand from the American market. Then there was a sharp upswing in British demand from the 1850s. Exports to Britain, particularly to Sheffield, by now the centre of a vigorous and growing steel industry, once again increased from a modest 10,000 tons in the 1840s to around 30,000 tons at the end of the 1850s. However, demand from the USA fell when English puddled iron replaced the more expensive Swedish product and the American domestic iron industry began to grow. These fluctuations in demand at the beginning of the nineteenth century essentially reflect changes in the use of the relatively costly Swedish bar iron, which was out-competed in markets where it could be replaced by cheaper puddle iron. But it held, and even increased, its share in markets where high quality was required for further processing to make steel products such as knives.

The increase in sales, particularly to Sheffield, can only be explained by the quality improvements of the first half of the nineteenth century. Gustaf Ekman's experiments with new blister steel at Lesjöfors were important here. Ekman's name is also linked to another important innovation that paved the way for a resurgence in Swedish iron-working shortly before the middle of the century: the Lancashire forge. This method used a different kind of crucible furnace which improved quality and reduced costs – the latter as a result of lower charcoal consumption. This method, which had its real breakthrough in the 1860s, was dominant in Sweden's iron and steel industry for many years.[27] Despite these advances, total production figures long remained fairly low, and iron export's share of total exports fell dramatically against, for example, wood exports. In the 1820s iron had perhaps a 60 per cent share of total export value, while only fifty years later it had fallen to

Figure 5.10 An innovator in Swedish steel manufacture: Gustaf Ekman, Lesjöfors Ironworks. KB.

only 20 per cent.[28] It was this decade, the 1870s, that was the real period of expansion for the iron industry in Sweden. Initially, this expansion was accompanied by a rapid increase in blast furnace capacity. The advent of the new English blast furnaces allowed production to increase and brought costs down. In 1870, 78 hectolitres of charcoal was required to produce a ton of pig iron. The same figure for 1915 was 58 hectolitres.[29] The production of pig iron, the basic material for further processing, rose from about 80,000 tons around 1813 to 180,000 tons in the early 1860s, 465,000 tons by 1885 to a total of 730,000 tons in 1913.[30] The other innovation of the 1870s was the introduction of the new ingot steel techniques. Henry Bessemer's methods, introduced in 1856, and those of Wilhelm Siemens and the brothers Emile and Pierre Martin somewhat later, replaced at a stroke the old method of repeated hardening in different forges. High-quality steel could be produced more continuously, on a larger scale and far more cheaply. When this steel came on to the world market from the 1860s onwards, only companies that were able to keep pace with these developments and take advantage of the benefits of large-scale production could compete with the Swedish producers.

G. F. Göransson, a merchant from Gävle, pioneered ingot steel in the Swedish iron and steel industry. He met Henry Bessemer in 1857 and the following year took over one fifth of his patent in Sweden. With the help of a loan from the Iron Bureau he completed a number of successful experiments with this new method. During his trip to England in 1858 he even managed to convince the English of the excellence of the Bessemer method, about which the English had been rather sceptical. Göransson's support was an important contribution to the international spread of this method. A number of Bessemer furnaces were then built in Sweden, the first being at

Västanfors (1860), Carlsdahl (1860), Långshyttan (1861), Siljansfors (1861) and Högbo (1862). The latter was also owned by Göransson.

But it was at Sandviken towards the end of the 1860s that large-scale production of Bessemer steel first began. Once again Göransson was the driving force here. In the following decade this method became firmly established when several new Bessemer furnaces were built, the main ones being at Svartnäs, Forsbacka, Iggesund, Nyhammar, Långbanshyttan, Ulfshyttan, Hagfors, Björneborg, Bångbro, Nykroppa, Domnarvet, Stjernfors, Avesta and Hofors. The Martin method came to Sweden some time after the Bessemer method; Sweden's first Martin furnace was built at Munkfors in 1869. These furnaces were also introduced in the 1870s at, for example, the works at Lesjöfors, Motala, Bofors, Domnarvet, Finspång, Kallinge, Kohhlswa and elsewhere. Modern rolling-mills were also installed, at least in the larger blister steel works. Finally, the Sidney Gilchrist Thomas method,

Figure 5.11 Sandviken Jernverks was the first in Sweden to produce Bessemer ingots on a large scale, largely thanks to the efforts of C.F. Göransson, a merchant from Gävle. Sandviken also led in new sales methods. A Sandviken Jernverks AB share certificate, 1897. KB.

or the Thomas method as it was known, which became widely used in the 1880s, allowed Sweden's rich deposits of high phosphor ore to be used. The Thomas method was first used at the Bångbro ironworks in 1880.

Taken together, the introduction of the blister steel processes caused an enormous upswing in Sweden's iron and steel industry. Production and exports doubled in the period from the 1870s until the beginning of the First World War. However, the success of blister steel did not cause the demise of Lancashire iron. On the contrary, exports of Lancashire iron increased at the same rate as blister steel, at least until the turn of the century. The continued success of Lancashire iron was due less to the scale of its manufacture and low unit costs and more its high quality, which attracted the Sheffield manufacturers and others. Lancashire bar iron continued to dominate iron exports, particularly to the most important export markets of Britain and the USA. But after 1900 the blister steel method was the most common, while the puddle methods (particularly the Lancashire method but also, to a lesser extent, Walloon forge production) lost ground. While some ironworks specialised, others combined the Lancashire forges with Bessemer and Martin production, particularly in larger works such as Domnarvet, Iggesundsbruk and Fagersta at the end of the 1870s. Even in the Lancashire works a growing proportion of the bar iron was rolled in rolling-mills.

The introduction of the blister steel processes, in particular, led to a dramatic structural rationalisation of the entire iron and steel industry, the so-called 'death of the rural ironworks'. The number of production units fell dramatically from 381 to 140 between 1870 and 1914. At the same time, average production per works increased tenfold. It was mostly the small puddle works that closed while some very large works emerged. In 1913 the largest of these was Domnarvet, with an annual production of over 100,000 tons of ingot steel, followed by Fagersta with 57,000 tons. Other large works included Sandviken, Degerfors, Hofors, Horndal, Storfors-Nykroppa and Forsbacka. Production from the largest Lancashire works was impressive: 14,000 tons at Boxholm, 13,500 tons at Ljusne, 12,000 tons at Horndal and 11,000 tons at Ockelbro.[31] In the process of industrial consolidation, many production units merged to form larger complexes of companies. Some of these complexes had been formed earlier, the largest being the Uddeholm and Fagersta works, whose operations now became even more concentrated. New complexes also came into being, for example Klosterverken in Dalarna and the works around Hofors and in Gästrikland.

Arthur Attman identifies the 'communications revolution' as perhaps the most important precondition for the concentration of the ironworks towards the end of the nineteenth century.[32] The larger and more distant works required a cheap and flexible supply of raw materials, and transport facilities for their finished product. The transport down to the weighbridges in the staple towns of Stockholm, Gothenburg and Gävle had been (to quote Attman again) 'a complicated system of horse and boat transport'.[33] Now the

Figure 5.12 Bessemer steel production at the Domnarvet Works in Borlänge. Halftone. *Ny illustrerad tidning*, 1884. KB.

railways could be used more instead. This was also partly true of the supply of coal and ore, although water and road transport, which often required costly investment, continued to play an important part.

This period also saw a revolution in the sales and financing of the iron and steel industry. As mentioned above, most financing was in the form of short-term credit, mostly provided by the merchant houses, which also handled the export of the product. Before the 1870s, more long-term credit was usually raised as promissory notes, and here too the merchants played an important role as agents. The bankruptcy of the old merchant house of Tottie & Arfwedson in 1867 was very much a sign of the times. Around this period it became more common for the sales operation to be run by the ironworks themselves, the first company to do so being Sandviken at the end of the 1860s. They dealt both with the increasingly important domestic market and with export sales. Both Henrik Göransson at Sandviken and Josef Michaeli at Horndal established personal contacts with the international market and set up systems of overseas agents.[34]

When the merchant houses lost their dominance as exporters they also began to lose their position as industrial financiers. In the 1870s the joint-stock company became a widely accepted business form in the industrial sector. However, in many cases most of the long-term capital came from foreign borrowings. After 1880, bank loans or bond loans appear to have come into common use. For the six works that Torsten Gårdlund examined in his study of early industrial financing, 52 per cent of total long-term capital in 1880 was in the form of these foreign loans, a figure which rose to 64 per cent in 1890 and 70 per cent in 1910.[35] When the merchant houses and the bond market went into decline, their roles were swiftly taken over by the commercial banks.

We have already seen that the sawmills were at their peak in the 1870s. At that time there were still only a few mechanical wood pulp mills. This raw material had already replaced linen rag in paper manufacture. But it was not until the nineteenth century that the *paper pulp industry* became firmly established. At the same time, mechanical processing of raw wood was gradually replaced by chemical treatments, either the basic sulphate or the acid sulphite methods. Towards the end of the 1890s, more mechanical wood pulp was used than sulphite and sulphate pulp together, but in 1913 chemical production – sulphite pulp in particular – was three times greater than mechanical pulp.[36] The sulphite method began to dominate, and the new cellulose industry was located largely in Norrland, close to the raw material. The real expansion of this industry came in the boom years of the 1890s, when twenty-four new factories were built. The biggest plants included the Ströms sulphite works in Harmånger, Wargön, Billerud, Kvarnsveden and Skutskär. Most of these works were enormous plants that represented very substantial capital investment. They were continuous operation plants and were entirely process-based. This industry had concentrated early on the export market, and at the beginning of the twentieth century paper and pulp exports overtook the export of sawmill products. Although paper and pulp manufacture were two separate and specialised operations, some works combined the two, particularly Billerud in Värmland, which was built in 1882 as a combined pulp- and paper-mill.

As we have emphasised, the late nineteenth century was a period of expansion not only for the exporting industries. The industries that produced for the domestic market also flourished, particularly in the boom years of the early 1870s and again in the 1890s. The foremost of these domestic market industries was the consumer goods sector, and its role in the industrial transformation is often underestimated. Focusing on the extensive technical advances and the large-scale factories built in the sawmill, iron and steel industries, for example, may divert attention from an industry that, measured in production value and size of the workforce, can easily compare with the export industries.

This picture is a rather fragmented one, but for *textiles* the period after 1850 was a transition from the rural protoindustry to factory production, especially in the Sjuhärads district where the factories gradually came to replace the old rural putting-out system. At the same time, cotton almost wholly replaced the traditional raw materials such as wool and flax used in this area. The mechanised cotton-mills were built with a relatively large number of machines. The technology came mostly from England. Both machinery and key workers, such as Alexander Malcolm at the Strömma mill outside Karlshamn, were often brought in from abroad. The first mechanised factories were simple cotton-mills which produced coarse yarn. By 1800 the first British-designed spinning jennies had already been introduced in Sweden, but it was not until the 1830s that the cotton-mills became firmly established. The best-known of them was the Rydboholms mill outside Borås, but another six or seven important mills opened in the same decade. Many of these, including the Rydboholm mill, were built in rural districts, in the centre of the traditional homecraft production area.

As Lennart Schön has emphasised, the trend from the 1850s onwards was for more and more cotton-mills to be located in the towns.[37] But there were other changes as well. The process of automation accelerated when the spinning mule was introduced, which allowed each worker to handle more spindles. This new technology made machine supervision more important, one effect being that the number of children working in the mills fell. It was not considered advisable to entrust these costly machines to children. However, the percentage of women working in the mills was still high, although it fell somewhat over time. But most of the key positions of supervisors and skilled machine-workers were taken by men, while the women had to content themselves with less skilled work.[38] At this time spinning and weaving was becoming more integrated, and factories began to produce finished cloth from raw cotton.

Up until the 1860s household weaving was still the dominant production method in the Sjuhärads district. But in the rapid expansion of the 1870s a growing number of factories were established solely for weaving or combined spinning and weaving. Cottage weaving declined at this time, but it did not disappear entirely.[39] The number of spindles per worker and the number of workers per work site continued to rise. At the beginning of the twentieth century it was not uncommon to find combined textile mills which employed upwards of a thousand workers. By far the largest share of production was still for the domestic market. To some extent, this certainly prevented the evolution of even larger companies. At the same time, the orientation towards the domestic market allowed cloths in a broad range of qualities and finishes to be produced. This, and the level of automation, also slowed the development of large-scale enterprises.

While the textile industry expanded in the Sjuhärads district, particularly through the establishment of a number of large (combined) companies in and around Borås, there was a move in the opposite direction in the other large homecraft production districts before the mid-nineteenth century. In Hälsingland and Ångermanland the situation was best described as one of 'de-industrialisation'. While forestry and agriculture grew, and presumably absorbed some of the protoindustrial workforce, there was a drastic fall-off in what had been a very active linen manufacturing industry. Since this industry had been dominated by women, its demise probably caused serious transition problems. Women could hardly be expected to simply move to a

Figure 5.13 A cotton-mill: the Norrköpings Bomullsväferi AB at Tuppen. The main weaving room in the Gryt factory, 1906. There were some 600 cotton looms on this floor. Norrköpings stadsmuseum.

wholly male-dominated, expanding forestry industry. The only way out, at least for unmarried women, was to relocate.

Several explanations have been put forward for the decline of the linen industry in Hälsingland and Ångermanland from the mid-nineteenth century, one being that the putting-out system was not widespread in these districts. Thus the considerable amount of autonomy the producers enjoyed presented a problem when competition from the factory-based production – particularly of the cheaper cotton – became competitive from the middle of the century. The absence of wealthy merchant-employers also meant that there was a shortage of capital available to invest in, for example, mechanised factories. An alternative (or complementary) explanation may be that the expanding forest and agricultural sectors attracted both workers and capital. The old homecrafts quite simply gave less profit and paid lower wages than could be secured elsewhere.

Parallel with the widespread practice of handicrafts, which was particularly intensive in the Sjuhärads and Hälsingland–Ångermanland districts, there was, even earlier than the mid-nineteenth century, wool production on a fairly important scale in Stockholm and Norrköping. From the mid-nineteenth century the Norrköping textile industry grew rapidly, while in Stockholm the decline that began, as we have seen, earlier in the century continued. As elsewhere, the first process to be mechanised in Norrköping was wool spinning. The first power looms were not introduced until the 1850s, but in Norrköping hand weavers still produced more than power loom weavers well into the 1860s. The real breakthrough for the large combined wool-mills was not until the 1890s, but once established their expansion was very swift. Between 1896 and 1900 alone, twenty-one new factories were opened, fourteen of which were combined factories. At the beginning of the twentieth century the industry became even more large-scale. The founding of Aktiebolaget Förenade Fabriker in Norrköping created a giant conglomerate which gathered in a single enterprise four of the biggest wool producers (Wahrens, Brück, Ström and Bergsbro).[40]

The rapid expansion of the *food industry* in the late nineteenth century is an often neglected feature of the industrial transformation. As may be seen from the above, in practice this industry represented a substantial part of overall industrial capacity in the period up to the First World War. Although this move towards more large-scale industrial forms was gradual, it became very marked in some important areas. The breweries and distilleries were among the first to centralise their production, as was the sugar industry. From the turn of the century onwards a number of larger factories were set up in what were formerly strongly craft-dominated sectors such as the flour-mills, slaughterhouses, bakeries and dairies. Before the mid-nineteenth century most of these activities were integrated parts of the agricultural sector, often in the form of a self-supporting household economy. In many sectors it is difficult to make a clear distinction between handicraft and 'industry' (see Chapter 2). But in several areas the trend was towards more factory-based manufacture that allowed both a division of labour and mechanisation, especially in the more process-oriented food industries such as the breweries and distilleries. Their constant expansion, particularly from the mid-nineteenth century, may be explained by a combination of factors. Obviously, the general rise in population and incomes increased demand. But the distilleries were helped by the ban on home distilling for household consumption and the introduction of monopolist companies licensed to retail liquor in the towns. Taken together, these factors laid the foundations of a spirits industry that was both highly concentrated and large-scale. Roughly the same factors applied to the growth of the beer breweries, but here in particular it is clear that the restrictions on the consumption of Swedish *brännvin* liquor from the 1850s caused a sharp rise in beer consumption. Already in the mid-nineteenth century there were large-scale breweries in the towns – they were often the first 'factories' in the area. This was particularly true of the large cities such as Stockholm and Gothenburg which had their own 'Bavarian' or 'Munich' breweries. At first, competition was keen among the numerous small breweries. As early as 1860 there were twenty breweries, but there was an inexorable move towards large-scale production and a smaller number of companies. New technology allowed the larger breweries to out-compete the smaller businesses by undercutting their prices. In Stockholm, this competition led to the establishment of a consortium of five large breweries in 1889, which operated under the name of AB Stockholms Bryggerier.[41] Cartel agreements then became the foremost method of reducing competition in the brewing industry.

Figure 5.14 The bottling room at Sankt Erik's brewery, Stockholm, in the 1890s. From *Svenska industriella verk och anläggningar 1896*.

The expansion of Sweden's sugar beet industry began in the 1880s and intensified in the 1890s. Before that time, imported cane sugar had been refined by companies such as D. Carnegie and Co. in Göteborg. Now several more refineries were built, most of them in south-west Skåne, but also on the island of Gotland (the Roma Sugar mill). The number of refineries rose from seventeen in 1900 to twenty-four thirteen years later.[42] Production rose sharply, and because all the product was sold on the domestic market, we may assume that the Swedish population's sugar consumption shot up. Per capita consumption of sugar was just over eight kilos a year in 1880. By 1913 consumption was almost twenty kilos. At the same time, prices fell sharply. Torsten Gårdlund gives us the following description of conditions in the sugar beet industry at the beginning of the twentieth century.

> The Swedish sugar factories were very large units, about the same size as those in Germany. They were, as a rule, easily the largest of Swedish enterprises. In general the share capital of sugar factories founded in the 1890s totalled about SEK 1 million. The number of workers at the raw sugar mills and the refineries totalled some 10,000 in 1910–11. However, just over a third of these workers were at work only for the season of two or three months a year, and worked in agriculture or other industries for the rest of the year.[43]

It was also in the sugar industry that we see the greatest concentration at the beginning of the twentieth century – a fusion that was *de facto* a single large sugar monopoly. But we shall return to this issue later.

Agriculture and industrialisation

The industrial transformation went hand in hand with a strong resurgence in the agricultural sector. As we have seen, agricultural production rose so quickly in the nineteenth century that, despite a rapid rise in population, fairly substantial quantities of agricultural produce (e.g. oats) were sold abroad at times. We have already discussed the causes of the agricultural expansion of this period. Although new land coming under cultivation continued to play an important part, after 1870 the greatest contribution was from mechanisation and other efforts aimed at improving productivity.

Thus it was in the final decades of the nineteenth century that machines came to be widely used in agriculture. Improved ploughs, harrows and threshers, and new aids such as sowing machines, haymakers, binding machines, muck-spreaders and threshing machines came into common use. At the end of the nineteenth century steam power was even installed in the larger farms to drive threshers and other machines. Although some of these machines were fixed installations, the mobile steam engines manufactured at the Munktells Works in Eskilstuna were even more common. This factory also produced the first motorised tractors in 1913. However, it was not until the inter-war years that the tractor became more widely used in Swedish agriculture, and its real breakthrough came even later, in the 1950s. Before then, almost all work in the fields and meadows was done by horses. But the trend was towards more mechanisation. There were major investments in training and information, in the form of public agricultural meetings, for example, where news of scientific advances was spread to the country's farmers.

The driving force in the expansion of the agricultural sector was ultimately the rise in demand from a growing market. The increase in national income per capita, despite the substantial population rise, was a central factor here. But there were other important changes as well, foremost the fact that a growing proportion of the population no longer had any land of their own to live off. This encouraged more protoindustry, which in its turn stimulated more efficient production methods and better-quality products. This then raised wages in the agricultural sector, and so on.

A generally observed effect of higher incomes that applies to broad population groups is that demand becomes more diversified. This is true of the agricultural sector as well. This is known as Engel's Law – formulated by Ernst Engel, the German statistician, in 1857. It says that people first tend to satisfy their most basic needs but then increase their consumption of other goods as their incomes increase. This theory explains the rapid increase in diversified animal products (meat, butter, cheese, milk) at the end of the nineteenth century. Of course, cereal and potato cultivation increased as well, but at far from the same pace as animal products.

It should be immediately added that it is difficult to separate the effects of 'Engel's Law' from the practical effects of another phenomenon: changes in

Figure 5.15 Munktells single-cylinder traction engine.

Figure 5.16 Munktells tractor, model 25, from 1934.

relative prices. The price of grain fell against animal products through the nineteenth century. This is probably in part a reflection of the fact that productivity increased faster in cereal farming than in other agricultural production. Most technical innovations introduced up to the end of the century were intended to increase cereal production. But competition from abroad also intensified, particularly the competition from the new nations across the oceans, notably the corn belt of the USA, and this factor had its greatest impact on cereals. Grain is easy to transport and the rapid expansion of railroads and shipping also made this commodity even cheaper. Keener competition brings down grain prices – but in the 1880s it also caused European states and their farmers to begin to demand higher corn tariffs to protect 'agriculture as the basis of the country's economy'. Sweden's corn tariffs rose sharply from 1888, but this did not prevent a relative shift towards more animal products. This in its turn encouraged improvements in animal husbandry, the application of new advances in genetics and more experiments with farming methods to improve yield.

The sharp rise in animal products may explain why the growth in productivity in grain and potato cultivation did *not* result in a rapid fall in the agricultural sector's labour requirements. As mentioned earlier, the labour requirement in this sector rose until the beginning of the twentieth century. Keeping milk-cows and raising young livestock for slaughter was labour-intensive at this time. This was also probably why most farm produce still came from small farms. Combining cereal and potato crops with animal production allowed farms to remain small and the farmers' incomes to rise. It is likely that small farms which cultivated only grain crops found it harder to compete with the larger farms that could use more efficient implements and machines. Cereal cultivation on the large farms undoubtedly gave some of the benefits of the economies of scale. But it is possible that these potential benefits were severely limited. Particularly towards the end of the nineteenth century, many theoreticians, Karl Marx among them, maintained that farms would become more industrial, i.e. they would turn into large-scale production operations. Since then, however, many have rejected this conclusion, advocating instead the advantages of medium-sized family farming in preference to large-scale agricultural production. This would mean that for ecological, technical or organisational reasons, the benefits of large-scale production in agriculture were not so great. The experiments with large-scale agriculture in the twentieth century, including large-scale experiments using paid labour, would in the best case appear to have generated short-term profits but, in the long term, poor ecological management, low efficiency and high transaction costs.[44]

The trend outlined thus far – the gradual introduction of innovations, more diversification and continued family-based farming – continued in all important respects to characterise the development of agriculture. However, the First World War was followed by some harsh years in the agricultural sector. As mentioned above, it is not until then that we begin to see a marked fall in the agricultural workforce in absolute terms. In the inter-war years this sector's percentage of the total labour force also decreased, falling for the first time to under 50 per cent. This was due to a combination of factors. First and foremost, accelerating mechanisation in agriculture resulted in an immediate improvement in per capita productivity. This allowed a rapid increase in agricultural production from fewer hands. It was mainly in the years immediately after the First World War that the improvements and investments of the previous half century began to bear fruit. However, the preference for combined farming, i.e. cereal crops and live-stock, delayed the fall in the workforce and halted the wave of closures of the smaller farms. Not until later did mechanisation begin to have a real impact on livestock farming. In the 1960s, in particular, the introduction of milking machines and the automation of feeding, etc., caused a sharp fall in the labour requirement.

But this does not fully explain the agricultural crisis of the 1920s and 1930s, a crisis which was accompanied by an overall rise in production and incomes for the agricultural sector as a whole. Although small-scale production continued, many small farms went to the wall. This structural transformation was caused partly by the fact that small, inefficient farms could no longer survive in competition with the larger and more efficient farms, and partly because of competition from foreign agriculture which, helped by the low tariffs of the 1920s could sell their products (especially grain) relatively freely on the Swedish market. In the 1930s a more protectionist policy was pursued, while farming co-operatives became firmly established. The pressure of competition lifted a little when these co-operatives managed to implement cartel agreements that fixed the prices of a number of agricultural products. The best-known price agreement was for milk, which was a result of the 'milk war' in the early 1930s, when a militant agricultural movement resorted to a milk strike to raise the price. The farming collective managed to present a united front, preferring to pour the milk away rather than sell it at the price offered by the privately-owned dairies.[45]

Another important factor was that the demand for a higher standard of living, combined with the real possibility of realising this hope, primarily by transferring to industry, caused many people to abandon their life on the land. This applied particularly to the younger sons and daughters from the farms and crofts who would otherwise have been forced to stay in a sector which, despite its rapid expansion, failed to keep pace with the wages paid in the industrial sector. Town life and better-paid work attracted these young country folk. This was the human aspect of the transfer gains discussed above. It appears that the first to move were usually the young women, for example in the small farming districts of inland Norrland, where farming was combined with forestry.[46] But this was probably also true elsewhere. The next stage was that the young men moved away from the small farms. With no women to marry and little chance of achieving a standard of living comparable to that of an industrial worker, they probably thought it better to leave.

The social consequences of industrialisation

In many respects, the consequences of industrialisation amounted to a social revolution. First, many people changed occupations and moved to a different area. The differences between sectors were considerable, and industrial work was radically different from agricultural work and the handicrafts (including the protoindustrial crafts). It is true that in the engineering industry, for example, there was still room for the older type of craftsman who religiously followed his craft traditions. But this was hardly the case in other sectors such as paper, sawmills, textiles or food, where the transition to work in large factories made entirely new demands of the worker: reliability, stamina and punctuality were needed rather than traditional craft knowledge and skills. This in turn sowed the seeds of a worker's identity, which was shaped more by the factory and the workplace than by the trade itself. Modern industrial workers were more oriented towards collectivism than their forebears in crafts and agriculture. Paradoxically, despite the greater mobility brought by an expanding communications network, these workers became more firmly rooted in their home areas than before. They became united by the conditions they shared in the factories; a kind of class consciousness began to appear, creating the conditions for an incipient trade union and political labour movement. Only through the collective could the individual rise towards the light.

Despite the stronger urge it created to put down roots, the industrial transformation caused many people to move away from their homes. The well-known 'migration from the land' was particularly marked in the inter-war years. But the percentage of the population living in the towns and urban areas had grown constantly since the mid-nineteenth century. New workers' suburbs grew up round the major industrial towns of Stockholm, Gothenburg and Malmö, but also in Norrköping, Eskilstuna and Västerås and other areas. Many workers' families were crowded into small areas in hastily built barracks. At the end of the nineteenth century there were reports, mainly from the industrial town of Eskilstuna, of overcrowded living conditions and an appalling lack of sanitation. There was often no clean water or drainage in these rapidly growing towns. In Eskilstuna many critics of the substandard social conditions blamed overcrowding and the absence of sanitation for the rampant tuberculosis and other infectious diseases such as the 'Spanish sickness' which claimed many lives as late as the First World War. In the case of Eskilstuna, however, the heavy and dirty work in the grinding shops, which because of the hazards associated with them were known as 'family burial plots', helped spread pulmonary diseases. By inhaling the dangerous dust from sharpening knives and scissors, the workers contracted a number of illnesses, among them the greatly feared silicosis, or 'stone lung'.[47]

However, as time passed, conditions in the workshops improved. The grinding shops in Eskilstuna, for example, were closed at the beginning of the twentieth century after action by both the trade unions and the newly founded Factory Inspectorate. Higher standards of reliability and efficiency – made all the more important by the costly investments in plant and machines – brought home to many employers the potential advantages of making improvements to the working environment. In the inter-war years, good progress had already been made on issues such as workers' health and safety, heating and sanitation. Although much remained to be done on handling hazardous substances, ventilation, etc., there were considerable improvements in this period in the housing conditions of workers' families. From the 1920s onwards what became known as the owner-occupier movement grew rapidly, a scheme which gave many workers financial assistance to

Figure 5.17 Workers' housing at Hybo. Drawing by Alice Nordin. *Svea* 19/10, 1895. KB.

build their own homes. In the following decade many modern, well-equipped, multiple family dwellings were built, usually with a water closet and sometimes even a bathroom. The outdoor environment was also improved. Public and private interests often co-operated in alleviating overcrowding and improving inferior sanitary conditions. Later in this book we shall discuss the public investment needed as a result of the industrial transformation.

In the international debate on the social consequences of industrialisation two different standpoints have emerged. According to the first, which has been called the 'pessimistic' view, the industrial transformation had largely negative effects on the vast majority of people, and there was a general fall in the standard of living. People were uprooted from their traditional homes and forced into unwholesome and overcrowded industrial towns. The second standpoint, the 'optimistic' view, sees the advantages outweighing the disadvantages. Here, the interpretation is that the standard of living rose, at least in the long term, and the industrial transformation produced living conditions that were superior to the old agrarian society. The reams of statistics which both sides have produced in the heated debate on this issue have failed to produce a satisfactory conclusion. But one may ask if the entire question has not been distorted. This is primarily a question of whether we are considering short-term or long-term trends. Even if the industrial revolution in Britain in the decades before 1848, for example, lowered the standard of living in the short term, measured in real wages, this does not mean that the long-term effects were the reverse, i.e. a substantial rise in real wages through the rest of the nineteenth century. On the other hand, the 'standard of living' is a difficult concept that may encompass many things. In the broad sense, it includes something that could loosely be called the quality of life. But, if so, the question is, how could the 'quality of life' in a pre-industrial society be compared with that of an industrial society? It is difficult to compare apples and pears. We may have to simply note that this transformation involved the creation of a new society which changed the basic criteria for what constitutes a decent and human life.

We can, of course, also apply a distorted definition of the 'standard of living' by expressing it as real wages, for example. From this viewpoint, Sweden can hardly be said to agree with the gloomy picture painted by the 'pessimists'. Instead, there is every indication that there were considerable increases in real wages for most Swedes in the period after 1850, and particularly after 1870. This was also true of the period between the wars, despite the major crises of these years. At times the rise in real wages was very sharp.

Thus Sweden was fortunate enough to combine industrialisation with improved living standards, at least in terms of wages and purchasing power. We have already discussed the reasons for this. Sweden's industrial transformation was able to benefit from a wave of higher demand for some simple raw materials and input materials from a Europe in the throes of rapid industrial change. Another crucial factor was the revolution in agriculture of the time and the beginnings of industrial manufacture. There were also the political and institutional reforms we have discussed above. It is at least likely that the great waves of emigration towards the end of the century accelerated this rise in real wages. It is at least possible that Sweden would otherwise have suffered from periods of falling real wages caused by underemployment and marginalisation in the agricultural sector. But we can only hazard a guess here.

Thus far we have not mentioned the gender aspect of the term 'quality of life'. Clearly, the industrial transformation did not always mean the same thing to men and women. The old society was founded on the family and the household, although there too a significant number of people were not part of that kind of community. Industrialisation, the spread of waged work and the growing quantities of goods and services distributed through the market all helped to debase this essential and central institution. In a reference to the author C. J. L. Almqvist's famous novel, *Det går an* (1839), Anita Göransson writes the following:

> The number of households headed by single women rose. In the mid-nineteenth century close to half the households in some towns in mid-Sweden were single women – mostly widows but also unmarried women from a variety of social strata. Many of them had to provide for children as well. This may be compared with the 15 per cent of households headed by single men. Thus little more than 35 per cent of them met the ideal of the time: the man-dominated two-parent home. Sara Videbeck's problem was so common in Sweden in the early nineteenth century that the authorities were forced to intervene.[48]

The difficulties women found in providing for themselves in the new industrial society forced changes that should have improved their position; the Resolution of 1846, in particular, gave women the right to start their own businesses upon obtaining a permit from a male guardian. Another step was taken in 1863, when women were declared of lawful age at the age of 25, whether they were married or not. For most women, the new job opportunities created by industrial expansion were, of course, more important than the chance to start their own businesses. A large number of women were in paid work, particularly in the textile, food and other consumer goods industries. In the 'heavy' and more craft-dominated industries, however, they were still virtually excluded. Towards the end of the nineteenth century some 'protective legislation' was introduced that *de facto* barred women from entering certain industries on the same footing as men. The well-intentioned aim to protect women and children from harmful industrial work caused laws to be introduced in the 1890s that banned night work for women and barred women from particularly hazardous work.[49]

The generally accepted view was that industrialisation was accompanied by the emergence of a family pattern in which the man worked in the factory while the woman stayed at home. But despite the acceptance at the ideological level of the 'family breadwinner ideal' towards the end of the nineteenth century, the 'housewife' was hardly a generally accepted phenomenon until after the First World War. Even then, they were not in the majority. Most women – in the working class – continued to work outside the home. Although more women were in gainful employment, it is still clear that the new industrial society enhanced the man's position of power rather than the woman's. Because women had to look after both children and family while also taking on waged work, they were effectively in a subordinate position. The woman's wages were usually seen as a supplement to the man's. The new industrial society, it is true, put a premium on work

Figure 5.18 Women mortar-carriers at the Stockholm Opera House in the 1890s. SSM.

outside the family and the household. But women were usually given the worst-paid and less-skilled work in the new factories. A dual, and contradictory, view emerged of women as labour. On the one hand, they were considered far too 'unreliable' and weak to be key workers, while on the other, women's 'deft fingers' and their stamina in repetitive manual work were emphasised. Moreover, the role of women as waged workers often came under threat. In periods of recession and unemployment, angry (male) voices often demanded that women withdraw to make way for the 'family breadwinners', i.e. men. Women were seen as only partly established in the modern industrial society – and were consequently accorded lower status.

6 Industry – dynamics and crises

Sweden's emergence as an industrial nation established the country firmly in the international economy. The effects of international capitalism's trade and monetary transactions had certainly been of great importance before this time. But it is the invasion of capital and its dominance over industry and production that gave these effects such an immediate and decisive impact. It was this combination of industrial endeavour and a capitalist appetite for profit that created the 'mighty force' that Gripenstedt, the minister of finance, described so eloquently in his visionary work, *Flower Paintings* (*Blomstermålningar*) from the 1850s.

Sweden's involvement in the economic crises that were, at least since the 1700s, a constant accompaniment to industrial expansion is tangible evidence of Sweden's integration into the international economy. The first crisis that had been honoured with the title of 'global crisis' hit the Western world in 1857 and 1858. It had been preceded by several years of intensive business activity, one result of which was an enormous increase in Sweden's exports of goods such as wood and iron. As with the rest of the Western world, the reverse in Sweden came quickly and hit hard. In 1856 there was general talk of 'overspeculation', not least in property, and warnings were issued about a shortage of money and a serious deterioration in the balance of payments. In the autumn of 1857, when a number of merchant houses and banks in Hamburg and England, among them Hoare, Buxton & Co. with its numerous contacts in Sweden, began to suspend their payments, the press reported the first bankruptcies in Sweden. The winter and spring of 1868 was a period of general business stagnation. In some sectors, notably mining, retailing and shipping, and to a lesser extent wood products, the crisis lasted several years. Conservative observers such as Mr Nordström, Keeper of the Public Records, were not slow to attribute the crisis to overspeculation; a 'virtually unlimited use of credit' combined with irresponsibly excessive consumption. Whatever the interpretation may be, most people agreed with Nordström's opinion that the speculation boom must be seen primarily as a 'ricochet from the world market'.[1]

In several respects, this crisis was an important turning-point. As Heckscher says, the events of 1857–8 brought Sweden into the international economic cycle from that time onwards. But equally important were the political consequences. As has already been shown, the crisis created the preconditions for a national-liberal economic policy – of the Gripenstedt and Wallenberg type – which did not hesitate to intervene in the economy when vital interests were threatened by, for example, a spate of bank failures.

The same policy was also pursued in the next major crisis at the end of the 1870s. These golden years of liberalism saw the emergence of the idea that government intervention was essential in periods of severe recession. An important motive was fear of what a rebellious lower class could do. For example, in 1855 an overheated economy had caused a sharp rise in cereal prices followed by widespread riots and strikes.[2] Two years later, the threat of unemployment was imminent and there was fear of even more serious social unrest. In December, reports streamed in of layoffs in the sawmill district of Norrland. Bergviks Sågbruk AB, for example, went into liquidation and threw 1,100 people out of work.[3] Undoubtedly Gripenstedt's interventionist policy could be attributed in part to the new group, feared by both the upper and middle classes, that had emerged: the proletariat.

Economic cycles

Agrarian society also had a set rhythm of upswings and downswings in production. Changes in climate and variations in annual growth rates formed the basis of cyclical changes over a single year, and from one year to the next. At the same time there were long cycles that could range over centuries and that were related to the balance between production, the utilisation of cultivated land and population pressure. Similar cyclical phenomena could be discerned in industrial society, although their causes were different. Here, too, there was a certain rhythm in which production seemed to alternate regularly between boom and recession.

The hidden secret of these cycles aroused the curiosity of economists at an early stage. As early as the mid-1800s the Frenchman Clément Juglar, for example, noted business cycles of seven to eleven years. These periodic variations have therefore come to be known as Juglar cycles. These are also what people normally mean when they discuss business cycles. Other, shorter cycles with a less severe impact can also be identified. One is the so-called Kitchin cycle of forty months, named after the Englishman Joseph Kitchin. Finally, there are also longer cycles of perhaps forty to fifty years. These are usually called Kondratiev cycles after the Russian economist of that name.

Taking as a starting point J.A. Schumpeter's theory on development blocks, the economics historian Lennart Schön and others have stated that the long cycles may be divided into the following three phases: transformation, rationalisation and crisis. The *transformation* that follows the crisis is characterised by renewal in the form of innovations in products, production methods and so on. At the same time, new institutional arrangements are added that facilitate growth. In the subsequent phase of *rationalisation*, growth is based on learning to make more efficient use of the earliest innovations. In this phase, competition increases as more and more people master the innovations. A feature of this period is usually an intensive 'struggle between the old and the new'.[4] After a time, a limit is reached on what can be achieved by efficiency-improvement within the framework of the technology and the production systems of the time. At this point the *crisis* occurs, which in its turn – following a period of company closures and the destruction of existing industrial capital – lays the foundations for a new period of transformation.

The underlying reason for these long cycles is often said to be technological advance. This is also true of the Schumpeter theory on development blocks mentioned above, which in Sweden has been refined by economists such as Johan Åkerman and Erik Dahmén. We have also come across the term 'technological system' which has often been seen to dominate a development block or a long business cycle.

According to this view, the transformation phase occurs mainly as a consequence of a cluster of technological innovations, the so-called development blocks. But these blocks hardly have a decisive effect on the Juglar-type short cycles. The explanation for these cycles has been a bone of contention among business-cycle researchers ever since the 1800s. Although some imaginative theories have been put forward – including that of W.S. Jevons, the famous English economist who maintained that business cycles were related to the periodic appearance of sunspots – the interpretations that have been presented fall into two main categories. The first is production-related, while the second is based on financial and monetary conditions. The first type is dominated by theories on overproduction introduced in the 1800s – all of which stem in some way or another from the theories of Malthus. Here, the basic idea is that, for some reason, production growth outstrips consumption. However, what makes this happen is a subject of debate even among the advocates of this theory. The adherents of the 'law of markets', named after Jean-Baptiste Say, the French economist, that says there is no reason to fear that in the long term supply will outstrip demand ('supply creates its own demand'), are even more critical. A certain proportion of production is always distributed in the form of income to different production factors to pay for their contribution to the production process. On the other hand, this does not prevent short-term disruptions: it may, for example, take time before higher incomes absorb an increase in supply. A variation on this theme is the idea that business booms are a period of 'over-investment'. In periods of general optimism, companies tend to build up far too large a capacity for the existing demand. This applies particularly if this larger capacity is financed by borrowing. The aggravated inflation that follows from the greater scarcity that arises when investments and consumption take off means that many of the new production plants become unprofitable when prices begin to come down again. Similarly, it is commonly assumed that optimism beguiles many entrepreneurs into investing money in projects that are not efficient and that under normal conditions would hardly be considered profitable.

The other interpretation considers the financial aspects, and attaches most importance to the factors that control fluctuations in the interest rate. According to the general equilibrium theory of economics, the interest rate is the mechanism that evens out fluctuations in the business cycle. Overoptimistic lending pushes up the interest rate, resulting in less borrowing. The reverse applies in the case of too little lending activity. According to this theory, the interest rate should then be low, which will stimulate more lending. But of course in reality the interest rate is affected by other factors as well, such as the size of the money stock. If this increases, as the American economist Irving Fischer and others have pointed out, there will be an immediate rise in the interest rate with the result that lending and inflation will increase in a rising spiral. This spiral can only be stopped by a general crisis, followed by deflation.

In most cases it is impossible to establish whether a crisis has financial causes or is caused by 'over-investment'. It is also clear that these two possible causes are closely related. One type of crisis may manifest itself in what may be seen as reckless financial speculation and far too rapid growth in industrial capacity. Both of these will lead to typical expressions of a business boom, such as rising interest rates and prices. Moreover, as Gustaf Åkerman pointed out, the theoreticians have been far too busy identifying common features in business cycles. Instead, one should perhaps focus on their distinctive features.[5] The 1857 crisis, for example, began with the Ohio Life Insurance and Trust Company in Cincinnati suspending payments on 24 August of that year. There is no doubt that large-scale swindling in railroad bonds and land lay behind this event, as well as the discovery of large gold deposits in California. This frightened many American banks into withdrawing their loans and ceasing to redeem their banknotes. As we have already suggested, the effects of this were felt even in the Old World. In Sweden, Stockholm's Enskilda Banken and the Skånska Banken were on the point of bankruptcy, but were saved at the last moment by Gripenstedt's government loans.

Coincidental events of this kind do not mean that there may not also be a connection between the Juglar type of short cycles and the longer, Kondratiev cycles. It would seem, for example, that the severity of the recession is stronger in the long term when the economy is in a crisis phase than in an upswing, and financial and monetary problems are also more serious.

From industrial revolution to mass production

In the period we are examining here, the Western world went through two longer phases of upswing and recession. By and large, Sweden conforms with the general pattern of trends, although as we shall soon see there are specific aspects to consider. The first phase ran from the 1850s to the beginning of the 1890s. The second phase is from the mid-1890s until the outbreak of the Second World War. The last year of the second Kondratiev cycle is thus rather arbitrarily set as 1939, the first year of the Second World War, when the conditions for all 'normal' economic activity underwent a fundamental change. As a result of, among other things, the development block generated by the war economy, a third cycle occurred which we shall discuss later.

In Western Europe as a whole, trends in the first cycle – up to the 1890s – may very well be analysed with the help of the concepts presented above: transformation, rationalisation and crisis. The mid-1850s was a time when a number of innovations generally associated with the industrial revolution – railroads, the textile industry, factory organisation, mechanical production processes and so on – came into widespread use. Industrial transformation was initially based on a consumer goods industry, which in its turn paved the way for the emergence of an industry which manufactured the means of production. The new cast steel processes, which were particularly important in Sweden, began to be introduced in the 1850s. The liberalisation of trade, as expressed *inter alia* in the Cobden Treaty, also greatly intensified economic activity in Western Europe.

But as early as the 1870s this powerful industrial upswing ran into difficulties. A period of rationalisation followed, which was succeeded by a more general crisis towards the end of the 1880s. In one country after another, small enterprises collapsed, their places taken by larger companies that could make better use of the resources. In countries like Germany and Sweden, the banks played an important part in this process of rationalisation, which expressed itself in more concentration, cartel agreements, etc. Clearly, it is against this background that protectionism in the 1880s should be seen, as should the increasing competition for the colonies – which culminated in the division of Africa at the Berlin Conference of 1888, and the increase in international aggression in the same period. Notwithstanding the emphasis on rationalisation and crisis in this period, important innovations were introduced, but their effects were not visible until some time later.

During the crisis, forces were created that would form the basis of a new block of important innovations which in their turn would pave the way for very rapid growth from the middle of the 1890s. After this period, the Western world experienced a period of intensive business activity which lasted until 1904, after which there was a Juglarian decline. As is often pointed out, this breakthrough was based on a series of revolutionising innovations: the internal combustion engine, the car, the ball-bearing, electricity and so on. Swedish companies were behind a number of these innovations, including the ball-bearing, the telephone, the milk separator, gas lighthouses, drilling equipment, etc. In a completely new way, these new products and production methods were based on scientific innovation. This was particularly true in Germany, which concentrated hard on developing scientific knowledge that had practical applications in industry. The government bore the cost of these efforts. But other countries followed suit, albeit on a more modest scale. Even in Sweden the first tentative steps were taken to improve technical research, one being the founding of the Royal Institute of Technology in Stockholm. Of at least equal importance was the introduction of a new business organisation and large-scale production methods of a kind that had hitherto been inconceivable. In the USA in particular, but also in Germany and France (though less so in England where the smaller, family-based company still had a strong position), the 1890s were characterised by what Alfred Chandler, the American economic historian, called the economies of scale and scope. Long production runs brought down unit costs. The economies of scope may also be defined as the advantages gained by producing different articles using the same technical equipment and the same input goods.[6]

Thus, beginning in the USA, the conditions were created in the 1890s for an industrial economy based on a number of new products which were often manufactured using radically new methods, in large plants and aimed at a mass market. Long production runs, standardisation and automation were the order of the day. Particularly in the process industries, the result was a rapid fall in unit costs. Instead of having many small companies in competition with one another, the 1890s saw the emergence of large companies that exploited the strategies of vertical and horizontal integration to win ever-larger market shares. In 'vertical integration' a company attempts to integrate several stages of the production process into its own organisation. To bring down transaction costs and gain greater control the organisation takes over the company that supplies raw materials, the company that supplies input goods and the company that distributes the finished product. In 'horizontal integration' the company, through purchases or mergers, attempts to reduce the number of competitors in its market. The effects of troublesome competition may, however, be reduced in other ways as well. A method that became increasingly common in the 1890s was to set up cartel agreements. Although these were often outlawed, it was impossible to stop companies dividing up the market among themselves or agreeing on a common retail price. Another method was to enter into more formal combinations in the form of various kinds of trust. In general, this meant that several companies of the same kind came under a single owner without actually merging. This, too, was often made illegal and was considered to lead to harmful monopolies, not least in the USA, where very strict antitrust legislation was enacted. After a number of well-publicised cases, which led among other things to the dissolution of the strongly monopolistic Standard Oil of New Jersey, tactics were changed, and formerly relatively autonomous companies merged to form gigantic corporations. Thus, the rigid legislation did not result in the perpetuation of competitive capitalism. Rather, it encouraged the formation of large integrated corporations that now gained an increasingly powerful position in the market.

The golden age of this new, mass-producing capitalism was the period up to the First World War. The period of rationalisation and crisis for the development block that originated around the turn of the century took place in the inter-war years. The Second World War then created a new development block that formed the basis for the growth and prosperity of the 1950s and 1960s.

The crisis of the 1870s

In the 1850s Sweden enjoyed a marked upswing in both its export and domestic market industries. An important precondition was the period of intensive growth that the Western European economy had entered at that time. As emphasised above, this growth phase moved into the rationalisation and crisis phases from the 1870s onwards. The 1870s were difficult times in Sweden too, although the decade began with a very strong upswing in the business cycle. In the spring of 1872 a sawmill owner reported the following: 'Sales this year have been excellent. Never before have I sold so many loads this early in the year. I can also sell at perfectly satisfactory prices that give a good profit.'[7] This growth was followed by a strong resurgence in industrial investments, which totalled close to 10 per cent a year in the first half of the 1870s, expressed in fixed prices. At the same time, prices rose rapidly. But from the mid-1870s the trend was reversed. The rest of the 1870s and the following decade constituted a period of serious unrest, in which there were a number of years of crisis. Among other things, this may be seen from the relatively low average rate of growth for the period as a whole. A decline in the growth rate was followed by an even steeper fall in industrial investments. These two figures were at a very low level until the mid-1890s – as were interest rates, particularly in the 1880s.[8] In Sweden and elsewhere the average price level fell at the same time. Deflation put both industry and agriculture under severe strain. One expression of this was the demand for protectionist measures that was often heard in the political debate of the 1880s. Demands were made for both industrial and agricultural tariffs, several of which were, as we have seen, introduced in this period. The tariffs were not only an expression of a successful special-interest policy, they were also an illustration of the vexatious competitive situation and the strained economy of the time.

In the contemporary debate at the close of the 1870s the opinion was often voiced that the boom at the beginning of the decade had led to an over-establishment of companies. Industrial capacity had quite simply grown too large. Or, as the entrepreneurs themselves put it, to quote Lennart Jörberg, there was 'overproduction'.[9] The sawmill owners and others thought that this overcapacity resulted in board and timber being stockpiled in foreign harbours. The ironworks owners were mostly concerned about the rapid growth in iron and steel manufacture, especially in the USA and Britain. The falling prices in particular were seen as a sign that supply was far too great, despite the steady increase in exports. This positive curve was only interrupted by the odd year here and there, and not even in the turbulent 1880s was this trend reversed.

Annual percentage growth.

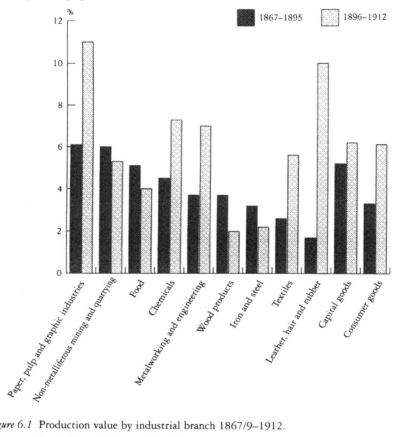

Figure 6.1 Production value by industrial branch 1867/9–1912.

Source: L. Jörberg, 'Några tillväxtfaktorer i 1800–talets industriella utveckling', in
R. Lundström (ed.), *Kring industrialsmens genombrott i Sverige*, Stockholm 1966,
p. 35.

Despite the lower growth rate of the 1880s as a whole, the continued
expansion of export industries suggests that the problems were not general
in nature but corresponded to the competitive struggle we have seen as a
general feature of the rationalisation phase in the cycle. We have already
observed that in the 1880s many sectors experienced a great leap forward
both in mechanisation and the introduction of factory-based production. The
statistical evidence for this is the sharp rise in the number of horsepower
consumed per workplace, particularly in the 1880s, even in such a strongly
craft-oriented sector as engineering. Behind this increase in the number of
horsepower used is both the installation of new workshop machines and the
rapid spread of steam engines as a new power source.

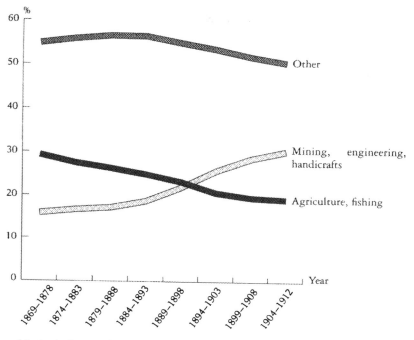

Figure 6.2 Agriculture, industry and other sectors, 1869–1912. Percentage of GNP.
Source: L. Jörberg, *Growth and Fluctuations of Swedish Industry 1869–1912*, Lund 1961, p. 23.

The main effect of competition, which grew steadily keener throughout this period, was further demands for improved efficiency. Only efficient companies can survive when better communications dramatically reduce the cost of long-distance transportation. In general, the local type of industry began to be replaced by companies that intended to expand their sales area. One way to counter this growing competition – mainly expressed as falling retail prices – was to try to bring down costs within the framework of a given type of organisation and technology. Many were successful in this. By lowering wages and other costs, the same quantity of goods was produced at a lower price. Another, more radical, method was for companies to improve their efficiency by altering their organisation and technology. More automation was one way to improve the cost efficiency of production. Larger-scale production could also bring down unit costs. But this involved more than simply making the production process as efficient as possible. Cost-effectiveness could also be improved by finding better ways of reaching the consumers, taking advantage of cheaper communications and so on.

Both these methods were used, of course, in different ways in different sectors. The general campaign to bring down wages in the sawmills of the

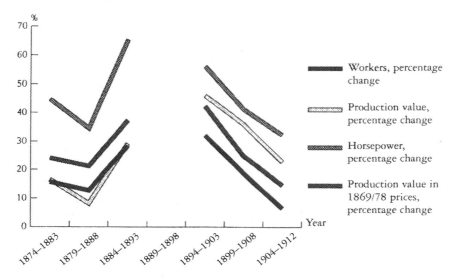

Figure 6.3 Manufacturing: percentage change in number of workers, production value, number of horsepower used and production value in 1869/78 prices.

Source: L. Jörberg: *Growth and Fluctuations of Swedish Industry 1869–1912*, Lund 1961, p. 40.

Sundsvall district at the end of the 1870s caused the famous Sundsvall strike of 1879. But perhaps the more common method was to improve efficiency by changing the company's organisation and/or by mechanisation. In several sectors, particularly outside the direct consumption industry, for example in iron and steel, paper, wood products and mechanical engineering, the result was an increase in the size of companies. But this was not a general trend. In reality, the larger companies' percentage of the total workforce from 1870 onwards *fell*. In relative terms there were more companies with over 100 and 500 workers in 1872 than in 1912. Seen as production value, however, the larger companies' proportion is higher, particularly those with a large workforce. This, and other factors, indicates the substantial amount of rationalisation and mechanisation that took place in this period.

Seen from an overall perspective, the ongoing process of industrialisation in Sweden cannot thus be described as a simple transition from small to large enterprises. In Sweden it was rather, as Lennart Jörberg pointed out, that large-scale enterprise was important from the very beginning. Already in 1872, close to 70 per cent of the industrial workforce were in companies with over 100 employees. This figure had fallen to 58 per cent by 1880, but in 1897 it was 60 per cent and in 1912 it was still 60 per cent. The figures for companies with over 500 employees were 15 per cent in 1872, 14 per cent in 1880, 14 per cent in 1897 and 15 per cent in 1912. There were, of course, considerable differences between sectors. The trend in some sectors,

Table 6.1 Industrial plant 1872–1912 by size, number of work sites, total number of workers and production value in each group. The whole of industry, percentage change

	Year	Size of plant (number of workers)						
		1–10	*11–25*	*26–100*	*101–250*	*251–500*	*501–1,000*	*1,001–2,000*
Number of	1872	44.4	20.1	22.1	8.8	3.6	1.0	0.1
work sites	1889	41.7	26.0	22.1	7.1	1.9	1.1	–
	1889	33.3	27.2	26.8	9.0	2.5	1.2	0.1
	1897	13.1	37.4	34.8	9.6	4.0	0.9	0.2
	1903	18.3	35.7	33.0	8.7	3.2	0.8	0.2
	1912	23.8	33.1	30.4	8.4	3.2	0.8	0.2
Number of	1872	5.3	6.7	22.7	27.45	23.0	12.3	2.6
workers	1880	6.2	10.7	25.5	25.8	16.8	15.1	–
	1889	4.1	8.7	26.0	27.0	16.4	15.5	2.4
	1897	1.4	10.4	27.7	24.2	22.0	10.6	3.7
	1903	1.9	10.7	29.4	23.9	20.0	10.3	4.5
	1912	2.7	10.2	27.0	24.1	20.6	10.4	5.0
Production	1872	6.7	8.2	20.7	30	19.8	12.4	2.2
value	1880	6.1	9.5	23.3	31.7	13.8	15.5	–
	1889	4.6	8.7	24.8	27.8	19.7	11.9	3.5
	1897	6.2	10.2	26.1	22.9	20.8	10.7	3.1
	1903	5.7	10.2	27.1	22.7	21.0	9.1	4.2
	1912	6.2	6.8	23.6	24.8	21.5	11.3	5.5

Source: L. Jörberg: *Growth and Fluctuations of Swedish Industry 1869–1912*, Lund 1961, p. 119.

Table 6.2 Percentage of the total number of workers in plants with more than 100 and more than 500 workers in 1872 and 1880

	1872		1880	
	>100	*>500*	*>100*	*>500*
Industry, total	69.3	14.9	59.5	16.0
Consumer goods	68.0	6.5	62.4	16.3
Capital goods	63.8	25.6	52.9	14.9
Food etc.	62.6		49.0	15.9
Textiles	78.0	10.9	76.9	15.4
Leather, hair and rubber goods	8.4	–	24.2	–
Wood, excl. sawmills	46.2	–	41.3	–
Paper and pulp	52.5	17.3	61.3	–
Non-metalliferous mining and quarrying	61.9	–	60.4	32.4
Chemicals	64.3	15.3	59.3	18.1
Metals, excl. iron	76.9	34.6	54.2	19.4
Engineering	69.1	44.3	59.2	22.8

Source: L. Jörberg: *Growth and Fluctuations of Swedish Industry 1869–1912*, Lund 1961, p. 151.

among them the food and engineering industries, clearly was an average fall in the number of employees. However, in most sectors the picture is the same at the beginning and the end of this period.

The reason why the percentage attributable to large enterprises did not increase is *not* that the absolute number of large companies fell, or that the existing large companies broke up into smaller units. On the contrary, the number of large companies rose in absolute terms. The stagnation of company size is more an effect of the rapid growth in the total number of companies, particularly small companies. In contrast to what Karl Marx, for example, thought, hardly anywhere does the process of industrialisation lead to the elimination of small enterprises in absolute numbers. Instead, they tend to increase, particularly during an upswing in the business cycle. This is what happened in Sweden at the end of the 1800s. Jörberg has estimated that there was a sharp rise in the total number of companies from roughly 900 in 1872 to 3,800 in 1897. These figures do not include one-man and purely craft enterprises.[10] Otherwise, the figures for the number of 'companies' during this time should be taken with a pinch of salt. The statistics vary between 'handicrafts' and 'factories', without stating clearly the criteria that were applied. In the 1870s this results not least in strange breaks in series of figures, where a large number of units that had previously be counted as 'handicrafts' were now counted as 'factories'.[11] Despite this, the trend is clear: industrialisation led to the formation of a growing number of small enterprises.

Here, however, we are in part dealing with a different kind of small business enterprise than before. For example, in the very extensive metal and forging industry in Eskilstuna, very small (craft) businesses could compete successfully with the larger factories up until the 1880s, even though the factories employed dozens of workers and used mechanical equipment. The small companies could quite simply market their knives, locks, tools, etc., at competitive prices. But in the 1880s many small companies closed down or were swallowed up by the larger companies, because the latter could offer cost benefits, either through more efficient production or better control of their sales. The small companies that survived and the numerous new companies that came into being could do so either because they found their own niches where there was no competition from factory-based industry, or because they began to supply the larger companies.

We should emphasise once again that the large number of new companies did not stop the absolute number of large companies from rising. It is this concurrent growth in both small and large companies that creates the fragmented picture that characterises the process of industrialisation. Similarly, we must emphasise the large scale of Swedish industry from its beginnings. Throughout this whole period many sectors were dominated by a small number of very large companies. This was true of a broad range of industries, including rubber goods and electricity. In most cases, however, the domestic market industries were more concentrated than those that produced for the export market. Although a large number of new small companies appeared, this was a special feature that Sweden would retain.

The much-debated crisis of the 1870s should therefore be seen foremost as a phase in the long cycle that began around the middle of that century. This does not fully explain its importance or its causes. In Western Europe as a whole, the beginning of the 'great depression' (1873–96) was marked by a number of crisis years. The period 1877–9 in particular was characterised by a sharp fall in the demand for both industrial and agricultural goods. In the financial market, the banks and private banking companies sustained severe losses. In Sweden, the effects of the international crisis were particularly intensive in 1877 and 1878. We have already seen that export sales fell and there were many redundancies, particularly in exporting businesses. In the boom years at the beginning of the decade, industrial investment had been high. Many companies had increased their capacity by raising loans, either from the commercial banks or in some other way – raising secured loans from private individuals was still a common practice. It was not unusual for the forecasts to be excessively optimistic, or for money to be borrowed for reckless speculation. The Hofors Works was saved in sensational circumstances by Stockholm's Enskilda Bank in 1878 – among other things,

Figure 6.4 Cuts in wages caused by short-term difficulties in the sawmills was the spark that set off the 1879 Sundsvall strike of about 5,000 workers, the largest action by workers in Sweden up to that time. It was a defeat for the workers in the short term – the County Governor in Härnösand, Curry Treffenberg, called in the Army. There were many arrests and many evictions. In the long term, this strike was the beginning of workers' organisation into trade unions. Historical illustration. KB.

Hjalmar Petré, the old owner and works director, was dismissed by A.O. Wallenberg. This crisis was brought on by Petré's extremely questionable investments in large Bessemer works to mass-produce cheap steel at the Avesta Ironworks.[12] Other companies that had built up their operations on borrowed money also found themselves in difficulties. For example, the AB Atlas engineering company was started in 1873, in what was perhaps the most intensive phase of the boom, with the idea of manufacturing railroad trucks and nothing else. Already in 1876 the company employed over 600 workers who used modern lathes, drilling machines and other mechanical aids that were advanced for the time. But as Torsten Gårdlund pointed out, the investments in AB Atlas had been made 'not only at the wrong time, but also in the wrong industry'. The basic problem was, of course, the cyclical downswing just as the company was in a position to begin to supply large numbers of railroad trucks. In addition, there were already several other companies established in the rolling-stock market, both in Sweden and abroad. Atlas's ill-advised investment, where once again A.O. Wallenberg was involved, together with the Crédit Mobilier company Göteborgs Handelskompani, collapsed ignominiously. For several years in the early the 1880s the company was forced to produce garden canes (!) and actively look for new business.[13]

When large enterprises such as Hofors-Avesta, Atlas or the even bigger Stora Bergslagsbanan railroad company, with their substantial borrowings, ran into difficulties, the effect on the banking sector was immediate. As we have seen, Stockholm's Enskilda Bank played a strategic part in the large investments in industry of the 1870s, and as a result the bank was in very serious trouble in 1878. The severity of its position was also underscored by the fact that the bank had acquired large quantities of railroad bonds. Their value, which had been inflated a great deal in previous years, now fell sharply. In general, it was obvious that the optimistic investment in extending the railroad system and other expansions had helped to inflate a financial bubble that was now about to burst.

For Wallenberg it was as if the events of 1857 were about to be repeated. The situation became extremely precarious when Stockholm's leading iron exporter, N.M. Höglund & Co., suspended payments on 2 December 1878. Three days later Stockholm's Enskilda Bank experienced its first (but not its last!) 'run', with the depositors losing faith in the bank and queuing to withdraw their savings. Wallenberg had to summon the support of all his contacts to stop the run of withdrawals. This strategy met with some success – a significant event here was that on 7 December, King Oscar II himself 'swam against the stream' and had SEK10,000 deposited in his account at the bank'.[14] But in the following year not even His Royal Highness could save the day. The otherwise almost dogmatically theoretical liberal minister of finance, Hans Forsell, had to intervene and 'bargain', as had Gripenstedt twenty years before, in order to raise a new government loan to shore up the bank and save it from insolvency.

The 1890s and the second industrial revolution

The development block of the 1890s is sometimes referred to as the 'second industrial revolution'. The period of rationalisation and crisis that Sweden had undergone had achieved what Hammarberg, a director of Sunds AB, had wanted in 1877. He wrote, 'I am convinced that our problems, and the way we have disposed of a great deal of dead wood in the business world, bodes very well for the future.'[15] This process of houseclearing had allowed many new and efficient enterprises to emerge that were well-placed to conquer new export markets. But there were also notable improvements in efficiency in the industries that produced for the domestic market, while companies also became more specialised. Against this background, the improvement in industrial productivity of the 1880s was also impressive. The resulting favourable growth figures were not long in coming. The downward movement in prices began to turn as early as the end of the 1880s, and a sharp upswing began some years into the 1890s.[16] Workers' real wages rose even faster from the middle of the decade.[17] There was also intensive activity in the agricultural sector. Put simply, all the curves pointed upwards.

Yet the aggregate figures do not fully reflect the major changes that took place in the industrial sector from the mid-1890s to the outbreak of the First World War. We have already described parts of this dynamic at the sectorial level. During this period there were not only evident advances in growth, productivity and exports, there was also increased automation, measured in, for example, horsepower. Among other things this meant that the number of machines increased; in the engineering industry the available power sources, measured in horsepower, increased from 0.5 per worker in 1899 to 1.2 in 1909, 1.76 in 1919 and 1.36 in 1939.[18] Similarly, the number of workers increased by 1.9 per cent a year between 1901 and 1907, while production grew by 5.5 per cent.[19] This means that a large part of this increase must be attributed to more capital investment in machinery etc., and/or to improved efficiency.

This, however, was not the most important factor. In vital industrial sectors such as iron, steel and paper, there was a breakthrough for a technology which, in its capacity and size, eclipsed most earlier experiences. The new electric power that now began to be used in industry was quite revolutionary. There had been a breakthrough as early as 1893 when, in co-operation with the newly founded ASEA in Västerås, Jonas Wenström, the engineer, built the first electric power link between the Hellsjön lake and Grängesberg. The introduction of the Thomas method had increased the consumption of Grängesberg ore in the 1880s. But pumping up water and extracting ore was very energy-intensive. For the first time, cheap and efficient electrical power, the so-called 'white coal', was available.[20] For natural reasons, it was mainly heavy industry that took advantage of this new technology at first. As early as 1894–5 the Hofors rolling-mills were electrified, as was a smaller plant in Boxholm. Later in the 1890s this technology spread to other industries, including paper pulp and engineering. In most cases, electricity was generated by turbines driven by local waterfalls. In Hofors a waterfall was used with a thirty metre fall from the smithy pond to the power station.[21] Special power companies which sold power to different subscribers were not established until some time later. When it came to the heavy process industries this new electrical power was indispensable. But it also had a revolutionary impact on other industries as well. Not only could far more power than before be used, but an equally important factor was that modern electric motors allowed a radically different and more efficient organisation of work. Machines and workers no longer had to crowd along central power drives and belts. The work processes could be dispersed through the shop in a way that better met the requirements of the production process. Against this background it is no exaggeration to say that the development block from which changes came after 1890 was based largely on a technological system that stemmed from electrical power. It was only with the help of this 'white coal' that paper, ore, iron and engineering goods could be mass-produced. Only in this way could the innovations in the engineering industry's 'black box companies' be exploited on a large scale. But the new technology also had different kinds of effect. We have already seen how production technology and various forms of organisation were modified to suit electric power. A series of commercial products were also developed more or less directly on this basis, including efficient electric motors and other electrical equipment developed by ASEA. Generally speaking, the upswing of the 1890s – in the Western world and in Sweden – was founded on a series of innovations such as the transmission of electric power and the development of electric motors, but also on the internal combustion engine. Many of these original inventions were put into different products, which in time conquered the world market.

This concentration of a small number of dominant companies in different sectors continued and even intensified. The strong inclination to merge companies helped lead to this – there was much talk of 'trustification'. But these activities extended beyond simple company mergers. Holding companies, in which companies retained their autonomy under a single owner,

Figure 6.5 Allmänna Svenska Elektriska Aktiebolaget (ASEA) in Västerås. The office and main workshops. From *Svenska industriella verk och anläggninar 1899/1900*.

Figure 6.6 Yet another advance: electric lighting is installed at the Näs sawmill, Dalarna, in 1878. The technical problems of 'the use of magneto-electric light for the illumination of large premises' were solved for the first time. *Ny illustrerad tidning* 1878. KB.

were not uncommon. In several cases this created an oligopoly or a pure monopoly. The best-known monopolistic combination at the beginning of the twentieth century was the so-called sugar trust. In 1907 the Svenska Sockerfabriksaktiebolaget was formed when three formerly independent sugar-beet processing companies merged. Up to the First World War there were in principle only three companies in the entire margarine industry. The same applied to the cement industry, which was also dominated by only three companies. Finally, the superphosphate industry should also be mentioned. Although at the beginning of the twentieth century it was made up of a number of autonomous enterprises, these companies had one common sales organisation. Lennart Jörberg, for example, said that the protectionist policy of the 1880s favoured this intensive process of concentration, foremost in the industries that produced for the domestic market.[22] The absence of foreign competition undoubtedly allowed this kind of monopoly to form. But the modest size of the Swedish domestic market also favoured the development of national monopolies and oligopolies. There was often no reason for foreign companies to compete in the limited Swedish market. This was particularly true of simple and cheap goods such as sugar, margarine and cement, where relatively local producers with access to local raw materials and located close to their markets had a considerable cost advantage. To distribute cement, for example, over a wide area has seldom been very profitable. We can also add to the above forms of intensified concentration cartels, which became very common during this period. The Swedish Tariffs and Treaty Commission's survey of the 1920s concluded that cartel formations were a characteristic of Swedish industry, perhaps more so than in any other country.[23]

Figure 6.7 The general strike of 1909. Demonstrations by locked-out workers filled the streets and roads throughout the country. The picture is from Stockholm. Photograph by Axel Malmström. From Ture Nerman's collection. AA.

After an almost sensational growth in production from the mid-1890s, the trend was broken in 1907. The downturn that hit so many Western countries in 1904 could only be seen in Sweden as a modest fall-off in export sales. But the downturn after 1907 was all the more severe. It was accompanied by a fall in production and export sales figures and a rapid rise in unemployment. Once again, the most spectacular consequence of this crisis was a strike. The notorious general strike of 1909, in which 300,000 workers were locked out, was a direct consequence of the employers' decision to cut wages. But towards the end of 1909 the cycle began to swing upwards again and both growth and export figures began to rise. The years leading up to the outbreak of the First World War were clearly boom years in which production, exports and prices shot up. The engineering industry was one of the sectors that experienced a strong upswing. Many engineering firms saw a major increase in exports in this period. As mentioned above, it was particularly the Russian and Eastern European markets that were behind this upswing.

The troubled 1920s

Thus far we have described the fluctuations in the economy since the mid-1800s as almost a natural phenomenon. This is correct inasmuch as each new development block appeared to lead, after a time, to a period of rationalisation and crisis. But how does a new development block actually occur, and what factors will hasten and slow its stagnation and decline? As we have said above, it is usually assumed that the cluster of innovations that start a new block derive from what Schumpeter chose to call 'economic destruction'. This process of destruction was an acid test which eliminated older plants in the rationalisation phase. But the exact content of the new development block is not known in advance. Neither is anything known about its power, or its ability to generate long-term growth. Here, of course, pure coincidence also plays a part, in the emergence of innovations, for example. But to at least as high a degree, political decisions, institutional reforms and revolutionary world events affect both how and when a new development block begins.

War is the kind of important world event that has always played a major part in economic life. It is no coincidence that in most accounts of the economic history of the 1900s the two world wars are chronological demarcation lines. Opinions differ on the extent to which war is a winnowing process, eliminating the old and allowing the new to emerge. Since war often involves a transition to a more closed economy – a kind of ultimate point of protectionism – it is more likely that war preserves an old structure. The underlying argument is that new development blocks are more likely to occur in open international competition. When Heckscher summarises the economic effects of the First World War in Sweden he quite correctly focuses on the conserving effect of government regulation and its negative effects on competition. The most important effect of the planned economy that the war led to was, in his view, the 'strong helping hand that was unintentionally given to those with monopolistic aspirations in the business world'.[24]

Yet this is only one aspect of the matter. It is also well known that war often generates a propensity for invention. Large investments in military technology often trigger other innovations. Neither is it unusual for peaceful applications to be found for military technology. Important examples of this include the civil use of modern aircraft technology and electronics after the Second World War. War also clearly encourages innovative thinking in the field of organisational solutions. Fundamental to all military activity for thousands of years is the handling of people and material as logistics problems. We can only guess at the number of advances in this area that have influenced our approach to economics and production.

Thus war may have a perpetuating effect, and it may also lead to new development blocks. In the case of the First World War there is little evidence of a new development block. In his description of Swedish industrial enterprise in the inter-war years, Erik Dahmén emphasises, it is true, the importance of the war. Both in terms of goods innovations (cars, radios, aluminium products, man-made fibres) and innovations of method (Taylorism), the First World War was a 'push forward greatly concentrated in time', he says.[25] Yet it is clear that this push consisted of innovations that had existed before the war being used more widely. The most important effect of the war was therefore to intensify the rationalisation phase of a development block that had originated as early as the turn of the century. In Sweden, the awakening that followed the wartime blockades was an unusually painful experience. The 1920s were years of dramatic struggle between old and new which in time led to structural changes and far greater competitive power.

The crisis of the inter-war years has often been associated with the Great Depression that followed the Wall Street Crash of November 1929. But the truth is that this crisis was a phenomenon that extended through almost the entire inter-war period. The 1920s began with a deep recession which, although short-lived, was one of the most intense the industrialised world had ever experienced. The upswing that followed was pronounced, but fairly weak and uneven in most countries. Clearly, it was not only Germany that had severe economic difficulties; they were also felt in the rest of the industrialised world. From 1929, the crisis once again became acute. The financial crisis in the USA spread to Europe in 1930. The financial sectors of many countries collapsed and the banks closed. There was a new recovery around 1933, but this was relatively weak. Both in the USA and Western Europe it was only when countries began to re-arm for war at the end of the 1930s that the threat of permanent mass unemployment and general depression lifted. The long period of stagnation and decline in the inter-war years may be read in the growth figures. They were generally poor, and on a completely different level than those from before the war.

Whether the Great Depression was a financial or an industrial crisis has been the subject of much debate. In fact it was both. The ultimate cause should be seen as a development block in regression. The crisis aggravated the political after-effects of the war. The war debt imposed on Germany caused troublesome financial and monetary unrest. Finally, the cautious deflationary policy that many countries pursued also reinforced the tendencies towards economic depression. The fact that countries such as Britain attached great importance to a return to the gold standard and a stable currency should be understood in light of the general unrest of the 1920s. People were quite simply worried that the unstable monetary and financial situation that followed the world war would cause galloping inflation.

By and large, Sweden also followed this general trend, but with some important distinctive features. First, for Sweden the war was hardly an 'acid test'. On the contrary, its industry enjoyed a virtually unbroken boom in the period between the wars. True, Germany's U-boat blockade of 1917 severely disrupted Sweden's exports, but as the war progressed the export traffic in both raw materials and industrial products was transferred to Germany, while domestic-market industries benefited from the blockade from the west. Some of the large quantities of imports from Britain were replaced by imports from Germany, but not to any great extent. As in other countries in this period, the world war led to some import substitution in Sweden. The general business boom was further accentuated by the considerable rise in

Figure 6.8 Times of war and inflation. Top: a potato queue in Stockholm. Bottom: The riots in Stockholm, 5 June 1917. The police charge in Gustav Adolfs Square. Just to the left of the centre of the picture, between the police horses, is Hjalmar Branting. AA.

prices that indicated a shortage of goods and a considerable demand surplus. The most acute shortages were of food, raw materials and fuel. Inflation and the commodity shortage caused real wages to fall. The truce between employers and employees announced in 1914 included a nominal wage freeze. Despite the introduction of weighting for high-cost areas at the end of the war, it proved impossible to compensate for the rapid rate of inflation. To curb speculation and the risk of inflation, among other things, rationing of some key commodities, particularly food, was introduced in the war years.

At the end of the war – in the autumn of 1918 – this period of high economic activity generated an extremely intensive speculation boom. This was very much a consequence of the international anticipation of high inflation after the end of the war, which led many businessmen to invest even more. At the same time, inflation led many to believe they were enjoying higher profits than was actually the case. They also overvalued their stock. The impressive figures, fuelled by inflation, in the annual accounts of 1918 fostered an atmosphere of recklessness. Despite the signs of growing congestion on the export market, production for stockpiling continued. When, in the spring of 1920, the inflationary trend suddenly turned into a sharp fall in prices, many people realised that their assets fell far short of covering the costs of the loans they had so generously allowed themselves. Wages and other production costs far exceeded the prices the goods would fetch on the market.[26]

Figure 6.9 A Scania coupé of 16 to 18 hp from Scania in Malmö. This new conveyance cost SEK17,500 or SEK33,000, depending on its horsepower. But as Petrus Nordberg, publisher of *The Book of Inventions* (*Uppfinningarnas bok*) (1907–9), notes: 'However high these prices may seem, they are not a deterrent when compared with the cost of a pair of carriage horses and harness . . . and a carriage that can match in comfort and elegance the automobiles illustrated here.' KB.

The sudden and dramatic downswing in 1920 was an international phenomenon which could hardly have been entirely unexpected. As Erik Lundberg writes:

> In general terms it is easy to understand how the scarcities associated with the boom of 1920 disappeared when the *supply* of goods and services increased. Harbours were re-opened, shipping became more and more efficient, the supply of coal and raw materials increased, and good harvests turned shortage into surplus. The speculative investments in stockpiling which largely supported the business boom could not be sustained... Once there was an international downturn, it soon became clear that the overcapacity in a number of strategic areas and the surplus of stockpiled goods had to be sold off, and this caused a cumulative fall in prices.[27]

Whatever the case may have been, the result was dramatic. In 1920 and 1921 industrial production fell by 25 per cent and unemployment rose by the same figure, according to the trade unions' own (not wholly reliable) figures. Many businesses went bankrupt or were forced to make drastic cutbacks in their operations. Other companies were amalgamated on the initiative of their lenders, the commercial banks. Hardest hit were the companies, among them sawmills and mechanical engineering works, that produced exclusively for export. But recovery after the lowest ebb in 1921 was speedy. The worst of the crisis was already over by the following year and production rose swiftly once again, but starting from a lower level. In the years that followed, large segments of the export sectors did very well, particularly iron ore, pulp and paper, and engineering products – but traditional exports such as iron and steel and sawn timber fared worse. Notwithstanding this fragmented picture, exports grew by 11 per cent a year through the rest of the 1920s.[28] This also generated a high level of growth: 7–8 per cent until 1929. But it took time for unemployment to come down. At first, the unemployment figures fell rapidly from the heights of the disastrous year of 1921, but levelled out at about 10 per cent for the rest of the decade, a far higher figure than in the pre-war years.

More than anything else, the relatively high unemployment figures bear witness to the fact that Swedish industry went through a period of consolidation in the 1920s. The spate of bankruptcies and mergers that followed the peak of the disaster in 1921 caused many less efficient production units to disappear, and much of the overcapacity was eliminated. But the problems were to remain throughout the 1920s. There was lively competition in the world market and Swedish companies were forced to improve their efficiency and productivity. This was true not least of the iron and steel industry, which was exposed to particularly keen price competition from larger-scale international industries. One way to improve their competitive position was to increase automation. Another was to find ways to improve the workers' productivity by introducing 'scientific management'. It became popular to speak of 'Taylorism' in these years, and many companies installed time-clocks and introduced time studies. A third, and perhaps more important, option was more standardisation and specialisation in production. Specialising in a product range allows longer production runs, more automation and improved efficiency. More specialisation and product refinement allowed the iron and steel industry, for example, to secure market niches that were less exposed to competition from large-scale foreign industry. An example of the way greater specialisation resulted in higher productivity and a better business result can be seen in the changes made in the Fagersta Group during these years. Production specialisation at the different ironworks in the group gave substantial gains through better co-ordination and capacity utilisation. At the Horndals Works in southern Dalarna this arrangement increased productivity by several per cent throughout the 1930s and 1940s without any new investments in plant. It was this production and product range specialisation that was the secret behind the famed 'Horndal effect'.[29]

Thus the demands of the 1920s were for efficiency improvements and more rationalisation. Many businesses managed to meet these demands. Specialised engineering companies, including ASEA, SKF Separator, L.M. Ericsson, Atlas Copco and Electrolux, now underwent another period of rapid growth. Times were also good for Ivar Kreuger's match company, Svenska Tändsticksaktiebolag (STAB). Conditions were less favourable for other companies and, as we have seen, for entire sectors as well. The agriculture sector was also under considerable price pressure, which caused many closures and brought about rapid structural change. The 1920s were difficult years indeed.

The golden 1930s

In all important respects the events of the 1920s were what we may expect of a phase of rationalisation. The export sector that was to grow rapidly and that had had its first phase of expansion at the turn of the century, through efficiency improvements and rationalisation consolidated and even improved its position. The repercussions of the Wall Street Crash of 1929 also appeared to confirm that the rationalisation phase was now over, and crisis was now imminent. As was the case at the beginning of the 1920s, the international crisis hit Sweden somewhat later, in 1931. It caused company cutbacks and closures and a sharp rise in unemployment.

The financial crisis that hit Sweden with full force in 1932 is often linked to the Kreuger crash in the spring of that year. Even before 1920 Ivar Kreuger had built up a considerable fortune from the building and match industries. In 1917 he brought together a large number of small match factories to form Svenska Tändsticks AB (STAB). In the same year, the Kreuger & Toll building company became a holding company. Using this as a base, he began to build an international match consortium in the 1920s.

Figure 6.10 Ivar Kreuger, head of the matchstick empire, before his fall in 1932. KB.

By offering generous loans to various governments he managed to acquire a monopoly on matchstick production in several countries. These loans were funded by new issues from Kreuger & Toll or the subsidiary companies, and from 1928, increasingly by borrowing from Swedish banks. In this way the Kreuger companies lent no less than a total of SEK1.25 billion to sixteen countries. At the same time, Kreuger acquired large shareholdings in important Swedish export companies such as Boliden, SCAB (Svenska Cellulosa AB), L.M. Ericsson and others. Moreover, Kreuger had become the major shareholder in Skandinaviska Banken. With the onset of the global depression, the Kreuger Group's enormous burden of debt could no longer be concealed. The banks quite simply refused to help. Neither could the American market be fed with bond issues at artificially high prices. The situation finally became untenable. After a fruitless attempt to raise loans in the USA and Britain, Kreuger once again turned to the Swedish loan market. But the Bank of Sweden and the commercial banks refused any more loans until they had received a statement of the group's financial position. Kreuger knew that after 1929 his corporation was built on sand. Efforts to 'tidy up' the balance sheet and profit and loss accounts were far too clumsy to avoid discovery. In this situation, Ivar Kreuger chose to take his life in his Paris apartment on 12 March 1932. There have been persistent rumours that Kreuger was actually murdered, but this theory can probably be attributed to the many myths that surrounded him from the 1930s onwards.[30] Whatever the case may be, the repercussions of the Kreuger crash were far-reaching. A number of the banks that had lent money to the Kreuger Group were on the brink of insolvency. Losses totalled no less than SEK828 million,

Figure 6.11 As with other industries that produced for the domestic market, there were great advances in the garment industry. The sewing shop at the Eiser stocking factory in Borås, founded in 1928. Photograph from the 1940s. The Textile Museum, Borås.

of which Skandinaviska Banken was responsible for over SEK410 million. The government had to commit substantial resources to save the banking system from total collapse. The Kreuger Group also had considerable holdings in large Swedish companies. These now had to be sold off at very low prices. The value of these shares fell rapidly and many people saw their fortunes evaporate, not to mention the losses facing those who had borrowed on their shares when they were at a high value.

The Kreuger crash was the great mass media event of the crisis of the early 1930s. But as we have seen, it also had very serious repercussions. The recession also led to a massive fall in export sales. Yet it is clear that the effects of the crisis were far less severe in Sweden than elsewhere. As early as 1933 production and export figures began to rise again and the worst of the unemployment crisis had passed.

Perhaps the main reason why the effects of the crisis were not so severe this time was that the international downswing was not followed by the kind of structural crisis we saw in the 1920s.[31] One possible interpretation is that the crisis had cleared a lot of dead wood from Sweden's industry and it now operated efficiently and without problems. But in some respects this is wishful thinking. Countries that had been hit hard in the 1920s found themselves is serious difficulties once again. Furthermore, some of the efforts to consolidate the engineering sector and other industries continued well into the 1930s. In 1932 there was, for example, a merger of two engineering companies with fine old traditions, Bolinders in Stockholm and Munktells in Eskilstuna. And throughout the 1930s productivity improvements in Sweden continued to be impressive from an international perspective.

Figure 6.12 The Electrolux vacuum-cleaner conquers the world. An advertisement for the Electrolux 'silent' Model XII (1929–), ca. 1930. The Electrolux Archives.

There are two schools of thought on why the Great Depression had a relatively mild effect on Sweden. In one view, Sweden's export industry benefited greatly when the Swedish krona came off the gold standard in 1931. This decision, which was in practice a major devaluation of the Swedish krona, at once gave Sweden's industry a competitive advantage. To understand the second factor we must examine more closely the segment of Swedish industry that actually expanded in the 1930s. First, we are dealing here with traditional export industries like the iron, paper and mechanical engineering sectors. But, second, we have an even higher rate of expansion in large parts of the segment of industry that produced for the domestic market. The garment industry and the building and food sectors were particularly successful, as were industries that produced goods that came under the general heading of consumer durables (household goods, cars, etc.). Despite the difficult years of the 1920s, the domestic market had evidently built up a level of buying power that now made itself felt. This increase in buying power may also have been related to the new patterns of consumption created when the level of activity in the agricultural sector fell sharply in the inter-war years and its workforce moved to industry. Unlike many other Western countries, agriculture was still dominant in Sweden in the 1920s. The resulting large transfer gains also expressed themselves in more purchasing power. Another explanation often emphasised in this context is a demographic one. In the 1930s there was a rapid rise in the number of younger people of working age in Sweden (particularly in the 20–29 age group). This undoubtedly fuelled demand for housing, food, clothing and other consumer goods. At the same time, throughout the whole of the 1930s there was a strong trend towards family-formation.[32]

Neither can we ignore the fact that greater protectionism and the relatively higher degree of isolation that reflected the general European political climate of the 1930s played a part here. As so often in situations like this, there was a great deal of import substitution which may help explain the rapid growth of the Swedish textile industry in the 1930s.

The role of the financial sector

The Stockholm Enskilda Bank, founded in 1856, and the Skandinavisk Kredit AB of 1864 (renamed Skandinaviska Banken in 1938) were Sweden's first modern commercial banks. The Skandinavisk Kredit was also a joint-stock bank along the lines of the French Crédit Mobilier, i.e. its owners had limited liability. As we have seen, the ever-diligent A.O. Wallenberg even had some part in bringing this bank into being. At the end of the 1880s these two institutes acted in some respects as competing central banks that were responsible for arranging credit for the smaller provincial banks that supplied the regions with venture capital. The Stockholm Handelsbank (later Svenska Handelsbanken) was founded in 1871, giving Sweden its third major bank. The Handelsbanken grew rapidly, especially in the troubled 1880s. As early as 1883 its level of lending had reached parity with the Enskilda Bank and Skandinavisk Kredit. After a few lean years following the building sector crash in 1885, the dynamic Louis Frænckel became head of the bank in 1893.

In addition to these three main commercial banks, there were two more important banks in Stockholm in the 1880s: Industrikreditaktiebolaget and Stockholms inteckningsgarantiaktiebolag.[33] As early as 1864 Sweden had forty-four modern-style commercial banks. Their number peaked in the 1910s; the bank statistics for 1913 show a total of seventy-four commercial banks. Towards the end of this decade, there was a powerful process of concentration as many of the smaller commercial banks amalgamated. In 1927 there were only twenty-eight banks left. This did not prevent continued growth of the number of branches from 630 in 1913 to 1,043 in 1927.[34] A number of savings banks were also founded which, however, were of little significance to industry and business during this period. Instead, they served as lending and savings institutes for private individuals, mostly from the middle and working classes.

From the 1860s the commercial banks began to play a more important part in supplying industry with venture capital. In time, they managed to squeeze out the merchant houses, wealthy private capitalists and the private banking companies. The crisis at the end of the 1870s made an important contribution to the dramatic expansion in the role of the commercial banks. During this crisis, several of the old merchant houses and private banking institutes became insolvent, among them the fine old houses of Tottie & Arfwedson, Guillemot & Weyland, with its extensive lending operation, and AB Gothenburgs Handelskompani.[35] As we have seen, the commercial banks also ran into considerable difficulties. Clearly, even more of them, including Enskilda Banken, would have gone under if they had not been shored up by the government. The government evidently chose to support the commercial banks but looked the other way when the merchant houses collapsed. The oft-quoted argument was that it was hard to predict how severe an effect the liquidation of an important commercial bank would have on the banking system as a whole. However, there were other factors under the surface that cannot be ignored, particularly A.O. Wallenberg's good political connections and the view that the commercial banks were more 'modern' than the old private banking firms. At the same time, the percentage of borrowings carried by the public institutions fell, particularly that of the Bank of Sweden and the Manufactory Fund (*Manufakturfonden*) that prior to 1850 had lent substantial sums to ironworks and other industrial businesses, for example. The mortgage banks also became far less important. In 1860, these banks, whose main purpose was to supply the agricultural sector with venture capital, answered for as much as 40 per cent of all funds lent to industry. As we have already seen, they advanced large sums to the industrial centres as well. By 1910 their share of total lending had fallen to 13 per cent.

Both Enskilda Banken and Skandinaviska Kredit (which was always the larger of the two) came to have a stake in the founding of many new industrial businesses from the 1870s onwards. They also played an indirect part in financing the rapid expansion of Sweden's railroad network. The government, it is true, stood for most of the loans, but private interests also invested in railway bonds. Wallenberg's Enskilda Bank's considerable holdings of these high-risk bonds became a heavy burden in the great crisis at the end of the 1870s. Added to this are the other commitments that the Enskilda Bank, in particular, was drawn into. As mentioned above, A.O. Wallenberg was close to some of the top people in politics. When he retired at the beginning of the 1880s (he died in 1886), Knut A. Wallenberg became head of the bank, with his brother Marcus as second-in-command. It was with their help that the 'theatre loan' of 1889 was raised to secure the future of the Stockholm Opera Company. The following year they helped broker a larger loan from foreign bankers to the Swedish government, a process they repeated in 1894. The 1890 government loan in particular was considered to benefit Sweden, and K.A. Wallenberg was duly praised in the Swedish press (*Aftonbladet* and *Post-Tidningen*). The usual procedure at this time was for the government to ask various Swedish consortiums to tender for raising foreign loans. Their good international contacts meant that the business often went to Knut A. and Marcus Wallenberg. However, the 1900 government loan was arranged by their competitor, Fraenckel, to the great annoyance of the Wallenberg brothers.

Finally, we should also mention that the Wallenberg brothers worked with the government to bring order to the complicated relations between the two companies that worked the iron ore deposits in Norrbotten – AB

Figure 6.13 The government becomes a half-owner of the Wallenberg-dominated LKAB in 1909. The Johan mine in Malmberget shortly before the turn of the century. From *Svenska industriella verk och anläggninar 1900.* KB.

Gällivare Malmfält and Luossavaara Kirunavaara AB (LKAB). Before these companies merged in 1903 to form a subsidiary of the Grängesberg Company, the Gällivare Company was controlled by Gustav Emil Broms, the wholesaler and financier, while the Wallenbergs controlled the Kiruna mine through its dynamic manager, Hjalmar Lundbohm. The conflicts between the Wallenbergs and the strong-willed Mr Broms were always vigorous – despite the fact that Broms was partly financed by the Enskilda Bank. The bank had a great deal of capital tied up in the Norrbotten iron ore deposits; at the turn of the century this was the bank's most important single investment. Already in 1890 Knut A. Wallenberg had arranged a loan for the Swedish government to take over the Gällivare-Luleå railway, owned at that time by an English consortium. This same consortium also owned the Gällivare mine before Broms took over. According to Olle Gasslander, K.A.

Wallenberg worked tirelessly to increase the government's involvement in the iron ore deposits of Lapland. There was great concern about what the wilful Broms would do. On more than one occasion he offered the Gällivare mine to foreign speculators. When bankruptcy threatened Broms in 1901, von Otter, the prime minister, suggested, with the approval of the Wallenbergs, that the entire Lapland ore deposits should be offered to the government at a price of SEK22.5 million. The idea was that the government would be the owner, while the mining and sale of ore should be put in private hands. This deal never coalesced. Instead, the Grängesberg company took over as the majority owner in 1903. After many ups and downs – the Grängesberg Company was far from stable and there was much speculation in its shares – the government finally went in as half-owner in 1907. Once again, this was obviously with the approval of the Wallenbergs, who realised they had much to gain from their close association with the political decision-makers.[36]

Throughout this entire period there was keen competition, particularly among the large commercial banks that had nation-wide operations. This competition often drew the banks into very risky projects with very uncertain long-term benefits. We have already seen, for example, how A.O. Wallenberg's involvement in Hofors-Avesta, Atlas and the Stora Bergslags railway almost cost him his bank. This knife-edge competition encouraged the heads of the commercial banks to establish more long-term credit relations between these banks and the industrial enterprises. A typical example was the increase in K.A. Wallenberg's involvement in the Hofors Works company, which was a problem child for the bank in the 1870s and on into the 1880s. Earlier, the bank's directors, as Gasslander observed, had intervened 'only sporadically' in the Hofors company's affairs. But after the death of his father, Knut A. Wallenberg took a position on the board to carry through a root-and-branch reconstruction of the company.[37] The same was true of Atlas, where the less dynamic Eduard Fränckel was replaced as director by Oscar Lamm, a 'well-educated theoretical and practical industrialist', in the words of Olle Gasslander.[38] There could, of course, be several reason for the bank to become involved in the running of a company to which it had lent money. However, the overriding interest was always to ensure that the funds advanced were protected. Particularly in periods of acute crisis this might require an active input from the bank. It was this, for example, that from the beginning of the 1890s motivated K.A. Wallenberg to take an active part in the reconstructions that followed the important Ferna and Korndals bankruptcies. Ferna was an industrial centre in Dalarna and Västmanland that became insolvent in 1891, and Korndal was a paper-mill on the River Mölndal that met the same fate the following year.[39] In the later ASEA crisis of 1900–2, Marcus in particular became involved in an attempt to reconstruct the company and appoint a powerful director. The man chosen was Sigfrid Edström who, with Marcus Wallenberg's backing, became a very successful industrial leader.[40] Gasslander notes:

'Edström's work was largely done in close co-operation with Marcus Wallenberg. He said that in the early years he was in the habit of visiting Marcus Wallenberg once a week, and they also engaged in lively correspondence.'[41]

However, the banks' involvement could also be more proactive. In several cases the commercial banks tried to help create more efficient companies – or reduce the pressure of competition – by actively promoting mergers. For example, since it was founded in 1871, the Handelsbanken had been the main source of credit for several of Stockholm's breweries. As a result of the 1894 retail crisis, the bank, under Frænckels' leadership, compelled the breweries to co-operate better with one another. This included establishing a cartel whose activities included common pricing, discounts and even sales quotas – the so-called guarantee association between Stockholms Bryggeri, Stora Bryggeriet, S:t Eriks Bryggeri and Münchenbryggeriet. As a lender to the sugar industry, around the turn of the century Louis Frænckel made vigorous attempts to prevent the establishment of new sugar refineries.[42]

From this we see that the commercial banks were involved in various ways in the industrial expansion that gained pace from the 1870s onwards. By intervening in crisis situations or taking a more active part in a recon-struction aimed at creating long-term improvements in efficiency and profit levels, the banks contributed to the process of consolidation discussed above. Of course, they were also actively involved in the development of the 'black box industries' that were to become so important. From the middle of the 1890s Stockholm's Enskilda Bank, for example, became one of the principal financiers behind Gustaf de Laval and his expanding separator business. This bank also increased its involvement in ASEA in Västerås towards the end of the 1890s. In 1899 the bank arranged a bond loan of SEK2 million for the company and shortly after approved a new loan of SEK300,000. This was the start of a long alliance between the Wallenbergs and ASEA.[43]

This banking policy continued largely unchanged until the 1930s. Through direct ownership or lending, the commercial banks continued to take an active part in structuring Sweden's industries. They played an important part not least in the reconstruction of the business world after the crisis of the early 1920s. Handelsbanken was one of the banks that was active in the reconstruction of the Munktell company after its crisis in 1892, and in the amalgamation with Bolinders in the early 1930s.

The banks themselves also got into severe difficulties during the 1920s. This was not so surprising in light of their heavy exposure in industry. Many of the large commercial banks, Skandinaviska Banken and Svenska Handelsbanken, in particular, suffered severe losses on their loans. The banks' large loans to industrial businesses, pushed up by inflation, now became worthless. As with the earlier demise of the ironworks and sawmills, there was widespread talk in the 1920s of a collapse of the banking system. As we have seen, many banks merged in this decade and by its end Sweden's commercial banking sector was perhaps more concentrated than in any other country.[44] Ultimately, the reason why depositors did not suffer more severe losses from the bank crisis was that the government refused to allow any of the major banks to become insolvent. In addition to the government, the larger commercial banks also helped save these organisations. Sydsvenska Banken, for example, was saved in 1922 when a special institute, AB Kreditkassan, was formed jointly by the Bank of Sweden and some of the larger commercial banks to take over the largest lending losses.[45]

From the end of the 1800s the banks' growing portfolios of industrial shares had been placed in special 'investment' or 'holding' companies. One example was AB Providentia, an investment company closely linked to the Wallenbergs, which was founded in 1899. The main reason for establishing this company was that under Swedish law, banks were barred from owning shares or 'dealing in real and moveable estate'. These were rules to protect depositors. Banks could not use the depositors' savings for risky speculation in shares.[46] This legislation was relaxed in 1912, when banks were allowed industrial shareholdings. But there were still numerous restrictions, and the investment companies continued to be active. In 1916 the Wallenbergs even took the trouble to set up a new company, Investor, for share dealings. Following the crisis of the early 1920s, further restrictions were introduced. At least on the surface, the total ban on banks owning shares that came into force in 1934 appears to have dealt a fatal blow to this activity. All shareholdings had to be disposed of by 1938. However, paradoxically, the 1934 Act by no means severed the ownership relations between commercial banks and industries. Instead, the management of shareholdings was transferred to investment companies such as the Wallenbergs' Investor, and Providentia. In the same way, the Skandinaviska Banken's share portfolio was managed by Custos, and Svenska Handelsbanken's by Industrivärden.

Figure 6.14 The Alfa Colibri hand separator. From *Svenska industriella verk och anläggninar 1896*, in the article on 'the world-wide success of the separator'.

Following the crisis at the beginning of the 1930s, the investment companies consolidated and concentrated their holdings. Investor, for example, offered to dispose of its insurance company shares in order to increase its industrial holdings.[47] The ownership relations between the different commercial banks that would leave their mark on Sweden's business world from 1945 onwards assumed its final form in the inter-war years.

7 Organised capitalism

The new capitalist industrial society that emerged at the end of the nineteenth century did not exist in a political and social vacuum. As the economy became based more on industrial work done by men and women in the towns and urban areas, changes had to be made to the society in which they lived. Dismantling the traditional family and community social safety net generated the need for a new order which would secure social reproduction. In the view published by Gustav K. Hamilton and others in 1865, the 'era of large enterprises, the division of labour, the introduction of machinery and the advent of a monetary economy weakened family ties, fomented mistrust between master and worker and caused widespread pauperism'.[1] New demands on central and local government were formulated by various special-interest groups that organised themselves to address the strains (and possibilities) associated with industrial change. Workers combined in trade unions and companies affiliated to employers' associations, not only to protect their interests against others in the labour market but also to demand support for 'the public interest'. Other groups made similar demands on 'society'. As Karl Polyani puts it in his work *The Great Transition* (1944), these 'counter-forces' are as old as the modern capitalist industrial society itself. Radical changes in the economy give rise to new institutional arrangements. Together, these forces are a clear incentive structure, which in turn form the basis for various 'new interests'.

In many ways the nineteenth century was a century of paradox. Its ideological writings and keynote speeches pay tribute to the individual in opposition to government and corporations. According to the doctrine of the economics of harmony of the mid-nineteenth century, the non-interventionist 'night-watchman' government was the highest ideal. But, as we have seen, this did not prevent the government playing an important part in industrial expansion in, for example, Sweden. The same paradox applies to individualism. Notwithstanding all the talk of the freedom of the individual, 'association' was perhaps the most powerful idea of the later nineteenth century.[2] In 1844 Gustaf Geijer and others saw the associations as the new society's 'advance guard of helpers' that would replace corporations such as the guilds that had hitherto been supported by the government.[3] In the words of Torkel Jansson, the swift advance of new, productive forces such as the 're-regulation' of government activities discussed above, created an 'explosive void' which had to be filled. Here is where the formation of free associations was needed: the workers' associations, the health insurance system, the consumer co-operatives, the adult education movement, the Rifle Owners' Association, the Scandinavian Association, and the religious and temperance societies. To some extent the reform of 1862 also meant that, unlike central government, the local authorities became voluntary associations of a kind.[4] The most important of the various associations that came into being in the nineteenth century was undoubtedly the joint-stock company. In practice, then, far from promoting individualism, the emphasis at this time was on the importance of voluntary association. Far more could be achieved by collective action than by an individual on his own.

At the beginning of this century Rudolf Hilferding, the Austrian Marxist economist, introduced the term 'organised capitalism'. He wanted to emphasise the differences between the free-trade-based laissez-faire brand of capitalism that was dominant until the 1880s and the more monopolistic capitalism that succeeded it. In Hilferding's view, the government came to have a superior and co-ordinating function in this new capitalist state. Since the days of Hilferding the term 'organised capitalism' has been defined and used in a number of different ways. A common definition is that introduced by Rolf Torstendahl as an 'in principle, liberal economy combined with a growing sphere of mutual interest to industry and government. The result is liberal-democratic interventionism organised by government bureaucracy.'[5] In the case of Sweden, it is often maintained that the question of tariffs in the 1880s drew a demarcation line between the restrictive and the interventionist state. According to Svenbjörn Kilander, this transition went hand in hand with a clear ideological shift. Before that time, there had been a theoretical line drawn between the private and public spheres. During the golden years of liberalism, the government was thought to be virtually incapable of action in the private sphere. But the tone of the debate changed.[6]

However, the question is whether it is possible to draw a clear line between two such 'stages'. We have already shown that at the peak of the liberal era, from the 1850s onwards, the government often intervened directly in business, for example during the financial crises of 1857 and 1877. We have also shown how people like Gripenstedt or Wallenberg deliberately attempted to devise institutional arrangements intended to favour the 'modern' forces at the expense of the old. Against this background it would seem that the term 'organised capitalism' (at least if compared with the earlier competitive capitalism, which was free from government involvement) is hardly an appropriate one. It may be true that before the 1880s greater care was taken to emphasise the differences between public and private; the government, for example, was not allowed to intervene to assist one sector in preference to another. But in practice that is precisely what happened. It is significant that government interventions in this period were always motivated by being 'in the public interest'. There could be intervention in the 'private sphere' if an unsatisfactory state of affairs could have seriously adverse effects on the 'public interest'. What the limits of 'public' or 'social' interests were varied a great deal from one case to the next. Most actions could be justified in this way, including the assistance given to the Wallenbergs' modern commercial banks at the end of the 1870s, while no help was available for the private banking interests that had gone into liquidation.

In an analogy to what we have already said, we may even say that 'capitalism' had always been organised. Capitalists have always tried to exploit the government and other 'public' bodies for their own purposes. They have always aimed to organise production, markets and forms of exchange in order to maximise profit. This requires appropriate institutions, laws and frameworks. As Göran B. Nilsson said, this was the very essence of the Gripenstedt system, in which capitalists like A.O. Wallenberg played a central part. But this very process of organisation also creates 'counter-forces' which will in time change the conditions for the actions of both capitalists and other actors in the market.

Changes in the roles of central and local government

The promotion of the status of the individual in the nineteenth century did not prevent the spread of 'association' and collective action, perhaps more than ever before. The simultaneous spread of a liberal doctrine of economic harmony did not prevent the role of the government and other public bodies becoming more important in practice. Increasingly, the state and 'society' were expected to create conditions that would encourage the growth of the new industrial society and, not least, solve the social problems that appear to accompany industrialism.

This dual view of the interventionist role of the state is particularly evident in the debate on the railroads. We have seen how a system of government-owned main lines and private branch lines came into being in the 1850s. Yet at the end of the 1880s the political debate and government committees repeatedly emphasised that government- or municipal-owned industries were perdition. According to the Economic Committee of 1886, 'the operation of industries on behalf of the government or direct action in their management, control or development' was unthinkable.[7] The only really major departure from this principle was when the government increased its holdings of LKAB stock to 50 per cent in 1907.

Despite the widespread criticism of the government's dominance of the railroads, the system was still defended by the most orthodox of liberals. Around 1870, however, Emil Key, the Agrarian Party's most prominent ideologist, mounted a vigorous campaign to stop the expansion of the government mainline network 'because it would be too expensive if the government both built and used the lines'. Another argument was that the authorities were not fully independent, but could fall under the influence of various 'private interests'. But Key and the other 'nihilists', so named because they wanted to reduce government influence, met with opposition from a number of well-known liberals such as the government ministers Hans Forsell and F.F. Carlsson, or S.A. Hedlund, editor-in-chief of the GHT, who felt that the main lines were more in the nature of a 'public welfare enterprise'. As such, they were intended, as had already been explained by Gripenstedt in 1857, to promote the expansion of all sectors. Thus the state railroads could be compared with the newly established telegraph company.[8] Hedlund, for example, said in 1881 that railroads in private hands could be very expensive for many of the country's provinces. If the government did not accept its responsibility, the alternative for the sparsely populated areas was either heavy municipal taxation or no railroad at all.[9] In economic terms, railroad construction benefited the whole country. It could even be justified by military–political considerations. In this case, the 'public good' justified this intrusion into the private sphere. That this could also be seen as the government's inability to stop meddling is evidenced by the bitter protests that came from various constellations of private interests that at the end of the 1860s considered forming large private companies to build the railroads.

Otherwise, the 'public good' was often cited as justification for different kinds of institutional reforms and changes. We have already discussed several of these initiatives which, from the mid-nineteenth century, put their stamp on developments. According to Torbjörn Nilsson, the conservative and national-liberal factions in the Riksdag's upper chamber were foremost among those behind the policy of institutional modernisation that was pursued to the benefit of industry. Nilsson shows how the upper chamber backed a number of initiatives of this kind. Its willingness to intervene in the private sphere may be seen not only as an expression of conservative, right-wing government officials' 'anti-capitalism'. On the contrary, there were many good liberals in the upper chamber and the atmosphere was often strongly pro-business. To give an example, an important initiative was taken in the question of forestry, where a restrictive felling policy was introduced in 1882 against the wishes of the ironworks owners, but coinciding at least in part with the wishes of the sawmill owners. It was intended to prevent the mismanagement and over-exploitation of the forests. The same limitation on ownership rights for the general good were claimed in the controversial issue of water policy. The men of the sawmill industries were among those in favour of improving waterways for log flotage and similar measures. Under Swedish law, the landowner has the water rights. An 1880 ordinance placed severe limits on the water rights of private landowners. In the matter of forest policy, most liberal forces were ranged against limiting felling rights. Yet when it came to limits on water rights there was silence from that quarter. The principle of ownership rights was clearly not worth defending in all circumstances, or by all 'interests'.

The demands for modernisation and institutional reform were reflected not least in the debate that began in the 1860s on the existence of the Board of Commerce. Many of its critics felt that this old government office had outlived its usefulness and should be replaced by a number of different government bodies – for agriculture, trade, industry and shipping. The idea was that the business world no longer had to be regulated in detail, and government agencies empowered to grant permits of the kind that the old, traditional Board of Commerce had, were no longer required. Instead, new agencies should be set up to assist in the development of different sectors through education and training, improving the complex of regulations, etc. Axel Bennich, Director-General of the Swedish Customs Board, who was generally regarded as a reliable liberal, said that the manufacture and transport of explosives, safety at sea, emigration and employer–worker relations required both legislation and the supervision of a government agency. He maintained, purely as a matter of principle, that:

> as a country develops, new matters arise that require examination. Freedom of trade requires new regulations if we are to avoid having this freedom extend to a point where it encroaches upon the liberty of others, and thus becoming a threat to the welfare of others.[10]

In one area after another, initiatives were introduced to improve general conditions for the business world, not infrequently by placing restraints on the rights of ownership and disposal. The main effect of the new legislation on patents and trade marks introduced in 1884, and the establishment of a new government agency, the National Patent and Registration Office, shortly after, was to strengthen entrepreneurs' rights of ownership to their own innovations. Put simply, modern legislation was introduced that gave protection against 'unfair competition'. On the other hand, this legislation was a direct intervention in the individual trader's right to freely carry on economic activities – patent rights were, after all, a kind of 'monopoly' for a given period of time.

The complex of regulations that governed the credit system had also developed since the reforms of the 1860s. In time, the power of the credit banks to acquire bonds was extended to include shares as well. But in this area legislation came later – the Act did not come into effect until 1906. After a debate lasting several decades, the private commercial banks' right to issue notes was withdrawn in 1897, effective from 1903. From this time onwards the Bank of Sweden would have a monopoly on issuing banknotes, which it was hoped would give better control of monetary flows. Further, a government agency, the Bank Inspectorate, had been set up, headed by the assiduous Robert Benckert, to keep a close watch on the commercial banks.

> According to its remit, the principal task of the Bank Inspectorate is to ensure that current regulations and the banks' articles of association are duly observed. This includes ensuring that the information and documentation issued by the bank to be published by the Bank Inspectorate

Figure 7.1 The Royal Institute of Technology in Stockholm, built in 1864. Architect: F.W. Scholander. *Ny illustrerad tidning* 1877. KB.

– monthly statements and annual reviews – are properly drawn up. It is foremost on these documents that the general public bases its judgement of the banks; if the documentation is incorrect, the public will be misled.[11]

There was, of course, also the expansion of the main railway lines, investments in telegraphy and telephones, improvements to the postal service, etc. The investments in improving primary and secondary education certainly played an important part as well, as did the founding of new technical teaching institutes, the most important being the Institute of Technology in Stockholm. Here, however, the part played by the vocational technical colleges was at least as important. In 1900, a total of forty-one vocational colleges offering engineering training had been founded.[12]

Most of these investments and reforms were carried through without serious controversy. There was, however, heated debate on the undertakings of central government and other public bodies when it came to what was known at the time as 'the social question'. In the 1880s the debate on social policy focused largely on the state's responsibility for the welfare of its citizens. Once again, government intervention in the 'private sphere' was justified by 'private' problems that could have 'public' repercussions. One of the best-known social reformers at the turn of the century, G. H. von Koch, emphasised that the purpose of social work was to remedy 'harmful shortcomings and unsatisfactory conditions that damage the social body'.[13] Gustav Cassel stated in his influential publication, *Socialpolitik* (1902), that social reform was essential to economic growth. In the first place, the social reformers were against a labour market wholly governed by free competition.

Figure 7.2 Adolf Hedin, the socialist journalist and author (1834–1905), who was active in the cause of political and social reform in the Riksdag. KB.

'City liberals' such as Adolf Hedin, S.A. Hedlund and Fridtjuv Berg advocated workers' health and safety and social legislation, clearly inspired by the complex of laws recently introduced in Germany. In the famous Bill he put before Parliament in 1884, Hedin branded this 'Manchester liberalism' as a 'false and immoral' doctrine. In his view, if one expected 'the working people to maintain in solidarity the existing body politic', then social reform was essential. His Bill resulted in the appointment of the 1884 Workers' Insurance Committee which led in turn to the 1889 Workers' Safety Act and the foundation of the Labour Inspectorate, as well as the 1891 National Health Insurance Act, under which the government funded the private sickness benefit schemes run by various associations. As stated above, in the same period protective legislation was introduced on female and child labour, and in 1913 the National Basic Pension Act, which laid the foundations of a modern pension system, came into force.

The issue of workers' insurance and workers' protection had originally been put on the agenda by liberals with a strong social commitment. There were many Conservatives who agreed with this line. The internationally renowned journalist Rudolf Kjellén, for example, well known for his geopolitical ideas, which were very well-received in Germany, maintained that the purpose of social policy was to eliminate the 'dark shadows of industrialism'.[14] But the Social Democrats increased their representation in Parliament, particularly after the voting rights reform in 1909, which gave the right to vote to far more working people and brought renewed vigour to reformist endeavours. The line that met with the greatest approval in the Social Democratic Party (SAP) was the demand for general reforms that would benefit all working people. This collectivist line was set against the orientation towards self-help and moral regeneration pursued foremost by non-socialist reformists. An important part of the debate on the social question was carried on in the Central Organisation for Social Work (formed in 1901) in which both lines were represented. The demand for better social security against unemployment and ill-health was thus an important 'counter-force' organised to remedy the most serious drawbacks associated with the modern capitalist industrial society.

Organised interests

Thus the industrial transformation also led to the emergence of organised interest groups. The most evident reaction to the new demands industrialism made of society was the emergence of labour market organisations with the main, but not sole, task of representing the interests of workers and employers. The growing working class soon organised into trade unions. The printers' union that was formed in 1846 was often referred to as Sweden's first trade union. However, it was 'not more than a copy of the apprentice associations that existed at the time of the guilds'.[15] It was not until the 1880s that modern-style trade unions really came into being. Behind the trade unions' Central Committee, formed in 1883, were the newly established trade unions for woodworkers, tailors, shoemakers and sheet-metal workers. It was not primarily the workers in the main export industries that spearheaded the formation of trade unions, it was rather the sought-after skilled workers in the craft industries that did so.

The prime purpose of the unions was to control the conditions under which labour was sold by reducing competition for labour. The unions should therefore be seen as a form of open cartel, i.e. their membership was unrestricted but they required 'solidarity' of their members.[16] Unlike open cartels, closed cartels do not offer free and voluntary membership, and they attempt to impose a strict division on the market. Of course, there have also been tendencies towards closed cartels in the history of the trade union movement, when egoistic, trade-centred unions with high membership standards attempted to control the allocation of labour. In the early twentieth century the Swedish Metal Trades Employers' Association (*Verkstadsföreningen*) accused several trade unions in the engineering sector of attempting to set up a compulsory employment exchange. Only unionised metalworkers could be given work, and they could only access the workplace through the trade union, it was said. The purpose was to boycott undesirable employers. But despite all the accusations, these arrangements only applied in exceptional cases. The open cartel was the norm. At an early stage, the need was identified to 'combine the practitioners of the different crafts to form a really strong labour party which will work for the implementation of the reforms that are essential for sensible social development' (according to the Trade Union Central Committee of 1883). Through the 1880s and 1890s the separate trade unions gradually amalgamated to form larger unions.

Until the Swedish Trades Union Congress (LO) was formed in 1898 the Social Democratic Labour Party (SAP) acted as the trade union movement's central organisation. The national leadership in the SAP and the LO strove to reduce trade egoism, particularly in the local and central craft unions. At the beginning of the twentieth century the so-called industrial union principle began to be widely accepted. Here, it was the large Metalworkers' Union, headed by Ernst Blomberg, that was the driving force. In time, this new principle of organisation led to all workers at a single workplace, i.e. workers with a trade skill, their assistants, smiths, carpenters and others, joining the same union. This principle was implemented in the face of considerable difficulties and local resistance. The decisive factor was the high degree of centralisation in the trade union movement. But the industrial union principle also reflected the fact that, as time passed, new groups of workers had gained influence in the trade union movement as a whole – the workers in modern large-scale industries.

In a similar way, the employers also organised their particular interest groups. However, the employers formed direct organisations rather later than the workers: the Swedish Metal Trades Employers' Association and the Swedish Central Employers' Confederation, for example, were founded in 1902. Further, the Central Employers' Association was formed in 1903, which initially organised mainly smaller companies in the building sector. Generally speaking, the centralised structure of the employers' organisations took shape somewhat later than in the trade union movement. Not until the Swedish Metal Trades Employers' Association affiliated to the Swedish Employers' Confederation in 1917 and the Central Employers' Association in 1919 did this organisation become the counterpart of the labour unions' LO. These organisations also preferred to act as open cartels. Their purpose was to attempt to set a common price for labour. Sometimes, however, they went further and tried to divide up the labour market among themselves; no employer was to compete for labour with other employers in a given area. However there were accusations from the workers that 'undesirable' employees were being blacklisted and local employment monopolies were being maintained. But these methods were not very common. 'Organised capitalism' evidently had its limits.

Although the emergence of special organisations for workers and employers was the salient expression of the organisation of interests that occurred from the end of the nineteenth century, these were far from the only attempts at organisation. A clear example of the way interests organised is the 'Norrland-sopinion' movement of the 1890s, whose main purpose was to counter the large forest companies' purchase of agricultural land. In a motion to the lower chamber in 1892, seven members of parliament from the Kopparberg and Gävleborg counties warned of a 'real danger threatening our country'. The threat to the existence of the land-owning farming population called for resolute government action. The question was tossed back and forth until 1906, when legislation banning the large-scale purchase of forest holdings

Figure 7.3 The Stockholm Phosphate Workers' Union gathered for a photograph, 1891. KB.

came into effect. The driving force behind this resistance to the forestry companies was a group of left-wing Liberals led by Carl Lindhagen. Through their work in the Norrland Committee (formed in 1901) these Liberals came to define the 'Norrland issue' as a separate special interest. However, this matter extended beyond the interests of the small farmers of Norrland. By generating a veritable storm of opinion, the Committee managed to win the support of many different forces that were opposed to large-scale industry and that wanted to improve the conditions of ordinary people in the craft and small-scale industries. Although its ideological expression was derided as 'incipient agrarian romanticism',[17] this did not prevent the Committee from capturing and giving voice to a special interest that was, for many years to come, a well-articulated response to the rapid pace of industrial change.

When it comes to the emergence of different groupings of special interests as a reaction to the demands of the industrial society, it is almost as important to emphasise the significance of the role they played in future developments. With the spread of democracy, various organised interests helped shape the laws and complexes of regulations that surrounded the 'free' activities of the business world. The more concealed and informal institutional arrangements were also affected. Some new standards were developed as to what was right, reasonable and just. Perhaps the most important development was that a number of 'interests', such as the organised workers' demands for a better standard of living, or the 'Norrlands opinion' demanding the retention of a particular way of life, were recognised as legitimate. Through the political process, such recognised, legitimate demands became a part of the institutionalised structure of society.

This was also true of the restrictions in the labour market. Here, setting up centralised trade unions and employers' organisations gradually led to the recognition of the legitimate interests of both sides. The employers recognised the employees' right to an 'equitable' share of the results of production, while the workers recognised the employers' right to 'direct and allocate work', as it was worded in the oft-quoted Clause 32 (originally Clause 23) of the Saltsjöbaden agreement. How 'equitable' was to be defined in this respect was of course the subject of much debate. But the recognition of legitimate interests was an important advance. This process actually laid the foundations of what was known as 'the Swedish Model' from the 1930s onwards (see also Chapter 9).

The public sector

As a whole, public sector expenditure as a percentage of Sweden's GNP grew steadily throughout the entire period from the mid-nineteenth century to the Second World War, as was generally the case in all other Western countries. Although some periods of unusual increase may be identified, they were usually periods of severe crisis and war, and there is no doubt that this is at least in part related to the fact that public sector spending often increases at such times. At the same time, the increase of the early 1920s may be explained mainly by the rapid fall in GNP caused by the acute economic crisis. Because public sector undertakings and expenditure are often difficult to change, at least in the short term, their percentage rises automatically in periods of crisis.

There was a fairly even rise in the number of county and local government employees, except in the years of crisis, public sector commitments and ambitions have tended to expand, ever since the birth of industrialism. Further, at least for a large part of this period they have grown faster than the average growth rate of the economy. This means that we have taken out an ever-increasing part of consumption in the form of public services. But the really large rise was not until after the period we are dealing with in this chapter, i.e. not until after 1945. In the inter-war years, the relative importance of the public sector to the economy was still fairly modest in terms of GNP, and particularly as a percentage of the total number of people in work.

Traditional expenditure items such as defence and the judicial system were major items in government budgets until 1900. But as we have already seen, government undertakings increased sharply in other areas in the second half of the nineteenth century. Over time, public investments in infrastructure, for example in the government-owned main railroad network and the telegraph service, became an ever-heavier burden. Interest on repayments of expensive foreign loans for railroad construction was also a growing burden on budgets. To this was added the more ambitious goals in education and, from the turn of the century, albeit on a modest scale at first, investments in expanding the social services. The cost of healthcare also rose. However, these items were covered by the municipal and county taxes levied on the population. And even if municipal and county government expenditure was very low, there was pronounced growth during this period.

All this means that incomes have to rise. As we have seen, a large part of the investments in infrastructure and railroads were financed by government loans. But taxes had to rise as well. Until the mid-nineteenth century the Swedish tax system had a traditional structure. A high percentage of tax income came from freehold farmers in the form of land taxes, and only a small part of tax revenues came from taxes on consumption or from charges or excise duties. There was no income tax, either progressive or proportional. There was also much conflict over the reform of this outdated tax system. The Agrarian Party, in particular, fought in the lower chamber for tax cuts and the abolition of the old land taxes, many of which dated back to the Middle Ages. The final repeal of these taxes in 1903 was, of course, an important historical milestone.

As time passed, the lifting of land taxes meant that a higher percentage of tax revenues had to be obtained from indirect taxes. These are usually levied as consumption taxes and excise duties, while direct taxes are defined as levies on income and wealth. In 1900, only 15 per cent of total government tax revenue was from indirect taxes, and these were mainly tariffs, taxes on alcoholic beverages, sugar and so on.[18] Being heavily dependent on indirect taxes was, however, generally regarded as a problem and a sign of weakness. There was therefore an intensive debate on the future structure of the tax system shortly before the turn of the century.

The basic principle of the tax system that began to take shape at this time was that public expenditure should be financed from a tax on incomes. There had been experiments with a regular income tax system, for example in 1713 and again in 1810. But they were introduced for a special purpose (war!) and were withdrawn when times were better. After a long debate, a permanent government tax on incomes was introduced in 1902. Unlike the tax of 1810, for example, this was to be a progressive tax system, i.e. with the percentage of tax levied rising with income. However, the tax rates were initially fairly low. A ceiling of 4 per cent was set for the progressive rate.[19] But this ceiling was raised as early as 1910, and at the same time a wealth tax was introduced which was extended in 1914 to include inheritance and gifts. But taxes on wealth, real estate and companies continued to be of fairly little significance. In the 1920s as much as 15 per cent of total municipal revenues came from corporate tax. From 1910 to 1913 corporate tax was progressive, and based on the relationship between profit and shareholders' equity, the so-called income percentage. From the time of the great tax reform of 1938, corporate tax was levied as a percentage of profit.[20]

Although this meant a marked rise in the proportion of revenues that came from direct taxation, indirect taxes continued to play an important part. Their share of total tax revenues was actually higher than that of direct

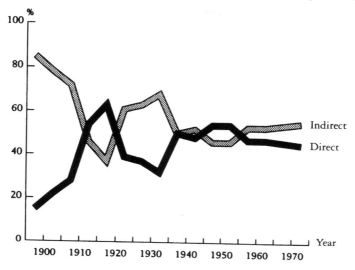

Figure 7.4 Direct and indirect government taxation, 1900–1975. Per cent.

tax for almost the whole period up to 1945. At the same time, the government agencies were, as always, interested in finding new objects for taxation. In 1914, for example, a special tobacco tax was introduced, and a vehicle tax in 1922. In the years between the wars, such consumption taxes provided between 20 and 30 per cent of total government tax revenues.

To this was added the largely proportional, i.e. non-progressive, municipal taxes that represented between 35 and 45 per cent of all government revenues.[21] There were large increases in these taxes, particularly between the wars, reflecting the higher ambitions of local government, particularly in the social services and the health service. In 1938 the average tax rate was

Table 7.1 Total taxation as percentage of national product in selected countries in the twentieth century. The years 1925 and 1933 as a percentage of national income

Country	1925	1933	1950	1960	1975
Sweden	16.0	18.9	21.0	28.7	46.6
Norway	20.9	25.1	–	32.0	44.7
Denmark	19.6	20.1	19.8	25.3	43.0
Finland	21.6	20.1	27.8	17.5	37.5
Holland	14.9	18.6	30.3	30.4	46.9
Germany	17.8	23.0	30.1	33.9	35.2
France	21.1	26.3	30.2	33.4	36.9
Italy	17.5	30.6	–	27.0	32.3
Great Britain	22.6	25.2	33.1	27.3	36.7
USA	11.0	23.4	23.9	27.5	30.3

Source: E. Rodriguez, *Offentlig inkomstexpansion*, Lund 1980, p. 25.

9.2 per cent of rateable income.[22] Compared with other countries, Swedish taxes were not high at this time. In 1925 'only' 16 per cent of national income was from taxes, a figure that reached 19 per cent in 1933. This was a lower level than in most other comparable countries. But taxes went up across the board in the 1930s. As mentioned above, this was true of both municipal taxes and taxes on consumption. The tax reform of 1938 also made the graduated scales of both income and wealth taxes steeper. This reform, which according to one observer 'intended to bring into the regular tax system the increases of the 1930s', in fact formed the starting point for Sweden's transformation into the high taxation country it would become after the Second World War.[23]

Economic (monetary) policy

An important part of what we today call economic policy is made up of an arsenal of counter-cyclical measures and a monetary and exchange-rate policy that benefits the country. After the 1930s, budget policy – or fiscal policy – was one method used to achieve at least the first of these goals. Both the British economist John Maynard Keynes and the Swedish Stockholm School advocated an increase in public spending in crisis years and spending cuts in good years which, it was thought, would 'tame' the business cycle. Before this period, economic policy was limited to an interest and monetary policy aimed at achieving stability.

Before 1900, however, it was in practice hardly possible for any country, least of all Sweden, to implement an effective policy of this kind. The first requirement is that the government actually has a chance to pursue an active interest and monetary policy. An independent central bank is an essential prerequisite. In Sweden it was only towards the end of the nineteenth century that the old *Ständernas bank* (from 1866 the Bank of Sweden) began to take on this role. It had formerly acted mainly as the government's commercial bank, and as a provider of loans to the general public. In this latter role it had to compete with the private banks. However, the Bank of Sweden's lending operations were heavily subsidised. Loans to both industry and agriculture could be arranged against security, and mortgages were charged at 2–3 per cent interest. Neither did this bank have a monopoly on issuing banknotes. As mentioned above, this monopoly was not granted until 1903. This meant, for example, that it was impossible to curb inflation or improve the exchange rate by limiting the money supply (see, however, the above description of the 'great reductions in the money supply'). Further, it was hardly possible to bring any direct influence to bear on the interest rates set by the commercial banks. Yet even in the 1870s, when the commercial banks ran into liquidity problems, they turned to the Bank of Sweden to borrow against treasury bonds. But not until some decades later did the Bank of Sweden seriously begin to rediscount bills of exchange for the private banks. It also took a long time after 1864 – when interest-rate

Figure 7.5 Knut Wicksell
(1851–1926). KB.

Figure 7.6 Gustav Cassel
(1866–1945). KB.

restrictions were lifted – before the Bank of Sweden became the body that set interest rates. True, from the 1870s the larger commercial banks began to consider the Bank of Sweden's discount rate when they set their own interest rates, but there was no clear breakthrough until 1890 when it was shown in practice that in an emergency it was possible to stop the outflow of currency by raising the discount rate from 4 to 6 per cent.[24]

Until the First World War Sweden was linked to the international monetary system that had been built up in the mid-nineteenth century: the common gold standard. Under this system the rates of exchange between different countries' currencies were regulated by the outflow and inflow of gold. If, for example, a country's foreign trade slumped and there was a deficit in the balance of payments, this was expressed in a lower exchange rate, an outflow of gold and falling domestic prices (deflation). At the next stage, the fall in prices would cause foreign demand to pick up, export sales to grow and the balance of payments to improve. In the same way, it was assumed that deflation would make foreign goods relatively more expensive, improving the balance of payments as imports dwindled. It was expected that this system of equilibrium would partly replace the need for a national exchange-rate policy. Before this time, such situations had called for drastic action – raising the excise duties or quite simply banning the export of money. It is generally accepted that the gold standard worked fairly well until the beginning of the twentieth century. The system was, however, very cumbersome in times of crisis. Rapid fluctuations in the business cycle were strong encouragement for many governments to influence the economy by pursuing an independent monetary policy.

Thus a series of measures gradually gave the Bank of Sweden wider possibilities to pursue a more proactive interest and currency policy. But this does not mean that the bank automatically took advantage of these possibilities, and this attracted criticism from the economists. In the crisis of 1908, Gustav Cassel accused the Bank of Sweden of passiveness and incompetence. The bank had not taken the opportunity to cut the interest rate, said Cassel. Without doubt, at that time the Bank of Sweden's board of directors was remarkably cautious and conservative. It quite simply did not dare intervene to influence the discount rate, for example to control the business cycle. According to the critics, Cassel included, this was essentially because the Bank of Sweden had fallen victim to its divided loyalties. As the government bank it was keen to keep interest rates down, while as a central bank responsible for economic stability it may have needed to raise them!

To the extent that the head of the Bank of Sweden had any clearly stated economic policy view, it coincided fairly well with both public opinion and the preachings of the academic economists. In Sweden, leading economists such as Knut Wicksell and Gustav Cassel advocated a low interest rate and price stability. According to the prevailing doctrine, much of which was formulated by Wicksell, there was a direct link between price stability, a low interest rate and a generally well-balanced economy. Balance was achieved when there was parity between interest and the yield on capital investments. If the monetary interest rate was higher than the real interest rate, investments would fall, as would wages and prices. If the opposite obtained, there would be a spiral of rising wages and prices as wages rose more sharply. In general, the ability of free-market forces were relied on to ensure that economic balance was maintained. Gustav Cassel said that it would be for the general good to keep the interest rate around 3 per cent, which was the 'normal' long-term yield on capital.[25]

However, the First World War would deal a blow to both the international monetary system, of which Sweden was a part, and to what was in essence a harmonic view that had dominated up to that time. Severe inflation, particularly towards the end of the war, gave rise to demands for a return to price stability. In Sweden, Eli Heckscher and others spoke of the 'capitalist bolshevism' that the inflationary economic situation had led to, i.e. that savers had seen their money confiscated by people who lived beyond their means. One way to achieve price stability was to return to the gold standard. And that was the policy recommended by the majority of the financial experts in a government report published in 1920 and backed by most of the heavyweight economists (but not Cassel). Accordingly, a policy was introduced that aimed to appreciate the value of the Swedish krona and force down prices and wages. By 1924 this policy had managed to write up the value of the krona against the gold standard to the level it was at in 1914. Then on 1 April 1924 a formal decision was taken to return to the gold standard. Events since 1920, including the gradual appreciation of the krona, were part of a gradual transition from an inflationary to a deflationary economy. Without doubt, this write-up of the krona strongly accentuated the downswing of 1921–2. All the actors who had expected prices to continue to rise now faced a radically different situation.

Another way to bring down inflation was to raise the discount rate. When inflation rocketed in 1919, prominent economists like Wicksell and Cassel attacked the Bank of Sweden for keeping the discount rate far too low, which in their view would simply accelerate the rate of inflation. When the Bank of Sweden persisted in its low-interest-rate policy, Eli Heckscher carried out his famous coup. In a newspaper article he called on the general public to redeem their Bank of Sweden banknotes for gold coin; the old right of redemption was still in force. There was a rush for gold coin, a rise in the discount rate (from 6 to 7 per cent) and the right to redeem banknotes for gold was withdrawn.

At the beginning of the 1920s there was a gradual return to the gold standard at the international level as well. By 1926 it had been introduced in almost all industrial countries. As in Sweden, the return to the gold standard led to rapid deflation in many countries, not least Britain where its return caused a very strong appreciation of the pound. However, in many quarters the return to the gold standard was seen as a necessity in light of the high rate of inflation during the war years, the post-war depression and hyper-inflation in Germany. The intention was also that this would reinstate the international equilibrium system which, in spite of everything, had worked well up to 1914. But despite a number of international agreements and conferences, in which Cassel and others were active as monetary experts, efforts to return to the old system failed. It was, in particular, what Erik Lundberg calls *the characteristic of symmetry* that was missing in the new system. Gold was not allowed to flow freely between countries to redress any imbalances. Countries with overvalued currencies, such as Britain, were forced to pursue a very restrictive discount policy to stop all their gold flowing out of the country. But according to Lundberg this had 'no equivalent in the countries that, due to a balance of payments surplus and an influx of gold, could and should pursue a more expansive policy'.[26] Instead, gold gathered in the treasuries of countries with a substantial balance of payments surplus, primarily the USA and France. Other countries suffered from a serious gold shortage. The ultimate reason for this asymmetry was undoubtedly the suspicion between countries that persisted after the war. Protectionism was also growing, as was economic nationalism, which was a strong feature of American policies in the 1920s. Nationalistic policy was at great variance with the 'old' rules of the gold standard. In practice, this trend meant that each country followed its own separate policy on the discount rate in the 1920s. The politicians had a very simple formula: interest rates should be put up in times of high economic activity and down in periods of recession. In Sweden, the discount rate was high at the beginning of the 1920s (7.5 per cent in 1921) but stabilised around 4.5 per cent from 1922.[27] In 1927 it was as low as 3.5 per cent. After the Wall Street Crash is rose by a few percentage points, but then fell back to the 3–4 per cent level for the rest of the 1930s.[28] In the 1920s and throughout the whole of the period in which the gold standard was maintained, the discount rate was regulated by the amount of money in the Bank of Sweden's banknote reserve. The issuing of banknotes was, in its turn, tied to the Bank of Sweden's gold reserves.[29]

The effects of the return to the gold standard have been painted in gloomy colours in the literature. In many countries, among them Britain, this is certainly a well-founded description. In the case of Britain, a contributory factor was that the gold exchange rate, which was in practice fixed, meant that the pound was overvalued. This was far from the case in Sweden. In general, it is difficult to make this uniformly dark picture agree with what we know about developments in Sweden in the 1920s. A few short years after 1921, Sweden actually experienced a strong, export-led upswing – while the economic situation was one of low inflation, a favourable balance of payments and relatively low interest rates. The main reason for this relatively positive development was presumably that the deflation of 1921 was so severe that the krona was undervalued at the nominal exchange rate set after 1922, even though the return to the gold standard increased the nominal value of the krona. According to Lundberg, the krona was undervalued by about 10 per cent in 1920, increasing to about 20 per cent some years later (in relation to 1913).[30] As we shall see later, this was not the last time that Sweden could benefit very much by depreciating its currency, officially or *de facto*. If Sweden was to benefit from undervaluation and *de facto* devaluation it was essential that wages could be adjusted without difficulty to the general fall in prices. As we have said, the major crisis of 1921–2 led to a sharp fall in nominal wages. During the rest of the 1920s wages rose largely in pace with the cost of living. So the final result was that, in the main, real wages – despite the shock of 1921 – were maintained at the same level.

The crisis policy of the 1930s

The official policy of keeping to the gold standard was still in effect in the summer of 1931. Yet it was clear that the crisis that started in the USA had spread to Sweden too. Unemployment had begun to rise sharply and the repercussions of the central European bank crashes had begun to make many investors nervous. At the same time, the political effects of the crisis were serious. When in the September of 1931 Britain abandoned the gold standard and devalued the pound, Sweden's currency and gold reserves were almost empty. But the Swedish government, headed by C.G. Ekman, made every effort to avert the inevitable. To save the krona, Marcus Wallenberg was brought in to help raise a large government loan abroad, but this attempt failed. On September 27, the Bank of Sweden abandoned the old krona gold exchange rate. Against gold currencies (such as the US dollar) the krona had depreciated by about 45 per cent by 1935. But since other countries had also devalued, the krona's depreciation against currencies that were important to it averaged only 25 per cent.[31] However, as in the 1920s, the krona was undervalued at this level. Erik Lundberg even spoke of a 'strong and lasting undervaluation of the krona from 1932 onwards'.[32] The chronic balance of payments surplus from 1932 (at 2 per cent a year) is compelling evidence in support of this statement.[33]

Under its 1931 decision, the Bank of Sweden gave up the struggle to maintain fixed exchange rates against other countries, but this was only a temporary setback. Some years later it was decided to link the krona to the pound. Yet it was clear that fixed exchange rates were not the highest priority. In future, the Bank of Sweden would act with full vigour to preserve the 'domestic buying power of the krona'. Ever since the early 1920s Gustav Cassel and others had advocated a policy of domestic price stability. In his view, stable prices were also important for international business. Using his purchasing power parity index theory that was so well known at the time, he was able to show that price stability led to stable exchange rates in the long term. When in 1931 the Bank was about to break the krona's link with a set gold value, the opinions of professors Cassel, Heckscher and David Davidsson were sought on how to handle the situation. They all recommended a policy of domestic price stability and advised on practical measures to achieve this goal.[34]

Most observers thought the devaluation of 1931 was one of the main reasons for the relatively mild effects in Sweden of the depression of the 1930s. The undervalued krona not only gave substantial gains from exports and laid the foundations for stable growth, it also afforded vital protection to the domestic market. At a stroke, all imports became far more expensive. As we have described in an earlier chapter, the result was a strong boom for Sweden's domestic industries. As in the 1920s, one of the main preconditions for depreciation to have such fortunate effects was the Bank of Sweden's ability to continue to keep inflation at a low level. An important feature of this programme, strongly emphasised by Lars Jonung, was the stabilisation of the money stock. Prices and wages could only be kept steady if there was no increase in the money stock.[35] But other interpretations are possible. The decisive factor may have been less the Bank of Sweden's 'monetary programme', and more the fact that from the summer of 1933 the exchange rate was fixed in relation to the pound. This was the main measure that caused the Swedish krona to be undervalued throughout the rest of the 1930s.[36] At this time, Britain was Sweden's most important trade partner, and there were strong links between the two countries in the world of finance and banking as well. Sweden's undervalued currency gave real advantages, not least in relation to Great Britain.[37] But it is remarkable that the high level of industrial growth in the 1930s – about 9 per cent a year – and the severe depreciation of 1931 did not trigger a rise in prices. The cost of living hardly increased at all before the end of the 1930s. Public awareness of the crisis certainly had some effect here by curbing people's spending and by the fact that the trade unions pursued an extremely cautious wage policy.

We must also include in the explanation for Sweden's swift recovery after 1933 the new 'crisis policy' that was applied from 1933 by the Social Democratic Party and Agrarian Party coalition government. Earlier interpretations of the Swedish 'miracle' of the 1930s have often seen the 'horse-trading' policy as arguably the most important factor. This is true to the extent that the economic policy the new government, and Ernst Wigforss, the minister of finance, wanted to introduce contained some new features. As mentioned earlier, before the 1930s there is very little evidence of fiscal, or Keynesian-style budget policy thinking. To use, for example, the budget to stimulate demand was an unfamiliar idea to the government. Rather, the rule of thumb was that the budget should balance each year. After the end of the war in 1918, Fredrik Thorsson, the Social Democratic minister of finance, made such drastic cuts in government spending, without the least thought of the economic consequences of this action on employment, for example, that a special 'Thorsson effect' was named after him. The same policy was also applied in the great crisis of 1921–2.

However, different voices were heard in the early 1930s. In the government budget proposal of 1933, Wigforss emphasised the possibility of using fiscal policy measures to reduce the effects of the crisis. A memorandum written by Gunnar Myrdal was attached to this proposal, which put forward the idea that the business downturn had caused a sharp fall in demand for goods and services. This low level of demand would in its turn create unemployment. In Myrdal's view, if government spending was increased in the short term, various multiplicatory effects would relieve the depression. Thus it was not necessary to balance the budget every year, and policy should aim to balance the budget over the full economic cycle instead. The main point was that the government's net capital should be maintained in the longer term. The kind of government measures that could have a counter-cyclical effect were, according to this budget proposition, public works, investments in infrastructure, etc. However, no radically different fiscal policy was introduced for some years to come. The government continued to exercise great caution in increasing its spending. The Wigforss budgets from 1933 onwards were rather more austere than the budgets of Ekman's non-socialist governments of some years before.[38] In the same way, the budget deficit was higher at the beginning of the 1920s – 3 per cent of GNP – than it was ten years later.[39] The 2 per cent deficit from 1932 was soon replaced by a surplus in 1934. At this time, unemployment was somewhat lower – but there was hardly full employment. Some social policy initiatives were also introduced by Per Albin Hansson's government. They included government-subsidised voluntary unemployment insurance from 1934, new legislation on national basic pensions, means-tested maternal benefit and the introduction of preventive health and medical care (such as child health centres). These reforms, which were not particularly costly, were motivated by socio-political reasons. No mention was made in the current debate of their potentially stabilising effects. Yet in one area there was a reverse that suggested a new attitude to the possibilities of fiscal policy. This was the unemployment policy. As early as 1914 a special Unemployment Commission had been set up to help the unemployed by running a relief work scheme. In the great periods of unemployment in the 1920s this commission intensified its work. Relief work was regarded as basic assistance and the pay was low. To avoid labour competition, wages were not to be higher than the lowest wage paid for manual labour in the district. This system was severely criticised by the labour movement. In particular, they said that relief work led to unfair competition for labour by undercutting wages. There was a risk that relief work would undermine the system of trade union agreements. Added to this was the detested clause in the Unemployment Commission's directive which made it possible in certain circumstances to send unemployed workers to places of work that were boycotted by the unions. Against this background the Social Democratic Party suggested in a Bill of 1930 that the Unemployment Commission should be disbanded. Instead, the government should take action to put unemployed people in proper jobs on the open market, with regular, agreement-based wages. The process of horse-trading with the Agrarian Party meant that this hated system introduced by the Unemployment Commission remained in place well into the 1930s, but in the spring of 1933 Per Albin Hansson requested SEK35 million for public works to be arranged on the open market. The government also requested SEK125 million for the relief work scheme. Most of these measures were to be funded by loans. This was a clear departure from the earlier policy under which the cost of relief work was to be carried forward to the next budget. To borrow money to finance work that was not regarded as profitable was considered far too irresponsible.[40]

It has often been assumed that the 'new unemployment policy' was inspired by economic ideas derived from Keynes. As we know, Keynes – and Myrdal in 1933 – maintained that high unemployment was caused by low effective demand. Most economists thought that the main cause of unemployment was that wages rose too high. But according to Keynes, lower wages were not a formula for success; this was a path that would only lead to a fall in demand. Instead, underbalancing the budget in periods of recession would increase demand, and the economy would pick up. The new unemployment policy introduced in 1933 can undoubtedly be seen as expansive. So the matter was settled. Keynes was the main source of inspiration for this programme![41]

However, the theory of the importance of Keynes has not gone unchallenged. It has been suggested that Sweden's own economists may have also have had an impact on Wigforss and others. The so-called Stockholm School, of which Gunnar Myrdal, Bertil Ohlin and Erik Lindahl were leading figures, issued a statement in 1930 that was in line with what Keynes had said. But Ohlin and Myrdal advocated a more expansive fiscal policy without having been directly influenced by Keynes in any way. An example of the independent stance of the Stockholm School was Alf Johansson's doctoral thesis entitled 'Wage Development and Unemployment' (*Löneutvecklingen och arbetslösheten*), presented in 1934 – two years before Keynes' General Theory. Johansson presents a detailed discussion of the way higher wage costs would gradually lead, through price rises, to higher demand. In fact, this thesis contained ideas that had never been proposed before – not even by Keynes.

Further, many people have pointed out that the attitude towards a more vigorous and aggressive government employment policy with clearly expansionist features had existed in the European Social Democratic movement at least since the 1910s. Even Wigforss himself pointed to the importance of 'social democracy's own traditions' in his government's employment policy.[42] The debate in England is often quoted in this context, where as early as the 1910s the radical couple, Sidney and Beatrice Webb, wanted more public measures to combat economic depressions. Or we may take a Swedish example from about the same time. Otto Steiger cites a Social Democratic parliamentary proposal from 1912 which suggests countering unemployment in recessions by 'better use of the natural resources of the state such as forests, hydro-electric power, the reclamation and cultivation of wetlands, etc.'[43] Here, in his view, were the foundations of the crisis policy that was given full expression in the Bill of 1930, and which the Swedish Social Democratic Party were to implement.

In a polemic exchange on this view, however, Nils Unga stated that the Social Democratic Party did not pursue an 'expansive' crisis policy in the 1930s. Such a view of the capability of fiscal policy to dampen fluctuations in the economic cycle – Keynesian or not – did not emerge until the 1940s, he said. He maintained that into the 1930s the Social Democrats showed no awareness of a long-term expansionist policy to counter unemployment and increase national income. 'In all important respects, views based on a pre-Keynesian economy were maintained.'[44] The 'new unemployment policy' had largely evolved from the Unemployment Commission's policy. It cannot be accepted unconditionally as the reason for an entirely new economic view.

There is much to suggest that Unga's interpretation is correct. The goal of 'sound finances' still had strong support in the 1930s. Wigforss, it is true, considered raising loans to finance more relief work schemes in the worst years of the crisis. But to use this method to increase demand was something he was presumably against. There are in fact few traces of what was assumed to be his expansive view in his budget proposals.

On the other hand, Unga almost overstates his case. First, it is clear that Wigforss, unlike many of his predecessors, realised that fiscal policy *could* be part of the arsenal of economic policies. In this sense, it is correct to regard this as a reversal. Second, there was undoubtedly a shift in theory at the beginning of the 1930s. The heated debate at the beginning of this decade between an older and younger generation of economists on unemployment and prices policy is an indication of the significance of this shift. Most of the older generation of economists thought the new policy to be an abomination. They clung to the view that unemployment could be remedied by bringing down wages, and that the danger of financing relief work schemes was that it would force out private investment by pushing up interest rates. To Gustav Cassel, for example, who saw the crisis as a natural reaction to the business boom with the attendant sharp rise in interest rates, the whole idea seemed ridiculous. He believed that this government action would push up interest rates even more, and delay the recovery from the recession. But the younger economists made light of these fears. Lower wages were not a way to get out of the crisis, they said. Because high unemployment was an indication of a low level of capacity utilisation, government investments did not compete with investments in the private sector. The younger economists saw the potential of a new, more aggressive fiscal policy. To the extent that this had any practical significance worth mentioning in the 1930s is, as we have said, a different matter.

Figure 7.7 Relief work: road construction in Småland in the 1930s.

8   Welfare capitalism

The period from the end of the 1940s to the beginning of the 1970s was one of very strong growth throughout the Western world. It is sometimes referred to as the 'golden years'.[1] Growth in Sweden was faster than in most other Western countries. In real GNP the growth rate was 3.3 per cent a year from 1951 to 1954, 3.4 per cent from 1956 to 1960, 5.2 per cent from 1961 to 1965 and 4.1 per cent from 1966 to 1970. After this period, growth moderated somewhat and after 1975 fell to barely 2 per cent a year.

The gross national product is not, of course, a 'measure of success' of all aspects of welfare. Yet this rapid upswing brought a revolution in living standards. A broad strata of the population were now able to enjoy the benefits of mass consumption. People bought their own cars and many of them even bought summer homes. There was an enormous improvement in housing standards. Most of the overcrowded tenement apartments, with an outhouse in the yard, were replaced by modern, detached owner-occupied houses. Much of this growth in prosperity was channelled into social reforms and improvements. A system of basic social security was introduced. No-one needed to feel cold or hunger any longer.

An important effect of this rapid growth was that incomes evened out. This tendency was noticeable from as early as the 1930s, and was very marked in the 1940s. It was largely due to the mass migration from the rural farming communities to paid work in the urban areas. In the 1950s and up to the mid-1960s this process of wage equalisation began to falter, only to pick up strongly again from 1967 onwards. It is, of course, a common phenomenon for growth to be accompanied by a reduction in the spread of incomes, largely because unemployment falls, which drives up the pay of the lowest income groups in particular. In periods of growth, or at least in business booms, the relative price of labour usually rises faster than that of capital.[2] Thus the spread of factor incomes shifts so that the wage percentage of national income rises at the expense of income from capital. There is evidence of both these effects in Sweden from the 1940s until the mid-1970s. The gap between the highest- and lowest-paid groups narrows while the wage percentage of national income increases. Of course, falling unemployment makes it easier for the trade unions to implement a pay policy that

Figure 8.1 Alva and Gunnar Myrdal. AA.

benefits their members. If the unions also want to close the wage gap – as did the LO from the mid-1960s – this process of equalisation is even swifter.

At the end of the war in 1945, no-one could predict this period of unparalleled success. On the contrary, many recalled the years after the First World War and feared that history would repeat itself. As late as 1944 Gunnar Myrdal, for example, who was soon to become minister of trade in the wholly Social Democratic ministry that followed the coalition government of the war years, warned of a major post-war depression. The same fears permeated the 'post-war programme', which had unanimous Social Democratic support. To counter a severe depression after the war, the government would have to intervene and shore up the economy. The popular view was that the only alternative to high unemployment was some form of planned economy. Gunnar Myrdal, for example, who at that time emerged as one of the Social Democratic Party's foremost ideologists, maintained that, 'at some point, in one area after the other, all the various government interventions must be co-ordinated into uniform systems of government regulations in a planned economy'.[3]

But no deep recession materialised after the war. This may have been why nothing ever became of the 'command economy'. Despite extensive government intervention, Sweden remained a capitalist market economy. Nonetheless, after the end of the war, serious adjustment problems had to be tackled. After the wartime blockades were lifted, it took time for the export market to recover. There had been considerable changes in Sweden's economy during the war years. Production had been directed mainly at

Figure 8.2 The suburb of Kristineberg, north-west Stockholm, is typical of the housing developments begun after the Myrdals had sounded the alarm about the falling birth rate. In a play on the Swedish name 'Myrdal', Olof Dahlins Street, which swarmed with children, was soon popularly known as 'Myrdalen' (the valley of the ants). SSM.

supplying the country's own needs. For example, a large percentage of the capacity in the engineering and textiles sectors had been used for military production. Now, when imports and exports slowly began to increase, major adjustments had to be made. Many companies faced the problem of either changing their product range or going out of business. Similarly, adjustments had to be made to a changed political world. Germany had been Sweden's most important trade partner, particularly when the wartime blockades were in effect. Despite the war, ore, wood products and engineering products had found a market in Germany. Further, the need for imported coal and other vital raw materials was met through Germany, at least until 1943.[4] To make this transition less painful, much of the comprehensive system of wartime regulations was kept in place for some years after the war. These restrictions were justified by the threatening economic scenario painted after the war of the risk of recession and decline. The system of regulations was an extensive one. A special ministry of supply (*Kungliga Folkhushållningsdepartementet*) was set up during the war and countless committees and councils were appointed at the both the national and local levels to make this system work. The main purpose of the system was to hold private consumption in check by introducing bans, luxury taxes and the like. The system also regulated the consumption of important raw materials and fuel, controlled production through subventions, introduced restrictions in the building sector (imposing a direct import ban in 1947), closely monitored foreign trade, controlled the use of labour, introduced price controls, etc. Various commodities in short supply, especially fuel and other raw materials and input goods, continued to be rationed for some years after the war. As late as 1949, butter, pork, beef and sugar were still rationed.

Figure 8.3 The ideal 1940s family gathered round the kitchen table in their bright new apartment. The wife, probably a housewife, two well-nourished children, one boy and one girl, and the radio in a prominent position. AA.

The building restrictions were in force until 1958. As mentioned above, foreign trade was also under strict regulation. As Erik Lundberg observes, in exports a 'jungle of bilateral trade agreements, and variations in prices and terms for import and export with different countries were very confusing. Moreover, new import and export opportunities opened up very rapidly, due to, among other things, unexpected payment difficulties between countries.'[5] The widespread demand for imported goods also caused a substantial outflow of currencies and gold in 1947. To counter this, on March 15 of that year, a blanket ban on imports was introduced. Exports in their turn were strongly encouraged by the 30 per cent devaluation against the dollar of 1949.

In time, these restrictions were lifted. Slowly but surely, the economy began to expand and by the early 1950s all the arrows were pointing upwards. Growth figures were very high, particularly for the early 1960s, and there was a correspondingly rapid rise in industrial productivity. Particularly successful sectors included metal and engineering, paper and pulp and the chemicals industry. There were, of course, a number of reasons for this rapid improvement in productivity. First, the period from the mid-1950s to the beginning of the 1960s was one of heavy real capital investment, mostly in new plant and machinery, and especially in the sectors with a very rapid rise in productivity. The second and even more important

Figure 8.4 An owner-occupied house in the 1940s. A 1½-storey detached house with room for two adults and two children, so far without either electricity or water. Ten years later this house was part of a completed urban housing development. Photo from 1941.

reason was the so-called technology factor. According to Yngve Åberg's calculations, 59 per cent of industrial growth from 1946 to 1964 may be attributed to this factor, while Bo Carlsson puts the figure even higher, particularly for the 1960s and 1970s.[6] The technology factor was also very important to the expanding industries mentioned above. This suggests a strong link between a positive technology factor and extensive capital investment. Labour inputs contributed very little to the improvement in production results. In most branches of industry, employment figures grew far slower than production. The number of employees even fell in some sectors, while there was a sharp rise in production. Despite this, the percentage of the total labour force employed in industry rose. At least 200,000 new jobs were created in the industrial sector between 1945 and 1965. Around 1965 the industrial workforce was just over a million. This year marks the peak of the classic industrial era. After this time both the absolute number of employees in industry and the industrial workforce's percentage of total employment has declined, and the public and private service sectors have grown.

Industrial growth and the new development block

For natural reasons, the post-war problems of economic transformation were more apparent in the countries that had been directly involved in the war. War damage was enormous and it took a long time for wartime economies to adjust to peacetime conditions. The Bretton-Woods system, officially recognised as early as 1944, introduced a monetary order that brought stability and allowed global trade to get under way again. In 1947 the first

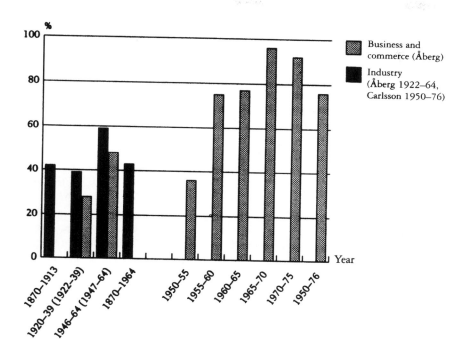

Figure 8.5 The contribution of the technology factor to production growth (percentage).

Source: O. Krantz: *Foreign Trade, Economic Growth and Structural Change after 1850*, Lund
           1987, p. 22.

Table 8.1 Productivity growth by sector 1950–83. Annual change (percentage)

Sector	1950–60	1960–65	1965–70	1970–75	1975–80	1980–85
Agriculture	3.0	4.8	6.4	5.6	5.8	7.1
Forestry	0.9	4.6	12.4	5.6	0.1	1.2
Industry	4.0	7.8	7.6	4.4	2.4	3.5
Electricity, gas, etc.	5.1	6.8	6.4	7.6	3.7	2.9
Construction	0.9	4.8	2.5	4.6	3.2	0.7
Distributive trades	3.0	4.8	3.8	3.5	2.5	0.7
Communications	3.9	4.9	4.3	5.9	3.7	−0.6
Housing	–	–	–	2.8	0.3	−3.9
Private services	–	–	–	4.5	1.5	0.7
Public services	0.0	−0.7	0.0	0.3	0.3	0.0

Source: *Sveriges industri*, Industriförbundet, Stockholm 1985, p. 52.

GATT treaty brought about general reductions in import and export tariffs in the world market. The fact that the USA was behind this agreement indicated that future policy would be less protectionist than in the inter-war years. This created the conditions for stability and confidence in the future. To alleviate the desperate situation in Western Europe, Marshall Aid was introduced, and large sums of money in dollars were transferred there from the USA. As part of the Bretton-Woods system, the World Bank was founded to arrange long-term credit for development purposes, and the International Monetary Fund for more short-term stabilisation policy measures. The Soviet Union and their allies in the Eastern bloc were not included in these arrangements, which created in Western Europe an institutional framework that laid the foundations of the strong economic recovery from the 1950s onwards. To avoid repeating the mistakes of the inter-war years, a number of bodies were set up in Western Europe for economic and political co-operation. The most important of these organisations was the Coal and Steel Community. This was the first step on the path to wider co-operation, especially between France and West Germany, that would subsequently be embodied in the Treaty of Rome in 1957, which formed the EEC (later the EG-EU). These initiatives also created the stability needed for investments and trade to flourish.

As with Sweden, growth in Europe was fairly moderate at the end of the 1940s. However, it rose very rapidly with the Korean War in the early 1950s. The 1950s and much of the 1960s were a golden era for the capitalist industrial system. Much of the honour for this should go to the very rapid upswing in world trade, which grew as never before. Its percentage annual growth – largely thanks to the GATT treaty – was in two figures. Of course, domestic demand was also at a high level after the war. Housing and roads, for example, had to be built. There was an acute and widespread need for investments in infrastructure. Taken together, these factors formed the basis for strong industrial expansion. One factor that emerged from the war was a new development block, undeniably generated by the USA. Not least the extensive federal investments in military technology led to the emergence of a series of innovations that began to be used after the war for civil purposes. We have already mentioned the importance of the aircraft industry and the modern electronics industry in this context. In the 1950s, in particular, the foundation was laid for the microelectronics revolution which was to radically change the worlds of information and production. New types of steel and metals were developed, as was a completely new material for mass use: plastic. Synthetic materials that could wholly or partly replace traditional raw materials became widely used in the post-war years. In addition, there was a veritable explosion of innovations in consumer goods, including goods which had come into use in the inter-war years but which now became very popular. These were 'consumer durables' such as cars, refrigerators, freezers, vacuum-cleaners, radios and gramophones. But the same was also true of foodstuffs, clothing and textiles, household equipment, furniture and the 'entertainment sector'. There was also an important innovation in the field of electronics – the television.

This new development block began in the 1950s. It spread until the mid-1960s, paving the way for the modern consumer society which we often take for granted today, but which actually has a very short history. The period we have referred to before as the 'rationalisation phase' of the development block took place in the mid-1960s. The following period has come to be associated with major structural rationalisation, severe competition and crisis. This was accentuated by the emergence of new industrial centres, particularly outside Europe. In the 1960s this was especially true of Japan, but also applies in the following decades to several of the NICs (newly industrialised countries) in Asia and Latin America. In the Western world, competition in the market and the drive to advance have resulted in large parts of the traditional industrial sector becoming leaner, or closing down completely. At least in the mass production of input goods such as iron and steel, cheap consumer goods, etc., raw materials and wage costs are important items. It is also a definite advantage to have access to the latest technology and to be able to run production on a larger scale than the competition. This also favours the countries that industrialised late while it works against countries with outdated capital stock. Whatever the case may be, the result of sweeping industrialisation outside the old industrial core area has been a geographical relocation of industrial sectors and industrial centres. Thus the old core area of heavy industry – iron, steel and coal – which ran through northern France, Belgium and north-west Germany (the Ruhr) has been almost entirely eliminated. We see in the late 1970s, and particularly the 1980s, a period of general crisis for the development block from the Second World War. The result was a constantly high level of unemployment and several years of deep recession.

Sweeping structural transformation

The high average growth figures in Sweden from the end of the 1940s to the beginning of the 1970s actually concealed an uneven spread between the different sectors of the economy and also between the different sectors of industry. If we examine the spread of growth between different *branches of industry*, we see that there was hardly any growth at all in the agricultural sector. From 1950, growth figures were even negative. After the 1940s Sweden was no longer an agricultural country with a high percentage of its population working on the land. The decline of agriculture and forestry is evident not least in the steady fall in the percentage of GNP these sectors answer for from 1950 to 1970. At the end of this period it was down to around 5 per cent. Before the Second World War, Sweden was still a largely agricultural country. Now we see a rapid drain of labour away from agriculture. From the 1950s until the 1980s the number of people working in this sector fell by 75 per cent. This was accompanied by numerous closures, mostly of small farms. From 1951 to 1966 alone, 100,000 of these formerly independent farming units disappeared. The average number of hectares per unit rose sharply and mechanisation became more widespread. From the 1950s onwards the tractor was a common sight in the countryside. By around 1970 almost all family-run farms had a tractor. The farmers who were left also invested in new mechanical equipment such as combine harvesters and modern milking machines. Specialisation was also a feature of this sector. The old mixed farms, most of which were self-sufficient, were gradually replaced by farming that specialised in either milk and animal products or cereal production.

Throughout the whole of this period the industrial sector's *percentage* of GNP stayed at about the same level, while there was some increase in the percentage of building, retailing and public services. But as GNP is calculated on changes in the value of production, these figures conceal the rapid expansion of industry, particularly in the 1950s and 1960s. Similarly, these figures exaggerate the decline in agricultural production. The reason is, of course, that the rise in productivity was very much higher in industry and agriculture than in the service sector – even if the figure for service sector growth is extremely difficult to calculate. This means that there was a relative fall in the costs and prices for production in these sectors in relation to the production of services. In short, one got relatively more for one's money when buying industrial products than when buying services!

The same picture of uneven development is also a feature of the conditions *within* the industrial sectors. Here, the mining industry, the metal industry, engineering, paper and pulp and the chemicals industry were strongly expansive, while growth in foods, textiles, garments and the shoe and leather industry was modest. This is clearly reflected in the trend in the employment levels of these different sectors. While, for example, the mechanical engineering industry, iron and metal manufacture, the electronics industry and chemicals expanded rapidly, the non-metalliferous mining and quarrying sector and the textile, shoe and leather industries lost workers from 1946 to 1967.

More interesting differences occur between branches of industry from the end of the 1940s. While the textile, garment and to some extent mining, shipbuilding and rubber goods industries, for example, enjoyed very strong growth from 1946 to 1950, the figures for the 1950s and 1960s were significantly lower. The reverse is true of the iron and metal producing sectors, iron and metal manufacturing, non-metalliferous mining and quarrying, and the paper goods and printing industries.

As a whole, the engineering industry was the major winner in the period up to the 1970s. It was without doubt the strong upswing in this sector that formed the basis for the considerable success Sweden enjoyed from 1950 until the end of the 1960s. At the same time, it was its more technically sophisticated sectors in particular that advanced the most. The engineering industry is, of course, a heterogeneous sector which in the industrial statistics

Figure 8.6 A milking machine – 'so simple a child can use it'. From *Lanthemmet* I, 1950, Landbild.

Table 8.2 Productivity growth by sector 1950–83. Annual increase in volume (percentage)

Sector	1945–50	1950–60	1960–65	1965–69
Agriculture	3.9	–1.4	–0.8	–0.1
Forestry	6.1	1.9	0.9	2.9
Industry	7.7	3.9	8.0	5.3
Electricity, gas, etc.	7.0	7.1	7.9	6.4
Construction	4.9	2.3	7.2	2.3
Distributive trades	7.5	3.9	5.7	3.4
Communications	4.0	3.9	4.3	4.6
Housing	3.2	5.8	5.7	4.9
Private services	3.8	3.6	6.0	3.1
Public services	5.1	3.5	3.3	4.8

Source: B. Södersten (ed.) *Svensk ekonomi*, Stockholm 1970.

cover everything from the manufacture of horseshoes and snuff boxes to advanced aircraft. From the 1950s onwards there were some sub-branches of the engineering industry that were particularly successful, foremost the mechanical engineering industry, the motor industry, the electronics sector and shipbuilding. At its peak in the 1960s the shipyards – Eriksberg, Götaverken and Lindholmen in Gothenburg, Kockums in Malmö and the Landskrona yard, to mention only the biggest – employed a total of 30,000 shipyard workers, i.e. about 8 per cent of the country's total industrial

Figure 8.7 Rape threshing in Väsby, Skåne, in the 1950s. Photo: Bertil Norberg/Landbild.

workforce. The expansion was fuelled by a high level of specialisation in the manufacture of larger and larger cargo ships, followed by oil tankers, many for foreign markets. In the electronics industry, both the high-tension sector (ASEA), the low-tension sector (L.M. Ericsson) and domestic appliance manufacture for the home market also expanded. The latter applied to, for example, rapidly expanding companies such as Electrolux with their refrigerators and vacuum-cleaners and Luxor with their radios, and later, TV sets. The motor industry was strongly dominated by two companies which, although founded far earlier, had their heyday in the 1950s and 1960s: Volvo in Gothenburg and SAAB in Trollhättan. Truck manufacture at Scania-Vabis in Södertälje also rose sharply. And a number of other products ensured the swift expansion of the engineering sector: ball-bearings (SKF), agricultural and dairy machinery (Alfa-Laval), typewriters and calculators (Facit), engines and mining equipment (Atlas Copco) and others.

Thus, relatively-speaking, most of this expansion was based on technologically intensive sub-sectors, while more simple metal manufacture and the metal goods industries found themselves in a backwater. In the first case, the value added to the product was relatively high. Goods with a substantial immaterial capital content are often unique and are therefore at a premium, commanding a high price on the market. Further, highly processed goods have strongly positive so-called link effects. The basis of this rapid expansion was in a fairly small number of large companies, and the high added value therefore created a strong demand for components from a large number of suppliers. Many of these suppliers also became highly specialised, leading to more mechanisation which in its turn created a demand for plant and machinery, etc. This was particularly evident in the motor, aviation and electrotechnical industries. The demand for service also increased. This could be met by less sophisticated or specialised engineering workshops. Taken together, this led to both strong growth and a sharp rise in the number of employees in the engineering sector.

Rising exports

The structural changes reflected by the shifts in the industrial sector from 1945 have a number of causes. At the general level it was ultimately a question of changing market conditions and demand trends. In the question of demand, foreign trade had become increasingly important. From the end of the 1940s, Sweden's imports and exports had grown considerably, at an annual rate of around 7–8 per cent, until the beginning of the 1970s. This meant a substantial rise in foreign trade's share of GNP. In other words, international trade played an increasingly important part in Sweden's economy. One result was an increase in the so-called export quota in the post-war years. This quota was, however, already fairly high in the 1920s.[7] Shortly before the First World War, foreign trade amounted to about 20 per cent of GNP. After falling during and shortly after the First World War it reached this level again towards the end of the 1920s. In 1946 the level was down again at just over 10 per cent. It then returned to around 20 per cent, where it has remained since. The reason why this percentage did not rise, even though the growth in export volume far outstripped growth in GNP, is that domestic prices for goods and services rose far quicker than world market prices. Thus the higher volume of exports did not cause an equally strong rise expressed in kronor and öre.

Since the Second World War there have been radical changes in the spread of Sweden's foreign trade by country. In the inter-war years, the USA became one of Sweden's most important trade partners – there was also considerable trade with Latin America. After 1945 there was a marked fall in the USA's share of Swedish trade, and Western Europe took over as Sweden's biggest export and import market. The most important countries were West Germany, Britain and the other Scandinavian countries. Norway, Denmark and Finland emerged as Sweden's most important export area from the 1950s, while Germany and England were the most important import countries.

The composition of foreign trade by type of goods also changed. Overall, the percentage of total exports that was made up of raw materials (ore, wood products, foodstuffs, etc.) fell, while there was an explosive increase in the engineering industry's percentage of exports. Thus, added value in Swedish exports increased in this period. Similarly, the percentage of cheap mass-produced products such as paper and pulp fell. Put in general terms, this was an expression of an international division of labour in a period of rapid change. In future, the percentage of Western European countries' production that was raw materials and cheaper input goods was to be lower. Instead, more and more of this kind of production moved outside Western Europe. In the 1970s and 1980s most mass production of cheap industrial goods moved to these new areas, and in Western Europe there was a gradual increase in the more advanced and high-technology industries. This new international division of labour was partly caused by rising production costs in the Western industrial countries, which in essence reflected the higher standards of living

Figure 8.8 Cars and refrigerators, which became standard in the 'people's home', were also important exports. Behind the car parked outside the owner's house, the town's new red brick secondary school may be glimpsed. The refrigerator is an Electrolux 40 from 1956–63 with typical contents for that time.

in this region, and partly by the fact that the most important markets for more sophisticated consumer goods such as modern electronics were to be found in the wealthy Western economies (and Japan). Proximity to these affluent markets was an important reason to locate these industries there.

As mentioned above, in the long term this shift in the international division of labour produced radical structural change that included the closure of large parts of the traditional raw materials industries and the branches of industry that concentrated on cheap mass production. This trend was of particular importance from the 1970s onwards, when the old development block had clearly entered its rationalisation phase. We shall therefore discuss this dramatic structural change and its expression in Sweden in the form of crises and company closures in a later chapter. But a decline in the traditional industrial sector began to be noticeable as early as the 1960s. Competition in the steel industry and associated sectors became increasingly intensive in this decade. By introducing more large-scale production and bringing down prices, the iron and steel industries in many countries tried to gain market advantages over other countries. But as western Europe's total percentage of the market fell, these countries found themselves competing for a smaller cake. One effect of this in Sweden was the widespread steel crisis that had dramatic consequences for the traditional iron and steel industry in the 1970s (see Chapter 10 below). Stiffer competition also hit the paper and pulp sector, a very important industry for Sweden. The struggle with countries such as Finland and Canada became

Figure 8.9 Swedish terrace houses with a rural flavour – sun, light, air, flowers and greenery. Left: A garden city development in Malmö. Building Contractor: E. Sigfrid Persson. Right: Off-road truck with a flexible chassis from Scania-Vabis. From: Vår tids uppfinningar (1950).

ever more intensive, and here too tougher competition was expressed in *inter alia* a fall in relative prices which forced rationalisation measures, mergers, etc. It is only logical that in light of this it was these very sectors that reported lower-than-average growth figures in the 1960s, while trends were all the more positive for the more intangible capital-intensive industries in, for example, the engineering sector.

The trend in Sweden largely followed the general pattern of development in Western Europe, i.e. from less to more intangible capital-intensive production. But the picture is a disjointed one. Raw materials and simple industrial product (including pulp, paper, wood products, ore, etc.) continued to be an important part of Sweden's exports. Thus towards the end of the 1960s Sweden's exports profile was a combination of traditional products that had been exported since the infancy of industrialism in the nineteenth century, *and* a number of sophisticated engineering products (among them cars, ships and machinery). Most of these latter export products were produced by a relatively small number of large companies that we have already listed above, including Volvo, SKF, L.M. Ericsson and Atlas Copco. As we shall see, this picture continued to be fragmented in Sweden through the 1970s and 1980s. The change in the import situation also contributed to the differences between sectors. The post-war years saw a marked fall in agricultural and food imports, from 20 per cent of total imports from the mid-1940s to 13 per cent in the mid-1960s. Instead, the import of a range of industrial goods, not least engineering products, increased. Here, Sweden's engineering industry could counter by specialising. But this was hardly a successful strategy for the textile and garment industry, another sector that had been exposed to tougher competition from foreign imports. This sector therefore became much leaner, a process which began as early as the 1950s. Thus at an early stage this sector felt the effects of a structural transformation that had no noticeable impact on other sectors in Sweden until the 1970s.

Industry, banks and Sweden's fifteen families

From its very beginnings, Sweden's industry was strongly concentrated. This degree of concentration, expressed as the number of companies that share the production of a given sector, appears, it is true, to have lessened somewhat around the turn of the century. Following the rapid introduction of industry, spearheaded by a small number of major actors, a broader industrial base evolved. Yet it is clear that a relatively small number of large companies or groups of companies came to dominate in most sectors. This was apparent in the paper and pulp industry, iron and steel, chemicals and some sub-branches of the mechanical engineering sector. Cartels also became common in some areas. As we have seen, cartel agreements were common even at the beginning of the twentieth century. There is no reason to believe that their importance diminished at all in the post-war years. An interim report published by the government commission on ownership concentration in industry confirmed that these agreements were prevalent in certain sectors.

This was often a question of a fairly stable number of large companies that dominated each sub-sector. Many of the large companies that were active between the wars – or even before the First World War – were still dominant actors in the 1960s. They included ASEA, STAB, SKF, Stora Kopparberg and L.M. Ericsson. Thus the large enterprises were stable and lasting. Companies that had grown large remained large. We can of course find some new arrivals such as Volvo, Electrolux, Skånska Cementgjuteriet, SAAB, Facit and others. Yet the continuity in the picture is still striking. This does not mean that there was not a lively process of mergers and restructuring that often resulted in companies changing their form without changing their name. As we shall see later, this kind of transformation was particularly common from the rationalisation and crisis years of the 1970s and after.

Another important observation is that between the 1920s and the 1960s there was a considerable increase in turnover and number of employees in the large companies. When it comes to the degree of concentration in industry it is difficult to find any uniform measurement that is comparable over time. The government commission on ownership concentration that studied conditions in the 1960s was, however, unanimous in its conclusion: the large corporations had increased their share and their power in industry as a whole. Of the 442 sectors studied (1963), 228 were dominated by a small number of companies. This investigation also included foreign competition through imports. Mining, metalworking, chemicals, electronics and paper and pulp were all largely in the hands of large companies. At the other end of the scale, large companies answered for a low percentage of operations in metal manufacturing, the ready-made clothing industry and the wood-processing industry.[8] The commission on ownership concentration also concluded that

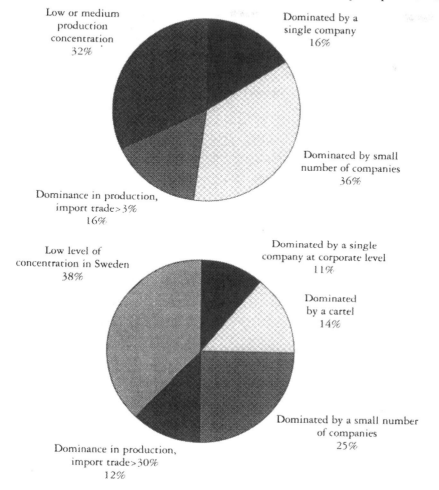

Figure 8.10 The structure and competitive relationships of industry. Concentration trends in large companies.

Source: C.H. Hermansson, *Monopol och storfinans – de 15 familjerna*, Stockholm 1971, p. 26.

the 100 biggest companies in Sweden answered for 46 per cent of value added in the whole of industry. The greater concentration of ownership in the post-war period further accentuated this picture.

There are several reasons why the large enterprises were so stable over time. First, it is common in economic literature to refer to the benefits of large-scale operations: large companies can maintain or increase their power simply by being large. This explanation can hardly apply in Sweden. In an international comparison, Swedish companies have always been small. Thus, this argument only holds if we assume Sweden to be a closed economy. Some of the successes of the large companies are attributable, it is true, to their unique products, where they were the biggest name from the beginning, and have usually managed to retain this lead (one example being ball-bearings). Yet this is still an exception. Most of Sweden's leading companies have maintained their status even though they were not particularly large nor had any decisive cost advantages over their competitors. In another interpretation, importance is attached to their success in investing in niches where quality and the guarantee of a reputable brand name were more effective than low unit costs keeping demand constant – not least in the home market. The high level of technological competence in Sweden's big companies and their ability to adapt swiftly and smoothly to changing conditions have often been cited in this context. A third interpretation of the stability of large companies focuses on the importance not of the size of the company *per se*, but on its access to various kinds of network. Large enterprises are good at connecting with unique competences and resources (technical, financial, etc.). Their networks are often better-developed than those of smaller companies. This creates stability over time, and gives large companies far better chances of surviving.

No less important here are the factors of ownership and financial resources. It is sometimes said that large enterprises have an advantage because they are linked to networks in which major shareholders with strong and long-term ownership-responsibility operate. In the case of Sweden, great emphasis has been given to the fact that the large banks acted as owners of this kind. According to this interpretation the support of different 'banking spheres' has been crucial to the survival of these companies. A quite different issue, and one that we shall return to, is whether or not this has helped Sweden's industrial growth.

We have seen that already in the infancy of industrialism the major commercial banks took an active part in the growth and development of industrial enterprises. This trend was further accentuated after the inter-war years, while the number of independent commercial banks fell. A new wave of mergers began in the 1970s when, for example, Enskilda Banken and Skandinaviska Banken merged, and Upplands Banken and Sundsvalls Banken became Nordbanken (1986), to merge again some years later with the government-owned Post- och Kreditbanken. As we shall see later, the major bank crisis of the early 1990s brought more changes. After the war the traditional banks' total share of all lending also fell – from 36 per cent in 1949 to 25 per cent in 1974. This was even more evident in the savings banks, where the percentage fell from 27 per cent to 14 per cent in the same period. Instead, the more specialised credit institutes, such as the mortgage banks and building societies, flourished. They had a 16 per cent share of total lending in 1949 and 34 per cent in 1974. The remainder (21 per cent in 1949 and 31 per cent in 1974) was spread among insurance companies, government lending institutes, etc.[9]

However, the large commercial banks increased their holdings in industry. Until the 1970s the three largest banks were the Wallenbergs' Enskilda Banken (with the Investor and Providentia investment companies) Skandinaviska Banken (with the Custos investment company) and Handelsbanken (with the Promotion and Industrivärden investment companies). As Jan Glete has shown, in the post-war years a growing number of large companies became dominated by a small number of major shareholders with strong links with one of these commercial banks. Particularly in the inter-war years, many economists believed that the kind of owner-controlled capitalism that had been a characteristic of the beginnings of industrialism was now on its way out, to be replaced by a form of capitalism controlled by powerful directors – managerial capitalism. But this theory has little relevance in the case of Sweden after 1945. In Glete's view it had even gradually become almost 'self-evident that large companies must have one or two major owners'. This was an important departure from the inter-war years, when 'management controlled' companies were in the majority.[10] After 1938, when the banks were no longer allowed to hold shares themselves in industrial companies, their power of ownership was exercised indirectly through investment companies that were closely linked to the large banks.

Stockholms Enskilda Banken was at the hub of the powerful financial and industrial complex that came to be known as the 'Wallenberg group'. From the end of the Second World War until the 1970s this empire was controlled by the two brothers Marcus and Jacob Wallenberg. It is well known that industrial matters were Marcus's special interest while the role of his older brother Jacob was more that of banker. As we have seen, this division between the brothers had its roots in the history of the Wallenberg family. A notable feature of the Wallenberg group's basket of large enterprises was its great stability. Already before the First World War this basket included companies like ASEA, Atlas and others. But it was mainly in the inter-war years that this industrial empire grew in size and power. In this period, major enterprises such as Separator, Stora Kopparberg, SKF, L.M. Ericsson, Astra and Scania-Vabis became connected to the Wallenberg group. In the financial reorganisation after the Kreuger crash many large companies became linked to the bank as long-standing clients. These ties were also gradually strengthened through ownership. Between the wars, SAAB, Electrolux, Nymölla, Bergvik & Ala, and others also joined this circle.

Against this background it is not surprising that emphasis has been given to the strong position of power that the Wallenberg group occupied in Swedish industry. In many respects it actually appears to be unique, even from an international perspective. At the end of the 1960s, perhaps one industrial worker in seven or eight was employed in a 'Wallenberg company'. Its dominance in large, successful, primarily exporting companies in engineering, iron and steel, and forestry was striking. The Wallenberg family has been closely associated with Sweden's industrial success since the Second World War, particularly in the export markets. This, as we have

already said, is hardly surprising. The Wallenberg family played an important part in many of the large companies that were behind the high rate of
industrial growth after 1945. Another characteristic of the Wallenberg
group is that it managed to build up a strong position of power despite what
were often fairly limited shareholdings. The so-called 'box in a box' or
'Russian doll' system of ownership made it possible with a relatively small
holding (10–20 per cent) in a large parent company to gain dominant
influence in a large number of subsidiaries as well. This dominance from
modest holdings cannot be attributed solely to a fragmented ownership
profile with a large number of small shareholders. It would certainly have
been possible for other owners to buy up shares to counter the dominance of
the Wallenberg group. But such hostile takeovers were unusual before the
1970s, for reasons that are difficult to see. It may be that potential competitors did not dare identify themselves for fear of reprisals from the
powerful Wallenberg group. Or people may have been prepared to respect
the unique position of the Wallenbergs in Sweden's business world, and
chose not to question the idea that some companies naturally belonged in
the Wallenberg sphere.

Until it merged with Enskilda Banken in 1971, *Skandinaviska Banken* was
an independent centre of power which exercised strong control over many
industrial companies. Unlike Enskilda Banken, Skandinaviska Banken had
no ownership ties with any family. The majority of the seats on its boards
were occupied by prominent businessmen. Also, unlike Enskilda Banken,
which had the nature of a capital city bank, Skandinaviska Banken had an
early interest in the business world of Gothenburg and the southern province
of Skåne. In fact, the bank consisted of three independent offices located in
Stockholm, Gothenburg and Malmö, and these offices had little contact with
one another. As Glete says, 'The bank's three regional boards functioned
largely as exclusive clubs for the top figures in the business world, and were
natural centres for co-operation and an exchange of information between a
large number of important Swedish enterprises that had no common links of
ownership.'[11] In Gothenburg between the wars, for example, the bank established connections through the shipping family of Broström with Gothenburg's
major shipyards, among them the Götaverken and Eriksberg yards. Until the
Kreuger crash – in which, as we have seen, the Skandinaviska Banken was
deeply involved – the Gothenburg-based firms of SKF and Volvo were part
of the Skandinaviska Banken's circle. Until 1932 the SKF Board and the
bank's Gothenburg board were largely identical. Dissatisfied with the
irresponsible dealings between Skandinaviska Banken and Kreuger, SKF and
its powerful leaders Sven Winquist and Björn Prytz, who were formerly
members of the bank's board, turned to the Enskilda Banken instead. When
SKF sold Volvo in 1935, Volvo did, however, continue its contacts with
Skandinaviska Banken. This very successful company never became a part of
the Wallenberg group.[12] Further, at an early stage the Skandinaviska Banken
had developed relations with a number of large companies based in Skåne:

Skånska Cement, Tretorn, the Trelleborg Rubber Works, Kockums, Höganäs, Klippans Fine Paper Mill, and others. Bofors had also been in the Skandinaviska Banken's sphere of influence. In the post-war years a number of important customers were added through Custos, the investment company, in which a shareholding was swiftly acquired. They included Boliden, the mining company, Mölnlycke, Hufvudstaden, the property company, and Uddeholms. The Skandinaviska Banken's industries were hit fairly hard by the crisis of the 1970s, and the great merger between Skandinaviska Banken and Enskilda Banken in 1971 thus did *not* result in a simple addition of these two banks' former 'industrial holdings'. Another important reason for the fairly large loss of companies was that the link between Skandinaviska Banken and Custos was dissolved at the beginning of the 1970s, when Custos became an independent investment company.[13]

Under the leadership of Louis Frænckel, *Svenska Handelsbanken* emerged as a major bank at the beginning of the twentieth century. As with Skandinaviska Banken, powerful industrialists were in a clear majority on the boards of Handelsbanken. But unlike Skandinaviska Banken, Handelsbanken was a city bank with interests in companies that had their head offices in Stockholm. Thus the large companies that were the bank's long-term clients came to dominate and control the bank. In common with Skandinaviska Banken, Handelsbanken had no main family or individual ownership interest. This only occurred in the mid-1970s when Anders Wall, the financier, acquired some holdings in the bank. In the post-war years up to the 1970s, Enfrid Browaldh and his son Tore served as managing directors. The Handelsbanken's sphere of ownership was in the iron and steel sector, and forestry in the north of Sweden. Important companies considered to be in the bank's sphere of interest included AGA, Sandvik, SCA, the large forestry corporation, Fagersta, PLM, Bolinder, Munktells (up to 1950, when this firm was bought by Volvo) and MoDo. L.M. Ericsson had also been an important client, although this company alternated between Handelsbanken and Enskilda Banken. After the war, Handelsbanken exercised its power of ownership through Industrivärden, the investment company. At the beginning of the 1960s even stronger links were forged between the bank and the investment company by a system of cross-holdings between the SCA and Industrivärden. This prevented the bank and its investment company from drifting apart, as in the case of Skandinaviska Banken and its investment company.

Thus the large commercial banks played an important part in Swedish industry and commerce. The literature on the history of banking usually identifies two different types of system for providing credit to industry: a market-oriented system and a bank-oriented system. In the first case the company is supplied with capital through an open share or bond market, while in the second system the emphasis is on the ties of ownership between a bank and its clients. Sweden is usually described as a country dominated by a bank-oriented credit system, i.e. one with close, long-term and often very stable relations between banks and industrial companies. One reason for this may be that because of their stable ownership relations and supply of credit, industries have attempted to introduce greater security into the system and avoid the effects of the vagaries of the market. Another possible reason is that the market for shares and bonds has traditionally been underdeveloped in Sweden. This may be natural for a small country, but may also, of course, depend on political factors, with shareholdings and the like being viewed with a certain amount of suspicion. Undoubtedly, the Kreuger crash and conditions in general in the 1930s meant that there was little interest in shares for a very long time to come.

A bank-oriented credit system undoubtedly helps create greater stability and security in industrial enterprises. One positive effect of this system is lower transaction costs, which are always high in a climate of general uncertainty. But in the same way, the long-term ownership responsibility exercised by the banks may also lead to less flexibility and a sluggish pace of change. Since economic growth is dependent on this kind of pressure for structural adjustment, this system may result in slower growth. But we cannot be sure of this. A relatively high degree of security may also have given companies the confidence to invest in high-risk projects that would have been out of the question in a more cautious market climate.

However, it was not only through the banks that the relatively high concentration of holdings in Sweden became so clearly visible. Small groups of owners are behind most of Sweden's large companies. Up until 1970 there was much talk of 'the fifteen families', and after this time the group became even smaller – people spoke instead of 'the ten families'. There were also new names among these families. Several surveys carried out in the 1960s, including the report on ownership concentration from which we have already quoted, identified a number of dominant groups: the families of Wallenberg, Söderberg, Wehtje, Bonnier, Johnson, Sachs, Kempe, Åhlén, Klingspor, Throne-Holst, Jacobsson, Åselius, Schwartz, Jeansson-Högberg-Hain, Roos, Dunker, Hammarskjöld, Broström and Wenner-Gren. As we have already said, the Wallenbergs were in a class of their own. In 1967 this sphere had direct ownership influence in companies with a total workforce of over 300,000 employees. But there was also the Bonnier family with their giant mass-media empire, including the Bonnier's publishing house, *Dagens Nyheter*, the country's biggest daily newspaper, Åhlen & Åkerlund, the magazine publishers, and others; or the Söderberg family which, through the publicly quoted investment company Ratos, has shareholdings in a very large number of companies. The Bonnier Group also exercised direct power of ownership in Holmens bruk, Bulten-Kanthal and Esselte. Another famous family was the Johnsons, headed by Axel Axelsson Johnson, which amassed a huge fortune, particularly between the wars, through retailing, shipping (Nordsjernan), oil trading – and Avesta Järnverk. In the same period, Johnson also bought a number of engineering firms that were on the verge of bankruptcy, including Motala, Karlstads (KMW) and the Hedemora mechanical engineering works, as well as Lindholmens shipyard in Gothenburg. After the crises of the 1980s, the Johnson family withdrew from their involvement in industry and concentrated on commercial companies instead. Finally, the legendary name of Axel Wenner-Gren must be mentioned. Wenner-Gren began his career as a salesman for AB Separator in Germany, but soon began his own manufacture of a new invention with a great future: the vacuum-cleaner. With this and the manufacture of refrigerators as a basis, in the few short decades between the wars Wenner-Gren managed to build up a large international enterprise, Electrolux. With this company as a springboard, he established himself in the 1930s as a world-wide financier. In this decade he bought clearly undervalued shares at a low price and managed to acquire holdings in a number of large Swedish companies, among them Boliden and SCA. However, Wenner-Gren's luck deserted him after the war. He gradually lost his huge fortune through a number of ambitious but failed investments in, for example, computers (Alwac) and monorails (Alweg). Some out-and-out fortune-hunters close to Wenner-Gren also helped to squander a fortune that was still huge in the 1950s.

Greater prosperity – and structural changes

From the end of the 1940s the high growth rate and healthy industrial expansion fuelled a very swift process of social change, one evident result being a sharp rise in consumption. Total consumption, which is estimated to have risen by close to 100 per cent from 1950 to 1970, was particularly high in the 1960s. A characteristic feature was that private consumption rose *at the same time* as consumption in the public sector (central and local government) increased rapidly. Notwithstanding this very sharp upswing in public consumption, private consumption rose by 1.8 per cent a year in the 1950s and 3 per cent a year in the 1960s. The fact that public consumption rose faster than private consumption means that the tax outtake on incomes was higher than before. We have already seen how a more efficient tax system gradually evolved in the twentieth century, particularly from the 1930s onward. From the same decade there was also a substantial increase in the tax rates, both in government income tax and municipal tax. Sweden changed from a low-tax country to a high-tax country, a trend that was further accentuated in the 1950s and 1960s. At the beginning of the 1970s the tax outtake began to approach the 50 per cent mark, even for ordinary incomes. At the same time, the ever-steeper progressive tax scales pushed 'marginal tax' on medium and higher incomes even further. Already in the 1960s there was mention of 'marginal tax' problems in the political debate. Although one of the most important taxes, the municipal tax was not actually progressive, yet a progressive tax system was ideal for the Social Democratic government of the time. The introduction of a 5 per cent sales tax in 1960 was a departure from this principle. This sales tax, which was later called value added tax, was gradually increased through the 1960s (and was already at 11 per cent in

1967). In general, indirect taxes became more important in this period. At the end of the 1960s they answered for about 55 per cent of total tax revenues (and they have become even more important since then).[14]

The rise in consumption meant not only that a larger proportion was taken out in the form of public services (see Chapter 9), there was also a major change in the nature of private consumption. The following are some of the most important discernible changes.

- Durable goods such as houses, cars and household equipment increase more than non-durables and foods.
- Goods that meet the most 'basic' needs (especially food and drink) take up less of the individual's budget.
- There is a sharp rise in the consumption of luxury goods and leisure expenditure (including holiday travel).
- Households spend more on processed products instead of raw materials (such as semi-processed food).[15]

Thus this higher rate of growth and consumption was based on – and in its turn caused – rapid structural change, the most spectacular feature of which was the decline in agriculture and the upswing in industrial production and services. Among the important effects of this change were the drastic regional consequences. But these would have been more complicated than the simple 'migration off the land' so often mentioned in the public debate. At least as important for the geographical relocation of the population were the changes in the industrial sector, and a phenomenon discussed in the next chapter – the emergence of the service sector. As we have seen, there were major shifts between different industrial sectors after the Second World War. Historically, many of these sectors had different geographical centres, and different growth figures in these sectors therefore had powerful geographical effects. The same is true of the spread of small and large enterprises, which also have different geographical profiles. Finally, the rapid pace of technical advance and automation can cause employment to fall in one sector, which in its turn affects the regional spread of the population.

Although the percentage of the labour force employed in agriculture fell steadily after the advent of industrialism at the end of the nineteenth century, this was far from a simple 'migration' from the countryside to the towns. Instead, two distinct patterns may be discerned from the inter-war period. From the First World War until the end of the 1940s there was a very strong expansion of old or new country towns and rural population concentrations. This has been called 'rural urbanisation'.[16] Growth, in the major cities, in particular, was slower in this period. Farm closures and the 'migration off the land' meant that people moved to a densely populated area close by and got work, often in a rapidly expanding industry. The closure of agricultural units in this period was also most common in the south of Sweden. In the same period there was also lively small business activity

Figure 8.11 A new element in the pattern of production: leisure products. The classic holiday picture, taken just after the Annual Leave Act came into force in 1938. Photo: Gunnar Lundh. NMA.

which often came to be located in small or medium-sized country towns.[17] Similarly, industrial growth had a fairly broad base, particularly in the consumer goods sector (from the 1930s). Undoubtedly the upswing in textiles, wood products, metal manufacturing and other sectors meant that many of the people no longer needed in agriculture could be absorbed into these activities in Sweden's country towns.

This picture changed dramatically after 1950. Until the beginning of the 1970s it was the large cities and the areas around them that grew most rapidly – Mälardalen, the Skåne region and Gothenburg. At the same time, there was a very obvious decline in the so-called forest counties of northern Sweden. For some counties, including Jämtland, Västernorrland, Västerbotten and Norrbotten, there were even periods in the 1950s and 1960s of population decline in absolute terms. This was clear evidence of a migration to urban areas. The percentage of the population in the urban counties of Stockholm, Gothenburg and Malmö increased from 29.7 per cent in 1940 to

35.8 per cent in 1977. The percentage of the population living in other counties fell. This migration ceased in the 1970s and we see the trend beginning to reverse. There are, of course, several reasons for this much-discussed 'green wave', in which the population of the rural areas increased once again. One main reason was the growth of public services production, which we shall discuss later in its proper context.

The relative (and sometimes even absolute) depopulation of the forest counties in the 1950s and 1960s had a strong impact on the political debate. Not least the Centre Party's strong advance at the beginning of the 1970s which reflects the great intensity of the debate. The problem of the sparsely populated rural areas was debated intensely from the 1960s onwards. There was much concern over the growth of the major cities and many saw in this population migration the danger of future erosion of the services which society could offer the inhabitants of the sparsely populated counties. Because this migration hit the northern counties so hard, the debate focused mainly on the status and position of that part of the country. Against this background, a special regional development policy was introduced that aimed to alleviate the worst effects of relocation by redistributing economic resources to the benefit of rural areas.

The continued closures of small farms was, of course, an important cause of this regional imbalance. Norrland was particularly rich in these small agricultural units. But this is by no means a full explanation. Even more important was the dramatic transformation of agriculture that took place at that time. Since the nineteenth century inland farming in the province of Norrland had been shaped in close interaction with the growth of the forest industry in that province. The forest workers combined felling work in the forests with the running of a smallholding that produced milk, butter, meat and potatoes. The forest worker also needed a horse, for which he grew a little hay and oats. But in the 1950s, in particular, the conditions for this combination of forest worker and smallholder changed. The rapid advance of mechanisation (chain saws and forestry machines) reduced the need for both people and horses. The forestry companies began to employ full-time forestry workers. The general improvement in living standards made the lot of the farmer in the forest regions seem all the worse. It was no longer possible to provide for a family in the traditional way. From 1944 to 1966 the number of cattle farms – in theory self-supporting family farms – fell from 100,000 to barely 25,000. In a purely forest district such as Jokkmokk, for example, the number of cattle farms fell from 650 in 1944 to 200 in 1961. In the 1960s almost all farming ceased in the Jokkmokk area.[18]

But the big city areas grew not only at the expense of the forest counties – even if migration from these areas epitomised what came to be known as the 'removal truck policy' of the 1960s. As we have seen, there was also a population drain from other counties. To some extent, this was a function of the shifts between different sectors of industry mentioned above. For example, a comparison may be made here between the strong upswing in the engineering

Figure 8.12 The problem of the sparsely populated rural areas was the subject of much debate in the 1960s. The 'forest counties' in the north of Sweden were hit particularly hard by the migration off the land. Like the horse, the small family farm was soon just a memory. Photo: Norrbottens museum.

Table 8.3 Private consumption. Annual increase in volume (percentage)

	1950–63	1963–75	1975–85	1985–92
Durable goods	5.7	5.1	0.3	2.4
Semi-durable goods	–	4.5	1.1	2.7
Non-durables	2.4	2.4	1.0	0.8
Services	2.6	2.6	1.7	1.3
Foreign net	9.2	7.3	–8.5	20.3
Non-profit organisations	–	–	–	3.8
Total private consumption	2.8	3.1	0.7	1.7

Source: B. Sandelin, *Den svenska ekonomin*, Stockholm 1994, p. 67.

industry – centred in the big city counties – and the decline in metal manufacture and the forestry sector. It was mainly the counties outside the main urban areas, foremost the Bergslagen district with is concentration of traditional mining, iron and steel, and forestry industries, and to some extent engineering production, which experienced a particularly severe decline in the crisis years of the 1970s.

But industry was only partly responsible for the growth of the main conurbations. In fact the percentage of people employed in industry *fell* in the big cities in the 1950s and 1960s. In the 1950s alone their share of the labour force fell from 26 to 24 per cent. While in total the engineering sector grew by 20 per cent in the same period, the increase in the Stockholm county was only 7 per cent, while the rise in Gothenburg and Malmö fell to just under the national average.[19] The gradual fall in the big cities continued throughout the 1960s and 1970s. At the end of the 1970s this 'de-industrialisation' had, in the case of Stockholm, resulted in its percentage of the employed industrial workforce falling to only 16 per cent, against Malmö at 24 per cent and Gothenburg at 25 per cent. This was well below the national average of about 35 per cent. Instead, the expansion in the big cities must be seen foremost as an effect of the expansion of the service sector after the Second World War. This applies particularly to public sector service, but to a significant degree to private services as well. Until 1970 the service sector grew faster in the big city areas than outside them. After this time, the trend reversed, the main reason being that local and county government public sector service production expanded faster outside the big city areas.

The rapid transformation after 1945 affected more than regional distribution. Equally revolutionary were the changes at the workplace. As we have seen, there was a shift between different branches of industry and commerce, and new and changed demands were made of the workforce. Many people who had left a relatively free job in agriculture and forestry found the conditions of factory work very different. But even for those who were already used to industrial work, the post-war years brought great change.

The world of work changed in pace with the growth in production and automation, and this in its turn led to more specialisation and other organisational changes that were often based on the principle of the extensive division of work tasks. The idea was that specialisation in the form of simple work tasks increased productivity. Large-scale production methods such as the assembly line became widespread. In several cases the extensive fragmentation of work led to a controlled and monotonous work situation. As early as the 1960s industrial sociologists warned that automation and an excessive division of labour would produce 'jobs with a low level of needs satisfaction'. As a result, there was, in their view, 'a low level of involvement in work and poor mental hygiene'. But there were, of course, advantages as well: 'For most employees, these conditions were justified by gains in productivity, thanks to which we have been able to improve living standards, reduce working hours and improve needs satisfaction in leisure time.'[20]

The improvements in the working environment that had begun before the war continued after it was over. Among other things, there was a real improvement in general hygiene at work, with better ventilation, less noise, etc. At the same time, automation had eliminated much of the hard manual labour. However, other 'health and safety problems' arose from stressful and monotonous work tasks which caused, among other things, repetitive strain injuries.

Although there were strong variations in the conditions affecting the different industrial sectors, the period from the 1950s onwards was still characterised by the breakthrough in Sweden of the technology of mass production and organisational forms that had come into being in the USA at

Figure 8.13 The Luxor assembly shop, Motala, in the 1970s. Photo: Luxor archive.

the turn of the century. The higher scale of production and long production runs was a basis for more standardisation and specialisation. This in its turn created the conditions for more automation. In the mass production industries such as iron and steel, paper and pulp, the sawmills and important parts of the engineering sector, this brought a move away from the craft-oriented type of work to more repetitive jobs. The machine-minder or the assembly-line worker replaced the skilled craftsman as the typical industrial worker. Compared with skilled and relatively varied craft work, the skill content of new work tasks was often impoverished. However, there already were a number of unskilled occupations in industry, craft workers' mates for example. As transporting and lifting operations became mechanised, these jobs tended to disappear. The departure of the old craft workers from the engineering industry had the same effect. Here, the workers' mates had acted as helpers to skilled foundrymen, forgers and machine-makers, people who now became machine-minders. As such, they needed more knowledge and carried greater responsibility. Together, the gradual exit of the craftsman and his helper from the factories made industrial work more homogenous and the clearly defined differences in status between different categories of worker became less important.

This trend towards the evening-out of differences in status was reflected at least to some degree in wages, which tended to level out between different occupational groups at the same place of work. This was also true of the LO collective as a whole, particularly in the 1940s, and again in the 1960s. But the differences from one sector to another were considerable. Even if the percentage of 'unskilled' workers fell in the engineering industry, for example, there was still a marked difference between these people and the so-called skilled workers. More skilled than unskilled workers were paid on a piece-rate system. In general, workers' pay on such incentive pay schemes tended to outstrip the pay of people on hourly pay.

As a result of automation and the fact that a great number of skilled 'intangible capital-intensive' tasks disappeared from the workshop floor, the numbers of another category of employee in industry – the white-collar worker – grew rapidly. This group expanded as the percentage of the employed labour force as a whole in salaried employment grew. This group grew strongly throughout the entire post-war period. When it comes to the increase in the number of white-collar workers in industry, the greater investments in the commercial sector played an important part, as did the new production methods that accompanied the advent of mass production technology. Growing production created the need for a more detailed division of office work.[21] In 1900 there were only some 8,300 white-collar workers employed in Swedish industry. Fifty years later the number was just over 189,000. Thus the percentage of white-collar workers of the total employed labour force increased in this period from 2 per cent to 15 per cent.

This expansion, which began in the 1910s, accelerated after the Second World War. According to Mats Greiff, from having been 'the manager's right hand', industrial salaried employees became a 'white-collar proletariat'.[22] The number of female salaried employees increased at the same time, above all among unskilled workers. Greiff gives the following description of SKF in the early 1920s.

> The work in the Tabulation Department was, as in the Punching Department, routine, and consisted mainly of extremely simple sorting work . . ..
>
> The routines that came to apply to office work were strictly form-alised. In the general systems instructions, every detail is meticulously regulated. . . . For deliveries in Sweden alone there are 20 pages of instructions. The form, of which there were eleven copies, was to be filled out by the Order Department from the letters, telegrams or tele-phone orders received. The form was to contain twenty-three separate items of information, including the customer, consignment and type of article. After this the copies were processed in different departments and circulated between these departments for verification and to have information added to and copied from them. This made the work reminiscent of assembly-line work in manufacturing.[23]

By the end of the 1940s the rapid pace of industrial expansion had created a substantially greater demand for labour. To some extent, this demand could be met by importing labour. There was a great deal of immigration in the 1950s, which intensified in the 1960s. Finns, Yugoslavs, Greeks, Poles, Italians and others streamed in to Sweden's major cities and many of the

Figure 8.14 The AB Nordiska Varuförmedlingen office. Photo: A. Malmström. SSM.

smaller towns. Most of these immigrants found work in the industrial sector. The early 1970s saw a fairly steep decline in labour immigration, partly because it became more difficult to find work. In the 1980s foreign immigration increased again, but most of the immigrants were political refugees. In 1980, 730,000 people, or just on 8 per cent of Sweden's adult population were immigrants or the children of immigrants.[24]

Women were another growing group of industrial workers. As we have pointed out, after the war there was a sharp rise in the percentage of female white-collar workers in the industrial sector. There was a general and dramatic rise in the percentage of women in the labour force from the 1950s onwards. While employment figures for the male workforce had remained constant at around 90–95 per cent since the First World War, or even fallen a little, the percentage of the female labour force in work rose from barely 40 per cent in the 1940s to about 80 per cent in 1980. Since then, the gap between men and women has closed even more, and the percentage of the female labour force in work in Sweden is unique in the entire Western world. Married women accounted for much of this sharp upswing (a large percentage of unmarried women had always worked outside the home). Barely 10 per cent of married women were in employment in 1930, this figure rising to 15 per cent in 1950, 36 per cent in 1964 and 64 per cent in 1980.[25]

At first, women's invasion of the labour market was attributed to industrial expansion and a concomitant rise in labour demand. In many cases, however, there was considerable doubt about employing women in industry. In some segments of the engineering sector women had only been employed as cleaners and the like.[26] But from the 1960s another factor pushed up gainful employment among women: the expansion of the public sector. After the

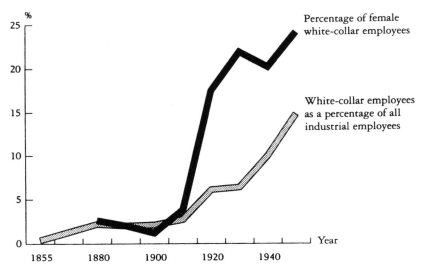

Figure 8.15 White-collar workers in industrial and craft production in Sweden, 1855–1950.
Source: M. Greiff, *Kontoristen*, Lund 1992, pp. 88, 89.

mid-1960s the percentage of women in the industrial workforce did not actually increase at all.[27] Instead, they were employed in the growing organised public service sector; in health and medical care, schools and child care. A far higher percentage of women than men also worked part time. By the mid-1960s a third of gainfully employed women were in part-time work, and two decades later almost half the female workforce had part-time jobs. The percentage of men in part-time work in these periods was, respectively, 3 and 13 per cent.

This and other indices suggest that conditions of work continued to be very different for men and women, even though women had greater penetration of the labour market. Although for many women going out to work was something of a revolution, they usually had to be satisfied with low-grade jobs – thus continuing the pattern from the earlier phase of industrialisation. The reverse was also true. If women took over a job the pay almost automatically became worse in relative terms. The market quite simply tended to put a premium on male labour.[28] The characteristics that were, either informally or in the formal type of job valuation systems, rewarded by the market forces were physical strength and technical know-how/qualifications. In both these respects women were at a disadvantage. Gunhild Kyle writes the following about women's work options:

> The traditional distribution of labour between the sexes proved to be enduring. Traditionally, women had worked in and around the home, including the care of children, the elderly and the sick. When these

tasks moved into the public sector, women followed them. . . . The ideology on which the distribution of labour was based endowed the woman with certain characteristics that were considered not only to make her suited to these traditional duties but also made her directly unsuitable for certain other tasks such as mechanical work.[29]

Although the principle of equal pay was widely applied in the 1950s and 1960s, women were still given low-paid jobs and were therefore over-represented in the low-paid bracket. They also acted to a higher degree than men as a labour buffer to absorb the effects of fluctuations in the business cycle. Similarly, the percentage of women was higher in low-paid segments of the industrial sector such as the textile or food industries. Their penetration in low-paid care work run by central or local government was also very high. Women continued to be conspicuous by their absence in the highly-qualified, top positions in the business world or public sector. Taken together, the events of the 1950s and 1960s were a large step towards better conditions for women. But there was still a long way to go before they achieved equality at work and in the community.

Figure 8.16 The ABBA factory, Kungshamn, in the 1970s. Photo: Jean Hermanson/Mira.

9 The Swedish model

The cautiously expansionist 'crisis policy' that Ernst Wigforss, the minister of finance, pursued from 1933 can hardly be said to have played an important part in Sweden's economic recovery after that year. A more important factor was the greater competitiveness achieved by the structural rationalisations of the 1920s and the devaluation of the Swedish krona in 1932. But the crisis policy must be considered in a broader context. It marks the beginning of a forty-four-year period of Social Democratic government power (until 1976), a record hard to beat in the history of modern Western parliamentarianism. What the short- and long-term effects would have been if the Social Democratic Party had not, through its famous process of 'horse-trading' with the Agrarian Party, been able to implement its crisis policy, is difficult to say. However, it is clear that in this long period of government power, durable institutional frameworks were put in place which enabled continued economic growth in Sweden. It is likely that it helped create the conditions required for the rapid growth and transformation that took place from the 1940s onwards.

It is against this background that the idea of developing a 'Swedish model' entered the debate in the 1930s. This term is used in several ways. In its narrower sense, the 'Swedish model' usually refers to the special relationship between employers and employees that developed from the end of the 1930s, which was expressed in the central wage negotiations between the LO (the Swedish TUC) and the SAF (the Swedish Employers' Confederation), the voluntary agreements between these parties under the provisions of the Saltsjöbaden agreement, the wage solidarity policy and the desire to avoid industrial conflicts. This term is also used in reference to the social welfare policy introduced in the 1930s. In this sense, the public welfare policy became the core of the Swedish model. In this interpretation of the term, Sweden was promoted in an international perspective as an example of the application of a sophisticated welfare policy, particularly in the fields of social policy and full employment. Sweden has been described as a country that takes a middle road between capitalism and socialism, with emphasis given to the importance of consensus and compromise as a prerequisite for this social structure.

Finally, the 'Swedish model' may mean what ultimately appears to be essential to peaceful relationships on the labour market and the continued construction of the Swedish welfare state, namely the 'historic compromise' between the different social classes in the 1930s, which was to leave its mark on Swedish politics and economics for the next half century. There is no doubt that it was this compromise between labour and capital that laid the foundations for Sweden's unusually peaceful industrial relations from the 1930s onwards. It also formed a basis for the public welfare policy with its strongly collective features that are characteristic of Sweden's social structure, which sees welfare as both a goal and a means. In addition to promoting a higher, more evenly distributed standard of living, the welfare policy aims to improve economic efficiency and stimulate growth. Cash assistance to the unemployed or similar simple relief measures are replaced by retraining and other proactive labour market measures. For this purpose a Labour Market Administration (AMS) was set up and given extensive powers. Even the trade union movement's wage policy (the so-called wage solidarity policy) was designed to create growth. In general, the 'historic compromise' creates a climate favourable to strong growth and rationalisation in Sweden. In exchange for a steadily improving standard of living, the organised labour movement recognises the need for profits in industry, as well as structural rationalisation and geographic relocation.[1]

From the perspective of the early 1920s there was little to indicate a future historic compromise. At that time, Sweden was one of the most strike-bound and conflict-prone countries in Western Europe. After the great strike of 1909, relations between the LO and SAF were cool for a long time. The bitter conflicts on compensation for the high cost of living during the First World War and the introduction of the 8-hour day at the end of the 1910s fuelled this mutual suspicion. But this attitude gradually changed in the 1920s. At the end of the 1920s the government initiated discussions between the employers and employees on ways of maintaining industrial peace. At the 1928 Industrial Peace Conference, the Industrial Peace Delegation was set up to promote a policy line based more on consensus. But the results were disappointing and in the depression of the early 1930s their differences flared up once again, and the number of industrial conflicts shot up.[2]

The central agreement between LO and SAF of 1938, the Saltsjöbaden agreement, was the beginning of a new period of compromise. The immediate background to this agreement was the government's threat of legislation on industrial peace. The Social Democratic government, led by Per Albin Hansson, saw industrial peace and more stable labour market relationships as essential to their own package of crisis policies. Many industrial conflicts had tended to have very adverse effects on the general public. In the troubled political climate of the 1930s, it was feared that these conflicts would cause the middle class in particular to show a preference for authoritarian political solutions. It was against this background that the government summoned the parties for talks. But the SAF's attitude towards legislation was negative – and the LO agreed. After a number of complicated political manoeuvres, the SAF and LO chose to bypass the government and attempt to negotiate a voluntary agreement instead. Both these organisations were now tired of conflict. The industrial conflicts of the 1920s and early 1930s had produced

Figure 9.1 The Saltsjöbaden agreement is signed at the Grand Hotel in Saltsjöbaden in 1938. Sitting, August Lindberg, LO (left); Sigfrid Enström, SAF (right). AA.

very few positive results for either employers or employees. There was every reason to try something new.

The result was the central agreement between the LO and SAF, the Saltsjöbaden agreement, which set out an agreed bargaining procedure for resolving conflicts. Together with the law on collective agreements passed in 1928, the Saltsjöbaden agreement made it considerably more difficult to start strikes and lock-outs. A national Labour Market Council, on which representatives from both the SAF and LO sat, was also a forum which could determine whether or not a conflict would endanger or harm the community. Industrial peace was thus considered fairly secure, and the threat to society lifted. But the term 'Saltsjöbaden agreement' encompasses something more. After 1938, a series of ancillary agreements were negotiated and a dialogue between the parties began in an atmosphere of consensus which put in place a bargaining procedure to resolve disputes that had formerly soured relations between these parties. Examples of these agreements include the Workers' Protection Agreement of 1941, the Apprenticeship Agreement in 1944, the Works Councils Agreement of 1946 and, the last of what are known as the Saltsjöbaden agreements, the 1948 agreement on time-and-motion studies. Taken together, these negotiations created a unique climate of co-operation that was an important precondition for the rapid economic and social development of the post-war period. In addition, the allocation of power and responsibilities vis-à-vis central government had now been determined for many years to come – until the mid-1970s. At the core of this balance of power was the understanding that the government would not intervene in labour market affairs, an area in which matters were to be regulated by the employers and employees themselves.

We need not look far for the general background to these efforts to achieve co-operation. Labour peace in itself was not the most important goal. To the trade union movement, the struggle for higher pay took precedence over all other goals. But could this goal be achieved? In the view of prominent trade unionists, in the long term higher pay required a higher rate of economic growth. This implied that they had to accept that company owners made profits and took action to improve efficiency, and that painfully tough restructuring measures would sometimes be implemented. This acceptance was not widespread in the trade union movement until after the Second World War. But other important arguments and motives lay behind this choice of direction. Trade union leaders understood that strong trade union organisations were the only path to success. Agreements, bargaining procedures and union–employer discussions gave the trade unions greater power – both in relation to their opponents and also over their own members. The growing trade union apparatus required more 'experts' and the national organisations had to be allowed to expand at the expense of the local-level organisations. This kind of centralist policy was applied by the LO from the end of the 1930s onwards. A milestone in this area was the report produced by a fifteen-man committee in 1941 which stated that the LO must be given the authority to ban the kind of strikes that could involve the entire LO collective in costly conflicts. Further, ever since its infancy the Swedish trade union movement had fought for agreements. The first collective agreement between the Swedish Metalworkers' Union and the Swedish Metal Trades Employers' Association, which was signed in 1905, became a standard for the whole labour market. The Swedish trade union movement's experience of such agreements was overwhelmingly positive. The Swedish Employers' Confederation's initiative in starting negotiations in 1936 was therefore seen as an opportunity to advance the positions of the trade unions.

Even the Swedish Employers' Confederation (SAF) saw the advantages of free bargaining with the Swedish TUC (LO). The power of central government, in the hands of the Social Democratic government of the time, in itself posed a threat to the interests of the SAF. The threat of legislation in the field of labour relations was a daunting one to the SAF which, as a matter of principle, wanted as few restrictions as possible in industrial relations. At the same time, it was in the employers' interest to bring down the number of industrial conflicts, and to achieve this, some bargaining procedure had to be put in place. A general regulation of the labour market also meant better calculability and restraints on 'unhealthy' competition in the long term.

The wage solidarity policy

In hindsight, the wage solidarity policy appears to have been the foremost expression of the new policy of growth. It became the cornerstone of Social

Democratic economic policy after the Second World War. The view that the trade union movement should attempt to reduce wage differentials became widespread as early as the inter-war years. In the 1938 publication, *Den solidariska lönepolitiken* (The Wage Solidarity Policy), Albin Lind, the editor-in-chief of the LO publication *Fackföreningsrörelsen* (The Trade Union Movement), stated that the trade union movement had to pursue a wage policy based on solidarity. This policy meant that the better-paid groups of employees should be restrictive in their pay claims to allow more to be awarded to the less fortunate. Albin Lind was not very successful in expressing in concrete terms how this was to work. Among other things, he thought that low wage increases in the highly-paid industries – which, in the 1930s, were the industries that supplied the protected domestic market (!) – would cause prices to fall, thereby benefiting the lower-paid (in the export sector). But his critics, who found his proposal far too utopian, thought this form of wage solidarity policy required a wholly socialised economy. Neither did the wage solidarity policy as it was shaped after the Second World War have, in essence, very much to do with Lind's ideas. The fact was that many leading trade unionists, including Arne Geijer, President of the LO between 1956 and 1973, rejected the idea of a high degree of wage equalisation. It was not until the advance of the political left at the end of the 1960s and the beginning of the 1970s that Lind's ideas were dusted off and brought out again.

The wage solidarity policy that was applied instead from the end of the 1940s was first formulated by the LO economists, Gösta Rehn and Rudolf Meidner, in a number of articles published in the Social Democratic journal *Tiden* and ratified by the 1951 LO Congress. Both Rehn and Meidner saw the central problem of Sweden's post-war economy as combining full employment with a high rate of growth and price stability – the classic dilemma of stabilisation policy. Rapid growth could only be created through improved efficiency and structural rationalisation. This required investments, which in turn presupposed a relatively high level of profits in the most efficient sectors. Full employment and price stability could only be combined if employers and employees brought a principle of solidarity to wage negotiations. Otherwise, high labour demand would simply have resulted in higher inflation. Neither did generally well-intended advice such as that offered by William Beveridge in England, that the trade unions should be restrictive in their demands for wage increases, have any chance of success. Instead, inflation had to be kept down through efficiency-improving measures, while the government ensured that company profits were pruned by keeping demand low through the application of a restrictive fiscal policy, which included high and selective corporate taxation.

In expansive sectors with a strong labour demand, the principle of wage solidarity meant that employees did not take such large pay rises as they could have according to the ability-to-pay principle. On the other hand, companies that could not afford to pay wages on the principle of solidarity

Figure 9.2 The powerful presidents of the workers' and salaried employees' national confederations. The LO's Arne Geijer (left) and the TCO's Otto Nordenskiöld (right) in a joint demonstration in support of trade unions in underdeveloped countries, 1963. AA.

went to the wall. But this was a risk that Rehn and Meidner had taken into account. An important purpose of the wage solidarity policy was to promote efficiency-improvement and structural transformation. The employees affected were to be persuaded to relocate and retrain. Thus an important component of the Rehn–Meidner model was that government should actively stimulate labour mobility. To meet these demands, the government labour market bodies, led by the Labour Market Board, expanded rapidly. In the field of industrial relations, what became known as 'workfare' or 'welfare-to-work' was introduced with dramatic speed. One result of this activism was the 'removal truck' policy, which its critics feared would de-populate the rural areas, while in the big cities the 'million programme' (a housing programme to build 1,000,000 homes) was put into effect to provide housing for the large numbers of people who came off the land.

The most important precondition for the Rehn–Meidner model was the policy of co-operation between the parties in the labour market that was already in operation. It also presupposed the high degree of centralism that had evolved both in the trade union movement and among the employers. Industrial peace and the era of central wage negotiations between the LO and

SAF that began in 1957 were therefore central to this new economic policy. The model for central wage bargaining that placed the entire structure of wage policy squarely in the hands of the national confederations – the LO and the SAF – was first put to the test in the bargaining round of 1951/2. It came to be applied in each pay bargaining round from 1955 until the mid-1980s. Even the trade unions were able to agree to this because wages rose at an acceptable pace and the economy was stable. The SAF also held the view that in the central negotiations the LO had a restraining effect on the national unions' demands.[3]

Keynesian demand policy

Economic policy faced a completely new situation in the post-war years. In the 1930s there was a breakthrough for a demand-stimulating policy. To attribute this to Keynes alone is, however, obviously inaccurate. In the USA, Roosevelt had introduced his expansionist New Deal without any knowledge of Keynes, and in Sweden Gunnar Myrdal and Bertil Ohlin had arrived at ideas similar to those of Keynes but from different points of departure. They all emphasised that the major problem was flagging demand. The remedy was to increase government spending and underbalance the budget in periods of depression.

As we have seen, at the end of the Second World War many experts expected a severe post-war depression and a fall-off in demand. But this depression never came. Instead, the central problem for Swedish politicians was to combine monetary stability with full employment, which there was, in theory, in the 1950s and 1960s. One of the main ideas behind the Rehn–Meidner model was to dampen the high level of demand by eliminating unprofitable companies and deliberately creating regional islands of unemployment. Gösta Rehn in particular said that a very restrictive fiscal policy had to be applied, i.e. expenditure had to be kept down while taxes were put up.

Thus, the principal method was more one of restraint than demand-stimulation. From the 1950s onwards tax policy became an increasingly important instrument in this context. We have already seen how the tax rates rose sharply in the 1950s and 1960s; indirect taxes, not least, shot up after the introduction of the new sales tax in 1960. But the Social Democratic government, particularly its minister of finance, Gunnar Sträng, applied other methods as well. In the 1960s, a system of investment taxes and investment funds was developed. The investment taxes were first used in two periods of high economic activity: 1952–3 and 1955–7. These short-term counter-cyclical levies reduced industry's planned investments by about 15 per cent – which of course slowed economic expansion.[4] However, since at the end of the 1950s these taxes were seen as politically controversial, the government relied more on the special investment reserve funds to influence investments. Tax relief encouraged the companies to place their profits in reserve funds – which could only be withdrawn with the permission of the

Figure 9.3 The new suburbia. As part of the so-called 'million (homes) programme', large new housing estates grew up round the big cities in the 1960s and 1970s. The Tensta-Rinkeby development under construction outside Stockholm. SSM.

Bank of Sweden. This was a simpler and more effective way of achieving the same objective as investment taxes.

Although Keynes' theories had to be turned upside down in the post-war years, the basic principle remained: economic policy instruments could be used to moderate the effects of cyclical changes. If, for example, the investment reserves were used largely to moderate cyclical peaks, they could also be used for the opposite purpose. On several occasions, in anticipation of a recession, Sträng instructed the Bank of Sweden to release the reserve funds to increase investment. This kind of counter-cyclical policy was the motivation for a range of fiscal policy measures. The main principle, as advocated by Keynes, Myrdal and Ohlin, was to use the national budget as an 'accordion' in response to fluctuations in the economic cycle. The budget reform introduced by Dag Hammarskjöld in 1937 cleared the way for budget policy to be used in this way in the future.[5]

The counter-cyclical aims of public investments, particularly in housing, were revealed in the same way. But as many critics have maintained, this was not a consistent policy. It was characterised 'more by expansion recession than by reduction in booms.'[6] As a result, public sector growth outstripped GNP growth during this period. In the 1960s, parallel to fiscal policy, labour market policy became the most important counter-cyclical economic policy instrument. From the 1950s there was explosive growth in the Labour Market Board's (AMS) budget – although unemployment was generally at a very low level. In the 1950s and 1960s it was only rarely over 2 per cent of the government budget's operational expenditure.[7] In 1950 the Labour Market Board had answered for 1 per cent of the operational budget, but by 1960 it had risen to 3.75 per cent, and 5.3 per cent in 1970. In the same period the Labour Market Board's expenditure in relation to GNP rose from 0.2 per cent to 1.5 per cent.[8] A number of measures, including relief work, retraining and relocation benefit, were introduced to eliminate local unemployment, stimulate labour mobility and alleviate the effects of economic downswings.

The most important goals of an economic policy are usually given as high growth, high employment, a balance of payments and stable monetary value. When it comes to the first three of these goals, politicians were helped considerably by the generally favourable economic expansion in Sweden in the post-war years. But the goal of combining high employment with low price increases was less successful. Despite lively experimenting with different stabilisation policy measures of this type, prices rose relatively quickly. Clearly, low unemployment and rising export figures caused a rise in demand and the 'inflationary pressure' of which many economists had warned. The Phillips curve, which gives the relationship between unemployment and inflation, was strongly positive for Sweden in the 1950s and 1960s.

Against this background, it was soon clear that neither the Rehn–Meidner model nor Keynesian counter-cyclical policies were entirely satisfactory. In the first case, it was evident that it was impossible to apply forcefully enough the restrictive fiscal policy required to create a combination of full employment and price stability. When it came to budget policy it was clearly easier to increase expenditure in recessions than to lower expenditure in times of high economic activity. In labour market policy, according to Rolf Andersson and Rudolf Meidner, despite all the good intentions to achieve the opposite effect, the model worked as follows.

> The pattern of Sweden's government budget declarations is thus very clear: when faced with an economic downswing, great weight is attached to the principle of reluctance to resolve employment problems by means of public measures that increase buying power. In periods of economic recovery and booms, where budget policy has proved time and again to be incapable of preventing overheating and inflationary tendencies, the preferred means is to intensify labour market policy measures as a way of evening-out regional and sectorial imbalances. In other words, the Swedish government prefers a constant increase in labour market policy investments, with the emphasis on employment-creating measures in periods of recession and adjustment measures in periods of high economic activity.[9]

At a general level, the reasons behind this dilemma were foremost political. The 1950s and 1960s were periods of growing expectations. The general public assumed that their standard would improve by several percentage points a year. And the politicians helped to lull the general public into the feeling that economic growth of this order was a natural condition.

The 'people's home'

The 'Saltsjöbaden spirit' that prevailed between the SAF and the LO was not the only result of the historic compromise of the 1930s. The idea that economic growth was an absolute prerequisite for having a larger surplus to share out was also the basis for the welfare policy that took shape from the 1930s onwards. Towards the end of that decade the leading ideologists in the Social Democratic Party and the trade union movement were in agreement that a distribution policy that favoured the less well-off could only be applied in times of rapid economic growth. This was strongly emphasised, not least in the strategically crucial reports produced by the LO's so-called fifteen-man committee (1941): 'The trade union movement must work for a strong commercial and industrial world and for its sound development, as only on the basis of strong commerce and industry can the working class hope to achieve better economic and social conditions.'[10]

In the 1930s the growth-stimulating distribution policy gave the Social Democratic Party the ideological renewal it so badly needed. In the 1920s it had appeared to be a party largely without an ideology. In practice the Social Democrats had abandoned the idea of a swift socialist transformation of society. This became quite clear when, for example, they mothballed the major report on socialisation at the beginning of the 1930s. But they had difficulties in finding any alternative to the general nationalisation of the means of production. There was, however, an ideological breakthrough for a renewed reformist socialism at the end of the decade. In 1928 Nils Karleby published a book entitled *Socialismen inför verkligheten* (Socialism Facing Reality) in which he did not see nationalisation as an end in itself – instead, the goal was the equal entitlement and participation of workers in society and its governing bodies. Neither did he see the Social Democrats as a purely class party. Clearly, the time was right for his ideas. The evolution from a class party to a broader party for ordinary people was strengthened by the agreement with the Agrarian Party in 1933. Per Albin Hansson's 'People's home . . . the cornerstones of which are a sense of community and accord', became a metaphor for the new efforts to promote co-operation.

After the Social Democrats came to power in 1932 the Social Democratic Party and the labour movement had in the ideology of the 'people's home' a new weapon that encouraged them to start an offensive in the field of social policy. The idea of the people's home encouraged the building of the social structure that eliminated social destitution. 'In the "good home" there is equality, consideration, co-operation and helpfulness', said Per Albin in his famous 'people's home' speech. In the 1930s, Gustav Möller, his minister for social affairs, was behind many of the reforms that gradually transformed Sweden into a welfare state. Möller's line was that the social reforms of which he helped to lay the foundations in the 1930s – unemployment, insurance, mother care centres, the government employment service, housing for families with children and one week's statutory annual leave – were to be available to all. It was this welfare policy based on 'solidarity' that became the most distinctive characteristic of the Swedish and the Scandinavian model.[11] These reforms were to be introduced as laws, and, in principle, applied to all citizens. In 1946 Möller was also the architect of the new

Figure 9.4 The builders of the 'people's home': the 1945 Social Democratic government. From left: Herman Zetterberg, Gunnar Danielsson, Gunnar Sträng, Ernst Wigforss, Östen Undén, Torsten Nilsson, Axel Gjöres, Per Albin Hansson, Tage Erlander, Gunnar Myrdal, Gustav Möller, John Ericsson, Allan Vougt, Nils Quensel and Eje Mossberg. AA.

national basic pension, which was to be the same tax-free basic entitlement irrespective of the recipients' income and wealth. Shortly after this, child benefit and free school meals were also introduced, again, available to all. Unlike Möller's view of welfare as a citizen's right, Gunnar and Alva Myrdal advocated a more selective line, in which the worst-off, especially poor families with children, were prioritised. According to the husband and wife team of Myrdal, the current 'population crisis', i.e. the worrying fall in nativity in the inter-war years, could be remedied by improving social services, for example by introducing crêches. This was essential not least because women too should now be inculcated into the new people's home as full and productive members. In general, the Myrdals advocated a strictly rationalist social policy which had science, order and planning as its guiding stars. Their social programme was set out in the famous publication *Kris i befolkningsfrågan* (The Population Crisis) (1934).

As we have seen, Sweden enjoyed a high level of economic activity from the end of the 1940s. Growth was good and it was a golden age for the export industry. Vigorous growth, combined with virtually full employment, allowed both private and public sector consumption to increase. The policy of consensus introduced in the 1930s – the historic compromise – was undoubtedly one of the preconditions of this rapid growth. At the same time, it is unlikely that this compromise would have survived without this consistently high rate of growth.

A number of the LO reports published in the 1940s and later, expressed very strong confidence in the ability of commerce and industry to create growth and prosperity. Two publications in particular, *Fackföreningsrörelsen och den fulla sysselsättning* (The Trade Union Movement and Full Employment) (1951) and *Samordnad näringspolitik* (Co-ordinated Industrial Policy) (1961), recommended that industry should generate a high and steady rate of growth. The task of the government was to distribute these increased revenues in as 'equitable' a way as possible. This also meant that the trade union movement supported the process of rationalisation and structural transformation essential to this philosophy of growth.

The golden age of welfare policy

The 1950s and 1960s represent a golden age of government-administered welfare. The 'welfare state' developed in Sweden had, of course, its counterparts in other developed capitalist countries in Western Europe. After the end of the Second World War, Sweden was inspired not least by the British debate on welfare – which was strongly influenced by William Beveridge's report in particular. Country after country designed welfare policies in which the common core, at least according to one authority (H.L. Wilensky), was 'a minimum level of income, nutrition, health, housing, and education, protected by the state, that should be guaranteed to all citizens as a right and not as a matter of charity.'[12] At the same time, the welfare policies of different countries varied in their characteristics and focus. Sweden focused on the 'people's home' model developed in the 1930s and the historic compromise of that decade that ultimately allowed this model to be put into effect.

After the Second World War the percentage of government revenues spent on public sector consumption rose sharply both in total and relative terms. From 1950 to 1980 this figure increased more than threefold, from 11 per cent to 34 per cent.[13] As we have seen, the foundations for this change were laid by Möller's reforms in the 1930s. In 1946 all the political parties supported the introduction of a new law on a national basic pension for all. The following year (1947) saw the introduction of general child benefit. The first legislation on annual leave, introduced in 1938, gave one week's statutory holiday. This was increased to two weeks in 1945, which was extended to three weeks in the 1951 Annual Leave Act. Subsequent legislation in this field increased annual leave to four, and even five, weeks. The working week was brought down to forty hours and work-free Saturdays were introduced. At the same time, the educational system was expanded. Comprehensive schooling was introduced in 1950 and in 1960 Parliament made nine-year basic education compulsory. In 1955 compulsory health insurance and more comprehensive insurance coverage for accidents at work were introduced. A law on public welfare was passed in 1957 to replace the old legislation on poor relief. A complex system of housing subsidies was built up. Reforms in the early 1970s included legislation on part-time

Figure 9.5 Social services were extended to include new old people's homes, later pensioners' homes, and pensions were also increased. Top: The new Sabbatsbergs old people's home in Stockholm, built 1945–50, and the Social Democrats' poster for the referendum on the introduction of the ATP supplementary pension system in 1957. Above: The expansion of the municipal day nursery service in the 1960s and 1970s was important for families with children. AA.

pensions (1974), more comprehensive health insurance (1974) and longer parental leave (1974).

Most of these reforms were introduced with broad parliamentary support. However, the proposal on supplementary pensions (ATP) was a call to battle. The Social Democrats wanted to apply the general welfare policy line here too. However, the non-socialists pressed for a voluntary policy on pensions. After lengthy discussions and a referendum in 1957 the proposal backed by the Social Democratic Party and the LO was finally carried by a single vote.

The result of this conflict on supplementary pensions seemed to settle the matter of a choice between a selective and a general welfare policy. Sweden continued to apply a general welfare policy until the 1970s – at least officially. In practice, however, the degree of selectivity increased, for example through housing subsidy and the charges levied by local authorities.

The public sector also expanded in other areas, particularly health and hospital care, which was financed through the county boards, and child care, which was part of the growing municipal service sector. Child care in particular grew rapidly from the 1960s. Without doubt the municipalities were the fastest growing area of public expenditure. This was largely due to an increasing proportion of the responsibility for public sector activities being delegated to the municipal authorities. The municipal authorities assumed responsibility for upper secondary education (1966) and social care (1968), and the county authorities took over responsibility for the district and local medical officers (1963, 1968), the transport of patients (1965) and care of the mentally ill (1967). In addition, from the 1950s the municipalities had to assume the growing responsibility for public housing. At the local level the municipal housing companies soon became by far the largest companies in this sector.

An examination of the spread of total social expenditure (both central and local government) over different items since 1950 shows the greatest expenditure to be on 'income protection'. After falling relatively sharply in the good years of the 1960s, these costs rose again in the 1970s. This heading includes the cost of pensions, health insurance, unemployment benefit, child benefit, local government housing benefit, etc. At the same time, the cost of health and hospital care slowly but surely crept up, while towards the end of this period there was a relative fall in expenditure on education. 'Social services' is always the smallest cost item, covering expenses such as services for children (including child care), the old and the handicapped, the employment service, workers' health and safety, etc.[14] However, expenditure here seems to have increased fairly sharply from the late 1960s too.

Thus the central and local government welfare sector came to offer a social service that affected every area of people's lives. The Social Democrats, in particular, spoke of 'the strong society', with its responsibility for people's welfare in matters both large and small. The view was that the government's long-term planning would eliminate any residual pockets of destitution. The Swedish author Sven Fagerberg's words, 'The future cannot be predicted – it has to be invented', became the motto of the time. Optimism about progress and faith in the 'art of the social engineer' were characteristic features of this utopian picture. The public sector was entrusted with the task of distributing the greater prosperity as evenly as possible. Against this background, 'more welfare' became the main slogan of the Social Democrats in the 1960s and 1970s. The 'benign people's home' that recognised 'no privileged or underprivileged, no favourites and no stepchildren' (Per Albin Hansson) appeared to be on the way to becoming a reality.

Experimenting with a mixed economy

From an international perspective, a unique feature of the burgeoning policy of co-operation in the 1930s was that it was based on voluntary agreements between the employers' and employees' organisations. But although the government refrained from direct intervention in labour market affairs, it still had a finger in this pie. As we have seen, the threat of legislation in industrial relations hung over the employers and employees. The political section of the labour movement – the Social Democratic Party in government – also brought influence to bear upon the LO and its national affiliates to accept more social responsibility in the stormy years of the 1930s. But the government and its administration came to play a very active role in the development of society in other respects. First, the government acquired more and more holdings in industry and commerce. However, as we shall see, government ownership was never dominant in Sweden. Second, efforts were made in macroeconomic planning to increase government influence in the largely privately-owned industrial sector. Third and finally – and here its efforts met with greater success – the government exerted influence through a comprehensive policy of regulation intended to steer the economy towards goals that were considered to be politically justified.

As an *owner* the state has its modern roots in the government utilities that were set up in the nineteenth century. As we had seen, that century saw the founding of a state telecommunications administration and a state transport company, the Swedish State Railways (SJ). Of course some of the utilities, such as the Post Office Administration and Forest Service, went back to earlier times. Others, such as the State Power Board (1911), were founded at the beginning of the twentieth century. Later in this century the National Lithographic Establishment (to produce maps) (1920), and the National Defence Factories (1940) and the Board of Civil Aviation (1947) were set up. The reasons for these agencies coming into being varied from case to case. However, in most cases it was unanimously agreed that they were to be responsible for activities that were essential to economic development, but could hardly be maintained by applying criteria of private profitability – for example, by ensuring that society had access to essential 'infrastructure'. Legislation was passed that gave some of these utilities an absolute monopoly. Until the 1980s, this was the case with the Telecommunications Administration, the Board of Civil Aviation and the Post Office Administration. Other utilities, such as the Forest Service and the National Defence Factories, operated constantly in a competitive market.

In addition to these public agencies, the twentieth century also saw the emergence of a government-owned joint-stock company sector. This sector expanded until the 1970s, after which time it went into decline. The first Swedish government-owned joint-stock company was the LKAB mining concern, in which the government acquired a 50 per cent holding in 1907 (the other 50 per cent was acquired in 1957). Much-publicised government takeovers of companies in the first decades of the twentieth century included the Swedish Tobacco Monopoly (1915) and the founding of the Central Wine and Spirits Company (1917). In the first crisis-hit years of the 1920s the government took over a number of joint-stock companies, including Kreditkassan, AB Svenska Lantmännens bank (a farmers' bank) and Kalix Träindustri (wood products). Similarly, in the 1930s the government acquired, for example, AB Motala Ström (electricity) and AB Gävle Vagnverkstad (railway rolling-stock). In the same period new companies were founded by the government, for example AB Industrikredit in 1930, AB Trafikrestauranger in 1938 and Svenska Penninglotteriet (the national lottery company) in 1938. Nationalisation and the founding of new government-owned joint-stock companies became even more common in the 1940s and 1950s. These included the National Forest Industries (ASSI) in 1941, The Swedish Football Pools Service in 1943, SAS in 1946, the Swedish Atomic Energy Authority in 1947, the Swedish Credit Bank in 1950 and the Swedish Mining Company, which was formed in 1950. This last company was formed to nationalise the so-called German mines in the Bergslagen region after the end of the Second World War.

Until the end of the 1950s most state-owned companies were set up to counter the threat of company closures and unemployment. It is evident, for example, that the government was particularly rigorous in its takeovers during periods of economic crisis, which, as we shall see later, was also the case in the 1970s. In some instances, another motive was to 'lend a hand' in operations that were considered to be at a disadvantage in a free market economy. It was on this pretext that the government became involved in, for example, Vin och Spritcentralen. For the same reason, these government-owned companies were given an exclusive monopoly.

By and large, this pattern came to apply through the 1960s as well. However, at times during this decade when government holdings increased enormously, this process appeared to be an end in itself. Lennart Waara and others maintain that the government-owned companies sector 'grew more in the 1960s than in any previous decade'.[15] But this hardly gives a true picture. In fact, the government's share of gross investments fell from 1950 to 1970. The number of employees in government-owned companies also fell during this period. Although there was a sharp increase in the number of industrial employees during this period in the country as a whole, the increase in the number of employees in government-owned companies was insignificant. However, this does not mean that there were not more government takeovers in the 1960s, which were often the subject of vigorous debate. There were particularly heated discussions about the takeovers of Svenska Durox, the building materials company, the Uddevalla Shipyard, the SMT Machine Company and AB Kabi Vitrum (pharmaceuticals) as well as the founding of the publishing company, Liber. When it came to the acquisition of the pharmaceuticals company Kabi Vitrum a government report claimed, for example, that 'A private economic system, left to its own devices, tends –

particularly in industries like pharmaceuticals – to fail to reach optimum performance in various respects, including the extent of research, pricing and production volume'.[16] For the same reason the Apoteksbolaget (The National Corporation of Swedish Pharmacies) was brought into the government sector in 1970 and the Pripps Brewery in 1975. In the latter case it was said that the government's alcohol policy goal – to bring down alcohol consumption – required more powerful government controls. It is true that in the 1970s the state's share of industrial holdings increased, and for the same reasons as had caused large-scale government intervention before: economic crisis and structural transformation. To a considerable degree this also applied to the rapidly increasing government involvement in the energy sector, for example through the founding of Svensk kärnbränsleförsörjning (nuclear fuel supply) in 1972, Petroswede AB (1975) and Svenska Petroleum AB (1975). This involvement stemmed from a real concern about Sweden's future energy supplies caused by the oil crises of the early 1970s.

In addition to these two motives for nationalisation, a third was particularly evident in the 1960s. During this period, the opinion was widely held that there were advantages in increasing the 'mixed economy' component, particularly in sectors and areas of activity that for different reasons could be considered strategic, such as the energy sector, high-technology operations, telecommunications, etc. In the same way, the founding of the PK Bank in 1973 may be seen as part of an effort to extend government influence in credit operations. But the advocates of a larger government enterprise sector *per se* were still in a minority.

As mentioned above, the government has never had very extensive holdings in companies in Sweden. Measured as number of employees, the government-owned sector has never exceeded 10 per cent. Methods other than pure nationalisation have been preferred to secure government influence on the economy. We have already seen how in the 1930s the Social Democrats in practice abandoned the path of nationalism. Instead, they chose a path that was subsequently called 'functional socialism', in which industry and commerce would remain in private hands but would be strictly controlled and surrounded by complexes of regulations to ensure that, from a political viewpoint, they operated in a satisfactory way.

At the end of the Second World War in particular, demands were put forward for the public regulation of industry and commerce. It is true that in the so-called 'planned economy debate' that followed the publication of the labour movement's post-war programme and the Myrdal Commission's interim report, there were calls for more nationalisation. But full employment was still the paramount goal of the Social Democratic government and other methods were recommended to achieve this. In part the economy was to be stimulated in a Keynesian spirit by more government expenditure, but the need for some *economic planning* was also emphasised, particularly when it came to investments. And it was to develop the forms of this kind of planning that the Myrdal Commission was appointed in 1944. The type of planning Myrdal had in mind was foremost of the indicative type, i.e. it aimed to guide developments towards pre-determined goals by means of voluntarism and a range of incentives. A more sophisticated 'planned economy' would have required more extensive government ownership, a direction in which people were obviously reluctant to go. The Myrdal Commission chose to work on a two-year planning period and devoted itself foremost to planning investments in housing as a way of countering unemployment. However, their ambitious plans went awry. Some years later the idea of a more sophisticated planning body was in effect discontinued. One important reason for this was political: in a powerful campaign against the idea of a planned economy, the non-socialist parties and the Swedish Employers' Confederation forced the Social Democrats to withdraw. But an equally important reason was certainly that the anticipated post-war depression failed to materialise. There was, therefore, hardly any pressing reason to stimulate production through investments in housing or elsewhere. Instead, in the long term, investments came to be governed through fiscal policy, in particular through the investment funds. From 1962, however, the so-called Long-Term Planning Commissions were appointed, which expressed some ambition in the area of indicative planning. The main purpose of these commissions was, however, more to develop a system for forecasting that could be used for advance economic/political planning. These bodies were never given any direct controlling function in politics.

Rather than a planned economy and government ownership, *regulations* have been the distinguishing feature of the Swedish model. These controls governed a number of different areas, but were particularly extensive in the housing, agriculture and financial sectors. The complex rules in the housing market which, as time went by, became very extensive, began with the introduction of general rent controls in 1942, which froze rents and introduced detailed rent controls for newly built dwelling units. Originally, these rent controls should only have been in effect until 1943, but they were extended, although with a growing number of exceptions, until 1975! The 1968 Rent Act was another step towards regulation. Negotiations between tenants' associations and landlords along the lines of the collective wage bargaining procedures became the norm. These parties were limited by a number of rules. Rents were to be set on the 'use value' principle, i.e. based on an assessment of the standard of the dwelling unit. In fact, the system meant that the rents set by the municipal housing companies formed the standard on which the private rental market was regulated. This is, in principle, still the case. There were a number of other regulations. The Rent Control Act of 1942 also granted tenants certain rights of tenure. This system was later refined, and the 1968 Rent Act introduced very strong tenant protection. The municipal authority housing office was also born of the rent controls of 1942. The growing municipal housing companies were obliged to register their apartments with the local housing office. However, despite intensive pressure from, *inter alia*, the municipal authorities, private landlords were never under any statutory obligation to register their properties with the municipal housing service. Further, as Mats Bladh notes, the municipal housing authority took on the task of 'ranking housing applicants'.

> They were to have a 'good housing culture', have no outstanding rent arrears, and they should be reliable and conscientious. The housing office undertook to screen the applicants on behalf of the landlords. Tenants are ranked according to different principles; the time they had waited, whether they belonged to one of the prioritised special-needs groups, a points system, and the allocation of different sized apartments to suit the size of the household. This last principle often meant that people without children were often passed over.[17]

Mention should be made here of the regulations that applied to residential construction. Housing standards complied with government building standards, which stipulated the size of the living area, the lowest acceptable sanitary standards and the like.

The effects of this extensive complex of rules have been widely discussed. Economists have often maintained that the rent controls in particular led to a distortion of the housing market which allowed criteria other than the household's private requirements to determine the actual choice of dwelling. It was one of the most important political considerations for introducing – and stubbornly retaining – the system of regulations: the concern that an unrestricted market would result in a greater segregation in housing and/or greater differences in the quality of the housing stock. On the other hand, at times the system also caused long housing queues, a low level of building and standardised building (compare this with the criticism of the uniform tenements of the 'million homes programme'!) which was undoubtedly seen as an undesired side-effect even by the proponents of this regulatory system.

Agricultural policy was another well-regulated area. Modern agricultural controls were introduced as part of the 'horse-trading' between the Social Democrats and the Agrarian Party in the 1930s. Agricultural policy had been firmly liberal through the 1920s, which led to a rapid pace of structural transformation. Instead, the tariffs were now raised, and a long list of subsidies were introduced to support farming. Food prices were therefore controlled by negotiations between the government and the special-interest organisations in the agricultural sector, rather than by the demands of the market. The Parliament of 1947 approved the 'incomes objective' as the main guideline for future agricultural policy. The goal would be to achieve parity in incomes between agricultural workers and industrial workers. The purpose of price regulations and subventions was thus to ensure that farmers could survive on medium-sized farms, i.e. mainly farms of 10–20 hectares. On the one hand, the policy of 1947 – much of which was in effect until the 1980s – generated some production surplus. This was justified largely by the

Figure 9.6 'Battery farming' in Säbylund, 1991. Photo: Ann Lindén/Landbild.

need for a state of readiness in times of national emergency. If war cut Sweden off from the rest of the world, it would be possible to be self-supporting in terms of food production. On the other hand, in adopting the agricultural policy 'incomes objective', the government supported the rapid elimination of the smallest farming units.

From the 1960s, in particular, agricultural policy was characterised by a comprehensive, complex and poorly ordered system of tariffs, subsidies, import charges, cereal regulations, fat and milk regulations, stockpiling subsidies and clearing systems. The main co-operative agricultural organisations (the LRF and the dairy, slaughterhouse and central associations) vigorously supported this policy and thereby gained a powerful hold over their members. Market regulations were further reinforced by the strong cartels that grew up in the food industry. In addition to the co-operative companies, Svenska Sockerfabriks AB and the oil-yielding plant interests should be mentioned here, which had virtually total monopolies in their respective areas.

The 1960 Agricultural Commission had, it is true, argued in favour of mergers to form larger units and an overall reduction of Sweden's agri-cultural sector, but the agricultural policy decisions of both 1967 and 1977 meant in practice a return to the old policy line of medium-sized family farms as the norm, a high degree of (potential) self-support, a continued substantial production surplus, etc. By and large, the principle of price regulations was also retained – as were the negotiations between the govern-ment and the special-interest organisations in the agricultural sector, which came to liken the trade union wage bargaining rounds. To the price regulations were also added different forms of investment subsidy and government loan guarantees. From 1977, regional policy played a prominent part in agricultural policy, with considerable subsidies being paid, mostly to farms in the north of Sweden. The policy of regulation in the agricultural sector continued more or less unchanged through the 1980s. However, towards the end of that decade there was a changeover to more price competition, while the ambition to make Sweden agriculturally self-supporting was severely moderated, a matter we shall return to below.

Another area which became surrounded by regulations after the Second World War was the credit market. Part of the economic policy of the time was the overall goal of controlling the amount of borrowing. Fluctuations in the economic cycle were to be countered by regulating borrowing, and investments were to be directed to certain high priority areas. The government acted mainly through the Bank of Sweden to control the commercial banks. One method was to raise and lower the official discount rate to influence the borrowing and lending of the commercial banks, and in this area the Bank of Sweden was particularly active in the post-war years. But this system had its limitations, and at the beginning of the 1950s the then deputy head of the Bank of Sweden, Mats Lemne, thought that attempting to prevent the ongoing credit expansion by moderate increases in the interest rate was virtually fruitless. Instead, in an influential memorandum from 1951 and in other publications, he advocated various kinds of regulations and a general control of share issues. The legislation on interest regulation passed by Parliament in 1951 introduced an effective control of new share issues that required a permit from the Bank of Sweden to be sought for new bond issues. More regulations were also introduced when Lemne became head of the Bank of Sweden in the autumn of 1952. He introduced so-called liquidity quotas from 1952 which set a borrowing limit based on the ratio of the bank's liquid assets (including treasury and housing bonds) to its liabilities, which allowed the commercial banks' lending to be very tightly controlled.[18] These liquidity quotas could also be used to influence the banks to give high priority to treasury and housing bonds. To quote Lars Jonung, for example: 'In time, the liquidity quotas had a significant effect on the composition of the commercial banks' portfolios'.[19] In general, a whole arsenal of techniques were introduced in the form of lending ceilings, punitive interest rates, cash quotas, regulations governing borrowing in the Bank of Sweden, agreements, not infrequently informal, and 'moral persuasions' to limit lending to non-prioritised areas. These regulations were applied very rigorously in the 1960s. The system of punitive interest on the amounts borrowed by the commercial banks from the Bank of Sweden became a particularly effective method of controlling the flow of credit in this decade. In 1962 an investment obligation was introduced for all investors, under which a part of available assets had to be invested in treasury and housing bonds.

Generally speaking, this system of strong controls remained in effect right up until the 1980s, after which it was rapidly phased out. From 1971 to

1974 and 1975 to 1976 the discount rate was, it is true, low and the commercial banks' lending almost entirely uncontrolled. But the outflow of currency and pressure on the krona forced the Bank of Sweden to abandon its liberal monetary policy. At the end of the 1970s the policy of strict controls was re-introduced. Throughout the whole of this period, a check on foreign currency transactions was maintained by means of the so-called exchange control. This control was a very important part of the total system. Ultimately, in fact, it was this exchange control that allowed control instruments such as the liquidity quotas to be applied – or, for that matter, the discount rate to be manipulated.

Finally, it should be mentioned that at the local level the authorities also had considerable latitude in governing the development of industry and commerce. Land policy (which rests on the right of redemption), municipal construction, the production of town plans, traffic policy and so on were effective municipal instruments of power that impacted not only on the physical environment but also on trade, public communications and industries. Even central government's national physical planning, which began in the 1960s, was significant in this context. This plan determined future land use: zoning areas for urban development, agriculture, industry and recreation.[20]

The Swedish decision-making model

In Sweden, the historic compromise between the LO and the SAF, the long reign of the Social Democratic Party, the hegemony of the 'people's home ideology' and a Keynesian economic policy laid the foundations for a decision-making model that is sometimes referred to as 'corporatist'. Corporatism usually means a power structure in which different special-interest organisations co-operate with the state (liberal), or are incorporated within the state (totalitarian). In Sweden, these special-interest organisations forged links with the state at an early stage, as in liberal corporatism. For a very long time the Swedish government's administrative bodies, particularly the civil service departments, have enjoyed a high degree of autonomy. The advent of parliamentarianism made no real change to this order. In the nineteenth century, civil service departments were controlled by 'experts'. After the turn of the century, organised interests gained more influence in government administration. As before, Parliament and government were bypassed when it came to the concrete implementation of policy. In the twentieth century, Sweden's citizens were guaranteed insight through their special-interest organisations, which enabled Sweden to develop strongly democratic features.

The special-interest organisations were drawn into the government machinery foremost through the boards and committees under the auspices of the civil service, and through the important parliamentary committees. The first corporative institutions on which the employers' and employees' organisations were represented were set up shortly after the turn of the century. For example, the Workers' Insurance Council of 1902 had five members representing the employers and five representing the workers. And when the National Board of Health and Welfare was founded in 1912, both employers and employees were strongly represented on its board. This model came to serve as a pattern. At the local government level, employers' and workers' representatives were also involved in the administration of, for example, the public employment service from 1903 onwards. At the beginning of the 1930s the corporative model, which was by then thoroughly tried-and-tested in Sweden, thus came to be applied in even more areas.[21] Through their work on these boards and committees, employers' and employees' representatives learned to take into account the best interests of the state when pressing their demands. They gained considerable experience of negotiations and working in a spirit of co-operation.

This model was widely used in the post-war years. For example, when the Labour Market Board (AMS) was set up in 1948, representatives from both the employers' and employees' organisations had seats on the board. The Bill which proposed the founding of the Labour Market Board had the following wording:

> Representatives of various organisations will take part not only in deliberations but also in decision-making. This is intended to give the individual representatives confidence, which will strengthen the authority of the Board. This is of particular importance in consideration of the nature of the decisions the Board will take, many of which must be regarded as sensitive and of far-reaching importance to large groups of the population.[22]

The special-interest organisations, especially the SAF and the LO, were also represented on the boards of a number of bodies, from universities and institutes of higher education to the National Environment Protection Board (founded in 1971) and the Swedish Television Corporation (in which several special-interest organisations also had holdings). By working on committees, government commissions of enquiry, and by producing official comments on government consultative papers, etc., considerable influence was brought to bear, especially in areas such as agricultural policy, where the government worked very closely with that sector's special-interest organisations. But this was also true of labour market policy and industrial policy, where the SAF and LO played an important part. The temperance organisations also had strong influence on the government's alcohol policy. And although the employers' and employees' organisations were not represented on the National Board of Education when it was appointed in its modern form in 1963, they still had significant influence on education – unlike other interested parties such as parents![23] A general characteristic of Swedish corporatism is that the interests of the producer came to have far greater authority than the interests of the consumer.

The expansion of the public sector

After the Second World War a growing proportion of Swedish people's incomes was distributed through the 'public sector'. The fact that a growing percentage of benefits came to be distributed in this way instead of through a market has had a number of important consequences. In a market it is, in theory, user demand that controls the way benefits are distributed, while 'user preferences' or 'the demand curve' ultimately reflect how much they have in their wallets. However, a different principle of distribution was applied to a large part of the swelling flow of revenues that were channelled into the public sectors after the war. Particularly in the medical health and care sector, the 'principle of need' has applied: i.e. politicians and government agencies have applied a set of criteria to determine different need levels, which have then been used in distributing public sector services. Those that were considered to have the 'greatest' need were given priority over those with a 'lesser' need. The degree of uncertainty in grading the needs of the individuals or families has varied from case to case. When it comes to a 'general' benefit such as child benefit, it is easy to identify the recipients: people with children. However, when it comes to other services, greater uncertainty is associated with the 'needs' principle. This is true, for example, of the health and hospital service, where it has sometimes been difficult to rank different 'needs' by priority. Here, for better or for worse, one has had to rely on the producer – that is to say, doctors and other experts – to make sensible and rational choices. Some more selective welfare services, such as social assistance and housing benefit, have been even more difficult to handle from the administrative viewpoint, particularly when government agencies have based their distribution of benefits on the net income of individuals or families. This has sometimes involved very arbitrary allocations while leaving the door open for some people to 'plan' their net income in order to maximise the benefits they receive.

The basic idea behind the needs system was that the market mechanisms were not capable of distributing certain services and benefits, such as 'care', in a socially acceptable way. To allow people's means to determine the preferences would result in broad social differences in, for example, medical and care services, according to the proponents of the Swedish welfare system. In these circumstances the lower income group would be forced to prioritise their daily survival. There would be nothing left over for health care and other needs. In theory, this also applied to housing. To allow a free market in this area would lead to strong segregation in housing, it was thought. It would be better to allow the 'use value' to determine rent levels and, at least to some extent, allocate the housing stock on the 'needs' principle.

Against this background, in the heyday of the Swedish model, which lasted until the 1970s, the market principle was forced into retreat to make way for the 'needs' principle. To some extent this meant a relative reduction in the capitalist sector of the economy. Private capital quite simply failed to gain access to important parts of the service sector that emerged after the war. On the other hand, the public sector became an important market for the products of private industry. Similarly, the major actors in the credit market could, through their ownership and management of treasury bonds – which was an effect of the growing public sector deficit – increase their capital. As we have already stated, capitalism is essentially something other than a market economy. Private capitalists can very well adapt to a mixed economy which has need-driven distribution as a strong component – even if their sphere of activity is, of course, reduced if they are excluded from some sectors of the economy, for example by public monopolies.

Whether or not a largely need-led economy will produce the growth required to generate a large surplus to share out, *inter alia* through a social welfare system, is quite a different question. Opinions are strongly divided here. Many critics of the 'huge public sector' have claimed that the incentives for growth and transformation are weaker when market forces are no longer in play. People will not work to increase their standard and improve their conditions if benefits are distributed according to centrally determined needs. Without questioning capitalism as an effective machine to generate growth, many advocates of a large public sector maintain that the Swedish model managed to combine a revolution in the field of welfare with a high and even level of growth. Consequently, there need be no direct conflict between a large public sector and a dynamic economy that generates growth and a high level of employment. But even the advocates of this model admit that it ran into difficulties in the 1980s. This may have been because some of the basic ideas in the Swedish model – particularly the emphasis on the need for economic growth in order to have something to distribute – had begun to fall into disuse. We shall discuss this and other matters in the next chapter.

Figure 9.7 Forces in the public sector. Left: Nurses and doctors performing surgery at a woman's clinic in Karlstad, 1992. Photo: Anders Petersen/Mira. Right: The Harsprångets power station on the River Lule – a vertical drop of 107m, 940 MW, built 1910–14. Photo: The State Power Board (Vattenfall).

10 A model in crisis

In the decades after the Second World War, Sweden rode a general economic upswing that swept over the whole of the Western world. The industrial sector expanded and the rise in productivity led to a rapid improvement in the standard of living of Sweden's citizens. At the same time, the low level of unemployment — supported by the wage solidarity policy and an increasingly ambitious social policy — ensured a more equitable distribution of this prosperity. Further, economic stability was an important feature of the 1950s and 1960s. Although inflation was a problem, it was no higher in Sweden than elsewhere. The stability of the economy was both a reason for and a consequence of Sweden's enduring industrial peace. Seen from an international perspective, the number of days lost to strikes was very low and, year after year, national wage settlements were negotiated between the LO and the SAF as the central labour market organisations. These two organisations had the common objective of combining economic growth and low unemployment with low inflation and balance in both domestic and foreign trade.

However, towards the end of the 1960s it became clear that there was sand in this well-oiled machinery. The 1960s ended with a large deficit in the balance of current payments which was interpreted as a sign that Swedish industry had begun to lose ground abroad. The recession of 1971–2 was unexpectedly severe and resulted in a sharp rise in unemployment. This was exacerbated by the severe credit restrictions introduced to improve the balance of current payments. At the same time, industry had stopped expanding, which resulted in stagnation in economic growth. The remainder of the 1970s was to be a troubled period which was, however, followed by an upswing in the 1980s. But this upswing in its turn paved the way for the severe economic decline — a fully-fledged depression — at the beginning of the 1990s. Something was seriously wrong. As time passed it became increasingly clear that Sweden's economy was in serious and long-term crisis.

The 1970s

The 'first' oil crisis at the end of 1973 and the beginning of 1974 has often been cited, with the benefit of hindsight, as one of the main reasons for Sweden's economic problems in the 1970s. But this theory overlooks several factors, the most important being the fact that the symptoms of crisis in the international economy predated the oil crisis. It was, it is true, clear that the 400 per cent rise in the price of oil as a result of the OPEC countries' decision of 1973 had serious repercussions in the industrialised countries, expressed in the form of balance of current payments problems and a slower pace of economic growth. But growth had begun to stagnate at the end of the 1960s: 1968 was not only a year of student revolts, there was also a rise in unemployment and a fall in economic activity in, for example, England and France. At the same time, the breakthrough of Western monetary co-operation through the Bretton–Woods system in 1971 brought disorder to monetary policy. The sharp rise in money stock in the Western economies – caused not least by the USA's way of financing the Vietnam War by printing money – led to inflation, while the growth rate fell and unemployment rose. Economists soon began to call this effect 'stagflation'.

Because the economic crisis was attributed to the oil crisis, the severity of Sweden's domestic difficulties was seriously underestimated. After 1973 the governments of the other Western countries chose to allow the higher cost of oil to bring down real wages and buying power. This led to a severe depression, which was accompanied by a great deal of structural transformation. The oil crisis made visible the gradual fall in profitability in many of the sectors that had traditionally acted as the industrial core of Western Europe: coal, iron, steel, shipbuilding and other mechanical industries such as textiles and other consumer goods industries. Cutbacks and restructuring in the traditional base industries led in turn to mass unemployment and the dismantling of entire industrial regions.

In direct contrast to other Western countries, Sweden attempted to avoid the consequences of the oil crisis by introducing a so-called 'bridging policy'. The parliamentary elections of 1973 had produced an even balance of power between the non-socialist and socialist blocks. Until 1976, when this 'balanced' Parliament fell after the non-socialist block made gains in the election, the Social Democratic government was forced to either progress through compromise or by lottery (from which this Parliament came to be called the 'Lottery Parliament'). The even balance of power in Parliament led to a series of settlements, negotiated at the royal residence at Haga (the so-called Haga agreements) from 1973 to 1976, between the government, the non-socialist block and the LO and the SAF. No party to these negotiations wanted to see the crisis cause a rise in unemployment and a fall in buying power. Instead, the parties involved wooed the electorate by publicly competing to out-bid one another on tax reductions, subsidies for industrial stockpiling, releasing investment reserves, etc. At the same time, the rise in

Figure 10.1 The end of an epoch. The world's biggest overhead traversing crane, built in 1976 and weighing 6,000 tons, is dismantled in February 1986, marking the end of the shipbuilding industry in Uddevalla. The Volvo assembly plant was built in its place. Photo: Pressens Bild/Tommy Svensson.

Figure 10.2 The Haga II talks between the leaders of Sweden's five parliamentary political parties. From the left: Gunnar Helén (Liberal), Torbjörn Fälldin (Centre) Gösta Bohman (Moderate), Olof Palme (Social Democrat) and C.H. Hermansson (Left Party Communist). Photo: Pressens Bild/ Stig. A. Nilsson.

inflation and the fact that 1974 was a good year for Sweden's raw materials producers (wood and ore) meant that the next pay bargaining round was expected to produce substantial wage increases. The result was a formidable cost explosion which at a stroke increased (real) wage costs from 1974 to 1976 by about 4 per cent (including the increase in social contributions introduced at the same time). The result soon expressed itself in the form of falling exports in the world market – a trend accentuated by an over-valued krona, which had been linked to the D-Mark since the beginning of the 1970s in the European currency snake. When, in 1976, the worst of the depression was over in the rest of Western Europe, Sweden was hit by a severe decline. To alleviate its effect, the non-socialist coalition government that had recently come to power decided in 1976 to devalue the krona, and thus leave the currency snake. The three devaluations of 1976 and 1977 wrote down the value of the krona by about 14 per cent. There was a fourth devaluation of about 11 per cent in the autumn of 1981. The aggregate effects of these devaluations was that Sweden had largely regained its competitive position by 1982.[1]

The worst consequence of this cost explosion was lost ground in export markets and the severest industrial crisis since 1920. The worst-hit sectors were shipbuilding, mining and iron and steel. The production value of Sweden's shipyards was almost halved from 1974 to 1977, Sweden's steel production fell by 30 per cent and most of the old mining industry of the Bergslagen district collapsed.[2] The shipbuilding industry went into total collapse: between 1975 and 1982 the number of employees fell from 32,000 to 17,000, the number of work sites fell from 46 to 26 and the sector's percentage of total value added fell from 3.2 to 2.3 per cent. A number of large shipyards with long and rich traditions, including Lindholmens, Eriksbergs Götaverken, and Öresundsvarvet, were closed down.[3]

Unlike the situation in the 1920s, for example, powerful government countermeasures were implemented to moderate the worst effects of this industrial crisis. Companies in crisis formed a queue to solicit government assistance from the Centre Party's minister of industry, Nils G. Åsling. Several billions of kronor were paid out after 1976 to restructure the ship-building, steel and other industries. From 1976 to 1983 a total of SEK19.6 billion was paid to the shipyards, which was about one third of the total amount paid in industrial assistance during the same period. This assistance in its turn led to the formation of the government-owned Svenska Varv AB which in 1977 took over almost all Swedish shipbuilding. The government also increased its involvement in the steel industry, particularly its least profitable segment, the labour-intensive commercial steelworks. The country's three largest ironworks – Domnarvet, Luleå and Oxelsund – were amalgamated to form a single giant company, Svenskt Stål AB (SSAB), in which the government had a 75 per cent holding. Many small units went to the wall at this time, either by being closed down or bought up by the larger enterprises. Even the special steel industry was hit by a wave of cutbacks and restructuring, the effects of which included a powerful concentration of the entire industry and more extensive product specialisation.

Thus, the decline around 1976 was unusually severe, and not in pace with the rest of the Western world. Industrial capacity fell more in Sweden than in most other countries, as was reflected *inter alia* in the unusually poor growth figures for this period as a whole. Together with the devaluation, this made real wages fall, particularly after 1980.

However, the positive effect of the devaluations in particular was that, as mentioned above, the competitiveness of Swedish industry was largely restored. But at the same time, unemployment became a concern and created – not least through the generous industrial policy of the time – a substantial budget deficit. Through the crisis years, central and local government had been forced to borrow large sums of money to fund their ever-growing undertakings. The fact that much of this money was borrowed from abroad led to a ballooning deficit in the balance of current payments. It was in this situation that a new Social Democratic government came to power under the leadership of Olof Palme and with Kjell-Olof Feldt as minister of finance. What kind of economic policy would this new government introduce?

The 1980s

After 1982 the new government's ambition was to create full employment, economic growth and reduce the budget deficit, while keeping inflation low. This was a difficult equation to balance. Despite these difficulties, Kjell-Olof Feldt designed what came to be known as the 'policy of the third way'. On the one hand, it was oriented towards the economic policy of the 'first way' as pursued in Margaret Thatcher's Britain. She had attempted to create the conditions for growth and low inflation by making massive cuts in social welfare and by allowing free market forces to come into play. A policy of this kind was obviously far out of step with the Social Democratic inheritance that the new Swedish government had to administer. On the other hand, neither did the 'second way' – whose foremost advocate at the beginning of the 1980s was the new Socialist adminstration in France, led by President François Mitterrand – appear to be a particularly realistic alternative. At the beginning of the 1980s, Mitterrand's expansive Keynesianism had resulted in a growing deficit in the balance of current payments and galloping inflation in France. Feldt's and Palme's 'third way' involved, like Thatcher's path, a supply-side policy. Growth was to be stimulated by a sharp rise in companies' profitability. The wage solidarity policy and the trade unions' traditional loyalty to a Social Democratic government would ensure that this increase in profitability was not eaten up by pay rises. This was to be guaranteed by a new compromise of the kind entered into by Swedish workers in the 1930s. In return, wage-earners would enjoy the fruits of full employment and the long-term benefit of a higher standard of living.

Figure 10.3 Black Monday. The New York Stock Exchange crash in October 1987 shook the world of finance. Picture of the Stockholm Stock Exchange in November 1987. Photo: Lars Säffström/Mira.

The method used to increase profitability was a very drastic and 'aggressive' devaluation. After the elections of September 1982, the new government started its term of office by devaluing the Swedish krona by an astonishing 16 per cent – Feldt had originally considered a 20 per cent devaluation but was advised against it by his colleagues in the other Nordic countries. The effects were not long in coming. Unemployment fell rapidly, and until the middle of the 1980s the substantial budget and current balance of payments deficits were reversed. At the same time, the profit share of national income grew very rapidly while inflation hardly exceeded that of other countries.

However, after the mid-1980s the 'third way' policy ran into more and more difficulties. The most important reason for this was undoubtedly that in the long term it became increasingly difficult to continue to impose a restrictive pay policy. Employees and their elected representatives in the trade union movement saw – partly as a result of devaluation – how company owners began to line their own pockets. Despite central government's active intervention in pay-bargaining rounds – something that the employers' and employees' central organisations called an 'incomes policy' and to which they vociferously objected – it was no longer possible to refuse the demands for higher pay. Instead, the conflict hardened, particularly between the government and the LO. Most wage increases were in the form of wage drift. The fact that wage drift became so important reflected the decline in the trade union movement's power to regulate wages through central agreements.

The disagreements between the government and the LO on distribution policy were aggravated by other aspects of the supply-side policy of the third way. The ministry of finance lifted a number of regulations, among them those governing the money and finance markets, with a view to creating better conditions for growth. In time, almost all restrictions on the credit market were withdrawn. Perhaps the single most important decision in this area was the removal of the commercial banks' lending limit in 1985. The result was a rapid rise in lending by these banks and other credit institutions, not least to the property market. As the tax scales became more steeply progressive, rising inflation and the growing difference between what the purchaser of a service pays and what the person who delivers that service retains after income tax, employer's contributions, value added tax, etc., provided the opportunity for enormous profits from speculating in, for example, property or securities (through so-called options etc.). The term speculation is often used about transactions that anticipate a rise in price and value. Critics of this economy of growing expectations subsequently described the 1980s as a 'speculators' economy', and the word 'yuppy' was an innovation introduced into the language at that time. The substantial profits in the financial sector exacerbated the disagreements in the field of distribution policy. It became clear that the world had changed since the 1930s, and there could therefore be no hope of a new 'historic compromise'. An important reason for this was undoubtedly that industrial growth, notwithstanding the year's sharp rise in profits, was far from as high as it was, for example, in the 1960s. In fact, the industrial sector continued to decline through the 1980s, despite the supply-side economic policy, according to which changes in certain factors that affect supply, including taxation, are a particularly effective means of stimulating economic growth and stabilising price levels.

Towards the end of the 1980s, the problems of the 'third way' became apparent on a broad front. Inflation accelerated and the economy showed every sign of overheating. In many sectors there was no longer full but 'surplus' employment. This was true, for example, of some segments of manufacturing – perhaps foremost the export-oriented engineering sector – which experienced a severe shortage of labour and a fall in productivity. An important reason for this labour shortage was competition from the public sector, which continued to expand, and also from a protected domestic sector that could often offer higher wages, one example being the building sector. An important effect of this was that the export-oriented sector hardly increased its employment level at all through the 1980s – at least not in Sweden. Despite its high ambitions, the policy of the third way did not succeed in transferring resources to the export sector.[4] Further, the devaluations had more long-term effects on industry, to which we shall return below.

The 1990s

In Sweden the 1990s began with an overheated economy: an employment surplus, a financial sector with an over-dimensioned borrowing profile ('secured' by means of a high level of borrowing against overvalued assets), high inflation and a failing export industry that was losing market share, mainly due to falling productivity.

Against this background, in the spring of 1990 the Social Democratic government produced a package of crisis measures aimed at cooling Sweden's overheated economy. These measures included a ban on strikes, a wage freeze and a ban on any increases in municipal taxation. Reactions were violent, not least from the LO. As a result, the so-called 'War of the Roses' between the LO and the Social Democratic government entered its most intensive phase. At the same time, this package of crisis measures was voted down in Parliament, and the government – which, after the death of Olof Palme in 1986 was led by Ingvar Carlsson – chose to resign. After a crisis that lasted eleven days, a new government was formed – but with a less severe package of crisis measures and without Kjell-Olof Feldt as minister of finance.

Instead, it was the international recession that served as a 'brake' in Sweden. Already in 1990 there was a very sharp decline in the economy. The anticipated price rises suddenly failed to materialise in the second half of 1990 and there was a drastic fall in the growth rate. At the same time, there were signs that all was not well with the Swedish credit market. In August 1990 the Nyckeln finance company announced substantial losses and the Gamlestaden and Independent companies were viewed with considerable suspicion. In the autumn of the same year, the short-term interest rate suddenly shot up. It was obvious that this rapid U-turn from inflation and overheating to recession and deflation would hit Sweden's economy very hard indeed.

The problems that such a swift change from inflation to deflation could create had been seen in the 1920s. But the decline from 1990 onwards was even stronger than anyone had expected. It was accentuated in several ways by the economic policy of the time. The radical change in tax policy, which introduced, among other things, generous tax benefits for the middle class and also reduced 'marginal' taxes, made speculation in property and securities less profitable. When the price rises ceased, the bottom fell out of both of these markets. The property market in particular was hit by severe falls in prices and values, which meant ruin for those who, for example, had mortgaged property to finance the acquisition of other assets. Another important factor that intensified this crisis was that the value of the Swedish krona was maintained against the main currencies in the EU as part of European currency co-operation, the EMS. Thus the Swedish krona was overvalued, and combined with the swift decline into recession this meant that Sweden lost export market shares. Speculation in the krona also caused a steep rise in interest rates. In the autumn of 1992, the Bank of Sweden's so-called marginal interest rate rose to an incredible 1,000 per cent. Shortly after, the new non-socialist coalition government led by the Moderate Party's Carl Bildt – that started its period of government with a solemn pledge to defend the value of the krona come what may – was forced to let the krona float.

Figure 10.4 Worried expressions in the Riksdag in February 1990. Kjell-Olof Feldt (minister of finance) and Ingvar Carlsson (prime minister) and behind them, Birgitta Dahl. Photo: Pressens Bild/Sven-Erik Sjöberg.

This swiftly led to what was in practice a 25 per cent devaluation – the biggest single devaluation in modern Swedish economic history.

Finally, the new Bildt government's talk of a 'system shift' created uncertainty about the future, particularly about the Swedish welfare system. This greater uncertainty was one of the main reasons for the almost total collapse of domestic demand after 1990. From the summer of 1990 to the summer of the following year the number of new cars registered fell by 20 per cent, and by a further 30 per cent the year after. In 1993, fewer cars were sold in Sweden than in the years of the 1950s – a clear indication of the dire domestic demand situation. Households preferred to save their money. What Keynes had once predicted appeared to be actually confirmed: to save money was the dominant strategy in the uncertain circumstances that had occurred.

The most spectacular aspect of the crisis of the early 1990s was without doubt the bank crisis. Beginning in 1990, one crisis followed the other in the finance companies that were closely linked to the commercial banks. Already in 1990 the Nyckeln finance company announced losses of around SEK2 billion. In the first six months of 1991, Gamlestaden lost SEK2.8 billion. In 1989 the total exposure of the finance companies was SEK134 billion. By 1991 these borrowings had fallen to SEK103 billion. The finance companies continued to register losses in 1992 and 1993. Several of these companies had to go into liquidation. Taken together with other credit losses, this brought the commercial banks under considerable pressure. In 1990 the banking sector as a whole suffered credit losses totalling SEK11 billion. In 1991 Första Sparbanken alone lost SEK4.5 billion, Gotabanken SEK3.7 billion and Nordbanken an almost inconceivable SEK10.5 billion.[5] To avoid involuntary liquidation, the major banks had to turn to the government for help. In this way the government 'socialised', in 1990 alone, aggregate credit losses in the banking sector that amounted to an incredible total of over SEK100 billion.

The third industrial revolution

As the powerful upswing in Sweden's economy in the decades after the Second World War can be linked to the trends in the international economy, the severe problems of recent years must also be seen in this perspective. As we have seen, there was what we may describe as a breakthrough for a new international development block after the Second World War. In Western Europe this was based on the mass production of consumer durables (including cars and aircraft), together with a heavy industry of steel, iron, coal and cement. These base industries also helped build up the infrastructure of Europe's war-torn economies. The dominant form of industrial organisation had been called 'Fordism', which emphasised the American example of long mass-production runs. In the 1950s and 1960s this development block generated high economic growth throughout the Western world. The growth figures in Sweden were not at all exceptional; seen in this light, they were in fact fairly modest. By the end of 1960s, however, this development block had clearly entered its rationalisation phase. Particularly in heavy industry (iron, steel, etc.) there was considerable overcapacity, and the acute post-war need for new infrastructure had now been met. Roughly at the time the oil crisis hit the Western economies it became clear that the old development block was in decline.

The clearest expression of this decline was the rapid process of restructuring and the wave of closures that hit Western European industry throughout the 1970s. As we have already noted, a significant proportion of heavy industry was eliminated. Formerly well-developed industrial regions such as the Ruhr in Germany, southern Belgium or Sheffield and Glasgow in Britain were hit by widespread 'de-industrialisation'. In the 1970s, industrial employment in Western Europe fell on average by over 2 per cent a year. The result was a sharp upswing in unemployment which stabilised at around 10 per cent in the major Western European countries. Growth in the 1970s and through most of the 1980s would only reach about half of the level it had achieved in the previous two decades.

In the economic debate the crisis for the 'old' development block has often been related to what has come to be called the 'third industrial revolution'. This has gradually come to supplant the 'first industrial revolution' of the early nineteenth century, in which handicrafts were replaced by mechanical

Figure 10.5 Modern electronics manufacture. Ericsson's newest plant in Kista outside Stockholm. Photo: Nyhetstjänst/Anders Anjou.

equipment, particularly in the consumer goods industry, and the 'second industrial revolution' of the turn of the century, which was based on mass production, heavy industry, electricity and new means of transport. The 'third industrial revolution' thus has its origins in the industrial overcapacity that we have already discussed, but is also a consequence of gradual changes in the international distribution of labour. Not least, against the background of a high level of wages and prosperity in Western Europe, an increasing percentage of heavy industry and the simple consumer goods industry that manufactures standardised goods at a low price has come to be relocated to low-wage countries both in, but particularly outside, Europe. In recent decades, substantial parts of what was formerly called the third world have – notwithstanding all the pessimistic forecasts of the reverse – undergone an industrial revolution. This is evident not least from the fact that growth has consistently been far higher than in the earlier industrialised countries. But the term the 'third industrial revolution' also refers to the emergence of a high-technology, more differentiated and customer-controlled industry in Western Europe. Instead of standardisation, long runs and low unit costs, flexibility, service and uniqueness are at a premium. A typical feature of 'Fordism' was the assembly line and long runs producing identical articles. The result was often an erosion of job content, lower qualifications required of the workforce and – as the ultimate consequence – unpleasant work from which most people attempted to escape. This led to a high turnover of workers and falling productivity, resulting in poor profitability and accentuating the trend towards changes in the international division of labour.

The emergence of a different international division of labour is not, however, the whole story. The discussion of the 'third industrial revolution' is also based on the emergence of a new development block since the 1970s. On the one hand, it has its origins in changed preferences, particularly among consumers in the highly developed industrial countries. The demand for standardised mass-produced goods has been replaced by a more individualistic demand that puts a premium on flexibility, unique products and higher quality. On the other hand, there are the changes on the production side. Perhaps the most important technological factor has been the revolution in micro-electronics which has paved the way for a completely new 'technological system' or 'technological regime', according to Christopher Freeman, the economist and historian of technology, and others.[6] The introduction of computers, combined with very extensive automation in production, has had far-reaching effects. For example, the old demarcation line between white-collar workers and blue-collar workers has become increasingly vague. Once again, high demands are made of skill and competence, while many of the old repetitive work tasks have been replaced by automatic machines. The wider use of computer power has meant that many old jobs – often monotonous in nature – have disappeared, while the revolutionary effects of the new 'technological regime' and micro-electronics have often been described in almost lyrical terms:

> Machines, such as the computer, can to an ever-increasing extent be controlled by the user. The intangible capital he brings to the work becomes more important for the order of production than the capital tied up in the machine. *Real capital loses its 'agenda-setting' role.* This has major consequences: the size of the workplace changes, forms of ownership will be different, the boundary between blue-collar and white-collar worker is shifted or eliminated, and the systems of management and rewards will be modified to suit the new conditions. The major element of human capital will also affect the company's ability to adapt and renew.[7]

But there is another side to the coin. The new revolution has been bought – at least for a long time into the future – at the cost of an overall reduction in the industrial sector, which is thus no longer able to generate as many jobs as before. Productivity in this 'modern' sector is constantly rising, and more value than ever before can be added by fewer and fewer workers, both blue- and white-collar. The only way out for the residual – and often poorly educated – workforce is to take employment in what is, after all, an expanding service sector. This is often a low productive sector and only offers low-paid jobs. At least in the medium term, the 'third industrial revolution' therefore appears to lead to greater differentiation between the labour market's 'insiders' and 'outsiders'. The effect is an overall increase in the gaps between, for example, incomes and living conditions. The relatively homogenous industrial employment that was a cornerstone of the Swedish model is, in other words, under serious threat.

Finally, it is also clear that the new development block is based on a powerful internationalisation of the world economy that has occurred in recent decades. In Europe, this trend has been accentuated through the development of the EU – particularly since the 1985 decision to create an internal market. The effects of this internationalisation have been dramatic. Shortly after the end of the Second World War, Keynesian economic policy was at its peak. In addition to the public investments that were recommended to increase demand, it emphasised the individual state's ability to pursue an economic policy that was in its own interest. In country after country, different systems of regulations were developed to stimulate growth and achieve high employment. Keynesianism also recommended that each country should have its own base industries; thus each country jealously guarded its iron and steel industry, for example.

From the 1970s however, this line has gradually been abandoned. Experience of both stagflation and the severe industrial crises, which had serious repercussions on countries' base industries, appeared to be good enough reasons to abandon the Keynesian formula. And it has become increasingly evident that in pace with the change from 'Fordism' and mass production to more flexibility, a Keynesian policy of stabilisation and growth has become more difficult to implement. We have also observed from this structural transformation that for the first time since the infancy of industrialism there has been a serious decrease in the size of companies (this, however, did not apply to Sweden; see below). Moreover, this has been a reciprocal process. As business became more international and more difficult to control, the chances of pursuing a Keynesian economic policy diminished, which in its turn hastened the process of internationalisation and the dismantling of the instruments used to control the economy. In sum, the Western European economies had become more open – but also more vulnerable.

Structural crisis and transformation in Sweden

Sweden is a shining example of our argument about the general crisis that has hit the 'old' industrialised world in recent decades. As in many other areas, the problems could be seen in a sharp fall in the rate of growth and – at least from 1991 – high unemployment figures. Seen from an international perspective, growth in Sweden since the mid-1970s has actually been unusually weak, both in relation to the advanced industrialised countries in the OECD as a whole, and also when Sweden is compared only with the European OECD countries. Although it is sometimes said that it is only natural that formerly advanced industrialised countries will in time fall behind in their pace of growth, while countries that started later can achieve higher figures in this respect,[8] there is no law of economics or statistics which says that early industrialised countries such as Holland, Belgium, Austria, Denmark and Italy must inevitably, from the beginning of the 1980s, overtake Sweden in GNP per capita. From having been among the absolute élite in the OECD countries twenty years ago, Sweden has fallen well back down the field. It is clear that Sweden has found the adjustment from the golden years of the 1950s and 1960s to be particularly difficult.

More clearly than ever before, the process of adjustment that has been under way since the 1970s is expressed in the decline of what has traditionally been called the industrial sector. In Sweden, according to the official national accounts, industrial production's percentage of GNP fell from 27 per cent in 1970 to 20 per cent in 1991. This fall was particularly sharp between 1974 and 1978, and despite the good years of the 1980s and the investments in the policy of the third way, growth in industrial production continued to be weak. Except for the period from 1982 to 1985, the pace of growth was markedly lower than the average for the European OECD countries. As we can see from Figure 10.6 this means that the number of employees in different branches of industry has fallen rapidly since the 1970s (at least, according to the official statistics).

However, this reversal should not mislead us into believing that the 1980s were a generally poor time for the Swedish enterprise sector. In effect, companies' production rose – but most of this increase was located abroad. A distinguishing characteristic of the second half of the 1980s, in particular,

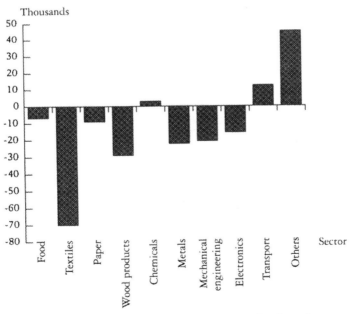

Figure 10.6 Employment trends in Sweden in thousands of employees, selected sectors 1970–89.

Source: T. Andersson *et al., Den långa vägen – den ekonomiska politikens begränsningar och möjligheter att föra Sverige ur 1990-talets kris*, Stockholm 1993, p. 67.

was the massive direct investments Swedish companies made abroad – especially in the engineering industry – to establish subsidiaries or buy up foreign companies. From 1984 to 1991 alone, the EU – in which most of these investments were made – received direct investments up to a value of SEK172 billion (against, for example, the SEK39 billion that went to the USA). If we confine ourselves to a study of industrial production in Sweden, we see that it increased by a modest 16 per cent between 1974 and 1990, but if we include foreign investments, it increased by 44 per cent. Much of this investment came from the technology and the intangible capital-intensive engineering sector.

At the same time as the industrial sector's percentage of GNP fell, the relative importance of other sectors, not least the private and public production of services, increased. This development is unmistakable – if we measure this growth with conventional methods. However, the problem is that the official national accounts *over-emphasise* the decline of the industrial sector in recent years. This is because it has become increasingly difficult to draw a clear line between industrial production and services production. In recent years, technological advances and, not least, the advent of micro-electronics have meant that a series of work tasks that were formally integrated into the industrial enterprise have been transferred to separate smaller companies, consultant companies, etc. An extensive 'industry-related' service production segment has emerged that should actually be included in the industrial sector. 'Revising' the estimate of the percentage of the different sectors in this way gives completely different figures than those in the official national accounts. In light of this, it is doubtful that we can see any decline in the 'industrial sector'.

The low level of growth bears witness to the severity of the problems that arose from the decline of traditional industry and the changeover to more flexible forms of production. To a great extent, this low growth rate reflects the various productivity trends in Swedish industry, including the 'industry-related production of services' in recent years. Thus, not all the blame for slow growth and low productivity can be laid at the door of the fact that a growing percentage of the GPD had been transferred to, for example, public services for which it is difficult to find any uniform measure of productivity, but for which all available studies suggest that the productivity trend has been very weak. The poor productivity trend in, for example, the second half of the 1980s, also applied to industry. The problem is not only that the industrial sector has become smaller, but also that it is no longer capable of generating higher incomes at the same pace as in the 1950s and 1960s, for example.

Figure 10.7 gives a clear picture of how industry-related services have increased in relation to industry itself. This suggests that the same process of transition towards increasingly intangible capital-intensive and flexible production that 'hit' Western Europe has also affected the Swedish economy. A growing percentage of investments were thus in the form of intangible

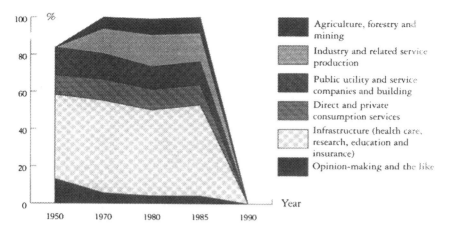

Figure 10.7 The real size of Sweden's industries. Percentages of GNP at producer prices 1950–90.

Source: T. Andersson *et al.*, *Den långa vägen . . .*, Stockholm 1993, p. 205.

capital formation, i.e. investments in research and development, sales and marketing, etc. In 1978, 55 per cent of investment in the five biggest corporations was in this kind of intangible capital formation.[9] The widespread concern that greeted the fall of industry's investment in fixed plant and machinery in the second half of the 1970s was therefore hardly justified.[10] This fact reveals, more than anything else, the changed face of the industrial sector, and that there had been a substantial increase in companies' R&D costs as a percentage of total company expenditure. At the same time, it was clear that much of this increase was in the large companies and that it was spread unevenly between different branches of industry, with about 70 per cent of the investments being in the telecommunications, transport and pharmaceutical sectors.[11] Surveys also show a considerable increase in the intangible capital content of Swedish production, particularly in the 1970s.[12] However, the trend reversed in the 1980s. In contrast to the trend in Western Europe as a whole, this suggests that Sweden specialised more in products with less value added per employee. If this trend proves to be sustainable in the long-term, it will undoubtedly have serious consequences for the long term development of Sweden's economy.

    In other respects, the trends we have already discussed in the development of the different economic sectors became, in general terms, stronger. The 'old' sectors such as agriculture continued to decline, while the service sector expanded. Similarly, in the industrial sector the textile and food industry continued to lose ground. From the 1970s onwards, this was also true of the mining, iron and steel industries. As we have seen, this sector became far leaner in the second half of the 1970s. In the 1980s the decline was stopped, but there was no real recovery in either absolute or relative terms. An exception among the 'traditional', often more material-based industries is the forestry industry, which has maintained its position. The engineering industry is, as before, an expanding sector, particularly if we include here this sector's considerable investments abroad in the 1980s as discussed above. The chemicals sector and transport, heating and power also expanded in the 1980s.

In an economy of the type we are discussing here, the production of services assumes ever-increasing importance. This is largely because people with rising incomes tend to spend higher percentages of their incomes on different kinds of welfare services, including recreation. This also means that much of the work previously done in the home is increasingly taken over by a private and public service sector. There is no doubt that the entry of women into the labour market was a decisive factor here. In Sweden, much of this production of services was under the auspices of a tax-financed public sector. As we have already seen, this sector's percentage of GNP has risen very sharply since the 1930s. That the production of 'welfare' in Sweden was allocated to the public sector was primarily a political choice. The 'law' on a constantly expanding sector formulated at the end of the nineteenth century by Adolph Wagner, the German economist, hardly applies to, or at least cannot explain, the considerable differences in the development of the public sectors in different countries or even how the public sector develops in different countries.[13] In the mid-1980s, the increase in public sector expenditure in Sweden was reversed, the main reason being that the transfers stopped

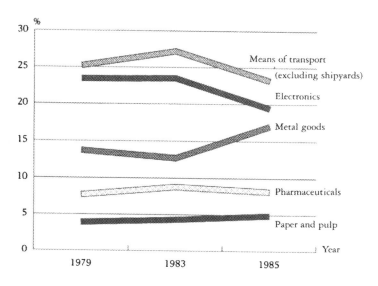

Figure 10.8 Percentage of total annual R&D in selected sectors 1979, 1983, and 1985.
Source: E. Ekstedt, *Humankapital i brytningstid*, Stockholm 1988, p. 43.

increasing and even began to decrease. However, this must not be interpreted as a sudden fall in the consumption of services (for example in 'welfare'). Instead, the explanation is that the percentage that was distributed through a private service sector began to grow. Here, too, the main reason was a political one. On more or less good grounds, Sweden's politicians decided that the aggregate tax outtake had hit a ceiling. In their view, any increase in taxes would prevent the economy from operating well enough to generate growth.

The political economics of adjustment

The crisis in the traditional industrial sectors and the low – more than halved – rate of economic growth in the 1970s manifested itself in a number of different ways. *First,* problems of economic balance occurred of a severity that was quite unknown in the 1950s and 1960s. These problems had certainly been aggravated to some extent by the domestic policies of the time – in particular the 'bridging' of the 1970s and the policy of the third way of the 1980s. Yet it is clear that these problems were ultimately related to the rapid pace of structural transformation. However, the balance problems were accentuated by the failure to downsize political expectations and ambitions in pace with the fall-off in the rate of growth. Both politicians and the general public assumed that the work of social reform would still be assiduously pursued, and that the automatic increase in prosperity would continue.

If the problem in the decades following the end of the Second World War had been to combine high unemployment with low inflation, the problem now, both in terms of balancing the national budget and the external balance, was to combine low growth with a high level of ambition in employment and welfare. The problem of the external balance manifested itself in rapid fluctuations in the balance of current payments, high rates of interest to counter excessive monetary outflow, and extensive foreign borrowing. The deficit in the budget and current account of the balance of payments may be seen partly as a phenomenon related to the economic cycle: they became particularly serious in the sharp decline at the end of the 1970s, and again in the acute crisis after 1991. But all the signs indicate that what has come to be called the 'structural' – i.e. more long-term – budget deficit increased steadily throughout this period, which suggests that political ambitions were too high for the resources available. Among other things, this means that through the rest of the 1990s the Swedish public purse will have to pay very high interest costs on loans raised to finance the current undertakings that Sweden's politicians voted in, often almost unanimously.

In the 1950s and 1960s the government was able to implement a traditional Keynesian policy of stabilisation to remedy the imbalances in the economy. Devaluation has been the instrument applied in these situations ever since the 1970s. As we have seen, Sweden has used this instrument on a number of occasions since the war to extricate itself from untenable situations. Devaluation was used primarily after a wage and price spiral that resulted in the loss of export market shares. But devaluations – at least those of the magnitude implemented in Sweden in 1976–7, 1981–2 and 1992 and onwards – can be troublesome in the long term. They may act as a time-bomb for future disturbances in the balance, for example in the form of galloping inflation via imports or exaggerated expectations of wage rises when, as a result of devaluation, profits rise in industry. More than anything else, the repeated devaluations demonstrate the problems that accompanied this long-term structural crisis – and how these problems were exacerbated by the fact that political ambitions failed to adapt to the new economic situations.

Second, structural problems can be seen in industrial relations and in the crisis of the Swedish model. At the beginning of the 1970s, this model appeared to be at its peak. The central pay-bargaining procedure was still in use. Both the LO and the SAF agreed in principle to the main content of the Rehn–Meidner model and the wage solidarity policy. But the period that followed was a dramatic one. The 1980s in particular were characterised by numerous labour market conflicts. The decade began with a widespread lock-out initiated by the SAF which affected close to a million employees. The public sector employees bore the brunt of the major conflicts in this decade, for example the public sector white-collar workers in 1985, and doctors and nurses in 1988. By the mid-1980s, it was increasingly difficult for the employers' and employees' national organisations to agree on the central pay-bargaining model. And from 1988, when the Swedish Metal Trades Employers' Association withdrew from the system of co-ordinated negotiations, this procedure in practice went out of use. As a result, the wage solidarity policy has been increasingly difficult to sustain, and the difficulties in the trade union movement have become more severe. In particular, suspicion grew between private and public sector white-collar and blue-collar workers. The public sector employees organised in the LO collective demanded compensation for the wage drift that had benefited workers in the private sector. The private sector workers in their turn strongly rejected these demands and put forward the view that wage drift was a result of increased productivity in their sector.

This 'vociferous bickering over distribution policy' that broke out in the 1980s occurred, of course, for more than one reason. Yet it is clear that the combination of low-level growth and poor productivity *at the same time* as full employment and an expected sharp increase in inflation played an important role in this context. All experience shows that when growth abates it becomes more difficult to find methods that give an 'equitable' distribution of the surplus among the different categories of employee. In this situation, we may expect so-called compensation effects to occur: higher wages for some people cause others to demand compensation which, because of the poor growth rate and failure to improve productivity, must quite simply result in higher inflation – which then generates new demands for higher

pay and compensation. In Sweden, this spiral was accentuated by an economic policy that aimed to maintain employment at all costs. The simple
law of supply and demand meant that this led people to expect higher
wages. In these circumstances a system of pay awards based on the principle
of solidarity meant that wage drift causes an even sharper rise in pay. The
general pay rise the central agreement awarded to all was regarded as a
minimum by some employee categories that were in a strong negotiating
position. To remain competitive, many companies were forced to pay far
more than the central pay award to keep their skilled workers. This caused
even more conflict between different categories of employees – not least
between public sector and private industrial sector employees.

The conditions required to apply a wage solidarity policy have changed over
time in other ways as well. The emergence of a new technological regime based
on micro-electronics, which requires greater flexibility, customer preferences
and shorter production runs, makes quite new demands on the competence
of the workforce. The core industrial worker can no longer be seen as the
worker at his machine; he is instead an operator who is in fact a hybrid of
blue-collar and white-collar worker, and who often possesses a great deal of
technical competence. The high-technology export sector requires education,
responsibility and flexibility. This means, for example, that it is no longer as
easy to evaluate an individual employee's input as it is expressed in a collective agreement. To an ever-increasing degree, wages will reflect individual
qualifications such as specialised training and the like. Against this background it is evidently more and more difficult to build on one of the cornerstones of the Swedish model, the wage solidarity policy. The problems
generated by the economic policy of the third way in the 1980s were largely
related to the failure to contain ever-growing pay demands. Since the middle
of the 1980s, wage differentials have begun to increase again in Sweden.
Until that time, the centralised wage bargaining system and the principle of
wage solidarity had resulted in a high degree of equalisation.

The domestic causes

Many people hold the view that the problems Sweden experienced from the
1970s onwards were accentuated by factors that cannot be directly related to
the restructuring of the international economy. One such factor is the break-
up of the basic preconditions for the Swedish model. As we have seen, the
lynchpin of this model was the historic compromise negotiated in the 1930s.
This compromise was based on a voluntary agreement in which the workers
recognised industry's need for profits and structural rationalisation, provided
the resulting growth produced higher wages and social reforms. But the
compromise was more profound than that. It also rested on the recognition
of industry as the driving force in the economy. All distribution must be
based on industry's ability to generate growth. Or, as Gunnar Sträng said in
the 1960s: 'What is good for business is good for Sweden.'

However, this compromise came under severe strain in the 1970s. Increasingly, both parties appeared to forget what the Swedish model was actually about. On the one hand, the workers – with the LO as their principal representative – departed from the policy of voluntary compromises and turned to the government to demand legislation as a way of securing improvements. In 1975 the LO commissioned Rudolf Meidner and Anna Hedborg to publish their ideas on collective employee investment funds. This proposal aimed to resolve the so-called surplus profits problem which was a result of wage-earners refraining, on the principle of solidarity, from claiming the entire margin for pay rises. But the report was not regarded simply as a technical solution to an internal trade union problem, and it generated great bitterness. The employers and the non-socialist political parties united in rejecting the employee investment funds which, in their view, would in the long term lead to a gigantic wave of socialisation. There were even differences of opinion within the labour movement on the employee investment funds. By the time the proposal was presented to Parliament in 1982 it had been considerably diluted. But the entire issue had caused strong antagonism between the labour market parties. The same applied to the offensive in the field of workers' rights initiated by the LO in the 1970s (the Act on Co-determination at Work, the Security of Employment Act, the Act on the Position of a Trade Union Representative at the Work Place, and others). These laws were pushed through Parliament in the face of opposition from the employers. The way the whole issue was handled was a break with the old principle of the immunity of the labour market from government intervention. This, too, brought the traditional allocation of roles into question.

It was in this atmosphere that the political confrontations between the LO and SAF intensified in the 1980s. The SAF response to the LO initiative was to demand more differentiated pay and the break-up of regulations governing workers' rights. From the mid-1980s they quite simply refused to enter into any central negotiations. Further, in a number of areas they broke off the co-operation that had been in effect between the parties in the labour market, and withdrew from a number of joint bodies.

This deteriorating climate between the employers' and employees' central organisations led not only to further and greater conflicts. It is likely that an even more important outcome was that many of the political and trade union actors appeared to suppress their understanding of how intimately wages and distribution were linked to economic results, i.e. in the first instance, industry's capacity to generate growth. They began to act both in politics and wage bargaining as if this link had never existed. At least until the end of the 1980s there were only a few people who saw any serious problem in the rapid increase in public sector costs or in a higher tax outtake. In the 1980s Sweden's politicians acted as if the country still had the growth rate of the 1960s. In this sense, the erosion of the Swedish model's strong emphasis on industrial growth and rationalisation was a serious problem.

Other domestic factors also influenced the picture, and are part of the explanation for this specific development in Sweden – and perhaps also for the severity of the crisis problems at the beginning of the 1990s. As we have already suggested, the economic policy of the third way played an important part in this context. In the short term, the substantial devaluation of 1982 brought good times to the Swedish export industry, and also generated full employment, but it also caused overheating and inflation. Here, deregulation, particularly of the credit markets, in the sound spirit of supply-side economics, also played an important part. The price paid for high profits and a 'speculation economy' was a fall in real wages for large groups of employees, which generated demands for substantial compensation and considerable tension between the employers' and employees' organisations.

Further, in spite of rising profits, the third way put long-term industrial development at serious risk. First, this policy resulted in a major shortage of skilled labour – one effect of which was the large numbers of Swedish companies that were set up abroad. These elimination mechanisms are probably also behind the fact that in the 1980s, the industrial sector's 'good years', the number of small enterprises did not grow. This same factor may explain why there was no rapid expansion at that time, in terms of production and number of workers, of the small companies that already existed. Instead, low transformation pressure was a characteristic of the industrial sector in the 1980s. As we have already noted, the average size of companies in Sweden did not fall as it did in other parts of the world. This low transformation pressure may well have been accentuated by the speculation in securities and property that broke out in the 1980s – and which was caused by the expectation of high inflation combined with the tax wedge – the (considerable) difference between an employee's take-home pay and the total cost the employer pays for the employee to receive this net wage.

Second, the large devaluation of 1982 meant that Swedish industry was 'protected' for several years from necessary structural rationalisation and the need to increase productivity by improving efficiency and introducing new technology. This may also have contributed to the relative stability that we have noted was a feature of Sweden's industrial sector in the 1980s. It is difficult to say whether it might even be the reason for the apparent fall in the intangible capital content of Swedish exports in the 1980s. Whatever the case may be, there is much to suggest that the 1982 devaluation made a simpler type of production profitable – that is to say, in direct contrast to what occurred in the 1950s, 1960s and 1970s, when Sweden was very much a high-wage country. The de facto devaluation after the krona was floated in the autumn of 1992 has further accentuated the picture of Sweden as a country with low wages. If this trend is allowed to continue, and the intangible capital content of production does not increase once again, Sweden will be forced to compete in the market with low price countries for relatively simply industrial products.

Can the Swedish model survive?

By the mid-1970s most of the force in Sweden's post-war economic expansion appeared to have been spent. An important condition for this expansion had been the strong demand from abroad for raw materials (ore, iron, steel, wood products, pulp, etc.) but also Sweden's ability to introduce technical development and renewal. This latter factor fuelled the rapid expansion of the mechanical engineering sector. But since the war, new competitors have emerged, both in Europe and in other parts of the world. After the record years of the 1950s and 1960s, there has been a marked fall-off in Sweden's economic growth. Further, Sweden was hit by a severe crisis in the mid-1970s. After this point, policies aimed to avoid excessively high employment figures. At first the policy of the third way appeared to succeed in the 1980s, but the attempt to reconcile economic growth, low unemployment and low inflation failed. Economic growth was moderate and inflation rose – while the pace of transformation in the economy was limited. This later led to demands for ruthless restructuring and efficiency-improvement. This failure was also visible in the sharp rise of unemployment at the beginning of the 1990s, when the relatively mild recession in other countries developed into something akin to a depression in Sweden. The policy of devaluation since the end of the 1970s has also brought matters to a head: will Sweden in future be marketed as an industrial low-priced country or will it, as before the 1980s, be a high-wage country which can compete with the help of its high level of technical competence and its capacity for industrial development?

If we choose the second alternative, there is no other path than to make serious efforts to restore the ability of the Swedish industrial economy to take initiatives in the future – in whatever form they may be. Essentially, this means that the intangible capital content of Swedish industry must be

Figure 10.9 Abandoned base industry: the Stråssa mine, 1995.
Photo: Olle Lindstedt/Mira.

raised. Only an economy with a high degree of added value can generate the high incomes that we need to distribute for different purposes. Only this kind of economy can generate a higher demand for services – a sector that must also be allowed to expand in order to absorb surplus labour from other sectors. This, it is true, requires radical – and probably also painful – changes. If we do not choose the low-wage alternative, there is, however, hardly any way back to the simple, standardised mass production that once appeared to be the driving force of growth. This means that the labour market – and the economic, education and welfare policies we intend to apply in future – must be adapted to meet new demands. It may also be a good idea to restore the historic compromise between labour and capital to reflect the new conditions that obtain, particularly if it can be based on one of the fundamental doctrines of the entire development of economies since the beginning of time: the intimate relationship between resources and distribution.

Abbreviations for illustration sources

AA   Arberarrörelsens Arkiv, Stockholm (The Archives and Library of the Swedish Labour Movement)

ATA   Antikvarisk-Topografiska Arkivet, Stockholm (The Antiquarian-Topographical Archives, Stockholm)

KB   Kungliga Biblioteket, Stockholm (The Royal Library, Stockholm)

NMA   Nordiska Museets Arkiv, Stockholm (The Nordic Museum Archives, Stockholm)

SSM   Stockholms Stadsmuseum (The Stockholm City Museum)

UUB   Uppsala Universitets Bibliotek (The Uppsala University Library)

Other sources are given unabbreviated in the captions.

Notes

Introduction

1 E.D. Clarke 1823, pp. 39f.
2 W.H.B. Court 1970, p. 156.
3 E.F. Heckscker 1936, p. 17.
4 C. Cipolla 1991, pp. 3ff.
5 W.H.B. Court 1970, p. 153.
6 See e.g. Beckman 1990.
7 D. North 1993, pp. 16ff.
8 K. Polyani 1991.

1 The agrarian revolution

1 G. Utterström 1957, pp. 694f.
2 L. Magnusson 1986.
3 L. Schön 1985.
4 S. Martinius 1970, p. 26
5 O. Hannerberg 1971, p. 73.
6 G. Utterström 1957, pp. 199ff.
7 F. Karlsson 1978; C.-J. Gadd 1983.
8 L. Schön 1985.
9 L. Magnusson 1982, pp. 53f.
10 M. Isakson 1979, pp. 168ff.
11 U. Herlitz 1988, p. 24.
12 Ibid., pp. 121ff. See also G. Fridlizius 1957.
13 G. Utterström 1957, pp. 1ff and 694ff.
14 L. Magnusson 1982, p. 17.
15 G. Utterström 1957, p. 74.
16 Ibid., p. 47.
17 C.-J. Gadd 1983, p. 243.
18 M. Isacson 1979, p. 168.
19 F. Karlsson 1978, p. 39.
20 U. Herlitz 1988, p. 207.
21 G. Bodvall 1959.
22 C.-J. Gadd 1983, p. 239.
23 L. Magnusson 1982, p. 20.
24 R. Jirlow 1939; A. Eskeröd 1973, p. 87; and H. A:son Moberg 1989, pp. 30ff.
25 A. Eskeröd 1973, p. 88.
26 H. A:son Moberg 1989, p. 37.
27 Ibid., p. 132ff; Eskeröd 1973, pp. 88ff.
28 Ibid., p. 101.
29 See the notes in P. Hebbe 1939, 1945.
30 H. A:son Moberg 1989, p. 158.
31 A. Eskeröd 1973, p. 202.
32 A. Eskeröd in: S. Carlsson 1956, p. 38.
33 B. Olai 1983 p. 228.
34 R. Pettersson 1983, p. 336.

35 S. Helmfrid 1961.
36 G. Utterström 1957, pp. 547ff; N. Holmberg 1939.
37 S. Smedberg 1972.
38 E. F. Heckscher 1957, pp. 176f.
39 L. Herlitz 1974, p. 162; N. Wohlin 1912.
40 V. Elgeskog 1945.
41 N. Wohlin 1912; V. Elgeskog 1945, pp. 171ff; K. Petander 1912.
42 L. Herlitz 1974, p. 166; N. Wohlin 1912.
43 L. Magnusson 1980, p. 145.
44 M. Fridholm, M. Isacson, L. Magnusson 1976, p. 29.
45 Ibid., p. 29.
46 L. Herlitz 1974, pp. 279f.
47 E. F. Heckscher 1949, pp. 270ff.
48 G. Rydeberg 1985, pp. 44ff; E. F. Heckscher, 'Ett kapitel ur den svenska jordbesittningens historia' ('A Chapter from the History of Land Occupation in Sweden'), in Heckscher, 1944.
49 E. F. Heckscher 1944, pp. 122ff.
50 Ibid., pp. 125f.
51 J. Kyle 1987, p. 1.
52 Ibid., p. 147.
53 Ibid., p. 49.
54 S. Svensson 1977, p. 49.
55 Ibid., p. 48.
56 V. Kotevski 119, pp. 96ff.
57 G. Utterström 1957, p. 705.
58 Ibid., pp. 598ff.
59 C. Winberg 1975; I. Eriksson and J. Rogers 1978.
60 C. Winberg 1975, p. 265.
61 S. Martinius 1977, pp. 137f.
62 C. Winberg 1975, p. 265.
63 Particularly E. F. Heckscher 1949.

2 Early industrialisation

1 Quote from M. Isacson and L. Magnusson 1983, pp. 77ff.
2 Ibid., p. 115.
3 C Ahlberger 1998, p. 38.
4 Ibid., pp. 49f.
5 For a discussion see M. Isacson and L. Magnusson 1983, Chap. 2.
6 C. Ahlberger 1988, p. 128.
7 L. A:sson Palmqvist 1988, p. 66.
8 K. Ullenhag 1982, p. 47.
9 Ibid., p. 63.
10 M. Morell 1982, pp. 87ff.
11 I. Jonsson, 1984.
12 Ibid., Chapter 9 in particular.
13 L. A:son Palmqvist 1988, p. 66.
14 Ibid., p. 65.
15 C. Ahlberger 1988, p. 21.
16 Ibid., p. 30.
17 L. A:son Palmqvist 1988, pp. 68ff.

18 C. Ahlberger 1988, p. 37.
19 K. Ullenhag 1982, p. 33.
20 Ibid., pp. 53f.
21 G. Utterström, II, 1957, p. 25.
22 K. Ullenhag 1982, p. 33.
23 G. Utterström, II, 1957, p. 93.
24 K. Ullenhag 1982, p. 17.
25 Ibid., p. 19.
26 E. Söderlund, II, 1949, pp. 221ff, and E. Söderlund 1943. See also L. Edgren 1987.
27 L. Edgren 1987, pp. 69ff.
28 Ibid., p. 78.
29 See J. Söderberg, U. Jonsson and C. Persson 1991.
30 L. Edgren 1987, pp. 11ff.
31 L. Mangusson, 1988.
32 L. Edgren 1987, pp. 119ff.
33 C. Persson 1993, p. 13.
34 P. Nyström 1956, pp. 122ff.
35 E. F. Heckscher 1937/38; P. Nyström 1956; K. Nyberg 1992; O. Kranz 1976.
36 K. Nyberg 1992, Chap. 6.
37 E. F. Heckscher 1949, p. 608.
38 C. Persson 1993, p. 97.
39 K. Nyberg 1992, Chapter 6.
40 Ibid.
41 Ibid.
42 L. Schön 1992, p. 32, and L. Schön 1979, Chapter 9.
43 A. Göransson 1988, p. 95.
44 Ibid.
45 J.-O. Jansson 1990.

3 Regulation, deregulation and adjustment

1 K. Petander 1912, p. 135, 139.
2 P. Frohnert 1994, p. 282.
3 J.W. Arnberg 1868, p. 10.
4 Ibid., p. 13.
5 Ibid., p. 18.
6 E.F. Heckscher 1922, pp. 246f.
7 Arnberg 1868, p. 25.
8 Ibid., pp. 36f.
9 Ibid., p. 79.
10 Ibid., p. 112.
11 A. Montgomery 1921, p. 6.
12 Ibid., p. 9.
13 Ibid., p. 64.
14 E. F. Heckscher 1949, p. 710.
15 K. Petander 1912, p. 30.
16 J. W. Arnberg 1868, p. 116.
17 E. Ekegård, 1924, p. 129.
18 L. Magnusson 1987b.
19 O. Gasslander 1949, pp. 111ff; L. Magnusson 1993.

20 P. T. Ohlsson 1994, p. 167.
21 Ibid., p. 100.
22 C. A. Agardh, II:2, 1856, p. 198.
23 J. Myhrman, 1994, p. 82.
24 A. Montgomery 1921, p. 73.
25 Ibid., p. 89.
26 P. T. Ohlsson 1994, p. 101.
27 O. Gasslander 1949, pp. 218ff.
28 P. T. Ohlsson 1994, p. 119.
29 O. Gasslander 1949, pp. 218ff.
30 P. T. Ohlsson 1994, p. 119.
31 Ibid., p. 112.

4   A transformed élite

1 S. Watts 1987, p. 33
2 S. Carlson 1973, Chap. 10.
3 G. B. Nilsson 1989, Chap. 10.
4 K. Samuelsson 1968, p. 204.
5 S. Högberg 1969, p. 21.
6 Ibid., p. 42.
7 For more details see K. Samuelsson 1951, p. 39.
8 Ibid., p. 21.
9 Ibid., p. 66.
10 Ibid., p. 65.
11 Ibid., pp. 82f.
12 Ibid., pp. 72ff.
13 Ibid., pp. 73ff.
14 I. Lind 1923, pp. 16ff.
15 P. A. Granberg 1815, pp. 176f.
16 E. F. Heckscher, 1949, p. 695. See also E. F. Heckscher, 'Sveriges framgångs-rikaste handelsföretag: Ostindiska Kompaniet' in Heckscher 1944, pp. 199ff; T. Frängsmyr 1976.
17 P. A. Granberg 1815, pp. 203f.
18 G. Utterström I, 1957, pp. 133ff; S. Högberg 1969, pp. 165ff.
19 A. Attman 1986, pp. 11ff.
20 See the discussion between Lars Magnusson and Per-Arne Karlsson in *Historisk Tidskrift* 1991: 13, 1991: 4 and 1992: 1.
21 A. Attman 1958, pp. 11ff.
22 K. Samuelsson 1951, p. 89.
23 Ibid., p. 91.
24 K. G. Hildebrand 1987, p. 10; A. Attman 1958, p. 35.
25 A. Attman 1958, p. 35.
26 P. G. Andreén 1958, p. 78.
27 G. Rydén 1990, Chap. 6.
28 A. Attman 1958, p. 59.
29 A. Attman 1986, p. 131.
30 A. Attman 1958, pp. 50ff.
31 S. Högberg 1969, p. 102. See also W. Carlgren 1926, pp. 35ff.
32 K. Haraldsson 1989.
33 M. Nyström 1982, pp. 47f. See also K. Haraldsson 1989, p. 47.

34 M. Nyström 1982, p. 51.
35 Ibid., pp. 51f.
36 E. F. Heckscher 1949, p. 350. See also W. Carlgren 1926.
37 S. Högberg 1969, pp. 159ff.
38 G. B. Nilsson 1989, p. 161.
39 R. Adamson 1968.
40 P. G. Andreén 1958, pp. 54f.
41 E. Dahmén 1961.
42 G. B. Nilsson 1989, p. 155.
43 Ibid., p. 184.
44 E. F. Heckscher 1944, pp. 239ff.
45 A. Nordencrantz, part IV, 1767–70, p. 21. See also L. Magnusson 1989b.
46 B. Dahlström 1942.
47 Ibid., pp. 66ff.
48 P. G. Andreén 1961, p. 84.
49 Ibid., pp. 66ff.
50 Ibid., p. 72.
51 Ibid., p. 154.
52 See also P.G. Andreén 1958, pp. 89ff.
53 Svenskt biografiskt lexicon: Arfwedson.
54 P. G. Andreén 1958, p. 91.

5 Industrial transformation

1 M. Berg and P. Hudson 1992; L. Magnusson 1994b, Chap. 1.
2 Y. Åberg 1969, p. 24.
3 See especially P. Deane 1965, Chaps. 6, 8 etc.
4 W. Hoffman 1958.
5 L. Jörberg 1966, p. 21.
6 Ibid., pp. 22ff.
7 L. Schön 1982, p. 31.
8 Ibid., p. 31.
9 L. Jörberg 1966, p. 35
10 H. Modig 1971, p. 122.
11 L. Magnusson, 1988.
12 S. Svensson 1977, p. 56.
13 L. Strömbäck 1993, p. 27.
14 See F. Crouzet (ed.), 1972.
15 T. Gårdlund 1947, p. 160.
16 A. Montgomery 1970, p. 105.
17 Ibid., p. 109.
18 T. Gårdlund 1947, p. 97.
19 E. Söderlund, 1966.
20 See e.g. B. Rondahl 1972.
21 *Iggesunds bruks historia* 1685–1985, II, p. 133.
22 Ibid., p. 110.
23 L. Magnusson 1987a, p. 47.
24 Ibid., p. 8.
25 M. Isakson and L. Magnusson 1983, Chap. 1.
26 L. Magnusson 1994b, p. 180.
27 G. Rydén, 1994.

28 A. Montgomery 1970, p. 69.
29 T. Gårdlund, 1947, p. 68.
30 A. Attman, 1986, p. 31.
31 Ibid., p. 108.
32 Ibid., p. 112.
33 Ibid., p. 113.
34 Ibid., p. 134.
35 A. Attman 1958, p. 500.
36 T. Gårdlund 1942, p. 120.
37 L. Schön 1979, pp. 104f.
38 A. Göransson 1988.
39 T. Gårdlund 1942, pp. 126f.
40 Ibid., pp. 128f.
41 K. Davidsson *et al.* 1978.
42 T. Gårdlund 1942, p. 140.
43 Ibid., p. 141.
44 E. Georgescu-Roegen, 1960.
45 Å. Gullander 1942.
46 D. Bäcklund, 1988.
47 L. Magnusson 1987a, Chap. 1; see also B.-I. Puranen 1984.
48 A. Göransson 1993.
49 See Karlsson 1995.

6 Industry – dynamics and crises

1 T. Hedlund-Nyström 1970, p. 15.
2 R. Karlbom 1967.
3 T. Hedlund-Nyström 1970, p. 35.
4 These are Erik Dahmén's words. See his 1950, I, p. 366.
5 G. Åkerman 1932.
6 A.F. Chandler 1990.
7 L. Jörberg 1961, p. 244.
8 V. Bergström 1969, p. 24.
9 L. Jörberg 1961, p. 247.
10 Ibid., p. 117.
11 For a discussion, see e.g. B. Öhngren 1974, pp. 27ff; cf. also L. Magnusson 1987a, p. 33.
12 G.B. Nilsson 1994, p. 215.
13 Ibid., p. 219.
14 Ibid., p. 273.
15 L. Jörberg 1961, p. 246.
16 Ibid., p. 268.
17 Ibid., p. 269.
18 E. Dahmén II, 1950, p. 65. See also E. Linder 1966, p. 93.
19 L. Jörberg 1961, p. 311.
20 F. Hjulström 1966, pp. 144f.
21 Ibid., p. 150.
22 L. Jörberg 1961, p. 172.
23 See the persentation in C.-H. Hermansson 1962, pp. 23f.
24 E.F. Heckscher (ed.), I, 1926, p. 28.
25 E. Dahmén, I, 1950, p. 363.

26 See e.g. K. Sågvall-Ullenhag 1970, pp. 98ff; A. Östlind 1945; L. Magnusson 1978a, Chap. 2.
27 E. Lundberg 1994, p. 41.
28 L. Ohlsson 1969.
29 M. Genberg 1992.
30 L.-E. Thunholm 1993.
31 This interpretation in B. Carlsson *et al.* 1980, pp. 71f.
32 J. Myhrman 1994, p. 130; E. Dahmén 1950, p. 379.
33 S. Fritz 1994, p. 98.
34 H. Lindgren 1988, p. 205.
35 H. Lindgren 1993, p. 251.
36 O. Gasslander, I, pp. 107ff; II, pp. 112ff.
37 O. Gasslander I, pp. 122ff.
38 Ibid., p. 130.
39 Ibid. pp. 131ff.
40 O. Gasslander II, pp. 149ff.
41 Ibid., p. 159.
42 S. Fritz 1994, pp. 197ff.
43 O. Gasslander I, p. 233.
44 H. Lindgren 1993, p. 257.
45 Ibid., p. 257.
46 H. Lindgren 1994, p. 9.
47 Ibid., pp. 78ff.

7 Organised capitalism

1 G. K. Hamilton 1865, pp. 36ff. For a discussion, see S.-B. Kilander 1991, pp. 71ff.
2 T. Jansson 1985; G. B. Nilsson 1994, pp. 552ff.
3 T. Jansson 1985, p. 10.
4 S.-B. Kilander 1991, pp. 64f.
5 T. Nilsson 1994, pp. 16, 50.
6 S.-B. Kilander 1991.
7 S. Oredsson 1969, p. 213.
8 Ibid., p. 214.
9 Ibid., p. 219.
10 T. Nilsson 1994, p. 207
11 *Benckerts testamente* 1993, p. 17.
12 G. Ahlström 1982.
13 S.-B. Kilander 1991, p. 93.
14 Ibid., p. 95.
15 S. Hansson 1938, p. 14
16 K. Åmark 1993, p. 64.
17 N. Edling 1994, p. 280.
18 E. Rodriguez 1980, pp. 46ff.
19 Ibid., p. 46.
20 V. Bergström 1969, p. 65.
21 E. Rodriguez 1980, p. 31.
22 Ibid., p. 48.
23 V. Bergström 1969, p. 66.
24 Ibid., p. 20.
25 L. Magnusson (ed.) 1990.

26 E. Lundberg 1994, p. 77.
27 Ibid., p. 56.
28 V. Bergström 1969, p. 40.
29 Ibid., p. 40.
30 E. Lundberg 1994, pp. 67f.
31 E. Lundberg 1953, p. 65.
32 E. Lundberg 1994, pp. 103f.
33 Ibid., p. 105.
34 L. Jonung 1979.
35 L. Jonung 1981.
36 V. Bergström 1969, p. 30.
37 E. Lundberg 1994, pp. 100ff.
38 B. Gustafsson 1974.
39 E. Lundberg 1994, p. 52.
40 N. Unga 1976, p. 157.
41 K.-G. Landgren 1960.
42 N. Unga 1976, p. 12.
43 Ibid., p. 14.
44 Ibid., p. 172.

8 Welfare capitalism

1 P. Armstrong, A. Glyn and J. Harrison 1991, p. 118.
2 For an example, see U. Olsson 1970, pp. 145ff.
3 After E. Lundberg 1953, p. 437.
4 S.-O. Olsson 1975.
5 E. Lundberg1953, p. 147.
6 Y. Åberg 1968, p. 78.
7 O. Krantz 1987, p. 33.
8 C.-H. Hermansson 1971, pp. 61f.
9 I. Nygren 1985, pp. 139ff.
10 J. Glete 1994, p. 291.
11 Ibid., p. 251.
12 Ibid., pp. 252f.
13 Ibid., p. 251.
14 Rodriguez 1980, p. 32.
15 B. Sandelin 1987, p. 73; R. Bentzel 1970.
16 J. Söderberg and N.-G. Lundgren 1982, p. 45.
17 E. Dahmén, I, 1950.
18 D. Bäcklund 1988, p. 190.
19 J. Söderberg and N.-G. Lundgren 1982, p. 45.
20 E. Dahlström, B. Gardell *et al.* 1966, p. 160.
21 F. Croner 1951.
22 M. Greiff 1992.
23 Ibid., pp. 245f.
24 J. Kuuse 1986, p. 20.
25 Ibid., p. 23.
26 M. Isacson 1987, p. 56.
27 B. Sandelin 1987, p. 56.
28 G. Kyle 1979, pp. 51ff.
29 Ibid., pp. 147f.

9   The Swedish model

1 A. L. Johansson 1989.
2 Ibid., Chap. 4.
3 H. de Geer 1986, pp. 323ff.
4 A. Lindbeck 1968, p. 95
5 Ibid., p. 73.
6 Ibid., p. 66.
7 R. Andersson and R. Meidner 1973, p. 40.
8 Ibid., p. 35.
9 Ibid., p. 46.
10 Landsorganisationen 15-man committee 1941, p. 4.
11 G. Esping-Andersen 1985, pp. 145ff.
12 H.L. Wilensky 1975, p. 1.
13 S.E. Olsson 1990, p. 125.
14 Ibid., p. 125.
15 L. Waara 1980, p. 163. Contradicted even by Waara's own empirics, pp. 198ff.
16 After L. Waara 1980, p. 158.
17 M. Bladh 1992, p. 278.
18 L. Jonung 1993, p. 298.
19 Ibid., p. 294.
20 E. Tobé 1972, pp. 97f.
21 Cf. B. Rothstein 1992, who speaks of a 'formative moment' in the 1930s (Chap. 6).
22 Quote from B. Rothstein 1992, p. 174.
23 Ibid., p. 302.

10   A model in crisis

1 L. Jonung 1991, p. 12.
2 B. Berglund 1987, p. 23.
3 *Sveriges Industri*, Svergies industriförbund 1985, p. 197.
4 See T. Andersson *et al.* 1993. See also SOU 1993: 16.
5 J. Lybeck 1992, pp. 56ff.
6 See the anthology, G. Dosi *et al.* (eds) 1988.
7 E. Ekstedt 1988.
8 W. Korpi 1978.
9 E. Ekstedt 1988, p. 37.
10 Ibid., p. 35.
11 SOU 1993:16 App. 1, p. 40.
12 E. Ekstedt 1988.
13 See M. Henrekson 1992. See also A. Forsman 1980, Chap. 2; A. Forsman in B. Gustafsson (ed.) 1977.

Bibliography

Adamson, R. 'Finance and Marketing in the Swedish Iron Industry 1800–1860', *Scandinavian Economic History Review* 16 (1968).

af Ugglas, C. R. *Lödöse. Historia och Arkeologi*, Gothenburg 1931.

Agardh, C. A. *Försök till en statsekonomisk statistik över Sverige, 11:2*, Karlstad 1856.

Ahlberger, C. *Vävarfolket. Hemindustrin i Mark 1790–1850*. Institutet för lokalhistorisk forskning, nr i, Borås 1988.

Ahlström, G. *Engineers and Economic Growth*, London 1982.

Andersson, R. and Meidner, R. *Arbetsmarknadspolitik och stabilisering*. Stockholm 1973.

Andersson, T. *et al. Den långa vägen - den ekonomiska politikens begränsningar och möjligheter att föra Sverige ur 1990–talets kris*, Industriens Utredningsinstitut. Stockholm 1993.

Andréen, P. *G Politik och finansväsen*, I och II, Lund 1958, 1961.

Armstrong, P., Glyn, A. and Harrison, J, *Capitalism Since 1945*, Oxford 1991.

Arnberg, W. *Frihetstidens politiska ekonomi*, Stockholm 1868.

Attman, A. *Fagerstabrukens historia, II. Adertonhundratalet*, Uppsala 1958.

—— *Svenskt järn och stål 1800–1914*, Jernkontorets bergshistoriska skriftserie 21, Stockholm 1986.

Beckman, S. *Utvecklingens hjältar. Om den innovativa individen i samhällstänkandet*, Stockholm 1990.

Benckerts testamente. Konfidentiella anteckningar angående bankinspektionens verksamhet, (Utg E Söderlund), Stockholm 1993.

Bentzel, R. 'Tillväxt och strukturomvandling under efterkrigstiden' in B. Södersten (ed.) *Svensk ekonomi*, Stockholm 1970.

Berch, A. *Inledning till Almänna Hushålningen*, Stockholm 1747.

Berg, M. and Hudson, P. 'Rehabilitating the Industrial Revolution', *Economic History Review XLV:i* (1992).

Berglund, B. *Kampen om jobben. Stålindustrin, facket och löntagarna under 1970–talskrisen*, papers from the Institute of Economic History 56, Gothenburg 1987.

Bergström, V. *Den ekonomiska politiken i Sverige och dess verkningar*, Stockholm 1969.

Beveridge, W. H. *Full Employment in a Free Society*, London 1944.

Bladh, M. *Bostadsförsörjningen 1945–1985*, Bostadsforskningsinstitutet, Gävle 1992.

Bodvall, G. *Bodland i norra Hälsingland Studier i utmarksodlingarnas roll för den permanenta bosättningens expansion fram till 1850*, Geographica 36, Uppsala 1959.

Bäcklund, D I *industrisamhällets utkant. Småbrukets omvandling i Lappmarken 1870–1970*, Kungl Skytteanska samfundets handlingar 34 (1988), Umeå Studies in Economic History 8, Umeå 1988.

292 Bibliography

Carlgren, W. *De norrländska skogsindustrierna intill 1800–talets mitt*, Uppsala 1926.

Carlsson, B. *et al. Teknik och industristruktur – 70-talets ekonomiska kris i historisk belysning*, IVA-meddelanden, IUI, Stockholm 1980.

Carlsson, S. *Bonden i svensk historia*, 111, Stockholm 1956.

—— *Ståndssamhälle och ståndspersoner 1700–1865*, Lund 1973.

Cassel, G. *Socialpolitik*, Stockholm 1902.

Chandler, A. F. *Scale and Scope. The Dynamics of Industrial Capitalism*, Cambridge Mass. 1990.

Chydenius, A. *Den nationale vinsten*, Stockholm 1765.

Cipolla, C. *Between History and Economics*, Oxford 1991.

Clarke, E. D. *Travels in Various Countries of Europe, Asia and Africa Part 3*, vol 2, London 1823.

Croner, F. *Tjänstemannakåren i det moderna samhället*, Uppsala 1951.

Crouzet, F. (ed.) *Capital Formation in the Industrial Revolution*, London 1972.

Dahlström, B. *Rikets gäld 1788–1792*, Stockholm 1942.

Dahlström, E., Gardell, B. *et al. Teknisk förändring och arbetsanpassning*, Stockholm 1966.

Dahmén, E. *Svensk industriell företagarverksamhet, I–II*, Lund-Stockholm 1950.

—— 'Innovationer i kreditväsendet under den svenska industrialiseringen', in *Money, Growth and Methodology . . . In Honour of Johan Åkerman*, Stockholm 1961.

—— (ed.) *Upplåning och utveckling, Riksgäldskontoret 1789–1989*, Stockholm 1989.

Davidsson, K. *et al. Münchenbryggeriet. En arbetsplats under hundra år*, Stockholm 1978.

Frohnert, P. *Kronans skatter och bondens bröd. Den lokala förvaltningen och bönderna i Sverige 1719–1775*, Lund 1993.

Frängsmyr, T. *Ostindiska kompaniet*, Höganäs 1976.

Gadd, C.-J. *Järn och potatis. Jordbruk, teknik och social omvandling i Skaraborgs län 1750–1860*, papers from the Institute of Economic History, 53, Gothenburg 1983.

Gasslander, O. *J. A. Gripenstedt statsman och företagare*, Lund 1949.

—— *Bank och industriellt genombrott. Stockholms Enskilda Bank kring sekelskiftet 1900*, I och II, Stockholm 1956.

Genberg, M. *The Horndal Effect. Productivity Growth without Capital Investment at Horndalsverken between 1927 and 1952*, diss., Department of Economic History, Uppsala 1992.

Georgescu-Roegen, E. *Economic Theory and Agrarian Economics*, Oxford Economic Papers 12, Oxford 1960.

Glete, J. *Nätverk i näringslivet*, Stockholm 1994.

Granherg, P. A. *Staden Göteborgs historia*, Stockholm 1815.

Greiff, M. *Kontoristen.Från chefens högra hand till proletär*, Malmö 1992.

Gullander, Å. *Bönderna vakna.Glimtar från 1930-talets genombrott*, Stockholm 1942.

Gustafsson, B. 'Perspektiv på den offentliga sektorn under 1930-talet', in *Kriser och Krispolitik. Nordiska historikermötet*, Uppsala 1974.

—— (ed.) *Den offentliga sektorns expansion*, Acta Universitatis Upsaliensis: Uppsala Studies in Economic History 16, Uppsala 1977.

Gårdlund, T. *Industrialismens samhälle. Den svenska arbetarklassens historia*, Stockholm 1942.

—— *Svensk industrifinansiering under genombrottsskedet 1830–1913*, Stockholm 1947.

Göransson, A *Från familj till fabrik. Teknik, arbetsdelning och skiktning i svenska fabriker 1830–1877*, Lund 1988.

—— 'Från hushåll och släkt till marknad och stat', in *Äventyret Sverige. En ekonomisk och social historia*, Stockholm 1993.

Hamilton, G. K. *Om arbetsklassen och arbetare-föreningar*, Uppsala 1865.

Hansson, S. *Den svenska fackföreningsrörelsen*, Stockholm 1938.

Haraldsson, K. *Tradition, regional specialisering och industriell utveckling – sågverksindustrin i Gävleborgs län*, Geografiska regionstudier nr 21, Kulturgeografiska institutionen vid Uppsala universitet, Uppsala 1989.

Hebbe, P. *Den svenska lantbrukslitteraturen, I-II*, Stockholm 1939, 1945.

Heckscher, E. F. *Ekonomi och historia*, Stockholm 1922.

—— (ed.) *Bidrag till Sveriges ekonomiska och sociala historia under och efter världskriget*, 1, Stockholm 1926.

—— *Sveriges ekonomiska historia sedan Gustav Vasa*. I:1 Stockholm 1935; I:2 Stockholm 1936; II:1–2 Stockholm 1949.

—— 'Den ekonomiska historiens aspekter', in E. F. Heckscher, *Ekonomisk-historiska studier*, Stockholm 1936.

—— 'De svenska manufakturerna under 1700-talet', in *Ekonomisk Tidskrift* 1937/8.

—— *Historieuppfattning. Materialistisk och annan*, Stockholm 1944.

—— *Svenskt arbete och liv*, Stockholm 1957.

Hedlund-Nyström, T. *Svenska kriser och internationella konjunkturer*, Lund 1970.

Helmfrid, S. 'The Storskifte, Enskifte and Laga skifte in Sweden – General Features', *Geografiska Annaler* 1–2, 1961.

Henrekson, M. 'Vad förklarar den offentliga sektorns utveckling', in B. Södersten (ed.) *Den offentliga sektorn*, Stockholm 1992.

Herlitz, L. *Jordegendom och ränta Omfördelningen av jordbrukets merprodukt i Skaraborgs län under frihetstiden*, papers from the Institute of Economic History, University of Gothenburg, 31, Lund 1974.

Herlitz, U. *Restadtegen i världsekonomin. Lokala studier av befolkningstillväxt, jordbruksproduktion och fördelning i Västsverige 1800–1860*, papers from the Institute of Economic History, University of Gothenburg, 58, Gothenburg 1988.

Hermansson, C. H. *Monopol och storfinans – de 15 familjerna*, Stockholm 1962.

Hildebrand, K.-G. *Svenskt järn och stål. Sexton och sjuttonhundratal. Exportindustri före industrialismen*, Jernkontorets bergshistoriska skriftserie 20, Stockholm 1987.

Hjulström, F. 'Elektrisk kraftöverföring och elektrifiering av tung storindustri', in R. Lundström (ed.) *Kring industrialismens genombrott i Sverige*, Stockholm 1966.

Hoffman, W. *The Growth of Industrial Economies*, Manchester 1958.

Holmberg, N. *Enskiftet i Malmöhus län*, Lund 1939.

Högberg, S. *Utrikeshandel och sjöfart på 1700-talet. Stapelvaror i svensk export och import 1738–1808*, Stockholm 1969.

Iggesunds bruks historia 1685–1985, II (ed. G. Utterström), Iggesund 1985.

Isacson, M. *Ekonomisk tillväxt och social differentiering 1680–1860. Bondeklassen i By socken, i Kopparbergs län 1680–1860*, Acta Universitatis Upsaliensis: Uppsala studies in Economic History 18, Uppsala 1979.

—— *Verkstadsarbete under 1900-talet.- Hedemora verkstäder före 1950*, Lund 1987.

Isacson, M. and Magnusson, L. *Vägen till fabrikerna*, Stockholm 1983.

Jansson, J.-O. *Arbetsorganisationen vid Motala verkstad 1822–1843. Den engelska tiden*, Acta Universitatis Stockholmiensis: Stockholm Studies in Economic History 13, Stockholm 1990.

Jansson, T. *Adertonhundratalets associationer*, Studia Historica Upsalensis 139, Uppsala 1985.

Jirlow, R. 'Till den svängda plogvändskivans historia', *Rig* 1939.

Johansson, A. *Löneutvecklingen och arbetslösheten*, Stockholm 1934.

Johansson, A. L. *Tillväxt och klassamarbete – en studie av den svenska modellens uppkomst*, Stockholm 1989.

Jonsson, M. *Linodlare, väverskor och köpmän. Linne som handelsvara och försörjningsmöjlighet i det tidiga 1800-talets Hälsingland*, Acta Universitatis Upsaliensis: Uppsala Studies in Economic History 35, Uppsala 1984.

Jonung, L. 'Cassel, Davidsson and Heckscher on Swedish Monetary Policy. A Confidential Report to the Riksbank in 1931', *Economy and History*, vol. 1979:2.

––––– 'The Depression in Sweden and the United States. A Comparison of Causes and Policies', in K. Brunner (ed.) *The Great Depression Revisited*, Boston 1981.

––––– *Devalveringen 1982: rivstart eller snedtändning?*, Stockholm 1991.

––––– 'Riksbankens politik 1945–1990', in L. Werin (ed.) *Från räntereglering till inflationsnorm. Det finansiella systemet och Riksbankens politik 1945–1990*, Stockholm 1993.

––––– (ed.) *Swedish Economic Thought*, London 1993.

Jörberg, L. *Growth and Fluctuations of Swedish Industry 1869–1912*, Lund 1961.

––––– 'Några tillväxtfaktorer i 1800-talets svenska industriella utveckling', in R. Lundström (ed.) *Kring industrialismens genombrott i Sverige*, Stockholm 1966.

Kadish, A. *Historians, Economists and Economic History*, London 1989.

Karlbom, R. *Hungerupplopp och strejker 1793–1867. En studie i den svenska arbetarerörelsens uppkomst*, Lund 1967.

Karleby, N. *Socialismen inför verkligheten*, Stockholm 1926.

Karlsson, F. *Mark och försörjning. Befolkning och markutnyttjande i västra Småland 1800–1850*, papers from the Institute of Economic History, Gothenburg, 41, Gothenburg 1978.

Keynes, J. M. *The General Theory of Employment, Interest and Money*, London 1936.

Kilander, S.-B. *Den nya staten och den gamla – En studie i ideologisk förändring*, Acta Historica Upsaliensia 164, Uppsala 1991.

Korpi, W. *Arbetaren i välfärdskapitalismen*, Stockholm 1978.

Kotevski, V. 'Med stambanan över ägorna', in J. Myrdal (ed.) *Alla de dagar som är livet*, Nordiska museet, Stockholm 1991.

Krantz, O. 'Production and Labour in the Swedish Manufactories During the 18th Century, 1–11', *Economy and History*, vol. XIX: i och XIX:2 (1976).

––––– *Utrikeshandel, ekonomisk tillväxt och strukturförändring efter 1850*, Lund 1987.

Kuuse, J. 'Strukturomvandlingen och arbetsmarknadens organisering', *SAF i samhällsutvecklingen*, Stockholm 1986.

Kyle, G. *Gästarbeterska i manssamhället*, Lund 1979.

Kyle, J. *Striden om hemmanen. Studier kring 1700-talets skatteköp i västra Sverige*, papers from the Institute of History, Gothenburg, 3 1, Gothenburg 1987.

Landgren, K.-G. *Den nya ekonomien i Sverige. J M Keynes, E Wigforss, B Ohlin och utvecklingen 1927–39*, Uppsala 1960.

Landsorganisationen (LO) *Fackföreningsrörelsen och den fulla sysselsättningen*, Stockholm, 1951.

––––– *Samordnad näringspolitik*, Stockholm 1961.

Landsorganisationens 15-mannakommitté *Fackföreningsrörelsen och näringslivet*, Stockholm 1941.

Lind, A. *Solidarisk lönepolitik och förhandsförhandlingar*, Stockholm 1938.

Lind, I. *Göteborgs handel och sjöfart 1637–1920*, Gothenburg 1923.

Lindbeck, A. *Svensk ekonomisk politik. Problem och teorier under efterkrigstiden*, Stockholm 1968.

Linder, E. 'Den mekaniska verkstadsindustrins utveckling under årtiondena närmast före världskriget', in R. Lundström (ed.) *Kring industrialismens genombrott i Sverige*, Stockholm 1966.

Lindgren, H. *Bank, Investmentbolag, Bankirfirma*, Stockholms Enskilda Bank 1924–1945, Stockholm 1988.

—— 'Finanssektorn och dess aktörer 1860–1992', in *Äventyret Sverige. En ekonomisk och social historia*, Stockholm 1993.

—— *Aktivt ägande. Investor under växlande konjunkturer*, Stockholm 1994.

Lundberg, E. *Konjunkturer och ekonomisk politik*, Stockholm 1953.

—— *Ekonomiska kriser förr och nu*, Stockholm 1994.

Lundström, R. (ed.) *Kring industrialismens genombrott i Sverige*, Stockholm 1966.

Lybeck, J. *Finansiella kriser förr och nu*, Stockholm 1992.

Magnusson, L. *Ty som ingenting angelägnare är än mina bönders conservation. Godsekonomi i östra Mellansverige vid mitten av 1700-talet*, Acta Universitatis Upsaliensis: Uppsala Studies in Economic History 20, Uppsala 1980.

—— *Kapitalbildningen i Sverige 1750–1860: Godsen*, Acta Universitatis Upsaliensis: Uppsala Studies in Economic History 25, Uppsala 1982.

—— 'The Rise of Agrarlan Productivity in Scandinavia 1750–1860', in P. K. O'Brien (ed.) *International Productivity Comparisons and Problems of Measurement, 1750–1939*, Ninth International Economic History Congress, Bern 1986.

—— *Arbetet vid en svensk verkstad – Munktells 1900–1920*, Lund 1987 (1987a).

—— 'Mercantilism and Reform Mercantilism: the Rise of Econormic Discourse in Sweden During the Eighteenth Century', *History of Political Economy* 19:1 1987 (1987b).

—— *Den bråkiga kulturen*, Stockholm 1988.

—— *Korruption och borgerlig ordning. Naturrätt och ekonomisk diskurs i Sverige under Frihetstiden*, Uppsala Papers in Economic History 20, Uppsala 1989.

—— 'Gustav Cassel, Popularizer and Enigmatic Walrasian', in B. Sandelin (ed.) *The History of Swedish Economic Thought*, London 1990.

—— 'The Economist as Popularizer: the Emergence of Swedish Economics 1900–30', in L. Jonung (ed.) *Swedish Economic Thought*, London 1993.

—— *The Contest for Control. Metal Industries in Sheffield, Solingen, Remscheid and Eskilstuna during Industrialization*, Oxford 1994.

Martinius, S. *Jordbruk och ekonomisk tillväxt i Sverige 1830–1870*, Meddelanden från, Papers from the Institute of Economic History, University of Gothenburg, 21, Gothenburg 1970.

—— *Peasant Destinies. The History of 552 Swedes born 1810–12*, Acta Universitatis Stockholmiensis: Stockholm Studies in Economic History 3, Stockholm 1977.

Moberg, H. A:son *Jordbruksmekanisering i Sverige under tre sekel*, Stockholm 1989.

Modig, H. *Järnvägarnas efterfrågan och den svenska industrin 1860–1914*, Ekonomisk-historiska studier 8, Uppsala 1971.

Montgomery, A. *Svensk Tullpolitik 1816–1911*, Stockholm 1921.

—— 'Tjänstehjonsstadgan och äldre svensk arbetarepolitik', *Historisk tidskrift* 1933.

—— *Industrialismens genombrott i Sverige*, Stockholm 1970.

Morell, M. *Bondeköpmän*, Örnsköldsviks kommuns skriftserie 4, Bjästa 1982.

Mun, T. *England's Treasure by Forraign Trade*, London 1664.

Myhrman, J. *Hur Sverige blev rikt*, Stockholm 1994.

Myrdal, A. and Myrdal, G. *Kris i befolkningsfrågan*, Stockholm 1934.

Nilsson, G. B. *André Oscar Wallenberg II. Gyllene tider 1856–1866*, Stockholm 1989.

—— *André Oscar Wallenberg III. Ett namn att försvara 1866–1886*, Stockholm 1994.

Nilsson, T. *Elitens svängrum Första kammaren, staten och moderniseringen*, Acta Universitatis Stockholmiensis: Stockholm Studies in History, Stockholm 1994.

Nordencrantz, A. *Bekymmerslösa stunders Menlösa och Owäldne Tankar om de Betydande Anmärkningar som en hedervärd Landtman . . . kallad Tankar om Yppighet och Öfwerflöd*, Del IV Stockholm 1767–70.

North, D. *Institutionerna, tillväxten och välståndet*, Stockholm 1993.

Nyberg, K. *Köpes: ull, Säljes: kläde. Yllemanufakturens företagsformer i 1780-talets Stockholm*, Ekonomisk-historiska institutionen, Uppsala 1992.

Nygren, I. *Från Stockholms Banco till Citibank. Svensk kreditmarknad under 325 år*, Stockholm 1985.

Nyström, M. *Norrlands ekonomi i stöpsleven. Ekonomisk expansion, stapelvaruproduktion och maritima näringar 1760–1812*, Umeå Studies in Economic History 4, Umeå 1982.

Nyström, P. *Stadsindustriens arbetare före 1800-talet. Den svenska arbetareklassens historia*, Stockholm 1955.

Ohlsson, L. *Utrikeshandeln och den ekonomiska tillväxten i Sverige 1871–1966*, Stockholm 1969.

Ohlsson, P. T. *Hundra år av tillväxt. Johan August Gripenstedt och den liberala revolutionen*, Stockholm 1994.

Olai, B. *Storskiftet i Ekebyborna. Svensk jordbruksutveckling avspeglad i en östgötasocken*, Studia Historica Upsaliensia 130, Uppsala 1983.

Olsson, S. E. *Social Policy and Welfare State in Sweden*, Lund 1990.

Olsson, S.-O. *German Coal and Swedish Fuel 1939–1945*, papers from the Institute of History, Gothenburg, 36, Gothenburg 1975.

Olsson, U. *Lönepolitik och lönestruktur. Göteborgs verkstadsarbetare 1920–1949*, papers from the Institute of History, Gothenburg, 19, Gothenburg 1970.

Oredsson, S. *Järnvägarna och det allmänna*, Lund 1969.

Palmqvist, L. A:son. 'Sjuhäradsbygdens bondefabrikörer', *Bebyggelsehistorisk tidskrift* 16 (1988).

Persson, C. *Stockholms klädesmanufakturer 1816–1846*, Acta Universitatis Stockholmiensis: Stockholm Studies in Economic History 17, Stockholm 1993.

Petander, K. *De nationalekonomiska åskådningarna i Sverige sådana de framträda i litteraturen, 1718–1765*, Stockholm 1912.

Petterson, R. *Laga skifte i Hallands län 1827–1876: Förändring mellan regeltvång och handlingsfrihet*, Acta Universitatis Stockholmiensis: Stockholm Studies in Economic History, Stockholm 1993.

Polanyi, K. *Den stora omdaningen*, Lund 1991.

Puranen, B.-I. *Tuberkulos. En sjukdoms förekomst och dess orsaker*, Umeå Studies in Economic History 7, Umeå 1984.

Quensel, C. E. in *Minnesskrift med anledning av den svenska befolkningsstatistikens 200-åriga bestånd. Statistiska meddelanden*, ser A bd VI:4, Stockholm 1949.

Rabenius, L. G. *Lärobok i National-ekonomien*, Uppsala 1829.

Rodriguez, E. *Offentlig inkomstexpansion. En analys av drivkrafterna bakom de offentliga inkomsternas utveckling i Sverige under 1900-talet*, Lund 1980.

Rondahl, B. *Emigration, folkomflyttning och säsongsarbete i ett sågverksdistrikt i södra Hälsingland*, Studia Historica Upsaliensia 90, Uppsala 1972.

Rothstein, B. *Den korporativa staten*, Stockholm 1992.

Rydeberg, G. *Skatteköpen i Örebro län 1701–1809*, Studia Historica Upsaliensia 141, Uppsala 1985.

Rydén, G. *Hammarlag och hushåll. Om relationen mellan smidesarbetet och smedshushållen vid Tore Petrés brukskomplex 1830–1850*, Jernkontorets bergshistoriska skriftserie 27. Stockholm 1990.

—— 'Gustaf Ekman, Jernkontoret och lancashiresmidet – ett inlägg i synen på teknisk utveckling', *Polhem* 1994:2.

Salander, E. *Salus Patriae eller Sweriges Wälfärd genom högstvärdande förbättringar wid the almänna näringsfång...*, Stockholm 1741.

Salvius, L. *Tanckar öfver den swenska Oeconomien igenom samtal yttrade*, Stockholm 1738.

Samuelsson, K. *De stora köpmanshusen i Stockholm 1730–1815*, Stockholm 1951.

—— *Från stormakt till välfärdsstat*, Stockholm 1968.

Sandelin, B. *Den svenska ekonomin*, Stockholm 1987.

—— (ed.) *The History of Swedish Economic Thought*, London 1990.

Schumpeter, J. A. *Theorie der wirtschaftlichen Entwicklung*, Leipzig 1912.

—— *Capitalism, Socialism and Democracy*, New York-London 1942.

Schön, L. *Från hantverk till fabriksindustri. Svensk textiltillverkning 1820–1870*, Lund 1979.

—— *Industrialismens förutsättningar*, Lund 1982.

—— *Jordbrukets omvandling och konsumtionens förändringar 1800–1870*, papers from the Institute of Economic History, Lund, 41, Lund 1985.

—— 'Kapitalimport, kreditmarknad och industri 1850–1910', in E. Dahmén (ed.) *Upplåning och utveckling*, Stockholm 1989.

Smedberg, S. *Frälsebonderörelser i Halland och Skåne 1772–1776*, Studia Historica Upsaliensia 39, Uppsala 1972.

SOU 1993:16 *Nya villkor för ekonomi och politik*, Stockholm 1993.

Strömbäck, L. *Baltzar von Platen. Thomas Telford och Göta kanal. Entreprenörskap och tekniköverföring i brytningstid*, Stockholm/Stehag 1993.

Svensson, S. *Från gammalt till nytt på 1800-talets svenska landsbygd*, Stockholm 1977.

Sveriges industri, Sveriges industriförbund, Stockholm 1985.

Sågvall-Ullenhag, K. *AB Åtvidabergs förenade industrier med föregångare*, Ekonomisk-Historiska studier 5, Uppsala 1970.

Söderberg, J. and Lundgren, N.-G. *Ekonomisk och geografisk koncentration 1850–1980*, Lund 1982.

Söderberg, J., Jonsson, U. and Persson, C. *A Stagnating Metropolis. The Economy and Demography of Stockholm 1750–1850*, Cambridge 1991.

Söderlund, E. *Stockholms hantverkarklass 1720–1772*, Stockholm 1943.

—— *Hantverkarna. II. Den svenska arbetareklassens historia*, Stockholm 1949.

—— 'Företagsorganisation och företagsledning inom trävaruindustrin', in R. Lundström (ed.) *Kring industrialismens genombrott i Sverige*, Stockholm 1966.

Södersten, B. (ed.) *Svensk ekonomi*, Stockholm 1970.

—— (ed.) *Den offentliga sektorn*, Stockholm 1992.

Thunholm, L.-E. 'Ivar Kreuger – Myter och verklighet', *Historisk Tidskrift* 1993: 1.

Tobé, E. *Kommunal planering*, Stockholm 1972.

Ullenhag, K. *Sörkörare*, Örnsköldsviks kommuns skriftserie, I, Bjästa 1982.

Unga, N. *Socialdemokratin och arbetslöshetsfrågan 1912–34*, Lund 1976.

Utterström, G. *Jordbrukets arbetare, I och II. Den svenska arbetareklassens historia*, Stockholm 1957.

Waara, L. *Den statliga företagssektorns expansion*, Stockholm 1980.

Watts, S. *Västeuropas sociala historia 1450–1720*, Stockholm 1987.

Wilensky, H. L. *The Welfare State and Equality*, Berkeley 1975.

Winberg, C. *Folkökning och proletarisering. Kring den sociala strukturomvandlingen på Sveriges landsbygd under den agrara revolutionen*, papers from the Institute of History, Gothenburg, 10, Gothenburg 1975.

Wohlin, N. *Den svenska jordbruksstyckningspolitiken i 18:e och 19:e århundradet jämte en översikt af jordstyckningens inverkan på bondeklassens besuttenhetsförhållanden*, Stockholm 1912.

Åberg, Y. *Produktion och produktivitet i Sverige 1861–1965*, Stockholm 1969.

Åkerman, G. 'Om konjunkturväxlingarnas nödvändighet och grundorsak', *Ekonomisk Tidskrift* 1932: 1.

Åmark, K. *Vem styr marknaden? Facket, makten och marknaden 1850–1990*, Stockholm 1993.

Öhngren, B. *Folk i rörelse. Samhällsutveckling, flyttningsmönster och folkrörelser i Eskilstuna 1870–1900*. Studia Historica Upsaliensis 55, Uppsala 1974.

Östlind, A. *Svensk samhällsekonomi 1914–1922*, Stockholm 1945.7

Subject index

administrative reforms 73
AGA 122, 219
agricultural controls 250–252
agricultural crisis 137
Åhlen & Åkerlund 220
Alwac 221
Alweg 222
animal husbandry 13, 136
animal production 136
Apoteksbolaget 248
ASEA 157, 158, 166, 174, 210, 214, 217
ASSI 247
Associations 177
ASTRA 217
Atlas Copco 122, 166, 213, 217
Avesta Ironworks 220

bank crisis 265–266
banking system 75, 99–101, 146, 169–177,
    181–182, 216–221
bar iron 91–94
Bergvik & Ala 217
black box companies 174
Bofors 219
Boliden 219, 221
Bonniers publishing house 220
Bothnian trade restriction 66
'box in a box' corporate ownership 218
Bretton-Woods system 204
Bulten-Kanthal 220
business cycles 155

cameralism 57
capital as production factor 9–12
capital association 86
capitalism vii, 80
capitalists 102
ceded tax land 23–25

child benefit 242
Clause 32 (23) 187
collective agreements 235
Commodity Act (*produktplakatet*) 62, 66
communications 73, 74
companies 86–89
competitive conditions, industry 215
concentration of ownership 220
consumer goods industry 55
consumption, private 221–222
consumption, public 221–222
corporatism 253–254
credit restrictions 252–253
crop rotation 15, 20
crop yield figure (*korntal*) 3
currency 72
currency controls 252–253
Custos 219

Dagens Nyheter 220
Dalarna 32
death of the rural industrial works 127
departmental reform 73
depopulation 223–224
depression 162, 164
devaluation 265
division of labour xv, xvi
division of labour, international 267–268
draught animals 13

East India Company 84
economies of scale 123
education 75
electrification 157–158
Electrolux 166, 214, 217
emigration to America 111
employee investment funds 277
employers' organizations 185–187

Index of names

Printed in the USA/Agawam, MA
January 20, 2011

556238.052